Nation-building in the Post-Soviet

The Politics of National Identities

This book examines how national and ethnic identities are being reforged in the post-Soviet borderland states. The first chapter provides a conceptual and theoretical context for examining national identities, drawing in particular upon post-colonial theory. The rest of the book is divided into three parts. In part I, the authors examine how national histories of the borderland states are being rewritten, especially in relation to new nationalising historiographies centring around myths of origin, homeland and descent. Part II explores the ethnopolitics of group boundary construction and the manner in which such a politics has led to nationalising policies of both exclusion and inclusion. Part III examines the relationship between nation-building and language, especially with regard to how competing conceptions of national identity have informed the thinking of both political decision-takers and nationalising intellectuals, and the consequences for ethnic minorities. Such perspectives on nation-building are illustrated with regard to substantive studies drawn from the Baltic states, Ukraine and Belarus, Transcaucasia and Central Asia.

GRAHAM SMITH is a Fellow of Sidney Sussex College, and Director of the Post-Soviet States Research Programme. He is a Lecturer in Geography at the University of Cambridge.

VIVIEN LAW is a Fellow of Trinity College, and a member of the Post-Soviet States Research Programme. She is a Lecturer in Modern and Medieval Languages at the University of Cambridge.

ANDREW WILSON is a Lecturer in Ukrainian Studies in the School of Slavonic and East European Studies at the University of London. He is also a Fellow of Sidney Sussex College, and a member of the Post-Soviet States Research Programme.

ANNETTE BOHR is a Fellow of Sidney Sussex College, and a member of the Post-Soviet States Research Programme.

EDWARD ALLWORTH is Professor of Turko-Soviet Languages, and a former Director of Soviet Nationalities at Columbia University. He was a Visiting Research Fellow at Sidney Sussex College, Cambridge in 1995.

Nation-building in the Post-Soviet Borderlands

The Politics of National Identities

Graham Smith, Vivien Law, Andrew Wilson,
Annette Bohr and Edward Allworth

PUBLISHED BY THE PRESS SYNDICATE OF THE UNIVERSITY OF CAMBRIDGE
The Pitt Building, Trumpington Street, Cambridge CB2 1RP, United Kingdom

CAMBRIDGE UNIVERSITY PRESS
The Edinburgh Building, Cambridge CB2 2RU, United Kingdom
http://www.cup.cam.ac.uk
40 West 20th Street, New York, NY 10011–4211, USA   http://www.cup.org
10 Stamford Road, Oakleigh, Melbourne 3166, Australia

© Graham Smith, Vivien Law, Andrew Wilson, Annette Bohr, Edward Allworth
1998

First published in 1998

Typeset in 10/12 Monotype Plantin   [SE]

A catalogue record for this book is available from the British Library

Library of Congress Cataloguing in Publication data

Nation-building in the post-Soviet borderlands : the politics of
national identities / Graham Smith ... [et al.]
      p.   cm.
Includes bibliographical references (p.   )
ISBN 0 521 59045 0 (hbk.) – ISBN 0 521 59968 7 (pbk.)
1. Nationalism – Former Soviet republics.   2. Ethnicity – Former
Soviet republics.   3. Former Soviet republics – Historiography.
4. Language policy – Former Soviet republics.   5. Former Soviet
republics – Ethnic relations.   I. Smith, Graham, 1953–   .
DK293.I56   1998
305.8′00947–dc21   97–32113   CIP

Transferred to digital printing 2000

Contents

Figures

Tables

Preface

Following the break-up of the Soviet Union, one of the most urgent questions to emerge from the critical confusion was how the newly emerging polities would set about creating convincing identities for themselves and their citizens. It was perhaps a foregone conclusion that Russia would inherit the lion's share of the symbols and the history of the USSR and the tsarist empire; on the other hand, it was unclear what resources nation-builders in the fourteen borderland states would have to draw upon. What new tensions would arise out of the choice of symbols and myths, and which old ones would be exacerbated, or alternatively suppressed? Which of the heady mix of religion, language, ethnicity and homeland would come to the fore in any given region? The elusive, ever-shifting nature of the answers to these questions, the separate elements rearranging themselves kaleidoscopically in the very moment when a coherent pattern seemed to be emerging, has become dismayingly plain in the years since 1991. And yet the more complex the picture, the greater the urgency of the task of understanding it.

It is clearly impossible for any one individual to be conversant not only with the languages, histories and diverse political and social cultures of the fourteen new or restored borderland states, but also with the disparate academic disciplines required to arrive at a balanced picture of the changes now underway. Hence, when in 1993 the then newly appointed Master of Sidney Sussex College, Professor Gabriel Horn, persuaded the Fellows of the College of the desirability of capitalising upon the multi-disciplinary nature of a Cambridge college by initiating an inter-disciplinary research project within the walls of Sidney Sussex, the post-Soviet states in transition, and more especially the restructuring of national identities within those states, were an obvious choice of subject. The founding members of the team – Graham Smith, a geographer with expertise in Russia and the Baltic states, and Vivien Law, a historian of linguistics with an interest in Georgian language myths – were joined by two College-funded Research Fellows, Andrew Wilson, a political scientist working mainly on Ukraine, and Annette Bohr, whose expertise lies in the political and social affairs of Central Asia, Uzbekistan in particular; and by a Visiting Fellow on sabbatical leave from Columbia University, Edward Allworth. We owe a very considerable debt to Dr Viktor Shnirelman, who spent a term with the Project as a visiting Fellow funded by the British Council. In addition to sharing his anthropological expertise with us during that time, and presenting a paper in our seminar series, he graciously agreed to contribute a chapter to this volume. We are most grateful to him for this, and hereby express our unreserved thanks.

Our research has been considerably furthered not only by the resources generously put at our disposal by the College, but also by the magnanimous support of the Leverhulme Trust and the confidence of its director, Professor Barry Supple. Thanks to Leverhulme funding we have been able to undertake field research in Estonia and Latvia, Ukraine and Belarus, Uzbekistan, Kyrgyzstan and Kazakstan, and Georgia. We are grateful to the Leverhulme Trust too for funding our invaluable Research Associate, Helen Morris, without whom the preparation of this book would have been far more laborious. Ian Agnew, of the Department of Geography, Cambridge, provided vital assistance in drawing the maps and figures for this volume.

In addition, Graham Smith would like to thank the Britia Mortensen Fund and the Scandinavian Studies Fund, Cambridge University, for their financial support. Vivien Law would like to thank first of all the very numerous Georgians who have given unreservedly of their time and effort to assist with the collection of materials for chapter 8. For reasons explained in note 7 to that chapter, it seems imprudent to thank them publicly by name. Others who have contributed include Patrick Hillery, Stephen McKenna, Patrick Sériot, Elizabeth Fuller, Vera Rich and members of the Post-Soviet States in Transition project. Andrew Wilson would like to thank Jim Dingley, Heorhii Kas′ianov, Oleksii Haran, and David Saunders for valuable advice. Annette Bohr gratefully acknowledges the financial support of the Nuffield Foundation in carrying out the field research and survey work for chapter 9. She also wishes to thank Vsevolod Rahr for his invaluable assistance in processing survey data. Viktor Shnirelman would like to thank the Central European University in Prague, where he was a Research Fellow in 1994–5, and the organisers of the 1995 symposium on 'Ideology, Warfare and Indoctrinality' held in Ringberg Castle, Germany, for their support.

We would also like to thank Michael Holdsworth of Cambridge University Press for his enthusiasm for this project and the three anonymous referees for their useful and encouraging comments.

As is inevitable with a multiauthored volume such as this, although each of the four Cambridge-based authors read and contributed to the final form of all chapters, individual members of the team took responsibility for particular chapters. The division of labour was as follows:

Chapters 1 and 5: Graham Smith
Chapters 2 and 6: Andrew Wilson
Chapter 3: Viktor Shnirelman
Chapter 4: Edward Allworth
Chapters 7 and 9: Annette Bohr
Chapter 8: Vivien Law

Where a standard English form of proper names or place names already exists, we have retained that spelling; in other cases, and in all transliterations of book and article titles, we have used the Library of Congress system for eastern Slavic Languages and Edward Allworth's system, slightly modified, for Turkic languages as set out in his *Nationalities of the Soviet East: Publications and Writing Systems* (New York and London: Columbia University Press, 1971). For Georgian, the system chosen is the one which most closely corresponds to that being used for Russian.

Graham Smith
Vivien Law
Andrew Wilson
Annette Bohr

Sidney Sussex College
Cambridge
July 1997

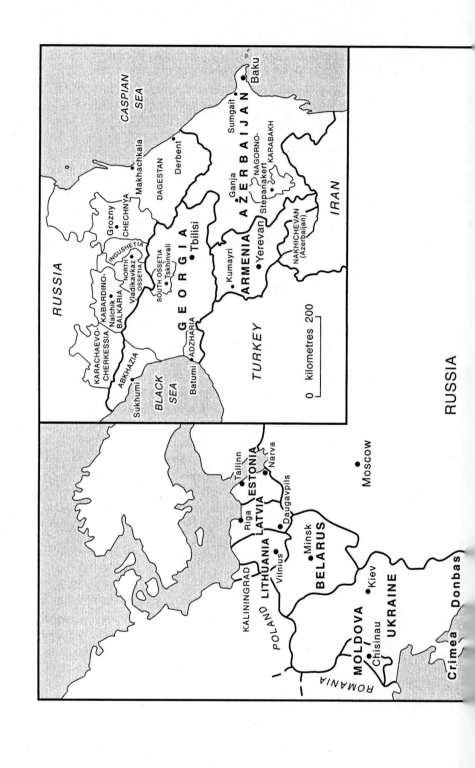

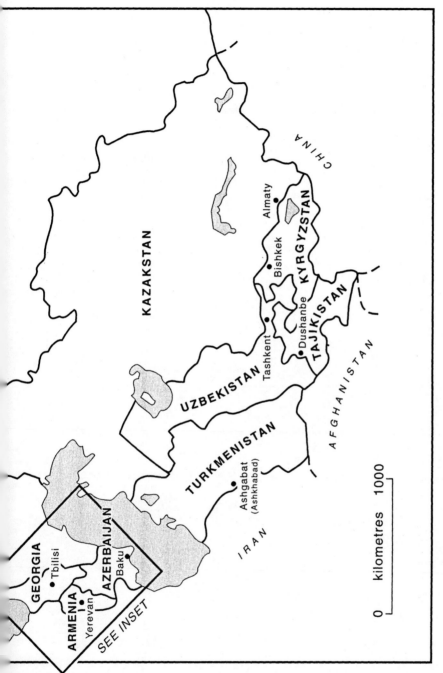

The post-Soviet borderland states

KAZAKSTAN

CHINA

Almaty

Bishkek

KYRGYZSTAN

Dushanbe

TAJIKISTAN

Tashkent

UZBEKISTAN

AFGHANISTAN

TURKMENISTAN

Ashgabat
(Ashkhabad)

IRAN

GEORGIA

Tbilisi

ARMENIA

Yerevan

AZERBAIJAN

Baku

SEE INSET

0   kilometres   1000

1   Post-colonialism and borderland identities

As the dust of the immediate post-Soviet transition settles, we are now better placed to begin to examine how national identities are being reforged in the fourteen borderland states of what up until December 1991 constituted the non-Russian union republics of the former Soviet Union.[1] Having secured sovereign spaces following the collapse of the world's largest multiethnic federation, the borderland states are now embarking upon nation-building. And herein lies the paradox. The post-colonial desire to recreate national identities can facilitate solidarity, play a positive role in state-making and form a basis for popular participation in politics. A politics defined in relation to a particular national community may not in itself be incompatible with processes of democratisation. The problem arises when national or ethnic identity is predicated on a form of imagined community that reifies the importance of national or ethnic boundaries to the detriment of the wider political community. In this regard, there is as yet only limited evidence to suggest that the post-Soviet borderland states are on the threshold of entering such a post-national era in which national and ethnic identities have been superseded by understandings of cultural difference based on a broader and more inclusive vision of political community. Rather, although the scale of inter-ethnic violence as witnessed in TransDniester, Nagorno-Karabakh and Georgia in the late 1980s and the first half of the 1990s has now diminished, national identities continue to be caught up in power struggles, leadership elections, legislative acts and in the state distribution of social goods. In short, the ethnification or even racialisation of identity politics remains an important ingredient of borderland politics and cultural life. If, as Simon During notes, 'the post-colonial desire is the desire of de-colonised communities for an identity',[2] then that identity in the post-Soviet borderlands is being shaped as much by the ethnic politics of exclusion and division as it is by inclusion and coexistence.

Throughout the multiethnic borderlands, there remains a predisposition amongst dominant national groups and minorities alike to recognise and overemphasise the importance of collective rather than individual actors as the constitutive elements of political community. Above all, this tendency is being played out through the state and its major institutions and is bound up with what Rogers Brubaker identifies as the tendency by political and cultural elites 'to see the state as an "unrealised" nation-state, as a state destined to be a nation-state . . . and the concomitant disposition to remedy this perceived defect, to make the state what it is properly and legitimately destined to be, by promoting the language, culture, demographic position, economic flourishing or political hegemony of the nominally state-bearing nation'.[3] Thus the articulation of interests and the design of public institutions and policies tend to reflect the interests of the dominant national group. Most straightforwardly, such 'a nationalising tendency' refers both to those states that explicitly define themselves in constitutional law as national homelands or the embodiment of long-held national goals of statehood, and to those states whose political policies and practices reveal similar 'nationalising' aspirations despite the lack of explicit words to this effect in their founding or other legal documents.[4] Thus, in the most extreme cases, nation-building has become caught up in a form of identity politics which is designed to produce and reproduce nationally defined contours of community and to reflect nationally defined interests and values predicated on fulfilling a normative concept of statehood in which nation and state should be spatially congruent. Such political practices have also resulted in members of national minorities being disadvantaged and in their informal exclusion from important spheres of public life.

While such nationalising tendencies centre on the political practices of the state, they are by no means confined to political elites. Rather, it is part of a far broader enterprise of nation-building in which cultural elites – especially intellectuals – play a crucial part in the production and representation of nationhood. Nor do the representatives or agents of such nationalising regimes necessarily understand or clearly acknowledge and articulate such a form of political rule; rather, the importance of the notion of a nationalising regime is that it has relational implications for those within the polity who are most affected by it, especially national minorities. In turn, the behaviour of nationalising states is also in part a product of reciprocal monitoring of 'the other', as a registering or transcription of what is happening *vis-à-vis* those whom it is argued do not belong. In addition, by our labelling of the borderland states as nationalising regimes it should not be inferred that they are all engaged in their nationalising projects to the same degree of intensity or that they all pursue the same policies. There is, for instance, a very different set of political and cultural practices taking place with regard to language policy in Belarus, where Russian is officially acknowledged as a state language, compared to Latvia where the Russian language now has no official status and where all citizens are expected to speak Latvian as a condition of citizenship.

The central aim of this book is not so much to question the significance that such a politics of national identity continues to play in structuring the social, political and cultural lives of those who live in the borderland states as to explore how such national identities are being reformulated, revitalised and contested as symptoms of the perceived post-colonial status of these states. The aim of this chapter is therefore to provide a conceptual and theoretical context for examining such national identities. As Roxanne Doty reminds us, 'national identity is never a finished product; it is always in the process of being constructed and reconstructed'.[5] In subsequent chapters, we will therefore have much to say about how such national identities are being refashioned by political and cultural elites in the light of their new and changing circumstances, of how a politics of nation-building is linked to practices of social inclusion and exclusion, and of how for post-colonial subjects the question of language has become a political, cultural and literary issue for both majority and minority groups alike. With this end stage in mind, this chapter turns to consider ways in which we can provide a conceptual and interpretative basis for understanding the interrelationship between identity, nation-building and post-coloniality.

A post-colonial politics

There is now a commonly held assumption in the literature that the post-Soviet borderland states, having secured sovereign control over their national homelands, have entered a new or post-colonial phase in their histories. To take 'post-colonial' only at face value, however, is to assume that the post-Soviet borderland states were once subjects of a colonial project, part of an empire-driven political formation named the Soviet Union, and that it is only as a result of their post-1991 status as sovereign polities that they have escaped from the vicissitudes of empire. Indeed, even from those commentators who during the late 1980s were uneasy about labelling the Soviet Union 'an empire', a historical revisionism is now underway in which, in the light of the USSR's collapse along multi-ethnic lines, the Soviet Union is busily being reinvented as empire 'since it now appears to have been an illegitimate, composite polity unable to contain the rising nations within it'.[6] For the borderland states, moreover, the colonial analogy is invariably treated in a less ambivalent and more forthright fashion. Indeed, for many in the borderland states, having experienced 'imperial disintegration', the question on the agenda is now one of 'potential imperial [Russian] reconstruction'.[7]

How then are we to interpret the place of these borderlands within the Soviet Union? Were they simply colonial territories of an empire similar to that ruled over by Britain or France and whose sense of national self was either wholly or partly structured by their subject status? After all, their sense of imagined community and the nature and form of post-1991 nation-building are bound up with their place, real and imagined, within such previous political formations. Thus any conceptual framing must take cognisance of the reality of the relationship of the borderland ethnorepublics as part of such a shared political formation and practices, while at the same time acknowledging that such a relationship to the Soviet state also constituted part of a discursive formation imbued with normative and subjective understandings of the nature of that state.

Most commentators are willing to accept that the relationship between the borderland ethnorepublics and the centre was in certain important ways unique amongst twentieth-century empires.[8] If we are to acknowledge as an empire a state in which a centre dominates a periphery to the disadvantage of the latter, then there seems little doubt that the borderland ethnorepublics were subject to subordination and inequality. The Soviet federation was certainly not the 'federation of sovereign and equal states' proclaimed by official Soviet discourse. Incorporation of the borderland territories was often extremely brutal, as in the cases of Georgia in the early 1920s and the Baltic states in 1940. Nor should we underemphasise the role that the coercive technologies of the centre and their deployment by the central state apparatus played in the pacification of the borderlands. It is hard to think of a worse crime perpetuated by an imperial power than Stalin's deliberate mass starvation of Ukrainians and Kazaks in the 1930s. Yet it is also important to acknowledge the paradox that reflected the relationship between the borderland republics and the centre, a relationship that might better be termed 'federal colonialism'.[9] In other words, explicit within such a labelling is the claim that the Soviet Union was neither wholly 'federal' nor 'colonial' but contained elements of both systems. Thus, while sovereignty resided with the centre rather than in the ethnorepublics, the particular nature of the Soviet federation ensured that nation-building took place at both the ethnorepublic and all-union levels. In short, it can be suggested that the 'federal colonial' nature and status of the borderland ethnorepublics were based on the following.

First, the centre denied the borderland ethnorepublics the *de facto* (although not *de jure*) right to national self-determination. Only a minimal degree of political manoeuvrability was granted to the local party-state machines in running their union republics. However, provided that nationalism did not become part of the local political agenda, a degree of localism was tolerated. For the union republic leadership, this meant that their role was far more complex than that of obedient lieutenants carrying out directives from the centre. Within the arena of fiscal federal politics in particular, native political elites were able and willing throughout the post-Stalin years to champion and politicise ethnorepublic economic interests and needs, but only in so far as such a politics did not undermine what the centre deemed to be politically permissible. In turn, local political leaders could be relied upon to ensure that nationalism remained off their ethnorepublic agendas. To be sure, there were occasions when this failed, most notably in Latvia and Estonia in the late 1950s and in Ukraine in the late 1960s. However, by and large, the local political leadership could be trusted to ensure the repression of nationalism. It was only when the centre under the reform-minded leadership of Mikhail Gorbachev relaxed these rules in the late 1980s in an attempt to facilitate local democratisation that nationalism inadvertently became problematic and subsequently capable of challenging the centre.

To conclude that the centre's policy of imposing limits on the degree of national self-determination that was permitted was part of a project designed to create a nation-state is therefore misleading. Although the centre did initiate policies of cultural standardisation, such policies were neither consistent through time nor uniformly practised throughout the ethnorepublics. Thus within the all-important arena of language policy, while the adoption of Russian as the state lingua franca provided Russians with greater opportunities for social and geographical mobility, it would be wrong to conclude that the Soviet state practised a language policy designed to promote the building of a Russian nation-state. Rather, a number of phases in the centre's attitudes towards language is evident: an initial post-revolutionary period in which the centre purposely encouraged the flourishing or even in some cases (as in Central Asia) the creation of literary languages other than Russian; the Stalin years, when in direct contradiction of Leninist federal principles, Russian was decreed as a compulsory subject in all non-Russian schools; a period from the late 1950s until the mid-1980s in which bilingualism was promoted but the choice of language of instruction became a feature of central policy, with the Russian language being held up as the hallmark of the Soviet people; and, finally, as a consequence of greater centrally initiated local democratisation in the late 1980s under the Gorbachev administration, a concluding phase in which local language laws were initiated by the ethnorepublics, which was to lead to titular languages becoming the state languages of sovereign statehood.[10]

Secondly, while the centre was engaged in institutional state-building and in creating all-union symbols of nationhood, one of the major paradoxes of the Soviet empire was that it provided the social space for nation-building at the ethnoregional scale.[11] Thus, in federalising what became the Soviet Union, Lenin in effect bequeathed to the ethnorepublics the institutional space to carry out limited 'nationalising' policies. This was affirmed in the practice of encouraging the upward mobility of natives within their own national homelands through affirmative action policies (*korenizatsiia*) that contributed to the indigenisation of the local political leadership and to the growth or consolidation of an indigenous intelligentsia through preferential access to higher education and to membership of the local Communist Party. As a result of union republic status, each of the borderland ethnorepublics was provided with a degree of institutional protection that enabled their native languages and cultures to flourish. Not only did such a form of institutionalised nation-building facilitate the preservation and reproduction of established niches for incumbents drawn from the indigenous cultures, it also enabled nationality divisions to remain an integral part and reference point of native public life and an organisational basis for reinforcing local national identities. Indeed, in some instances, notably in Central Asia, by federalising ethnic homelands into ethnorepublics, the Soviet state actually created nations whose sense of nation-ness had previously barely existed.[12] Moreover, this form of nation-building also encouraged ethnorepublic nation-builders to think of the ethnorepublic as the identity-marker of their homeplace. Where the centrally imposed federal map did not co-incide with national boundaries, where ethnic minorities either found themselves on the wrong side of an ethnic border or found their ancestral homeland incorporated into such an ethnorepublic, such encouragement to selective nation-building was to prove highly problematic following the collapse of the Soviet Union. In short, the nature of the federation exposes the post-Soviet nationalist myth that for the borderland states the process of nation-building was interrupted by Soviet rule and could begin again only with statehood in 1991.

This borderland bias towards nation-building also carried implications for both Russia and the Russians. Unlike the borderland ethnorepublics which possessed their own national institutions (including their own Communist Party, Academy of Sciences and even KGB), neither Russia nor the Russians possessed an obvious national homeland endowed with such national institutions. Consequently, the idea of the Russian Federation 'was not taken seriously by Russians or non-Russians as the Russian nation-state or the national homeland of the Russian people'.[13] However, like the other nationalities, they were encouraged to think of the Soviet state as their homeland (*sovetskaia rodina*) and to believe that what was central to their national sense was what Khrushchev in the late 1950s had first referred to as to the emergence of a new Soviet community, that of the Soviet people (*sovetskii narod*).[14] The difference was that, while the institutional supports of nation-building inadvertently provided the peoples of the borderland ethnorepublics with a choice of identity, for Russians, given the absence of a particular association between union republic status and nation-building, there was a far greater tendency to identify with the Soviet Union as homeland. As John Dunlop notes, 'the concepts of "Union" and "Russia" in the minds of Russians were one and the same'.[15] This notion that the boundaries of the Soviet Union coincided with a Russian sense of identity was further reinforced by the encouragement that the centre gave to the migration of especially Russians into the borderland ethnorepublics; by 1991 some twenty-five million were residing outside the Russian Federation. It may therefore be not that surprising that, more than any other nationality, the end of the Soviet empire affected the Russian sense of national identity: whereas the borderland nations felt that they had finally regained their homelands as a result of the collapse of the Soviet empire, for many Russians the abrupt end of the Soviet Union marked the beginning of an intense crisis of identity.

Finally, despite the fact that the fourteen borderland nations that emerged in 1991 as states had all been designated as union republics and enjoyed the same level of institutional supports as part of the Soviet federation, they differed in their relations with the centre. They were not all treated uniformly by the centre, nor in turn were relations between the ethnorepublics and the centre predicated on similarity. The nature of such relations was based on a whole host of criteria. These included the differing nature of incorporation. Whereas support for becoming part of a Russian-dominated Soviet Union was at least ambiguous amongst urban elites in Armenia, Ukraine or Belarus, the incorporation of the Baltic republics and Georgia, in contrast, was achieved through unreserved force: hence the idea of Russia as an expansionist metropole was always going to remain far more central in their relationship with the central government in Moscow. Similarly, for some of the ethnorepublic titular nations, the sense of imagined community transcended the boundary markers of nationality, as in the case of many Ukrainians and Belarusians with regard to their Slavic brethren, the Russians, whereas for Georgians or Latvians such a sense of overlapping identity with Russians remained weak. Moreover, the ethnorepublics also differed in their perceived economic relations with the centre. While by the late 1980s nationalists in the economically more advantaged Baltic republics and Ukraine could claim that redistributive economic policies had worked against their people's material prosperity, for the Central Asian republics, which were net fiscal beneficiaries of Soviet rule and which had gained most from the 'welfare federalism' of the Brezhnev era,[16] the idea of being subjected to a straightforward form of economic colonialism could hardly stand up to scrutiny. In contrast to the Baltic republics or Ukraine, this difference thereby weakened the argument that their polities could easily adjust from dependency on Russia, and undermined the appeal of secession-ist–nationalist politics in the region.[17] Instead, the rhetoric of local nationalist discourse in Central Asia tended to focus on the claim that the central authorities in Moscow had exploited the region's raw materials for the centre's own ends. The differentiated nature of such relations between the centre and the ethnorepublics therefore sheds light on why the mobilising potential behind the idea of nation-statism was to become a less problematic affair for the Baltic states and Georgia than it was for even Ukraine or certainly Central Asia.

Coloniality and post-coloniality, however, cannot simply be reduced to 'objective criteria'; like empire, state or nation, they are also social con-structs, a set of value judgements bound up with the very constitutive nature and meaning of national identity. Thus, despite claims to the con-trary, few of the centre's political elites took the view that they were pre-siding over a Soviet empire. Similarly, with the possible exception of far right-wing Russian nationalist parties, few within post-Soviet Russia would recognise or judge Russia's activities in Tajikistan, TransDniester or even Chechnya in the mid-1990s as part of a grand scheme to rebuild a Russian Empire. By introducing into post-Soviet studies Bourdieu's notion of *habitus*, Beissinger enables us to take on board such a per-spective by rethinking how 'empire-building', 'state-building' and 'nation-building' are products of how relations between different group-ings are formed and become highly contested and politicised.[18] For Bourdieu, the notion of *habitus* is defined as a system of embedded dis-positions, anticipations and expectations. In turn, they are themselves the products of social and cultural practices that structure the ways in which actors construe the social and political reality that they confront.[19] Thus *habitus* constitutes a kind of 'feel for the game' that is produced as a result of experience and which is itself the product of history. People tend to 'read' their future through a set of expectations and inclinations built up through the past. In the post-colonial context, what therefore becomes important is how the borderland states and their peoples envisage the Soviet experience within such discursive worlds in which meaningful action takes place on the basis of perceptions, values and culturally formed expectations. Thus the borderland post-Soviet states can be con-sidered as post-colonial in the sense that they are constructed and labelled as such by their nation-builders. Post-coloniality does not need to follow from an actual 'colonial situation'. Rather, as De Alva notes with reference to Latin America, 'post-coloniality is contained both within colonialism . . . and outside of it, by its questioning of the very norms that establish the inside/outside, oppressor (colonising)/oppressed (colonised) binaries that are assumed to characterise the colonial condition'.[20]

In acknowledging the significance of such experiential lenses in shaping the post-colonial condition, it is important however not to see such relations only in interactive terms between post-Soviet Russia and the borderland states. Rather, as we have already signalled, we also need to take on board the role of national minorities that are judged neither by the nationalising state as 'the Russian other' nor by Russia as part of 'the nationalising other', but whose colonial and post-colonial experiences have also been shaped by understandings of 'nation-building' and 'empire-building'. Thus through the construction of the 'other' as 'empire', we can begin to comprehend how the borderland states' interpretations of their previous and current relations with the Soviet Union help structure the idea of empire as a continuing and uninterrupted Russian project, of how Russia itself responds to the actions of the post-1991 borderland states as nationalising regimes, and of how the experiences of national minorities are constituted in relation to such projects of empire-building, state-building and nation-building. Thus *habitus* is above all about the environment in which such boundary concepts as empire, state and natioń are imbued and interpreted with deep identific and historical meanings by communities, and which in turn helps us to make sense of how such experiences have got inside post-colonial identities.

The borderlands inside Russia's identities

There are good reasons why post-Soviet Russia has found it more difficult than other empires to come to terms with the loss of 'the big homeland'. Russian political elites have not brought to decolonisation a clear awareness of the distinction between nation and empire as did, for example, British elites following their empire's eventual decolonisation.[21] As a consequence, the question of what and where is Russia, what is its sense of national self, remains highly ambiguous. It is therefore within this context that we need to begin to understand how such competing discourses of identity within Russia concerning its relations with the borderland states have emerged and unfolded. In this regard, three such political discourses can be identified.

First, there is what we can refer to as the liberal discourse, one which dominated Russian politics in the 1990–2 period and which represents a break with both the Soviet and tsarist past.[22] It is a discourse which, in embarking upon the wholesale de-Sovietisation of Russia, acknowledged the sovereignty of the post-Soviet states and which, despite having declared itself the successor state of the Soviet Union, accepted that it has no claims to the borderland territories. It is a discourse which emphasises the idea of *Rossiia* (the post-1991 boundedness of Russia), and which made Russian state-building its top priority. Although the liberal ideology held that all citizens of the former Soviet Union, irrespective of nationality or place of residence, have an equal right to citizenship of the new Russia,[23] none the less it was overwhelmingly a discourse that accepted that Russian citizens should become citizens of their place of residence. In short, the homeland for Russia was firmly redesignated as *Rossiia* and relations with the borderland states were to be based on co-operation, mutual respect and partnership.

This conception of respecting the sovereign difference of the borderland states has from the outset been challenged by what we can label a discourse of 'return to empire'. Instead of setting the bright future of post-communism against 'a dark past', it sets the identity crisis of the present against an earlier 'Golden Age'. There are two variants here. The first, that of the neo-nationalist right, looks back to pre-1917 and of a Russia associated with the empire-past, although the issue of exactly which boundaries of that empire (1772, 1913, 1917) should again exist remains hotly contested. Embedded in this vision are a whole variety of ethnic codes, the most vital of which is the idea of the Russian nation as a special world in itself, one based on an association between the Russian nation (*russkii narod*) and Slavdom's and Russia's historic homelands. What cannot be given up are 'the historic Russian lands', meaning Ukraine, Belarus and parts of neighbouring republics long settled by the Russian nation (northern Kazakstan, north-eastern Estonia, Crimea). However, although the criterion for inclusion remains ambiguous, it is made clear only *vis-à-vis* the ethnicised 'other' who do not belong. In contrast, the other variant, the neo-Soviet version, wants to recover *sovetskaia rodina*. The main organisational force of this form of neo-Sovietism is the Communist Party of the Russian Federation (CPRF), a political party which since its revival in 1992 has combined the rhetoric of socialism with an appeal to Russian nationalism.[24] It embodies a conception of Russia in which Russians again reside within a socialist multiethnic homeland. Extolling the virtues of inclusion through expressing universalistic aspirations of an 'international brotherhood', equality and common homeland for all citizens of Russia and the borderland states alike, it is committed to repealing the Belovezhskaia Agreement of December 1991 that recognised the formal dissolution of the Soviet homeland. In its place it wants 'to provide conditions for the gradual restoration of a union-state on a voluntary basis'.[25] Yet while ostensibly a discourse of inclusion, equality and universalism, neo-Sovietism none the less contains its own inherent limitation: Russia itself is the embodiment of exemplarity. Soviet socialism, while embracing universalistic ideals, is held up to be a singularly Russian idea and aim. As the motherland of socialism, Russia is the advanced point of exemplarity. A major theme in this discourse is that of Russia's national greatness, which coexists uneasily with the theme of international brotherhood. There is therefore a tension between universalism and particularism, as well as between identity and difference, that involves on the one hand the claim that 'we' and 'they' are the same, a universal brotherhood, and on the other hand the claim of difference that is implicit in these terms. So although the core aim is to rebuild a socialist society, it is based upon strengthening Russian statehood through which 'the Russian people should bind together all nations and people by their common historical destiny'. After all, it is argued that 'Russia is not Russia outside the [Soviet] Union, nor can it exist as a fully fledged state.'[26] The appeal of this largely unreconstructed form of communism therefore relies on re-establishing Russian hegemony. Hence the 1917 revolution is interpreted as a Russian revolution, reflecting the innate characteristics of the Russian people based upon a strong collectivist spirit and well-developed sense of inter-communalism.[27] Russia, it is argued, can again lead the way amongst the post-Soviet nations to re-establishing socialism. So, just like the Soviet Union, the restorationist political order would be quintessentially a Russian achievement, one that elevates Russia to playing a proactive role in recreating a Soviet world in which it would again become first amongst equals.

By 1993, an important sea change had occurred concerning Russia's relationship with its former borderlands or with what was increasingly being dubbed in Russian foreign policy circles as 'the near abroad' (*blizhnee zarubezh'e*). Such a change was bound up with the emergence of a third discourse, that of the so-called statists (*gosudarstvenniki*). It constitutes a hybrid of the two former discourses, 'not only double-voiced and double-accentuated . . . but also double-languaged; for in it there are . . . two individual consciousnesses, two voices, two accents . . . two epochs . . . that come together and consciously fight it out on the territory of the utterance'.[28] While accepting the boundaries of the new Russia, it reflects an unease within foreign policy circles in particular over certain events in some of the borderland states. As Andrannik Migranyan, one of Yeltsin's former foreign policy advisors, put it, 'As a result of miscalculations in assessing the role and place of Russia and the deep-seated nature of relations between Russia and the countries of the near abroad, officials of the

Russian Foreign Ministry and other political leaders in the country drew the strategically erroneous conclusion that Russia should return inward . . . thereby openly and publicly renouncing any special rights and interests in the post-Soviet space outside the Russian Federation . . . However, the events that occurred in Russia and in the republics during 1992 made some serious adjustments in the understanding of Russia's role and place in the post-Soviet space . . . A significant proportion of the political establishment . . . began to realise more and more clearly that a special role in the post-Soviet space belonged to Russia.'[29]

Within some of the borderland states, notably Moldova, the Baltic states of Estonia and Latvia, and Ukraine, Russophone minorities were being reclassified by the centre as victims of nationalising states. Within Russia, Russians began increasingly to think about their larger ethnolinguistic community and of the way in which their co-nationals were being treated and castigated as 'colonisers' and 'occupiers'. In the case of Moldova, the Russian state even went so far as to intervene militarily in support of the breakaway Russian-speaking enclave of TransDniester. In addition, the introduction of citizenship legislation in Estonia (1992) and Latvia (1994) that limited the rights of their substantial Russian minorities evoked in Moscow highly emotive accusations that these states were guilty of implementing policies of 'social apartheid' and 'ethnic cleansing' and that the only way such a situation could be resolved was to introduce trade embargoes and economic sanctions, as well as for the centre to clearly signal its unwillingness to withdraw Russian troops from either state until their governments enforced what Russia coded as 'the end of human rights abuses'.[30] Russian statists also began to talk about their 'compatriots abroad' and calling the protection of the rights of such compatriots 'one of the fundamental factors in Russia's foreign policy'.[31] Indeed, a notable refinement in the centre's language of citizenship had also occurred: although citizenship was still to be offered by the Russian state to any former Soviet citizens, what now clearly concerned Russia was the repatriation of ethnic Russian speakers.[32]

In recodifying Russians outside Russia as a diaspora (*Rossiiskaia diaspora*), statists are in effect signalling two things. On the one hand, Russia no longer lays claim to a larger homeland and no longer seeks sovereignty beyond *Rossiia*. Thus *Rossiia* is the political homeland and, in labelling Russians outside Russia as a diaspora, such a homeland stance accepts that what were the boundaries of either the tsarist empire or the Soviet Union no longer compose the natural extent of Russia. On the other hand, such a change in policy also signals that Russia has a clear part to play as the historic homeland (*rodina*) of the Russians, and that, for the *vykhodtsy* (literally, 'those who have left'), Russia is their 'natural' homeland (*otechestvo*). The upshot is that the Russian diaspora have become a central concept in defining Russian national identity, as a Russia which is the 'historic homeland' of the Russian-speaking communities with Russia directly responsible for their well-being. In both senses, then, the idea of Russia has been reinvented in relation to its diaspora. For *Rossiia*, Russians will be homeless no more. Yet by offering extra-territorial citizenship to all those who have a connection – ethnic or historic – to the Russian homeland, Russia has attempted to redefine the nation while at the same time acknowledging the inviolability of the borderland states' sovereign spaces. Besides fulfilling a communitarian logic of protecting co-nationals, such a refocused willingness to safeguard the diaspora has also been motivated by a reluctance either to get further embroiled in costly irredentist wars involving Russian speakers as in TransDniester, or to encourage in Russia's present economic situation the wholesale 'gathering in' through the return migration of the diaspora.[33] The regime has therefore attempted to create a Russian nation without restoring the homeland-empire, something which Russia had failed to fully implement when it was part of either the tsarist empire or the Soviet Union.[34]

Colonialism inside borderland identities

The nationalising regimes that constitute the borderland states have been informed and structured by the shared legacy of Soviet rule. Thus, any understanding of how national identities are being reshaped and appropriated by nationalising elites must acknowledge that they are also a product of this shared history and its consequences, part of the contemporary social and political complexion of the post-colonial condition. Thus, just as for Russia, the Soviet past and its consequences also raise questions for the borderlands about identity, about cultural sameness and difference and about the boundaries between peoples. Consequently, nationalising regimes in effect draw upon and bring into the public sphere of the post-colonial present the codes of colonialism to debate and legitimise the reshaping of social and political life and to justify political actions of inclusion and exclusion. Three perspectives on such a discussion can be identified and briefly explored: de-Sovietisation, the reinventing of boundaries and cultural standardisation.

'De-Sovietisation' refers to the way in which nationalising political elites have been keen to remove the symbols, political institutions and representatives of Soviet power from the social and political landscape, and to replace them with new national symbols, political institutions and social practices in order to safeguard what is claimed as 'the national interest' against the colonial 'other'. Throughout many of the borderland states, notably in the Baltic states, Georgia and some of the Central Asian republics, the main institution of Soviet power, the Communist Party, has been banned. While of considerable symbolic significance, this move is also bound up with the self-interests of new ruling political elites, of the need to distance the polity (and themselves) from the previous political formation, and can be legitimised on the basis of securing geopolitical security and encoded in terms of 'protecting the nation'. Thus, in a number of the borderland states, those political elites who had held positions of power within the Communist Party during the Soviet period have been subject to purges or electoral humiliation. For those political elites who have survived, most notably in the Central Asian republics of Kazakstan, Uzbekistan and Turkmenistan, the only way to remain in power has been to distance themselves from the previous regime by switching to employing ethnic codes.

De-Sovietisation is also bound up with mistrust of 'the other', of questioning the place of migrants – particularly, although not exclusively, Russians from the former metropole region – within the borderlands. As Morley and Robins note elsewhere, 'it [the homeland] is about conserving the fundamentals of culture and identity. And, as such, it is about sustaining cultural boundaries and boundedness. To belong in this way is to protect exclusive and therefore excluding identities against those who are seen as "aliens" and "foreigners". The "other" is always and continuously a threat to the security and integrity of those who share a common home.'[35] To varying degrees, nationalist discourses in the borderland states draw upon a vision of the Russians as 'the colonial other', as erstwhile agents of Soviet rule whose presence is still treated with suspicion and unease. While some Central Asian political elites have been keen, out of economic necessity, to play up the positive side of the Russian presence as a way of stemming the tide of Russian emigration from the region, in the Baltic states of Estonia and Latvia many share the view that the de-Sovietisation of their homelands will be complete only when the Russians return to Russia.

De-Sovietisation can also serve as an instrument for privileging certain members of the nationalising state in which the utilisation of ethnic codes provides an important resource for indigenous social mobility and political status and position. Thus not only has the removal of 'the other' ('the Communist Party', 'Russian nomenklatura', 'those associated with Soviet rule') created spaces for career advancement, but such marginalising practices have also remained crucial for major political parties in the winning of national elections. In order to secure power, the key has been to politically outbid other political parties by deploying ethnic codes in order to secure the electoral support of the titular nation. Thus, while such practices have become a feature of successive national elections in Estonia, Latvia and Georgia, there are limits to the success of such practices, as in Ukraine where the successful political outbidding of the nationalist right has been circumvented by the large proportion of Russophones and Ukrainianised Russians within Ukraine's electoral constituency.

Nation-builders are also engaged in reinventing, defining, clarifying and homogenising boundaries. 'The meaning of boundaries', writes Passi, 'is accentuated by the fact that collective identities are typically produced through boundaries and the social continuation of demarcations, since identity is typically defined in terms of a difference between "us" and "them".'[36] It is part of 'a dialectic of inwardness and outwardness': the dialectic of inwardness concerns the nation's uniqueness and is termed in the first person plural, we. Yet, at the same time, the first person plural identification is closely linked with the third person plural, that is, the other.[37] Thus the social production of boundary markers and the issue of how they are taken up through practices of representation have become crucial to the reshaping of national and ethnic identities. In this regard, three such boundary marker tendencies can be identified.

First, there is the tendency to *essentialise*, to identify one trait or characteristic in codifying a national or ethnic grouping. Here it is assumed that there is some intrinsic and essential context to any identity which is defined in terms of oppositions by either a common origin (our homeland, language community) or a common structure of experience (colonised/colonisers; immigrants/indigenes) or both. Thus the representation of identity takes the form of offering one fully constituted, separate and distinct identity of 'us' which is different from 'them' (e.g. the titular nation as 'the chosen people', Russian settlers as 'fifth columnists'). In such essentialist accounts of the past, identities are therefore represented as linear, continuous and above all singular, part of a project bound up with 'primordialising the nation' through searching for and delineating a pre-colonial cultural purity for the nation which is juxtaposed to the more recent heterogenising and transformed colonial past that threatened or destroyed the nation's culture.

The second is to *historicise*. This can entail rediscovering an ethnic past or selective history, especially of a 'Golden Age' that can act as an inspiration for contemporary problems and needs, but it can also be linked to rediscovering or inventing national heroes. 'These pasts', suggests Anthony Smith, 'then become standards against which to measure the alleged failings of the present generation and contemporary community.'[38] Particular periods and places are thus valorised,[39] creating a hierarchy amongst past, present and future in which a particular moment in history becomes 'the single source and beginning of everything good for all later times'.[40] Thus for Lithuanians, a valorised epic past is configured by idealised images of a harmonious pre-colonial social order of Lithuanians running their own state (either the medieval Polish-Lithuanian Commonwealth that at its apogee stretched from the Baltic to the Black Sea, or the more recent inter-war (1918–40) Lithuanian state), replete with an overly romanticised view of the Lithuanian peasantry and their folk–rural culture. The distance of this absolute inter-war past from the present is marked by the break of (Soviet) colonialism; but simultaneously, this past is represented as a constituent part of the nation's post-colonial status, one that can again be more fully realised if political leaders follow the model of the inter-war period. By representing the past–present relationship as entailing both break and continuity, distance and proximity, conservative-nationalists in Lithuania in effect modernise the pre-modern and pre-modernise the modern, turning continuity into the nation's fate.

The third tendency is to *totalise*, that is, to turn relative differences into absolute ones. Individuals are thus collectivised and ascribed to or squeezed into particular categories: one is either a Tajik or a Russian; one cannot be both. Inter-ethnic sameness is repackaged and fetishised as difference. Thus nation-builders engage in creating or manufacturing distance between the colonial past and the post-colonial present, between the colonisers and colonised. In this regard, language often becomes an important symbol of national identity even when its actual distance to the language of the 'colonial other' is not great. Thus, in terms of etymology, syntax and pronunciation, the distance between Russian and Ukrainian or between Romanian and Moldovan is limited compared to the distance between Estonian and Russian, or Georgian and Abkhaz. In feeling some unease about their linguistic similarities, some nationalising elites call for the privileging of those variants of vocabulary and syntax whose distance from the language of the colonial other (Russian for the borderland nations or Romanian for Moldovans) is deemed the greater. In a similar manner, albeit with more far-reaching consequences for inter-ethnic relations, political elites in both Armenia and Azerbaijan manage the territorial struggle over who gets Nagorno-Karabakh by reifying the importance of religion, presenting it as a struggle between 'Islam' and 'Christianity', when in effect from the 1920s up until the late 1980s the two communities coexisted in a common homeland.

The idea that cultural standardisation provides a necessary building block for the post-colonial state's economic and political modernisation is rooted in the claim that, historically, successful nation-state building (and here western Europe is seen as the model) was bound up with making the nation and state spatially congruent. Linguistic, cultural and educational standardisation is therefore held up as commensurate with the running of a more efficient national space-economy, 'a scientific state bureaucracy', and with the producing of a more harmonious and loyal citizenry. For nationalising elites in the post-Soviet borderland states, such a conceptualisation of people as living within a single, shared spatial frame in which one national culture predominates is thus viewed as commensurate with creating the conditions for the rational and modern state. 'Baptised with a name, space becomes national property, a sovereign patrimony fusing place, property and heritage, whose perpetuation is secured by the state.'[41] Of all the nationalising tendencies of cultural standardisation, the goal of creating a national language within such 'a shared spatial frame' is for the borderland states amongst the most important. As During notes, 'the question of language for post-colonialism is political, cultural and literary, not in the transcendental sense that the phrase as *differend* enables politics, but in the material sense that a choice of language is a choice of identity'.[42] Thus the institutionalisation and promotion of the titular language – in the state bureaucracy, politics and education – are at one level bound up with reversing the one-time 'colonial other's' policy of asymmetric bilingualism in which the titular nations learnt Russian while those Russian migrants who moved into the borderland ethnorepublics during Soviet rule had neither the need nor an incentive to learn the titular language. If Russophones want to become part of post-colonial society, then they have little choice but to learn the now appointed language of position and status. It is therefore not surprising that, under these circumstances, as David Laitin notes, there is a propensity for individuals from the minority groupings to behave as rational actors in encouraging their offspring to learn the titular language in order to secure the longer-term privileges that accrue from language mobility and from gaining a prerequisite resource for entering the middle-class job market before it is saturated.[43] There are, however, other incentives to conform: in some of the borderland states, 'for the post-colonial to speak or write in the imperial tongues is to call forth a problem of identity, to be thrown into mimicry and ambivalence'.[44]

'The other' inside national minorities

For national minorities, however, the idea of conforming to cultural standardisation, of becoming part of the project of the nationalising state, has so far had little impact in transforming them from minorities into national citizens in which the identity markers that distinguish 'them'

	REGIONALISED COMMUNITY	
	YES	NO
STATE PATRON — YES	Russians in TransDniester, North-East Estonia, Crimea; Armenians in Nagorno-Karabakh; Lezgins in Azerbaijan; Poles in Lithuania; Uzbeks in Osh region of Kyrgyzstan.	Russians in Belarus, Uzbekistan, Georgia.
STATE PATRON — NO	Abkhazians, Adzharians, Crimean Tatars, Gagauz in Moldova.	Gypsies in Moldova, Belarus, Lithuania, Ukraine; Meskhetian Turks in Central Asia.

Figure 1.1. Minority groupings in the borderland states

from 'us' have dissipated. In understanding the dynamic relationship between such nationalising regimes and minority groupings, two perspectives in particular are important.[45] The first concerns the extent to which minorities constitute a regionalised community. This is especially vital for those groupings which inhabit a particular region with which they have had a long association or which they regard as their ancestral homeland. Other things being equal, such regionalised communities are more likely to possess stronger social networks and greater opportunity through these social networks to articulate collective grievances compared to those minorities who are more spatially scattered throughout the borderland state. The second important variable is whether a minority possesses a patron state, that is, one which considers its co-nationals living in a borderland state as part of its geopolitical responsibility and which is willing and able to devote considerable economic, political and even military resources to protecting or advancing their interests. On this basis, by juxtaposing these two perspectives, we can distinguish between four types of minority groupings (figure 1.1).

In the first grouping, a secessionist potential exists although, with the exception of TransDniester, this potential has not been fully utilised by the local ethnoregional community. Of all the minorities, it is this grouping, because of the potential to question the territorial integrity of its sovereign boundaries, which is invariably perceived by the nationalising state as the greatest threat. Here inter-communal tensions have often become explosive amongst minorities who may receive greater material, organisational or moral support from a state patron, and whose sense of community and social networks are stronger in part due to being embedded in a regionalised community.[46] However, it is important not to under-estimate the constraining role that either local or national institutions play in political mobilisation. In some instances limited political opportunities to articulate grievances at either the local or the national level can inhibit the ethnic mobilisation of minorities. In other instances, the existence of political institutions, especially regional ones, can mobilise minority groupings. As Philip Roeder has noted, 'The most successful ethnic chal-lengers to the central governments have tended to emerge within the regional administrative apparatus of the state itself.'[47] In a number of such instances, it has been the pre-existing local Communist Party which has acted as a basis for ethnic mobilisation, as in the Donbas (Ukraine) and, in the period before it was formally banned, also in the Russophone enclaves of south-east Latvia (Latgallia) and in north-east Estonia.

In the second grouping, nation-state aspirations exist amongst a regionalised community but with no external support (e.g. Crimean Tatars, Abkhazians). Due to the absence of a state patron, the organisa-tional, material and symbolic resources available are therefore either more limited or non-existent, which makes such ethnoregional groupings more likely victims of a potentially nationalising state. Certainly such regimes are less persuaded of the need to let the region secede. It is these minorities that have often been most prone to the extreme policies of ethnification, including population transfers, refugee migration and state-sponsored decolonisation from their ancestral territory. However, as in the case of Abkhazians in Abkhazia in the post-1991 period, such popula-tion transfers under conditions of civil war can occasionally involve an exit of the larger state nation from a region, as with the Georgians.

The third grouping is likely to be of less geopolitical concern to the state patron principally because there are no obvious geopolitical benefits or issues at stake. Minorities in this grouping tend to be less organised collectively, in part due to their more dispersed nature. Due also to the lack of regional community that potentially could provide the basis for some form of local autonomous administration, they are least likely to be accorded special status by such nationalising regimes. Amongst this grouping we find high incidence of 'return migration' to the patron state homeland, especially amongst Russians from the Central Asian states of Uzbekistan, Turkmenistan and Kyrgyzstan.

The final grouping includes those minorities who have no obvious state patron and who lack any sense of regionalised community. The classic case is the Gypsies in Moldova, Belarus, Ukraine and Lithuania who are so poorly integrated into the legal, political and national culture of the majority society that they do not even manage to lay effective claim to the rights of citizenship and self-defence through the use of organisation and mobilisation.[48] Included in this category are several 'dispersed peoples', like the Meskhetian Turks, who were forcibly moved eastwards under the Stalinist regime but whose one-time homeland does not possess an obvious patron state.

Plan of the book

The rest of this book is divided into three parts based upon what can be considered as three key perspectives in the reconstruction of national identities in the borderland states. In part I, we examine how the national histories of the borderland states are being rewritten, especially in relation to new nationalising historiographies. Prominent within such national-ising historiographies, it is argued, are mythic narratives, including myths of origin and descent which serve as a means of legitimating current boundaries of homeland in the face of counter-narratives by 'others', who question the legitimacy of such myths of national destiny and who are themselves engaged in putting forward alternative interpretations of their place within the borderlands. Part II explores the ethnopolitics of group boundary construction both at a formal level through such means as the codification of citizenship and through nationalising policies, and at an informal level through the characterisation of 'other' groups as part of an inter-group discourse. In particular we consider the role that minority groupings as 'the constitutive other' play in shaping nationalising policies and the consequences that follow for ethnic relations, democratisation and the rights of minorities from such a politics of inclusion and exclu-sion. Finally, part III examines the relationship between nation-building and language by exploring the politics both of language and language policy, and of how the reconstruction of national identities and the search to secure a central, even hegemonic, role for revitalised national cultures are bound up with the way in which nationalising elites are engaged in socially reconstructing their national histories to legitimise the key role for a national language within the borderland states.

Part I

Rediscovering national histories

2 National history and national identity in Ukraine and Belarus

This chapter seeks to examine the relationship between historiography and the nation as an 'imagined community' in Russia's two east Slavic neighbours, Ukraine and Belarus. The focus of the analysis is on the mythic[1] structures of national historiography as a key influence shaping evolving national identities, and on the tug on identities exercised by rival narratives of the past, here classified for convenience's sake as 'Ukrainophile'/'Belarusophile' and 'Russophile' or 'pan-Slavic'.[2] The former have come to the fore since independence in 1991, but Russophile myths have proved powerful and persistent, particularly in Belarus but also amongst the half of the population of Ukraine that is either ethnic Russian or Russian-speaking (see chapter 6). The historical, or historiographical, component of national identities in the region is therefore in transition. The single narrative of the Soviet era has given way not to monolithic new national alternatives, but to a fluid situation characterised by competing myths and dissonant voices. Whereas a potentially strong, if controversial, historiographical mythology is under construction in Ukraine, a key reason for the relative weakness of the Belarusian national movement to date has been its inability to displace hegemonic Russophile myths and anchor a new Belarusian identity firmly in a rival historiography.[3]

Russophile historiography, on the other hand, has so far failed to address seriously the fact of Ukrainian and Belarusian independence, and has remained content to recycle the myths of the tsarist and Soviet eras. Although this provides the ideological ammunition for postures of denial, it does not help promote a politics of practical engagement. Moreover, it has granted Ukrainians at least more of an ideological space for 'nation-building' than they enjoyed in 1917–20, and has left the large potential middle ground (largely Russophone Ukrainians) ill equipped to adjust to their new status.

The chapter begins by providing an analytical taxonomy of the key myths that form the building blocks of the rival historiographies. The Ukrainophile and Belarusophile versions of history are then examined in

23

detail before being compared to the rival Russophile conception.[4] The chapter concludes with an analysis of the potential comparative strength of the three strands.[5]

The mythic structure of Ukrainophile and Belarusophile historiography

The way a nation describes its origins reveals a lot about its modern-day priorities. The search by nationalist historians for proof of national uniqueness tends to begin with the identification of an ethnic substratum that encapsulates the modern nation in embryonic form. For the Belarusians this is the Krivichian people who dominated what became the north-western marches of the early medieval Kievan state; for the Ukrainians it is the Polianians of the same era. The nation's pre-history is then told as a *myth of ethnogenesis*, which begins a narrative of separate development and myth of national character, serving to liberate both peoples from the myth propagated in the Soviet era that they shared a common origin with the Russians as a single 'old Rus´ nation'.[6]

Homeland myths are closely tied up with notions of ethnogenesis. They tend to be of two main types. Either the eponymous group is deemed to have occupied its given national territory since time immemorial, or, if it arrived as a result of migration or land seizure,[7] then those whom it displaced are depicted as marginal peoples who left no claim on the land they fleetingly occupied. The main task of homeland myths is therefore the fixing of a given bounded territory as the national patrimony, which is always imagined at its greatest supposed historical extent. The subsequent loss of national territory to other groups or polities does not change its eternal status. Thus a 'Greater Ukraine' would include areas such as the Kuban´ in the north Caucasus and Lemko Poland, a 'Greater Belarus' the Lithuanian capital of Vilnius (Vil´nia), Bialystok (Belastok) in Poland and even the Smolensk region in Russia. On the other hand, contrary claims, such as the Russian assertion that Crimea and the Donbas are historically Russian territories, are rejected by seeking to demonstrate the regions' long, unbroken connections with the eponymous nation.

Foundation myths serve to sanctify the national myth of descent by providing a concrete beginning that announces the arrival of the national group on the historical stage. 'Foundation' is normally dated to the first significant polity established on national territory, even if alternative histories have ascribed that polity to an alternative national group or mocked its claims to statehood. For the Ukrainians, their national history therefore formally begins with the foundation of Kievan Rus´ in the ninth century AD. For the Belarusians the lack of a resonant starting point is a serious problem. Hence the history of Rus´ is rewritten to claim that its north-western territories were really the autonomous kingdom of Polatskaia-Rus´.

Myths of antiquity and *myths of descent* are another important means of establishing that the eponymous nation is more than just an artificial construct. National history is therefore stretched as far back in time as possible, and discontinuities in national history are bridged by the construction of a continuous narrative through the centuries (or even the millennia). Where necessary, periods, individuals and events that traditionally belonged to other narratives are reclaimed to create *polity myths* that assert the nation's long and continuous tradition of statehood. A rich and fulsome chronology thereby replaces tsarist and Soviet historiography, with its long gaps and silences during which the Ukrainian and Belarusian peoples were deemed not to act as historical subjects at all. Ukrainophile historians fill in the lacunae between the decline of Rus´ in the thirteenth century and the Cossack 'revival' four centuries later by arguing that Ukrainian traditions, even statehood, persisted into the Galician and Lithuanian periods. The Belarusians have to make do with hyphenation, reinventing the medieval Lithuanian-Belarusian kingdom as an ersatz Belarusian polity, whose Belarusian essence supposedly survived both dynastic (the Union of Krevo in 1385) and eventual political union with Poland (the Union of Lublin in 1569). Remnants of both Belarusian and Ukrainian statehood supposedly persisted right up to the final annexation of national territory by Russia in the late eighteenth century.

'National revival' in the present is normally predicated on the restoration of past glories. *Myths of a 'Golden Age'* therefore invoke the embodiment of the national genius at its zenith to provide proof that the nation can rise again in the present. The establishment of a 'Golden Age' serves to refute the assertions of detractors that the eponymous nation is somehow lacking in tradition or culture, or is an artificial construct of nationalist ideologues. Ukrainians therefore point to the Kievan and Cossack periods as times when their nation was at a peak of cultural creativity and a leading member of the European concord of states. The Belarusian Golden Age came between the Unions of Krevo and Lublin, when Belarusian language, culture and legal and political traditions held sway over the largest state in eastern Europe.

For Ukrainophiles and Belarusophiles their nations possess a distinct and glorious heritage. *Myths of national character* and *myths of the other* are therefore a vital means of delineating a separate past and providing boundary markers to distinguish the eponymous nation from its neighbours.[8] The three most common character myths in both Ukrainian and Belarusian historiography are that their nations are democratic, demotic and European. Their democratic character is supposedly exemplified by the tradition of popular assembly and sturdy individualism. Their demotic nature lies in the manner in which national character was preserved by the local peasantry despite the (often forcible) assimilation of national elites. Finally, it is argued that natural intercourse with (the rest of) Europe was rudely and unnaturally severed by Russian occupation. Both nations therefore see themselves at the dawn of the twenty-first century as *returning* to Europe and to their associated democratic traditions.

These myths also constitute boundary markers to distinguish Ukrainians and Belarusians from Russians, the main traditional 'other', who are portrayed as natural despots and imperialists, with an 'Asian' political culture that is even in crucial respects non-Slavic. Subsidiary stereotyping casts Poles as perfidious aristocratic interlopers, Lithuanians as pagans civilised by the Belarusians and so on. *Myths of aggression* and *exploitation* and *myths of empire* replace the traditional narrative of the 'Great Friendship' of the east Slavic peoples. The Pereiaslav 'reunion' between Russia and Ukraine in 1654 is reinvented as a contract of convenience subsequently betrayed, while Russian attempts to 'liberate' Belarus from the Polish-Lithuanian yoke are painted as a series of bloody wars of aggression. Subsequent relations are characterised via *myths of colonialism* and *myths of suffering* that depict the nation as the hapless victim of systems of imperial rule.

On the other hand, *myths of national resistance* and *myths of revival* are designed to prove that the nation retained its character under occupation, and demonstrate its existential urge towards freedom from foreign rule. The achievement of statehood in 1991 is therefore legitimated by presenting it as the result of a long, arduous and heroic period of struggle, rather than historical accident or the self-interested manoeuvrings of politicians. National history under foreign 'occupation' is reinterpreted retrospectively as a teleological struggle towards inevitable national revival, and different narratives obscured or occluded. For the Belarusians (and the Lithuanians) the great Polish national hero Adam Mickiewicz was actually a fighter for Belarusian (or Lithuanian) national rights. For Ukrainians, Gogol was a true patriot, despite the fact that he wrote in Russian. Moreover, national revival is always the restoration of the Golden Age and the reaffirmation of the national character, the 'rediscovery' of submerged tradition rather than the invention of national intellectuals. Independence in 1991 was the natural culmination of these processes.

Pan-Slavic or Russophile myths

However, local nationalist narratives are far from being the only historical discourse available. National identities are not necessarily *tabulae rasae* awaiting the imprint of new national myth-making; in both Ukraine and Belarus the *myths of the tsarist and Soviet eras* persist and enjoy deep-rooted popularity. Furthermore, they are not just external in origin – that is, the product of the ideologues of a potentially revanchist Russian state – but are also the work of historians and publicists in Ukraine and Belarus themselves. In particular there is considerable resistance to attempts to disentangle Ukrainian and Belarusian history from that of Russia and to depict Russia exclusively as the imperial 'other'.

Pan-Slavic or Russophile historiography has its own mythic structure. First and foremost is the persistent *myth of the common origin* of the three east Slavic peoples, reinforced by *myths of separation* that claim that their divergence between the thirteenth and seventeenth centuries was solely the result of artificial political divisions and, in any case, was only skin-deep. Second therefore are *myths of reunion* in the seventeenth and eighteenth centuries, alongside *myths of common Orthodoxy* and the consequent existence of a community of fate as the main inspiration for reunion. It is denied that only 'empire' brought the three peoples together.

The Ukrainian and Belarusian national revivals of the nineteenth century are explained away via *myths of foreign intrigue*. The true 'other' for all the east Slavs is depicted in myths of the Tatar, Polish, German/Habsburg or papal threat, and *myths of common endeavour* are built around the joint resistance of all three peoples to such outside dangers. The final myth is the idea that whatever statehood Belarusians and Ukrainians now enjoy is in fact a product of their joint labours in the Soviet period.

The above short outline demonstrates the potential for wholesale contradiction between rival versions of east Slavic history. The analysis now turns to a detailed examination of the alternative mythologies, starting with the Ukrainophile/Belarusophile dimension.

The local version of Ukrainian and Belarusian history

National history has a much longer pedigree in Ukraine than in Belarus. In Belarus, despite limited work by a handful of predecessors,[9] the first truly 'national' historians were Vatslaŭ Lastoŭski (1883–1938) and Usevalad Ihnatoŭski (1881–1931),[10] although even Ihnatoŭski has been criticised for his Marxist-influenced approach and for his failure to carry the narrative of separate Belarusian development past the Union of Lublin in 1569 (see p. 35, n. 76). Moreover, after a brief flowering in the 1920s, the 'national' historiographical school was suppressed with much greater thoroughness than its equivalent in Ukraine.[11] Ihnatoŭski was therefore unable to establish a canon of national historiography in the manner of Franciszek Palacký in the Czech lands or Mykhailo Hrushevs´kyi in Ukraine (see below).

The roots of Ukrainian national historiography, on the other hand, go back at least to the Cossack chroniclers of the eighteenth century, such as Samiilo Velychko (1670–1728) and Hryhorii Hrab´ianka (1670?–1738).[12] However, early historians such as Mykola Kostomarov (1817–85) were still influenced by theories of the common origins and joint development of the Ukrainian and Russian peoples.[13] It was left to Mykhailo Hrushevs´kyi (1866–1934)[14] to establish a complete schema of Ukrainian ethnohistory, which was developed and refined by his disciples in the Soviet 1920s, in western Ukraine between the wars and in the Ukrainian emigration. The 'Hrushevs´kyi school' has been the single most powerful influence on modern Ukrainian historiography, although certain emphases and aspects have been added in the 1990s.

On the other hand, the historical bifurcation of Ukrainian culture between Ukrainophones and Russophones (see chapter 6) has been a factor preventing the Ukrainophile schema from becoming hegemonic. Whereas historiography in Belarus is polarised between Belarusophiles and Russophiles, in Ukraine there are many historians and archaeologists who have attempted to combine moderate Ukrainian patriotism with elements of traditional Russophile historiography, and indeed those from all points of the spectrum who have attacked the tendency of nationalism to displace scientific method.[15]

Myths of origin: Ukraine

The key premise of the Ukrainophile myth of origin is that 'the Ukrainian people are autochthonous (aboriginal) on their native land. This means that they have lived on the very same territory [the lands of the middle Dnieper] since the beginning of their existence.'[16] Whereas Hrushevs´kyi tended to begin his narrative of Ukrainian 'ethnogenesis' with the main precursor of the Polianians – the Antes tribal federation of the fourth to seventh centuries AD – many modern Ukrainian archaeologists and historians have gone back much further into the pre-Christian era (ironically the Ukrainians have been able to take over earlier tsarist/Soviet myths of the autochthonous origin of the local Slavs),[17] arguing that the Ukrainian ethnos developed through the mixture of early proto-Slavic and a succession of Iranian and Ural-Altai (mainly Turkic) elements.

Ukrainian civilisation is therefore deemed to be one of the oldest in the world. Some historians have even made the hyperbolic claim that the lost Arcadian '"Golden Age" [or "second Babylon"] described by the ancient Greeks most probably was neither in Egypt nor in muddy Mesopotamia, but on the territory of Ukraine', thanks to 'its warm climate, fertile black earth, flat fecund steppe, the clean waters of its rivers and its masses of wild animals'.[18] The first group deemed to have created a more or less settled society to take advantage of these natural riches was the neolithic Trypol'ean (in Ukrainian Trypillian) pottery culture which existed from around 4000 BC to approximately 2700 BC. As well as being the first true 'substratum of the Ukrainian people, which provided the basis for our national worldview', the Trypillian culture is held to have been 'the most developed civilisation [of the time], not only in Europe but in the whole world', whose achievements included the first domestication of the horse.[19] It has even been claimed that an early Trypillian state, 'Arrata', existed on the middle Dnieper,[20] and that it served as the cradle of all subsequent Indo-European civilisation. Ukraine, then as warm as 'today's Africa', was 'the original Indo-European home', and 'Kiev the oldest city of the people of the White race [sic]'.[21] Much of the canon of classical (Greek) mythology was allegedly derived from the Trypillian store of myths and legends.[22]

As Trypillian culture was not literate, however, most of this is pure speculation, based on the methodologically dubious discipline of 'cultural-historical archaeology', that is, the practice of imputing ethnic and/or linguistic identities from the 'evidence' of pottery or grave sites.[23] In the absence of proper written records there has been little to restrain such flights of fancy.

The Trypillian culture eventually declined, but Ukrainophiles claim that its traditions were preserved amongst the local population, who re-emerged as first the little-known Cimmerians (? to 700 BC), and then the Scythians (750 to 250 BC). Contrary to the claims of other historians,[24] it is argued that only one part of the polyethnic Scythian mix were Iranian migrants from the east; most were the direct descendants of the Trypillians and therefore 'proto-Slavs'.[25] Once again, it is claimed that the Scythians, 'our ancestors', established 'the most cultured country in Europe' of the time.[26]

Natural limits to this ethnic melting pot were provided 'from the Belarusians by the Pryp''iat' marshes, and from Russian terrain by massive forests';[27] a decisive pattern of separate local development was therefore already set. When the Scythians were succeeded in turn by the Sarmatians (second century BC to second century AD),[28] this was once again a case of renaming and re-emergence rather than wholesale replacement (although again with an Iranian influx), as was the emergence of the Antes federation in the fourth century AD. The Antes federation is described (following Hrushevs'kyi) as the first true 'eastern Slav political union', even 'the first Ukrainian state', 'upon whose ruins' Kievan Rus' eventually arose in the ninth century.[29] The final link in the chain is the direct successors of the Antes, the Polianians (*poliany*), who were to play 'the leading role in establishing the old Rus´ state'.[30]

The Ukrainophile myth of origin therefore claims a long and continuous path of indigenous development over several thousand years. Some have even asserted that 'the Scythians–Ukrainians are the oldest nation in Europe, and possibly in the world'.[31] In addition, it is argued that 'since ancient times each new wave of migrants, traders and other displaced peoples on Ukrainian territory has somehow merged into the stream of previous cultures . . . providing their own elements' to the Ukrainian character, but never displacing that which came before.[32] Alternative theories of Gothic influence in the region are emphatically rejected.

Myths of origin: Belarus

For Belarusophiles there is a similar need to disentangle a myth of national ethnogenesis from Russophile historiography in order to provide a separate starting point for their myth of national descent. In essence the Belarusophile myth of origin is a variant of the 'substratum' theory shared with most Ukrainophiles,[33] according to which different groups of Slavic tribes mingled with local non-Slavic elements to create the basic ethnic characteristics of the three east Slavic peoples. In the same way as the Iranian admixture created Ukrainians and Finno-Ugric blood the Russians, the 'symbiosis of Slavic and Baltic cultures became in turn the basis for the formation of Belarusian culture'.[34] Belarusians have consequently always had one foot in the Western world. (In the 1920s Lastoŭski and others even argued that Dacian and Getic elements formed part of the Belarusian ethnic substratum.)[35]

In contrast to the traditional Russophile view, Belarusophiles therefore claim that the various tribes that made up the east Slavic world of the second half of the first millennium were already highly differentiated. The main proto-Belarusian tribe, the equivalent to the Polianians for the Ukrainians, was the Krivichians (*kryvichy*), along with the Drehovichians (*dryhavichy*) and Radmichians (*radzimichy*). Archaeological studies and the evidence provided by local toponyms and hydronyms demonstrate that their culture, although kindred to that of neighbouring tribes, was nevertheless unique.[36]

Foundation myths: Ukraine

For both Ukrainophiles and Belarusophiles, national history proper begins with Kievan Rus´. However, while Ukrainians have sought to invert traditional Russian historiography by claiming the entire tradition of Rus´ as their own, Belarusians have challenged the conception of Rus´ as a centralised state and argued that the north-western territories inhabited by the Krivichians were autonomous and in a more or less constant state of warfare with Kiev. Both, however, seek to refute the myth prevalent in tsarist and Soviet times that all three east Slavic peoples were originally one (the different versions of this myth are examined in greater detail in the section on Russophile historiography below, p. 43).[37]

The Ukrainophile claim is that, in the words of the 1991 declaration of Ukrainian independence, the Ukrainians have a 'thousand-year tradition of state-building', beginning in the ninth century AD.[38] As in Russophile historiography, the 'Normanist theory' that Rus´ was in fact established by Viking envoys, is rejected as a German invention.[39] However, it is further argued that the ancestors of modern-day Ukrainians played a dominant and the ancestors of contemporary Russians a marginal role in the foundation and governance of Rus´.[40] Rus´ was founded by the Polianians and therefore embodied the local cultural traditions in development since Trypillian times.[41]

The culture, religion and spoken language of Rus´ were all therefore in essence proto-Ukrainian. Following the theory first developed by Mykhailo Maksymovych in the nineteenth century, many Ukrainian nationalists argue that the original east Slavic (proto-) language had already split into three branches by the middle of the first millennium AD (most historians would date linguistic differentiation no earlier than the fourteenth or fifteenth century),[42] and that 'proto-Ukrainian' existed as a language even before the monks Cyril and Methodius introduced their alphabet in 863 AD. Although 'Church Slavonic or Old Bulgarian' were used for literary and ecclesiastical purposes, supposedly 'the basic conversational language of the people who lived from Transcarpathia to the Don and from the Pryp´´iat´ [marshes] to the Black Sea steppe was Ukrainian', albeit not 'of course the Ukrainian of today' but still fundamentally recognisable as the same tongue.[43]

As regards the Russians, some Ukrainians have even suggested that they are not true Slavs at all, but linguistically adapted Ugro-Finns.[44] Alternatively, it is argued that the formation of a separate Russian nation began only after the northern regions lost cultural contact with Kiev in the thirteenth century,[45] when the north-eastern inhabitants 'went native' amongst the local population until Kiev reacquainted them with its traditions in the seventeenth century. Above all, the idea that there was a single 'Old Rus´' nationality is decisively rejected.[46] 'We' and 'they' already existed and were often in conflict, as when Andrei Bogoliubskii's northern armies sacked Kiev in 1169.

The idea of Rus´ as a (proto-) Ukrainian state is not, however, uncontested. Some of Ukraine's most distinguished scholars have continued to emphasise the multiethnic, or anational, character of Rus´ history and culture,[47] and have argued that 'it [would be] premature to speak of Ukrainians, Russians or Belarusians in the ninth to thirteenth century', and 'scientifically incorrect to attempt to "present" the Old Rus´ heritage to only one of these modern peoples'.[48] Viewed in such a light, Kievan Rus´ could serve as a model exemplar for a modern-day multiethnic Ukrainian society and broaden the mythological foundations of the state. The narrower ethnographic conception, however, appears to be winning ground.

Foundation myths: Belarus

For Belarusian nationalists, just as the Polianians founded Kiev, so the Krivichians founded the city, later principality, of Polatsk. Moreover, the north-western territories of Rus´ that were under the control of Polatsk were 'not dependent, either politically or economically, either on Novgorod or on Kiev'.[49] There was not one single Rus´ therefore, but several. Belarusophiles like to refer to what they term 'Polatskaia-Rus´' as 'a completely independent old-Belarusian state, with all the corresponding attributes – a sovereign ruler and assembly [*kniaz´ i vecha*], administration, capital, armed forces, monetary system, etc.'.[50] It is even argued that Polatsk was founded before Kiev, and that elements of Belarusian statehood existed as early as the sixth century AD.[51] A separate 'eparchy' of the Kievan Church was supposedly established at Polatsk in 922 AD.[52]

Polatskaia-Rus´ flourished under the dynasty established by Prince Rahvalod, especially Usiaslaŭ (1044–1101), and reached its apogee as a centre of culture and learning under the patronage of St Euphrosyne/Eŭfrasinnia (1104–73).[53] During this 'Golden Age', the territories under Polatsk's control reached as far as modern Poland and the upper Volga. Only during the reign of Volodymyr the Great (980–1015) were Polatsk and Kiev under the same single authority; at other times, as in 1127–9, the two were at war.

Myths of descent: Ukraine

It is important that a national history should be continuous. 'Statehood' is therefore found where previously it was held to be missing, and myths of institutional, societal or cultural continuity are used to link together otherwise disparate links in the national chain of descent.[54] The 'claim to statehood' (in Ukrainian *derzhavnist'*, in Belarusian *dziarzhaŭnasts'*) became a particularly strong theme after independence in 1991, as, in comparison to nineteenth-century populist historians, the main task was to legitimate political institutions inherited from the Soviet era rather than to identify the national character of a stateless people in the under-culture of the *narod*.

The task is easier for Ukrainophiles. If Kievan Rus' is included, the period after 1990–1 is routinely described as Ukraine's *fourth* period of statehood,[55] after the Cossack Hetmanate of the seventeenth and eighteenth centuries and the Ukrainian People's Republic of 1917–20. Historians merely have to plug the gaps in between. For Belarusophiles, however, statehood has to be reclaimed from different historiographical traditions (the Belarusian People's Republic of 1918 is difficult to depict as a real state).

According to Ukrainophiles, the effect of the Tatar incursion in the thirteenth century has been exaggerated by Russian historians seeking to claim that nothing of significance survived in the Kievan territories after 1240, and that the traditions of Rus' were forced to transfer to the north.[56] On the contrary, it now tends to be argued that Ukrainian society and Ukrainian institutions survived largely unscathed after 1240. In the west the 'centre of [Ukrainian] statehood passed to' the Kingdom of Galicia-Volhynia, which flourished until the 1340s.[57] Further to the east, the territories around Kiev enjoyed virtually complete autonomy under Lithuanian rule from the fourteenth century until the Union of Lublin in 1569. According to one account,

the Grand Principality of Lithuania was a polyethnic state. The Lithuanians' main priority was that the ruling Gediminas dynasty should come from the Lithuanian feudal order. In the other spheres of state and social life Ukrainians and Belarusians were equal with Lithuanians (the feudal classes as a semi-sovereign state, the Orthodox clergy, military retinues and so on). The languages of government, the courts and education were old Belarusian and old Ukrainian. All this provides the basis to consider the Grand Principality of Lithuania as a form of Ukrainian statehood which was lost [only] as a consequence of the Union of Lublin in 1569.[58]

This in turn makes it easier to claim the Cossack period was a direct revival of the traditions of Rus', rather than a phenomenon unique to the seventeenth century.[59]

The Cossack era is therefore the crucial link in Ukrainian historical mythology. Three myths stand out in particular. First, the Cossack rebellion led by Bohdan Khmel'nyts'kyi in 1648 is depicted as an ethnic Ukrainian 'war of liberation', rather than a mere *Jacquerie*.[60] Secondly, it is argued that the 'Hetmanate' established by Khmel'nyts'kyi was in fact a Ukrainian 'state', rather than merely the semi-autonomous military encampment of the Cossack army, the Zaporozhian Host (despite the views of some Ukrainian historians such as Panteleimon Kulish and Volodymyr Antonovych, who criticised the Cossacks for their inattention to 'state-building').[61] Thirdly, elements of that statehood supposedly persisted until the late eighteenth century,[62] leaving a relatively short gap before national revival in the nineteenth century culminated in the establishment of the Ukrainian People's Republic (UNR) and West Ukrainian People's Republic (ZUNR) in 1917–18.

The UNR, in turn, has assumed increasing importance in the post-Soviet period. Unlike the Baltic states, modern Ukraine does not claim legal descent from its post-revolutionary 'predecessor',[63] but the state symbols, hymn and currency of the UNR (themselves supposedly descending from the Kievan and Cossack periods) have all been appropriated to underpin the legitimacy of the modern state. In the historiography of the period, the UNR and ZUNR are idealised and their internal problems (and failure to co-operate) downplayed. Other events unfolding on Ukrainian territory after the 1917 revolution are less prominent in the analysis, and local support for the Bolsheviks is minimised.[64] Once such cross-currents are pushed to the margins, it can be asserted that 'what we are used to calling a civil war in Ukraine in 1917–20 was in fact a Russian–Ukrainian war – an imperialist [war of] conquest on the part of Russia, a [war of] liberation on the part of Ukraine',[65] and that the eventual collapse of the UNR in 1920 was due to 'Russian chauvinist Bolshevism unleashing a war of conquest against the young Ukrainian state',[66] rather than the inherent weaknesses of the Ukrainian national movement. The drama of 'us' (Ukraine) against 'them' (Russia) is therefore replayed.

Even the autocrat Pavlo Skoropads'kyi, who temporarily usurped power from the UNR in 1918 and eventually sought refederation with Russia, is described as earning 'himself a separate page in the history of the liberation struggle of the Ukrainian people in the twentieth century' through his support for the development of Ukrainian education and culture.[67]

Myths of descent: Belarus

Belarusophiles divide national history into four key periods: Polatskaia-Rus' from the ninth to the thirteenth centuries; a Lithuanian-Belarusian period from the reign of Mendaŭh (Mindaugas) to the Union of Lublin in 1569; a Polish-Belarusian period from 1569 to 1795; and the

Russian/Soviet period from 1795 to 1991.[68] They argue that continuity of Belarusian quasi-statehood was maintained throughout the first three periods, and was only finally extinguished in the 1790s. The 1994 constitution of Belarus therefore referred proudly to the 'centuries-long tradition of the development of Belarusian statehood'.[69]

The rudiments of statehood bequeathed by Polatskaia-Rus´ were supposedly relatively well preserved after the Tatar onslaught of the thirteenth century, as the north-western territories of Rus´ were the only ones to escape occupation. Many Belarusophiles argue that this is the origin of the prefix to their proper name: Bela-rus´ or White Rus´, meaning pure or unoccupied.[70] The key role in establishing the early Lithuanian kingdom in 1316–85 was played by the principalities of Polatsk and Novaharadok, not by ethnic Lithuanians.[71]

Supposedly, therefore, 'Belarusian was the state language of the Lithuanian Kingdom, because the Belarusian ethnic element dominated the political, economic and cultural life of the Kingdom, and our [Belarusian] lands were the basis of its greatness.'[72] The name for the inhabitants of the state (*litviny*) referred at that time to the Slavic Belarusians, not to the Lithuanians, who were known as *zhamoity* (*zhmudziny*).[73]

The Union of Krevo in 1385 which formed a dynastic union (only) between the Lithuanian-Belarusian and Polish kingdoms did not materially change the situation, as it was primarily a defensive measure designed to resist the pressure of the Teutonic Knights,[74] gloriously defeated by an international army depicted as under Belarusian leadership at the Battle of Grunwald in 1410.[75] Only with the (political) Union of Lublin in 1569 did Belarus begin to experience serious Polonising pressure, although even then elements of Belarusian independence persisted right up until final incorporation into the Russian Empire in 1793–5.[76] The Belarusian writer Maksim Bahdanovich was therefore able to claim in 1914 that Belarusian language and culture had remained fundamentally unchanged from the earliest times to the beginnings of forcible Russification in the 1840s.[77]

Belarusophiles have also attempted to play up the importance of the Belarusian People's Republic (BNR) established in 1918, portraying it, like the UNR in Ukraine, as a manifestation of the popular will towards national self-determination.[78] However, its existence was brief and the influence of German occupying forces more manifest than is the case of the UNR. Emphasis is therefore also placed on the 1920 'Slutsk rebellion' of Belarusian forces against the Red Army in order to promote the myth of forcible (re)incorporation into the Russian sphere.[79]

Homeland myths: Ukraine

Nationalist historiographies tend to develop myths of irrevocable association between a people and a particular territory, 'a rightful possession
from one's forefathers through the generations'.[80] The states of postcommunist eastern Europe, however, tend to have newly established
boundaries, few of which neatly coincide with the territorial limits of
nations as 'imagined communities'. The local nationalist vision of the
Ukrainian and Belarusian 'homeland' is therefore both expansive, in so
far as its definition of the national patrimony includes territory now occupied by other states (including each other), and defensive, as the national
homeland must be protected from the claims made by rival nationalisms.

In the Ukrainian case, the current borders of the state do not coincide
with any previous incarnation of Ukraine. The claim to long-standing
occupation of particular territories therefore ranges far and wide, especially with reference to what is now southern and eastern Ukraine. Some
Ukrainophiles go as far back as the Scythian and Sarmatian periods, as
their centre of gravity lay more in the open steppe than in the lands
around the middle Dnieper.[81] Most accounts, however, begin with
Kievan Rus', whose western borders are deemed to have included
Transcarpathia, Bukovyna and TransDniester and reached as far as the
regions of Peremyshyl and Cherven (now in Poland and Slovakia respectively).[82] In the south-west the Galician kingdom is depicted as controlling the region around Bessarabia. In the south-east, it is argued that Rus'
succeeded in dominating the steppe, establishing mini-states in the
eastern Crimea (on the basis of the earlier Bosphoran kingdom) and at
Tmutorokan' in the Kuban' after the defeat of the Khazars. The latter
supposedly lasted from 965 to 1117 AD.[83]

However, the key period for establishing a Ukrainian presence in the
steppe and Crimea is the Cossack era. In the south-east it is argued that
two waves of Cossack settlement to the east (Kharkiv or Slobids'ka
Ukraine) and south-east (the Don basin) established a Ukrainian presence *before* the rival wave of Russian colonisation from the north, and in
much greater numbers.[84] In the south, Ukrainophiles stress the role of
Kiev in helping to establish the Crimean Tatar state in the fifteenth
century, and the importance of subsequent links between the Cossacks
and Tatars.[85] The Ukrainian orientalist Ahatanhel Kryms'kyi even
argued in the 1920s that the Ukrainians/Slavs played a vital role in establishing and running the Ottoman Empire.[86] The Russophile myth that
Slavic settlement of both regions began only after Russia's defeat of the
Crimean Tatars and Ottoman Turks in the late eighteenth century is
therefore rejected.[87]

Homeland myths: Belarus

As in Ukraine, Belarusian nationalists have relied on a mixture of history and ethnography to construct their image of homeland, which, like that of Ukrainian nationalists, is not contained by the current borders of the state.[88] In the East, it is pointed out that the state borders of 'Lithuania-Belarus' extended east of Smolensk, which was only definitively lost to Russia in 1667.[89] Belarus' natural ethnographic borders therefore reach to within 200 miles of Moscow. In the West, it is stressed that Vil′nia (Vilnius) was established as the state capital of the *litviny* in the fourteenth century when it was already an ethnically 'Belarusian city'.[90] In the Belarusian case, the shrinkage of national territory in the present is therefore felt more acutely than in Ukraine, where the shoring up of the national territorial imagination is mainly a defensive task.

Significantly, Belarusian and Ukrainian historians even have conflicting histories of their mutual borderlands. Belarusian nationalists claim that much of the population of north-west Ukraine are in fact denationalised Belarusians who were once part of the medieval 'Lithuanian-Belarusian' state. Ukrainian nationalists, on the other hand, press the counterclaim that the population of areas such as Brest in south-west Belarus are denationalised Ukrainians, as reflected by the decision of the 1918 Treaty of Brest-Litovsk to grant the area to Ukraine.[91]

Myths of national character and myths of the 'other': Ukraine

In terms of their main singular 'other', Ukrainophiles and Belarusophiles share a similar view of Russia (although subsidiary stereotyping exists for Poles, Jews, Lithuanians, etc.). Common themes are that Ukraine and Belarus are by nature 'European' civilisations, the last frontier against 'Asiatic' Russia (as with Poland and Russia, or Germany and Poland, civilisation is deemed to finish at the state's eastern border). Moreover, Russia is characterised as an inherently despotic and expansionist imperial state, in contrast to the strong democratic (and demotic) traditions long nurtured in Ukraine and Belarus. Muscovy/Russia has therefore been forced to use Belarus and Ukraine as a 'bridge to Europe'.

While Rus′ was an integral part of European concord of states, and Ukrainian and Belarusian lands in the Polish-Lithuanian Commonwealth were open to influence from both the Catholic and later the Protestant worlds, Moscow's contact with Europe proper was limited until the seventeenth century.[92] The 'Tatar Yoke' therefore served only to widen a cultural gap that was already in existence. Supposedly, 'before its union with Russia, Ukraine was already a European state' with 'a level of development of literature, music and architecture' far in advance of Moscow, where 'more than half of even the members of the Boyars' Duma were illiterate'.[93] The 'Europeanness' of Ukraine and Belarus was reinforced by their long struggle with the East, whereas Moscow was forced to ape its invaders. The idea is often expressed that the rest of Europe owes a common debt to Ukraine and Belarus for their long and spirited defence of 'Christian civilisation',[94] during the Cossack period in particular.[95]

The democratic cultures of both Ukraine and Belarus were supposedly demonstrated by the practice of Magdeburg Law, and their more limited experience of serfdom, which had to be 'reimposed' after Russian conquest.[96] Both nations also had traditions of popular assembly and limited government that were supposedly alien to Moscow. For the Ukrainians the self-government practised by the Cossacks exemplified the individualistic Ukrainian national character, marking them off from the aristocratic Poles and collectivist Russians.[97] The 1710 Cossack constitution of Hetman Pylyp Orlyk is claimed to have been 'the first European constitution in the modern sense of the term', providing a model blueprint for popular democracy well before the American and French Revolutions.[98]

In the religious sphere, Ukrainian nationalists claim that during the six '[eleventh to seventeenth] centuries when the Kievan Metropolitanate was in practice autonomous from Constantinople' a complete 'national style' of Orthodoxy was developed, with Ukraine having its own rituals, mode of administration and style of art, architecture and music, as well as a 'greater tolerance of other believers'.[99] Moreover, the gap supposedly widened still further after the fifteenth century. Moscow regarded Constantinople itself as apostate after the temporary reunion with Rome in 1439 (the Union of Florence) and clung to an idealised version of original Orthodoxy by unilaterally establishing its own Metropolitanate in 1448,[100] while it has been claimed that most Ukrainians initially accepted the terms of the Union, or were at least unopposed.[101] With Constantinople's authority in decline after its occupation by the Ottomans in 1453, the Ukrainians were increasingly open to Renaissance, Reformation and Counter-Reformation influences, producing a 'Golden Age' of Ukrainian Orthodoxy in the seventeenth century, in sharp contrast to the *raskol* in Russia provoked by Patriarch Nikon's reforms.[102]

Although the Ukrainian Orthodox Church was suppressed in 1686, it was revived in 1921–30, 1941–4 and 1990. Ukrainophiles have attempted to 're-Ukrainianise' the Church and restore pre-1686 traditions, but have largely been stalled since the election of Leonid Kuchma as president in 1994, with both hierarchs and faithful divided between supporters of the rival 'Kiev' and 'Moscow' Patriarchies.

Since the Union of Brest in 1596, Ukraine has had a second national Church, the Uniate or Greek Catholic Church.[103] Historically, the Church has been based in western Ukraine, where nationalists have credited it with preserving national identity under the difficult conditions of first Polish, then Habsburg, next Polish again and finally Soviet rule.[104] However, it is also true that Uniate and Orthodox have frequently been in conflict and that the division between the two creates an awkward fissure in Ukrainian national identity. Tentative attempts at reconciliation between the two Churches have come to naught. Significantly therefore, some nationalists have harked back to the ccumenical unity of the era before 1596,[105] or even flirted with a Ukrainian 'neo-paganism', which glorifies the period before Christianisation in 988 AD as a time when all 'Ukrainians' were spiritually united and Ukrainian culture already highly developed.[106]

Myths of national character and myths of the 'other': Belarus

Many of the same points are made about Belarusian national character.[107] Because Belarusian lands escaped Moscow's '240 years under the Golden Horde', native traditions such as the *veche* (assembly), 'the [key] institution of medieval democracy', were able to survive, while 'an Asiatic despotism was established in the Muscovite state'.[108] In contrast to Russophile historians' depiction of Russia's western wars in the three centuries before 1795 as wars to liberate the Orthodox from Catholic oppression, Belarusophile historians have argued that they were in fact wars against the Belarusian people, defending their traditional liberties against the alien Muscovite autocracy. The Union of Lublin in 1569, far from being a 'Polish plot', was therefore essentially a defensive measure against Russian pressure during the Livonian Wars (1558–83), to which the Belarusians happily agreed.[109]

Furthermore, Belarusian nationalists argue that Russians and Belarusians, not Russians and Poles, were the main combatants in the wars of this period. During the war of 1512–22 some 30,000 Belarusians supposedly routed 80,000 Muscovites at the Battle of Arsha (Orsha) in 1514, putting 30,000 to 40,000 to the sword. At the battle of Ulla in 1564 Ivan IV was defeated, losing 30,000 men to the Belarusians' 10,000,[110] as revenge for the bloody massacre of Polatsk in 1563. On the other hand, it is estimated that during the 'Commonwealth' war of 1654–67 some 53 per cent of the population of Belarus perished (numbers fell from 2.9 million to 1.35 million).[111]

Some Belarusophile historians stress the struggle to preserve local religious traditions in the face of the Moscow Patriarchy's claim to a monopoly inheritance on the Church of Rus´ (Protestant influences were also strong during the Reformation), but in essence the claim to a religious difference between Russians and Belarusians rests on the assertion that most Belarusians adopted the Uniate Catholic faith after the Union of Brest in 1596. Supposedly, '80 per cent of the rural population' were still Uniate in the 1790s and remained so until the Church was forcibly dissolved in 1839.[112] However, the desire to maintain Catholic traditions led many Belarusians to assimilate to the Polish nationality in the nineteenth century, and the Uniate Church was extirpated much more thoroughly in Belarus than in Ukraine.

Myths of empire and colonialism

'Empire' and 'colony' are not absolute givens. They are socially constructed concepts whose application to any given context is a matter of social choice.[113] While Ukrainophiles and Belarusophiles have therefore freely characterised the Romanov and Soviet polities as 'empires',[114] this claim has been vociferously denied by Russophiles (see below, p. 46). The former have also claimed that it was only the experience of empire that led to a forcible diminution of the cultural gap between Ukrainians, Belarusians and Russians, whereas Russophiles assert that it was cultural closeness that brought them together in the first place.

For Ukrainophiles and Belarusophiles, 'empire' is therefore characterised by *myths of oppression* and forcible 'Russification'. The experience of 'empire', because it led to the abolition of institutions, the assimilation of elites and the suppression of all markers of separate identity, is used to explain the weakness of national identity in the present. National Churches were forcibly dissolved and languages either banned outright or damaged in purity (see also chapter 8 on the Georgian language).[115] Physical losses are also stressed and characterised as 'ethnicide', as with the upwards of seven million who died in the 1932–3 Great Famine in Ukraine,[116] and the victims of Stalin's repressions in Ukraine and Belarus.[117] Economic exploitation is also a standard theme, with both nations being characterised as 'internal colonies' of first the Romanov state and then the USSR.[118] Lastly, the 'empire' tends to be characterised as ethnic, a specifically 'Russian' dominion rather than a Romanov *Hausmacht* or an ideology in power, providing a means of characterising Russian behaviour in the present as merely repeating the patterns of the past.

Myths of resistance and revival: Ukraine

The other side of the depiction of the 'imperial' experience is the assumption that oppression and the continuing gap between the cultures of the metropole and the 'colony' bred strategies of resistance rather than assimilation. As in most nationalist mythologies, heroes and martyrs, and the depiction of the strivings of the nation towards eventual redemption, tend to play a prominent place in the Ukrainophile and Belarusophile schema.

Ukrainophile historiography, in contrast to the 'Little Russian' stereotype of voluntary Ukrainian absorption into the Russian cultural sphere, tends to portray the entire period since 1654 teleologically as one long defensive struggle (*rukh oporu*) for national liberation.[119] 'Resistance' (*opir*) can be found in every age, from the struggle of eighteenth-century hetmans such as Ivan Mazepa and Pavlo Polubotok to uphold the rights granted to Ukraine by the Pereiaslav Treaty (Mazepa was traditionally demonised in Russian historiography for siding with Charles XII of Sweden against Peter the Great at the Battle of Poltava in 1709),[120] through the leaders of the nineteenth century national revival movement and the UNR,[121] Mykhailo Hrushevs´kyi in particular (see above, p. 28),[122] to the dissidents of the 1960s and 1970s.[123] The pantheon of national heroes has even been expanded to include socialist leaders of the UNR such as Symon Petliura and Volodymyr Vynnychenko (vilified by nationalists in the 1920s) and the 'national communists' of the Soviet era, in particular Mykola Skrypnyk and Oleksandr Shums´kyi, who promoted Ukrainianisation policies before their removal in the early 1930s.[124]

Otherwise discrete events are made to fit into the schema of national resistance and revival. Peasant rebellions, such as the 1768 *Koliïvshchyna*, are now argued to have been provoked by national rather than class grievances.[125] When women are lauded for their contribution to Ukrainian history, it is characteristically mainly for their role in the national liberation movement.[126] The workers' movement in 1917–20 is made to seem more pro-nationalist or at least 'passive and neutral' than was undoubtedly the case.[127]

However, the most important, and most controversial, Ukrainian liberation myth concerns the campaigns of the Ukrainian Insurgent Army (known by its Ukrainian acronym, UPA) between 1943 and 1954. In Soviet times the UPA was derided as a neo-Nazi and collaborationist force, composed entirely of fanatical Galicians fighting a Red Army composed mainly of other Ukrainians. Now the UPA is lauded for its bravery in fighting against first the Poles and Germans and then continuing to engage Soviet forces against overwhelming odds until the mid-1950s.[128] Moreover, it is claimed that the vast majority of UPA fighters were simple patriots rather than ideological zealots, and that recruits came from all over Ukraine rather than from Galicia alone.[129] The total number of UPA soldiers, estimated at around 90,000 in Western sources, is put as high as 400,000.[130] The attempt has even been made to rehabilitate those who fought with some degree of direct German support, such as the SS-Galicia division formed in 1944.[131] While this new line is vigorously promoted in western Ukraine and to a lesser extent in Kiev, it is extremely difficult to export to the rest of Ukraine, where the traditional myth of the Second World War as a Soviet Ukrainian victory against fascism and its collaborators still holds sway.[132]

Myths of resistance and revival: Belarus

In Belarusophile historiography the first major national rebellion occurred in 1794, immediately after the first seizure of Belarusian lands by tsarist Russia in 1793.[133] The Russian general, Count Suvorov, who thanks to his traditional depiction in Russophile historiography as the 'liberator' of Belarus from Catholic Poland has scores of streets and squares named after him in Belarusian towns, is painted instead as the uprising's bloody suppressor.[134] The 1863 Polish revolt is claimed to have been locally primarily a struggle for the re-establishment of Belarusian rather than Polish independence, and its leader Kastys´ Kalinoŭski lionised as the founding father of the Belarusian national revival.[135]

However, the Belarusian People's Republic of 1918 enjoyed only a fleeting existence (see above, p. 35). The Belarusian pantheon is not as crowded as the Ukrainian. Moreover, Belarusophiles have no Second World War myth to displace, even at the price of divisive controversy, the Soviet myth of common endeavour against the Germans. The Polish Home Army fought on Belarusian territory,[136] but there was no Belarusian equivalent of the UPA or Baltic resistance movements.

The Russophile version

Conscious Russophile historiography on the Ukrainian and Belarusian 'questions' developed in parallel with the rise of the latter two nations' national movements, as it was in essence an attempt to refute the historical claims they made, although far less attention was paid to the arguments of the much weaker Belarusian movement. Before the late nineteenth century, the assumption of Russian historians such as Karamzin, Sovoliev and Kliuchevskii that the three east Slavic peoples were naturally one was more or less unconscious.[137] In the early nineteenth century, therefore, most Russians had no great antipathy towards 'little Russian' writers such as Mykhailo Maksymovych or Panteleimon

Kulish, although Russian attitudes were predicated on the view of 'Ukraine as different from Russia but at the same time a complement, not a rival, to Great Russian culture' and the assumption that 'little Russian' local patriotism was perfectly compatible with loyalty to the tsar.[138]

However, after the Crimean War, there was a greater sense of the fragility of the empire, and the rise of an organised Ukrainian national movement produced an at first unsympathetic and, after 1905, a distinctly hostile response.[139] The events of 1917–20 further deepened Russian antipathy to Ukrainian 'separatism',[140] at first amongst Russian émigrés,[141] but then also amongst the official Soviet historical establishment from the mid-1930s onwards.[142] Significantly, however, hardly anything new has been produced since 1991, with Russian historians and politicians content to recycle old arguments.

Myths of origin

Russophile historiography begins with a myth of common origin, namely that at the time of Kievan Rus´ there existed a single 'ancient Rus´ nation' (*drevnii russkii narod* or *tri-edinaia russkaia natsiia*). Even before the foundation of Rus´, it is argued that all the eastern Slavs shared 'a single language and a common culture and religion' and were drawn together in collective struggle against common enemies to both the east and the west.[143] By the time of Vladimir (Volodymyr) the 'national monolith' had therefore 'developed such extraordinary strength and solidity' as to last through the subsequent centuries of division.[144] The sack of Kiev by Andrei Bogoliubskii in 1169 was only due to 'fratricidal struggle amongst the Rurik [the ruling dynasty]'. 'The foreign, threatening power for the Russia [sic] of Kiev was not then Moscow, but the Tatars and Poland', and before them the Khazars, Pechenegs and Polovtsians, against whom all the inhabitants of Rus´ fought in a common front.[145]

Slightly more sophisticated versions of Russophile history hold that the identity of the inhabitants of Rus´ was 'pre-national', and/or that (partial) differentiation between the three east Slavic peoples came about only as a result of artificial political divisions imposed in the thirteenth–fourteenth or even fifteenth–sixteenth centuries.[146] As the Dnieper territories were depopulated (even in Kiev there were 'only 200 houses' at the end of the thirteenth century),[147] they were extremely vulnerable to temporary Polish influence. However, despite 'the denationalisation and Catholicisation of the upper classes . . . the broad popular masses preserved their Russianness [*russkost´*] and their desire for unity with the rest of Russia'.[148]

Myths of separation and reunion

In the Russophile view, just as Polish domination of the eastern *kresy* was an artificial phenomenon, the Grand Duchy of Lithuania was established only by the forcible conquest of Ukrainians and Belarusians, who began to seek reunion with Russia as early as the fourteenth century, after the Union of Krevo in 1385 led to a loss of faith in the Lithuanian state's ability to 'defend the Orthodox and unite all Rus''. The persecuted Orthodox now naturally looked to Moscow for salvation.[149] Reunion in 1654 or 1793–5 is of course prominently celebrated,[150] and would have come earlier, had not 'a new factor came onto the scene, – Polish Imperialism, – and the natural march of events, the political unification of the Russian [sic] people, [been] checked' by the Union of Lublin in 1569.[151]

The long wars fought against the Rzeczpospolita until 1795 were therefore supposedly fought for the liberation of the Orthodox. The Uniate Church is viewed as a creature of the Vatican, while the idea of 'separate' Ukrainian and even Belarusian branches of Orthodoxy is dismissed as an uncanonical absurdity. Although some local Orthodox magnates may have fought against Muscovy in the wars of 1507–8, 1512–22 and 1534–7, this was in the nature of warfare at the time, which was largely a 'collision of leaderships'. Kindred states often fought one another, but there was no evidence that the popular masses were involved.[152]

As the prime motivation of Belarusians and Ukrainians was then to seek reunion with Russia, there was no point in their establishing separate states. Lithuania was never a Slavic state; 'Lithuania-Belarus' was a fiction invented by nationalist historians. Nor was the Ukrainian Cossack polity ever a 'state'. The anarchic traditions of the Cossacks prevented it from developing an 'administrative apparat',[153] and it remained a loose geographical entity occupying a far smaller area than the fictional 'Ukraine of Brest-Litovsk'.[154] Slobids′ka Ukraine had little connection with the Hetmanate, and the Cossacks' military adventures further afield were only 'incursions' that never established 'permanent lordship'.[155] There was therefore no real Ukrainian presence in what is now south-east Ukraine before the area became 'New Russia' after Russia conquered it from the Tatars and Turks at the end of the eighteenth century.

It is worth noting that one of the founding fathers of the 'Eurasian' school in the 1920s, Nikolai Trubetskoi, accepted that Ukrainian and 'Great Russian' culture had indeed diverged to an extent before 1654, but, in an ironic twist to the Ukrainophile argument, argued that 'at the turn of the eighteenth century *the intellectual and spiritual culture of Great Russia was Ukrainianised* [as a result of the reforms of Patriarch Nikon and

Peter I]. The difference between the West Russian [i.e. Ukrainian] and the Muscovite versions of Russian culture were eliminated through the eradication of the latter. Now there was only *one* Russian culture.'[156] (The earlier Ukrainian influence from south to north made subsequent 'Russification' from north to south easier.)

Myths of foreign intrigue

For most Russophiles, Ukrainian and Belarusian history therefore ends in 1654 or 1793–5, union with Russia having 'saved the people of Ukraine [and Belarus] from extinction' at the hands of the Poles.[157] On the other hand, subsequent occasional manifestations of 'separatism' are explained away as the result of 'foreign intrigue', originally by Uniate Catholics and Jesuit Poles, then by Habsburg and German 'agents of influence'. For some 'the Poles can really by right be considered the fathers of the Ukrainian doctrine' working through Kharkiv university to re-establish their claim to the eastern *kresy* in the first third of the nineteenth century.[158] For others, 'there is no doubt as to the Austro-German origin of the legend of the existence of a separate Ukrainian nation'; historians should 'look for the Ukrainian Piedmont in the Foreign Offices of Berlin and Vienna, not in dear Galicia'.[159] All would agree, however, that foreign influence moulded the Galicians, introducing an artificial nationalist virus into Ukrainian–Russian relations. By the twentieth century 'in terms of name, blood, belief and culture, Galicia and Ukraine had less in common than Ukraine and Belorussia, or Ukraine and Great Russia'.[160]

In any case, the nineteenth-century Ukrainian national revival is depicted as a marginal movement, involving only 'a few tens of youths'.[161] Similarly, it is argued that the UNR collapsed within months through lack of popular support and was resurrected only by German force of arms.[162] In any case, the leaders of the UNR were not elected and 'had no formal or moral right to speak in the name of the people of Ukraine'.[163] The 1918 Belarusian People's Republic (BNR) is dismissed as a rootless 'bourgeois-democratic' experiment, 'formed by an [unrepresentative] group of the intelligentsia on an unconstitutional basis'. It had no support amongst 'the popular masses', as demonstrated by the mere 0.3 per cent of the vote won by the Belarusian national parties in the 1917 Constituent Assembly elections. It existed for so long only by virtue of the support of the 'German occupying administration'.[164]

Also dismissed is the idea that the BNR and Belorussian Soviet Socialist Republic were 'two parts of the same process'. Instead it was the Bolsheviks who made 'best use of the revolutionary energies of the Belarusian people', who sought and achieved 'self-rule on a Soviet basis',[165] thereby reiterating the key pan-Slavic myth that the first real Belarusian state/republic was a gift of Soviet rule.

Myths of joint endeavour

Instead of the discourse of 'empire' and 'colony' prevalent in Ukrainophile and Belarusophile historiography, Russophile history aims to present the experience of Ukraine and Belarus since 1654 or 1793–5 as one of 'fraternal union' with Russia and to celebrate their subsequent joint labours to mutual benefit. The link with Russia is also characterised as bringing 'progress' and 'development', economic growth, the spread of literacy and the establishment of modern welfare services,[166] in contrast to the tendency of Ukrainophiles and Belarusophiles to idealise the *status quo ante*. Traditional narratives of 'socialist construction' (or occasionally its opposite, 'joint suffering' under communism)[167] and the three peoples' joint victory in the Second World War therefore loom proportionately larger in Russophile historiography,[168] as does opposition to all attempts to rehabilitate 'outsiders', such as, pre-eminently, the UPA, who are still depicted as tools of the Nazis.[169] The dissolution of the USSR is blamed, when the question of causality is seriously addressed at all, on the machinations of self-interested politicians (in Solzhenitsyn's words, 'the agile Führers of several national republics')[170] and third parties.[171]

Conclusions

The Russophile schema is totally unwilling to concede any of the building blocks of a separate Ukrainian or Belarusian identity. There is no real engagement with rival narratives, just denial. On the other hand, this very inflexibility has left Russophiles ill equipped to respond to the realities of east Slavic disunion. Since 1991 the Ukrainians at least have therefore had relative freedom to develop their 'national idea', while the only option for ethnic Russians or Russophiles in Ukraine and Belarus has been root-and-branch opposition to the local mythologies.

In Belarus this is less of a problem, as the Belarusian 'national idea' is comparatively weak and the recycling of old myths is for the moment at least sufficient to keep it at bay. Something more is needed for Russophiles in Ukraine, however. Even in the east and south, Russophile historiography is being squeezed out of the official arena, although it can still be found in the press and in partisan party publications,[172] and there is a much greater need to produce a version of history that addresses the reality of being Russian- (or Russophone-) in-Ukraine (see chapter 6 on the crucial importance of the Russophone Ukrainian identity). Cognitive dissonance and passive resistance to the Ukrainophile schema amongst Russophones is considerable, but by sticking to traditional all-Russian historiography, which allows virtually no place for any separate Ukrainian identity, Russophiles may well be narrowing their appeal to the large potential middle ground.

In Belarus, national historiography was penetrating the official sphere only gradually before new president Alexander Lukashenka's *de facto* restoration of Russophile mythology in 1995.[173] Moreover, the comparative weakness of key aspects of Belarusophile mythology has hampered its dissemination.[174] In Ukraine, Ukrainophile ideas have dominated both school texts and official discourse to a much greater extent.[175] Significantly, although new president Kuchma dropped most references to more controversial subjects such as the UPA after his election in 1994, he maintained many key elements of the Ukrainophile schema, in particular the eulogisation of Khmel´nyts´kyi and the UNR.[176]

Where it has come to predominate, Ukrainophile and Belarusophile historiography provides a framework for justifying separate development and for characterising Russia's current actions as 'imperial'. On the other hand, it is the very sharpness of the divide it creates against Russia that makes such mythology difficult for many Russophiles and/or Russian-speakers to accept. Even in Ukraine it is unlikely that historians or politicians seeking historical legitimation will speak with one voice.

3   National identity and myths of ethnogenesis in Transcaucasia

In the post-Soviet period Transcaucasia has been especially prone to violent inter-ethnic conflict, as communities have sought to redefine their relations with neighbouring 'others' in localities characterised by a mosaic of interwoven communities whose understandings of sovereign space do not sit easily with the complex realities of ethnic geography. Three large-scale wars have been fought in the region since the late 1980s: between Armenia and Azerbaijan over the enclave of Nagorno-Karabakh, between Georgia and Abkhazia and between Georgia and South Ossetia. The aim of this chapter is not to explain why these wars occurred, but to explore how rival myths of homeland and overlapping 'claims to indigenousness' have informed the identities behind such contested understandings of sovereign space. It also seeks to explain the manner in which such myths have contributed to local ethnonationalists' belief in 'the inherent right of native peoples to exercise hegemony and fulfil their destiny in their ancestral homeland'.[1]

'The [home]land', as 'the place wherein memory is rooted', has always been a key building block of national identity, as part of what we have termed the tendency to territorialise ethnic boundary markers.[2] However, it can also be argued that 'homeland' is the place where pseudo-memory is encouraged to flourish and where a given group becomes infused with primordial ideas about the eternal state of their nation and the inalienable link with the land that is a gift of trust from their fore-fathers. As Stephen Velychenko has argued, this psychology was nurtured by Soviet historiography on the national question, which, despite its Marxist veneer, was profoundly primordialist in its approach.[3] Moreover, the loosening of the constraints imposed by formal Marxism in the post-Soviet period has allowed local successor historiographies to become even more ethnocentric and teleological, as is also often the case with new nationalising regimes.

The current literature on ethnicity and nationalism emphasises the importance of national myths in cementing a would-be monolingual and monocultural group as a solid cohesive community.[4] Although some authors are optimistic that this task can be accomplished 'without viewing the others as competitors and antagonists',[5] homeland myths in particular tend to be exclusive, squeezing out rival groups from the picture and delegitimating their claims to the territory in question. Moreover, the more a group insists on its distinctiveness and peculiarities for the sake of stronger consolidation and solidarity, the more it tends to oppose itself to other 'alien' groups.[6] In the modern world 'difference implies hierarchy' and 'otherness . . . implies a moral judgement' more often than not.[7] Previous rivalries are revived and catalogued in order to assess a group's current state of security.[8] As a result, a group either establishes hierarchical relationships between itself and others in order to take a superior position, or dehumanises the outsiders in general.

Cementing a sense of 'otherness' is therefore a key goal of alternative ethnocentric versions of the past.[9] This phenomenon was well understood by William Sumner, who developed a theory of ethnocentrism at the very beginning of this century,[10] later enriched by Camilla Wedgwood and other anthropologists,[11] who argued that ethnonationalist ideology always tends to be associated with a double moral standard: peace and order have to be maintained within a given group, but everything is permitted with respect to the out-group. Sumner's theory has been severely criticised from various points of view, and, with a few exceptions, has to date been applied only to pre-modern cultures, although Sumner himself insisted on its universal character. However, with some revisions and improvements,[12] his approach can help shed light on post-Soviet conditions and on the role played by ethnogenetic mythology in legitimating collective claims for material property or privileges, territory, political status or political power, cultural or linguistic domination, and the like, particularly in multicultural states where the temptation to use absolutist myths to close off claims to a privileged position in the polity is considerable.

On the other hand, it is important to bear in mind that these claims are not perceived in instrumental terms. Contemporary ethnogenetic myth-making tends to be the work of patriotic intellectuals, professional historians, archaeologists, linguists, researchers and university professors, who advertise their own constructions as the received truth. They therefore violently reject any characterisation of their own activity as mythological, although they are perfectly prepared to level the same accusation at their opponents. Moreover, the consumers of these sorts of myths treat them as end truths. Different and often opposite and incommensurable versions of history therefore clash with each other as if they were primordial shibboleths, as ethnic groups who use the versions in question charge each other with the falsification of the past.

In this chapter we shall discuss the manner in which ethnonationalist historiography is used to claim the right to a given national homeland. We shall focus primarily on three cases, which demonstrate how ethnocentric ethnogenetic mythologies contributed to ideologies of confrontation in the late 1980s and early 1990s: the Armenian–Azerbaijani, Georgian–Abkhazian and Georgian–South Ossetian conflicts. The focus is mainly on the historiography of the distant past, as our subject is ideas of 'ethnogenesis' rather than more recent history.

The Armenian–Azerbaijani conflict

Ethnogenetic studies began in both republics in the 1940s, but their starting points, goals and basic historical resources were quite different.[13] First, the relatively rich Armenian historiographical tradition can be traced back to the first millennium AD, whereas the Azerbaijani historiographical tradition was really established only in the twentieth century. Secondly, the Armenians can plausibly refer to the Kingdom of Tigran the Great (95–56 BC) as the cradle of their statehood, whereas Azerbaijanis have no real past polity to celebrate before the establishment of the Azerbaijani SSR. Finally, the Armenians have been known as a distinct ethnic group with their own proper name since the first millennium BC, whereas the consolidation of the Azerbaijanis as a coherent ethnic group took place only after the 1920s.

Therefore from the very beginning ethnogenetic studies have had different meanings for Armenians and Azerbaijanis. For the Armenians, their purpose was to help recover from the genocide of 1915 and to provide psychological protection against the 'Turkic threat', in part by identifying the Azerbaijanis indiscriminately and erroneously with the Turkish people. On the other hand, for the Azerbaijanis the purpose of ethnogenetic studies was to establish their own distinct national identity, as the Soviet authorities were deeply hostile to any manifestations of pan-Turkism.

Most Armenian scholars therefore initially felt more comfortable with the 'migration theory',[14] which argued that proto-Armenian speakers first arrived in the Tigris valley in the twelfth century BC, before merging with the local inhabitants shortly afterwards. Azerbaijani scholars, on the other hand, argued that the Azerbaijani people were descended from the local Albanians, who were Iranianised in the first millennium BC and began to assimilate with Turkic-speaking newcomers during the first millennium AD (although most modern scholars accept that the Albanians were Christian). However, although the indigenous inhabitants were formally 'Turkified' by the eleventh to twelfth centuries, senior Azerbaijani scholars argued that this was largely superficial, and claimed that the 'Albanians' managed to retain the basic aspects of their traditional pre-Turkic culture.

The growth of nationalism in the last few decades has pushed territorial issues to the fore, and ethnogenetic arguments have had to be revised and rearranged accordingly. However, the revisionist historians who began to appear on both sides in the 1960s and 1970s tended to be more junior and less careful, albeit ambitious, scholars. Modern Armenian versions of ethnogenesis have attempted to integrate narratives of the ancient Hayasa polity, arguing that it played a central role in the emergence of the contemporary Armenian identity. Despite the serious objections of many scholars,[15] younger Armenian historians began to identify Hayasa with the Armenian self-names 'Haj' and 'Hayastan', and claim that it was the most ancient polity established by the Armenians, dating back to the middle of the second millennium BC. Rafael Ishkhanyan has gone even further, claiming that the Armenians and the Armenian language were already well established in Asia Minor in the third, even the fourth, millennium BC. In other words, the Armenians are the only 'true' (i.e. primordial indigenous) inhabitants of the Armenian plateau.[16]

The Armenian historian Khachatrian has argued that in spatial terms Hayasa corresponded to Nairi and later to Urartu-Armina, all of which were ancient polities of the late second and early first millennia BC.[17] His aim is to prove the widespread belief in contemporary Armenia that Armenians made up the majority of the population in the state of Urartu (ninth to seventh centuries BC), whereas the Urartians themselves were only a small elite group whose language circulated solely in the official sphere. A. Mnatsakanian goes even further and argues that many of Urartu's rulers were in fact ethnic Armenians.[18] Finally, Suren Ayvazian has claimed that the Armenian language was transmitted by the Urartian cuneiform.[19] Ayvazian also identifies the Armenians with the famous Aryans and Hyksos, and claims that they were the inventors of the first alphabet (most scholars would date the codification of the Armenian alphabet to the fifth century AD). Armenian historians have also tended to minimise the extent of Turkic/Azerbaijani settlement in 'historical Armenia', especially in Nagorno-Karabakh, despite widespread evidence that many areas still had a majority Muslim population when they were finally definitively transferred from Iran to tsarist Russia in 1826.[20]

In parallel to the rise of a new generation of Armenian scholars, a new historical school emerged in Azerbaijan after the Second World War, which insisted that the Turkic languages in general and the Azerbaijani language in particular spread throughout what is now Azerbaijani territory long before the eleventh and twelfth centuries AD (when most Western historians would date their arrival). Moreover, the same historians consciously downplayed the role of the Iranian and north Caucasian languages in the ancient polities of Albania and Atropatena, which were situated on what is now Azerbaijani territory more than one thousand years ago. They accept the well-attested fact that non-Turkic groups inhabited the area in question in the first millennium AD and earlier, but argue that the role of these groups in Azerbaijani ethnogenesis was of secondary or even tertiary importance.

Modern Azerbaijani historians also argue that the Turkic family of languages was always predominant in the region of western Asia, where their use was already widespread by the third to first millennia BC. A. Mamedov, for example, is convinced that the original home of the 'proto-Turkic ethnos' and therefore of *all* the Turkic peoples was in western Asia.[21] Iu. Yusifov has argued that such proto-Turkic groups (in essence proto-Azerbaijanis) helped to establish the Kura–Araxes archaeological culture of the early Bronze Age in Transcaucasia,[22] and that when the Huns arrived in Azerbaijan they were able to mingle with their close relatives. This school of thought identifies the Scythians, Sakas, Sarmatians and Massagetae with local Turkic-speakers,[23] and argues that the Turks were the indigenous inhabitants in western Asia and in Transcaucasia from the third to second millennia BC onwards.[24]

An especially important point of dispute between Armenian and Azerbaijani scholars concerns the status of the ancient Albanians. Armenian historians tended to treat them as barbarous tribes who were partly Armenianised as a natural result of the expansion of Armenia's higher and more civilised culture in the region,[25] whereas Azerbaijani scholars have identified the Albanians as the direct ancestors of modern-day Azerbaijanis and have rejected all theories of their supposed 'Armenianisation'.[26]

The most crucial issue of current Armenian–Azerbaijani controversy, however, involves rival claims to be the true owners of the present-day territory of Nagorno-Karabakh, and therefore to be the legitimate heir of the legacy of its ancient population.[27] These disputes became especially sharp after 1988 when the dispute left the confines of academia and was taken up by the mass media, and by open letters and public petition campaigns. Significantly, both of the 'revisionist' historical schools in Armenia and Azerbaijan became closely affiliated with their respective national-democratic movements, Armenian scholars with the Armenian National Movement, and the Azerbaijanis with the Azerbaijani People's Front.[28]

The Armenians place a special value on Nagorno-Karabakh because, after the division of Armenian lands between Russia and Persia in the sixteenth century, it was the one region which preserved an element of autonomy under Armenian princes subordinate to Persia (until 1828). Moreover, during the subsequent period of Russian rule, Nagorno-Karabakh became an area of refuge for many Armenians fleeing from Persia and the Ottoman Empire. As a result, the region, the one common denominator 'homeland' for the Armenians, became a symbol for Armenian unity and consolidation.

On the other hand, the Azerbaijanis consider Nagorno-Karabakh to be the very place where their modern identity emerged under the Muslim khans.[29] Moreover, it was the first centre of the Azerbaijani national revival at the turn of the century. Indeed, it could be argued that the struggle over Nagorno-Karabakh has itself been the most important factor in stimulating the growth of Azerbaijani national consciousness in the twentieth century.

The Georgian–Abkhazian confrontation

In attempting to understand the role of mythological struggle in the Georgian–Abkhazian case, the following five aspects of the distant past are especially pertinent: the question of who was the first to develop iron production, the origins of local statehood, the dispute over the ethnic composition of the ancient and medieval population of the Colchis Lowland, the question of who founded the Abkhazian Kingdom in the eighth century AD, and finally the manner in which Christianity came to the region.

The origin of iron production

According to the Georgian version of local history, as developed by the historian Teimuraz Mikeladze,[30] iron was first invented by the Chalibs/Chalds, who occupied north-central Anatolia before the Hittites. Later the Chalibs migrated to the area at the south-east corner of the Black Sea as the ancestors of the Chans (Mingrelians), one of the groups that eventually became in turn the modern Georgian people. Mikeladze argued that these very Chalibs were reported in the Book of Genesis, and that it was they who first supplied the Hittites, the Mittani Kingdom and Ancient Egypt with iron. Mikeladze's argument served two purposes: first, he 'confirmed' the existence of early Georgian tribes across a vast territory of north-western Asia as early as the middle of the second millennium BC (in general Mikeladze assumed that the origins of the proto-Kartvelian –

that is, Georgian[31] – community should be dated to the period before the end of the third millennium BC).[32] Secondly, Mikeladze argued that the Chalibs, as the ancestors of the Georgians, made a massive contribution to human culture by, in effect, introducing the Iron Age.

The Abkhazian version of events was developed in the 1970s by the professional historian Vladislav Ardzinba,[33] who in the early 1990s became the Abkhazian president. He argued that iron was in fact discovered by the ancestors of the Abkhazian–Adyghe peoples who lived in the second millennium BC, just where Mikeladze located the Chalibs and some other 'Georgian' tribes.[34]

The origins of local statehood

Mikeladze also argued that the powerful Kingdom of Colchis (the mythical home of the Golden Fleece) began its existence in western Georgia as early as the middle of the second millennium BC.[35] Moreover, he claimed that Colchis was governed by an independent ruler and comprised many large towns with well-developed crafts. According to Mikeladze, this was the key reason restricting Greek colonisation in the region and preventing the Greeks from making a serious impact on the local economic and sociopolitical environment.[36] In particular, Mikeladze attempted to argue that ancient Dioscurias (the modern Abkhazian capital Sukhum, known to Georgians as Sukhumi) was initially a Colchian (i.e. Georgian) city. He therefore insisted that Georgian statehood grew directly out of the Kingdom of Colchis, which survived and developed quite independently on the same territory for almost two millennia (from the twelfth century BC until the sixth century AD). Nobody could subjugate it, neither Assyria, nor Urartu, nor Media, nor Persia. Since the 1970s and 1980s many Georgian scholars have presented this version of the history of Colchis as an incontrovertible truth,[37] a view that has even found its advocates in modern science fiction.[38]

Most Abkhazian historians, on the other hand,[39] cast doubt on the very existence of the Colchis Kingdom, as would most other scholars. The Georgian version was evidently forged with certain political ideas in mind, as will be demonstrated below.

The problem of the population of ancient Colchis

During recent decades there has been a trend in Georgian scholarship to argue that the ancient population of Colchis, including what is now Abkhazia, was made up entirely of Georgian tribes. More cautious Georgian scholars used to distinguish between two components amongst the local population of the Colchis Lowland about two thousand years ago, namely the Georgians and the Abkhazians–Adyghes.[40] Even then, however, it was argued that the Abkhazian–Adyghes were highlanders who had only recently moved to the plain,[41] which meant that only Georgians had lived there before.

However, by the 1980s the ethnocentric version became the dominant one in school curricula and in the Georgian mass media. It was first explicitly formulated by the Georgian philologist Pavle Ingorokva,[42] and then developed by historians such as Mikeladze, who went so far as to argue that only Colchians (i.e. ancient Georgians) lived in Dioscurias and on the Black Sea coast in the distant past.[43] Thus, according to Mikeladze, the Colchis Lowland was an ethnically homogeneous and politically integrated territory as early as the middle of the first millennium BC.[44]

Similarly, the contemporary Georgian historian Marika Lordkipanidze has argued emphatically that only the Georgians were the autochthonous inhabitants of Colchis, and that the ancestors of modern Abkhazians arrived much later.[45] She doubts that the Apsilae and the Abasgoi of the first to second centuries AD, mentioned by classical writers as living on what is now Abkhazian territory, can be considered the ancestors of the modern Abkhazians, and prefers to treat them as if they were Kartvelians (Georgians). In her view, one must distinguish between the local ancient Abkhazians and 'Apsua' who arrived later and gave roots to the modern Abkhazians. Thus she is inclined to identify indiscriminately with the Georgians both ancient Abkhazians and some other tribes of ancient Colchis (for instance, Sanigae and Missimians), whose ethnic identity is in reality obscure and is the subject of continuing controversy.[46] Following Ingorokva, she insists that the ancestors of the modern Abkhazians were backward highlanders who reached Abkhazia only in the seventeenth century, when the region was temporarily devastated and 'cleansed' of its Georgian inhabitants by Turkish raiders. With these arguments, she is able to present the Georgians as not only the original autochthonous population in Abkhazia, but also the dominant majority from time immemorial.[47]

According to Abkhazian authors, on the other hand, the ancestors of the Abkhazian–Adyghe peoples were the original inhabitants of the whole of north-east Asia Minor and south-west Transcaucasia. It was the Kartvelians who moved to the area much later, pushing the Abkhazian–Adyghe groups to western Transcaucasia.[48] The present Abkhazian president Vladislav Ardzinba frequently repeats these claims in his political rhetoric.[49] The Abkhazian version of events (arguably with more historical support) links the Apsilae and the Abasgoi directly to the ancient Abkhazian–Adyghe groups: the Apsilae are associated with the Abkhazian self-name 'Apsua', and the Abasgoi with the Abazinian self-name 'Abaza'. The Sanigae and the Missimians are treated as related populations rather than as Kartvelians.[50]

These tribes supposedly ruled the Black Sea littoral up to the modern city of Sukhumi and even further to the south, where they came into contact with the Mingrelians. In other words, it is argued that the Abkhazians already occupied all their modern territory by the first millennium AD. They were therefore the true local inhabitants rather than newcomers, with roots going back at least one and a half to two thousand years and possibly even longer.[51] Moreover, Abkhazian historians have used tsarist and Soviet ethnodemographic data to claim that it is only the tremendous changes in the ethnic composition of the area during the last century and a half that have turned the Abkhazians from a natural majority of the population into (before the war of the early 1990s restored their majority status) an artificial minority. Extensive Mingrelian resettlements into Abkhazia took place only in the 1930s–1950s, i.e. during the lifetime of the present generation.[52]

In reaction to Georgian mass media propaganda, in May 1989 the Abkhazians asked a well-known oracle, who lives in a famous cave, to adjudicate on the question of when their ancestors came to settle in Abkhazia.[53] Not surprisingly, the oracle confirmed that the Abkhazians were indeed the autochthonous inhabitants of their own territory, providing a timely boost to morale in the face of rising Georgian pressure.

On the founders of the Abkhazian Kingdom and its inhabitants

The main point of controversy between Georgian and Abkhazian historians is the problem of the Abkhazian Kingdom (end of the eighth to the early tenth century AD), in particular the questions of who founded the Kingdom and the ethnic composition of its population. The Abkhazian Kingdom as an independent sovereign state came into being in the 780s as a result of the unification of the earlier principalities of Abkhazia and Egrisi, and their liberation from Byzantine vassalage. The Georgian version of history considers this Kingdom to have been in all key respects ethnically Georgian.[54] As Lordkipanidze puts it, 'the Abkhazian Kingdom was a Georgian state as regards the vast majority of the population, language, culture, writing system and state policy, and the Abkhazian kings were ethnic Georgians, according to the same data'.[55] For her, the cultural identity of the Abkhazian Kingdom can be demonstrated by the following: the Georgians made up the majority of the population, the state established its own Georgian episcopate with a Georgian liturgy, thereby turning the Georgian language into the Kingdom's state language, and, finally, several masterpieces of Georgian literature and architecture were created in Abkhazia at this time.

All the population, including both the Georgians and the Abkhazians, were then referred to as 'Abkhazians', but only because of the name of the state (see chapter 2 on similar claims concerning the 'Belarusian-Lithuanian Kingdom'). It is therefore extremely difficult to judge the ethnic identity of the various population segments which were mentioned by medieval authors as resident on Abkhazian territory. Nevertheless, while recognising this fact, Lordkipanidze goes so far as to argue that the terms 'Abkhazia' and 'Abkhazian' stood mainly for 'Georgia' and 'Georgian' both in medieval Georgian and in foreign sources.[56]

Abkhazian authors may agree that the great majority of the Abkhazian Kingdom's population was made up of Kartvelians (Georgians) and that it was therefore at this time that the Georgian language gradually turned into the language of literacy and culture.[57] They may also agree that the term 'Abkhazian' was used in a broad sense at this time, and began to be applied to all the Kingdom's population in western Georgia. Nevertheless, they argue that the population was multiethnic in composition. Moreover, the popularity of the Georgian language amongst the aristocracy, including its Abkhazian element, by no means prevented the commoners from speaking their native Abkhazian language.

Abkhazian authors argue that it was precisely the establishment of the Abkhazian Kingdom that caused the consolidation of the Abkhazian tribes into a cohesive community, which then played the leading role in the life of the Kingdom. From their point of view it is of great importance that the unifier of Abkhazia and the founder of the ruling dynasty, Leon the Second, is referred to in the sources as 'the Abkhazian ruling prince' (*vladietelnii kniaz*). In other words, all these facts are considered in the Abkhazian schema to prove that the first true state on the territory of modern Georgia was founded by the Abkhazians,[58] providing powerful ideological underpinning to the Abkhazian struggle for sovereignty. It is no accident that President Ardzinba refers in his speeches to the ancient Abkhazian state as having been founded 'more than 1,200 years ago'.[59]

From the Georgian side, on the other hand, Lordkipanidze argues that the ethnic identity of the first Abkhazian king is obscure.[60] In her view, the title of 'Abkhazian king' meant only that the dynasty originated from the country of Abkhazia. In fact, Leon the Second could have been of either Greek or Georgian ethnic origin. However, she insists that the kings of the Abkhazians were Georgians in terms of culture and language.

The academic discourse in question demonstrates how ethnocentric attitudes all too glibly furnish definitive answers to obscure problems of the distant past, where modern scholarship has declined judgement given the lack of firm evidence. The dispute over the existence or non-existence of the Kingdom of Colchis is a typical example where the vacuum of evidence has allowed both sides to take up completely incompatible positions.

The problem of the Christianisation of western Georgia

In the late 1980s when the atheist communist regime in the USSR was in decline, an identity crisis manifested itself in a strong movement amongst various peoples towards the restoration of their traditional cultures and religions, given the latter's close links with folk cultures. Since the late 1980s Georgian nationalists have attempted to present Georgia as the main stronghold of Christianity in the Caucasus, a Christian island in a hostile Muslim sea. The Georgian mass media and the propaganda of the first informal Georgian political organisations unanimously characterised the Abkhazians as Muslims who were eager to unite with other anti-Georgian forces under the green banner of Islam.[61] Lordkipanidze in particular painted all Abkhazians as the natural enemies of Christianity in western Georgia.[62] This trend towards the radical 'othering' of the Abkhazians became particularly strong under President Gamsakhurdia (1990–2).

In fact the religious situation in Abkhazia is complex: Islam dominates in the north and Orthodoxy in the south, but neither has penetrated deep into folk culture, despite a long history of their development in the area. The core of Abkhazian folk culture still preserves many pagan traditions. Moreover, Georgian accusations that the Abkhazians were anti-Christian have forced the latter to re-evaluate their Christian legacy. In recent years this trend has established a new field of Georgian–Abkhazian confrontation, connected with rival interpretations of the legend of the Christianisation of Georgia by the early Christian missionary St Nino (fourth century AD).

According to the Georgian version, St Nino travelled all over Georgian territory. In contrast, the Abkhazians believe that she arrived in Transcaucasia by sea and first entered the Caucasus in Abkhazia, where she started her missionary activity. In essence the debate focuses on who was baptised first – the Georgians or the Abkhazians.[63] Abkhazian scholars have used this and other myths to present Abkhazia as a country with deep Christian roots dating back to at least the third to fourth centuries AD.[64] During the Georgian–Abkhazian war the Georgian charges had the paradoxical effect of provoking a movement for the restoration of old Orthodoxy amongst some Abkhazians.

Thus, an ideological struggle between the Georgians and the Abkhazians has been waged: first for cultural supremacy (who was the first to discover iron and to be baptised, whether the Abkhazians had an ancient writing system or not, who erected the old churches in Abkhazia, and what was the ethnic origin of the famous cultural activists of the past);[65] secondly for territorial supremacy (who is indigenous to Abkhazia); and finally for state supremacy (who founded the first state in western Transcaucasia).

For both sides, their particular versions of these myths have helped legitimate their claims to the sole ownership of Abkhazian territory, and have been used as key resources in the local struggle for political power, especially in the early 1990s when the Abkhazian struggle for sovereignty reached its climax. The Georgian–Abkhazian historical dispute therefore has much wider implications, particularly as both sides treat the other's myths as a form of blasphemy. Thus, as Mikhail Chumalov has already noted, the Georgian–Abkhazian war of 1992–3 was preceded by 'an ideological struggle' focusing on different interpretations of the Abkhazian past.[66] Moreover, despite the fragile peace achieved in 1993, each side views the other's case as fundamentally illegitimate, and long-term coexistence will be difficult to maintain.

The Georgian–South Ossetian confrontation

The role of historical myths in dramatising inter-ethnic conflicts is also recognised by South Ossetian authors. As one of them has claimed, 'disagreements [between] powerful contemporary historians, their suppression and falsification of the truth, have led to a dramatic uneasiness between our peoples [the Georgians and the South Ossetians]'.[67] This section will therefore examine the key myths employed by Georgian and South Ossetian authors and compare them with the Georgian–Abkhazian example.

The South Ossetian Autonomous District was established by the Bolsheviks in 1922 on the territory of Shida K'art'li, one of the central provinces of historical Georgia. Georgian authors argue that it was granted to the Ossetians in return for their assistance in the struggle against democratic (Menshevik) Georgia. The Georgian version also interprets this event as a contrivance to favour local separatists, as this territory had never previously been a distinct administrative unit, let alone a separate principality. According to the Georgian version, the Georgians were the original native inhabitants in the region, whereas the first

Ossetian groups settled permanently only after the late thirteenth century AD.[68] The large Ossetian communities in northern Georgia were probably established only in the seventeenth to eighteenth centuries,[69] or the fifteenth to sixteenth centuries at the earliest.[70] The most radical contemporary Georgian version of events is that the Ossetians came to Shida K'art'li only in the twentieth century.[71] At the very least, Georgian authors proceed from the supposition that the Ossetian people were formed only in the sixteenth to eighteenth centuries.

Obviously, this theory was unlikely to satisfy the South Ossetians, as it deprived them of their autochthonous status. Several Ossetian historians have therefore been working for several decades in the attempt to deepen the Ossetians' roots in Transcaucasia. This problem was first addressed in late 1950s and early 1960s by Iurii Gagloev,[72] who tried to identify the local Dvals of the pre-Mongol era with the Ossetians. As Georgian scholars vehemently attacked this interpretation,[73] Zakharii Vaneev,[74] one of the founders of Ossetian historiography, adopted another approach.

Vaneev sought to establish linguistic and cultural continuity between the Ossetians and the ancient Iranian-speakers of the Eurasian steppes (the Scythians, the Sarmatians and, especially, the Alans), and attempted to trace the migrations of all these nomads to Transcaucasia in the early Iron Age. He even argued that such movements could have started as early as the Bronze Age, in the late second millennium BC. Supposedly, the Cimmerians and the Scythians crossed Transcaucasia from the north to the south in the eighth to seventh centuries BC, and traces of Scythian culture can still be found in South Ossetia and some other areas of Georgia.[75] The next wave of expansion in the Caucasus was identified by Vaneev with the Sarmatians. In his interpretation of the classical authors,[76] in some periods Iranian-speakers accounted for the great majority amongst the highland population of the Caucasus. Moreover, Vaneev argued, the ancient Iranians brought a higher culture to the Caucasus, rather than simply being cruel conquerors and robbers. In his opinion, it was they who made the local inhabitants familiar with iron-working.[77] Vaneev also supported the idea of a local 'Alanian Kingdom', which supposedly emerged even earlier than its Abkhazian counterpart.[78]

By basing his arguments upon his own interpretation of the personal names mentioned in the classical sources, Vaneev claimed to find 'Ossetian chiefs' amongst the first Georgian and Abkhazian princes (sic).[79] Georgian rulers used to recruit Ossetian noblemen as mercenaries, resulting in the resettlement of the Ossetians to Georgia throughout the medieval period.[80] Moreover, in those days the Alans–Ossetians would frequently invade K'art'li (Georgia), driven first by the Mongols, then by Temur (Tamerlaine) and finally by the Kabardinians. But this was only one part of a much longer process of migration.[81] While making no distinction between the Alans and the Sarmatians, Vaneev argued that the latter settled all over the northern Caucasus and made a great contribution to the formation of many local peoples besides the Ossetians.[82] He insisted that it was the Alanian–Sarmatian newcomers who assimilated and Iranianised the local population in the central-northern Caucasus rather than vice versa.

In his view, this process was complete by the first century AD.[83] In other words, the Ossetians are the direct descendants of Alanian migrants rather than Iranianised natives.[84] Moreover, by identifying the Ossetians with the Alans and the Sarmatians, Vaneev sought to provide the Ossetians with deeper roots for a sense of their separate identity and a means of overcoming traditional Georgian claims of cultural superiority.

Thus, Vaneev's schema, which was developed in order to 'restore justice' to the much-debated problems of Ossetian ethnogenesis, was in obvious contradiction to the Georgian version of events. It was no accident that Vaneev's manuscripts, which began addressing these problems in the early 1960s, were first published in South Ossetia only in the late 1980s, after the Georgian authorities had lost control over local scholarship. Undoubtedly, Vaneev's works contributed to the development of the national idea amongst the South Ossetians, which itself resulted in first the growth of a separatist movement and, finally, in the Georgian–South Ossetian war of 1991–2.[85]

These works first rehabilitated the territorial claims of the South Ossetians by insisting on their immemorial roots. Secondly, they reversed traditional stereotypes by arguing that the Ossetians, who had contributed much to the development of Caucasian culture and the formation of many local peoples, were the true 'elder brothers' to the Georgians. Thirdly, they purported to prove that the Alans–Ossetians had enjoyed their own statehood even earlier than the Georgians, thereby legitimising the recent struggle of the South Ossetians for sovereignty. Lastly and arguably most importantly, it was argued that the Ossetians were the direct descendants of ancient Iranian-speakers rather than simply Iranianised natives. This helped to upgrade the status of the Ossetians since, in folk belief, a shift to another language lowers the status of a group.[86]

Vaneev's arguments have been picked up and developed by other South Ossetian authors in recent years. They have demanded the restoration of a 'true' history of the Ossetians, which they identify mainly with the glorious Scythian–Sarmatian and Alanian periods, and have stated openly that 'only the efforts of nationalist-thinking historians can help to restore this history in its completeness'.[87] In their view, the reason for the miserable conditions of the South Ossetians today lies in 'the haphazard attitude to studies and representation of the people's past, that is profitably used by our opponents who confine us to the small plots of land which [are all that] remain with us from our vast former domains'.[88] Furthermore, they insist that the South Ossetians have never been a part of the Georgian people, and that South Ossetia has never previously been included in an independent Georgian state. Moreover, it was South Ossetia (now in Georgia) rather than North Ossetia (now in Russia) that was the historical homeland of the South Ossetians.

South Ossetian scholars have attempted to substantiate these statements by using archaeological and linguistic data as well as written evidence. At a conference on Ossetian history held in Vladikavkaz in 1994, Iurii Gagloity tried to prove that the Sarmatians spread all over the southern slopes of the Great Caucasian ridge in the last centuries BC, and that the great majority of the 'Caucasians' of the central and western Caucasus, mentioned by Strabo, were therefore Iranian-speaking Sarmatians.[89] Iurii Dzitstsoity put forward the idea of the extraordinary antiquity of some Ossetian dialects.[90] He related the Dzhava dialect to the Scythian language and the Yron dialect to the Sarmatian language. Using such arguments, he concluded that the Scythians, the speakers of the Dzhava dialect, settled in southern Ossetia as early as the seventh to sixth centuries BC. On the other hand, the mass migrations to the south since the thirteenth century were carried out by the Yron dialect speakers, from where the development of the modern Tuala and Chisan dialects of South Ossetia began.

Finally, in terms of the struggle for their historical priority on their own territory, the South Ossetians consider the ethnic identification of the Koban archaeological culture (KAC) to be of crucial importance.[91] The culture in question flourished in the central Caucasus between the late Bronze and early Iron Ages (the late second to the first millennium BC). Its close relationships with contemporary sites in the Colchis Lowland are well attested.[92] Until very recently therefore the famous South Ossetian archaeologist Boris Tekhov accepted that the KAC was established by the Kartvelians (i.e. the ancestors of the Georgians) who expanded from the south and mixed with the local north Caucasian inhabitants, whereas the Iranian-speakers arrived somewhat later.[93] Not surprisingly, most Georgian scholars still advocate this view and argue that the ancient Georgians inhabited all of what is now Ossetia long before the arrival of the Ossetians' ancestors.[94]

The growth of inter-ethnic tensions in the Caucasus made Tekhov change his opinion. Since 1987 he has argued that the Indo-Europeans and, especially, Iranians were the autochthonous inhabitants in the Caucasus, especially in its central region.[95] According to his new concept,[96] the KAC was formed mainly by the Indo-Iranians who came from the north. Rafael Gagloity developed these arguments along the same lines while attempting to trace continuities between the KAC, the Scythians–Sarmatians–Alans and the Ossetians.[97] Vaneev linked the KAC with the local Caucasian tribes from whom the Alans later emerged.[98] This line of reasoning reaches its extreme point amongst some South Ossetian authors who have claimed to find evidence that 'the ancient Ossetians' already lived in southern Ossetia in the early Bronze Age, that is, in the third millennium BC.[99] One such author has even sought to prove that close contacts between the Indo-Iranians and the Western Semites were established in the early second millennium BC,[100] allowing him to date the early period of the Ossetian prehistory to the third to early second millennium BC, arguing that at that time they controlled a vast territory comprising the whole of the east European steppe, the Caucasus and all of modern Syria.[101]

In order to demonstrate the unique importance of South Ossetian territory, one of the leaders of the South Ossetian national movement, the historian Alan Chochiiev,[102] argues that its capital Tskhinvali and adjacent areas served as the most important sacred lands for the ancient Aryans, the site of many of their sanctuaries, a place for religious ceremonies, a habitat for martyred heroes and even 'an Aryan homeland' since the time of the Koban archaeological culture. Chochiiev hints that it was just here where Jesus Christ learned the wisdom of sacrificial behaviour in his teens and youth.

Whereas Chochiiev confines himself to this hint, two other authors, Valerii Khamitsev and Aleksandr Balaev, claim that the Galileans were Iranian-speaking descendants of the ancient Aryans, 'the Israeli Scythians', and that Jesus' mother was 'a Scythian'.[103] It follows from this argument that both Jesus Christ and eleven of the Apostles (save Judas) were in fact close relatives of the Ossetians, and that Christianity formed the original core of the culture of 'the Ossetians, the Alans of the Caucasus'. Thus Galilea is depicted as a land of 'the Scythians–Alans'. It is also claimed that Georgia was baptised four hundred years later than Ossetia, and that Ossetia, rather than Georgia, was the main original stronghold of Christianity and the bulwark against Islam in the Caucasus. This line of reasoning is also used to legitimate the demand to re-establish an independent 'Alanian eparchy' in Ossetia.

Finally, the Ossetians place major stress on the existence of an early independent Alanian state. It is of course of vital importance to them to prove that this state emerged no later than the Abkhazian Kingdom,[104] in order to try to legitimate their political and territorial rights against the similar claims of their neighbours.[105]

Ossetian historical mythology is therefore constructed using the same strategies as the Abkhazians. The Ossetians have attempted to deepen their past on their modern territory, to demonstrate their huge contribution to Caucasian history (the introduction of iron, their contribution to the development of the Alan state, their direct participation in the formation of many groups of Caucasian highlanders) and to mankind in general (the introduction of Christianity). They also stress the existence of early statehood amongst their Alanian ancestors.

The South Ossetian version of the past has its particularities, however. First, in the face of the powerful opposition of Georgian historiography, and lacking in reliable historical evidence, Ossetian authors consciously exaggerate their mythology, lending it fantastic features. The latter include the claims for the earliest adoption of Christianity, for an enormous past territory and for a central place in the Aryan (Indo-Iranian) tradition. Secondly, there is the attempt to combine an association with the glorious deeds of the ancient Iranians (Scythians, Sarmatians, Alans), who were unquestionably newcomers in the Caucasus, with a stress on the Ossetians' autochthonous origin.

This difficult task is accomplished in the following way. It is well established that many Caucasian highland peoples, including the Ossetians, were of heterogeneous origin; that is, both newcomers and local groups participated in their formation. Ossetian authors, however, have tried to maintain their Iranian cultural and linguistic legacy by insisting that their ancestors were also Iranians in blood and that the newcomers assimilated comparatively small groups of the local inhabitants. To prove this, the Ossetians try to pre-date the presence of the ancient Iranians in the Caucasus as far back as the late Bronze Age (the Koban archaeological culture), if not earlier. Once again, this is an explicitly primordial approach; Ossetian authors have identified without any reservation the Ossetians with the Alans, the Sarmatians and even the Scythians.

Conclusions

Different peoples use similar strategies when searching for historical arguments to legitimate their modern political claims. They attempt to confirm their historical supremacy in the fields of culture (invention of iron-working, creation of the Koban culture, erection of monumental buildings etc.), religion (early adoption of Christianity) and politics (establishment of early statehood). They also try to defend their territorial rights through deepening their roots in a given 'homeland'. At the same time, they associate themselves with the glorious deeds of distant real or imagined ancestors, where possible those mentioned by classical authors. Identification with the ancient Iranians ('Aryans') has a crucial significance for the Ossetians, and recently the Abkhazians have started to emphasise their distant links with the ancient Hattians, the pre-Hittite population of Asia Minor.

Since all the ancient groups in question originally lived outside the territory of their contemporary descendants or relatives, ethnonationalists tend to date their ancestors' resettlement to the national 'homeland' as early as possible in order to prove their autochthonous roots. Additional claims to linguistic continuity are especially important since it is widely believed that a language is a 'people's soul' and that a shift to another language deprives an ethnic group of its originality and therefore its creativity. This misfortune lowers a people's perceived status, and its political and cultural claims lose their persuasive power.

A stress on the external, so-called objective traits of ethnicity – language, culture, blood – lies at the basis of this sort of argument. It is assumed that archaeological cultures can be identified with modern ethnic groups.[106] However, if any of these 'objective' criteria threaten to contradict the mythology in question, it is unceremoniously dropped, as when Vaneev refused to consider the somatic features and burial rites, which, in his view, were highly unstable and, thus, of subsidiary importance for any study of the Ossetian past.[107] It is perhaps worth mentioning that in the opinion of the great majority of experts it is just these traits which are highly persistent.

The historiographical mythologies analysed above do not necessarily move explicitly to the conscious denigration of opponents. Just the opposite: opponents appeal to each other for peace and friendship. However, the assertion of ethnogenetic priority, the complete disregard of opponents' positions and their claims on the local cultural legacy all tend to produce a worsening cycle of accusations of historical falsification and ideological confrontation. In the multiethnic mosaic of Transcaucasia it is practically impossible to construct an ethnocentric version of ethnogenesis without encroaching upon the cultural legacy of neighbouring peoples and, by asserting a prior claim to the 'homeland', placing them in the unequal, inferior position of 'a younger brother'.

Under the hierarchical ethno-administrative structure that was practised in the USSR, the cultural status of any particular ethnic group was strictly connected with its political status, resulting in unequal prospects for further development.[108] Historians from peoples blessed with high administrative status have concentrated on mythical justifications for maintaining that position; historians from peoples lower down the hierarchy have sought to provide arguments to advance their status. Feelings of inferiority have been cited by Abkhazian authors[109] in the face of

Georgian denials of their very existence as a people at the same time as appeals were made for 'peace' and 'friendship'. In 1989 the author was provided with a whole list of Georgian academic literature which was considered 'hostile' by Abkhazian scholars. Curiously enough, even a jubilee encyclopaedic volume devoted to Georgia in which both the Georgian and Abkhazian versions of early history were included (written by Georgii Melikishvili and Marika Lordkipanidze for the Georgian side, and by Zurab Anchabadze for the Abkhazians)[110] was classed by the Abkhazians as an 'anti-Abkhazian' book.

To conclude, it is worth stressing that, although primordial traits such as an ancient common territory, language, religion, blood and cultural legacy can be recently created myths, popular belief in the veracity of such myths establishes propitious conditions for the growth of ethnonationalist movements and in bloody clashes between them.[111] The mythological foundations of mutual antagonism in Transcaucasia will have to be studied with care if lasting peace is to be restored to the region.

4   History and group identity in Central Asia

During most of the late modern and post-communist period, official guidelines or religious ideology shaped the writing of Central Asian general history. In this way, extra-historical motives constantly encroached upon what might have developed as a historiography evolving in the research, interpretation and critique appropriate to an open, educated environment. Some authors accepted such close guidance. Uncoopted historians and like-minded intellectuals ordinarily could not trust the establishment and its communications outlets to express nonconformists' interpretations and presentations of the region's history. This forced dissenters to seek alternative ways of conveying their views under rather dangerous conditions.

The following discussion about the making and writing of contemporary and very recent history in post-Soviet Central Asia examines precedents for the latest historiographic configurations and the continuing covert competition between political and cultural leaders over the basis for and nature of post-communist group identity in the region and in certain of its subdivisions.

We call this covert, because official historiography remains the order of the day, and its form persists largely as before, a collective, controlled academic enterprise amongst Central Asians themselves. This exposition contends that the political leaders of Central Asia have used the habitual method of prescription in the field of historiography persistently and purposefully. They seem to do so especially in order to divide and confuse the cultural elites of the area, and thereby stifle rival visions of imagined community – supra-ethnic or ethnic – that could strengthen and focus the foundation for group identity in the region.

This investigation will evaluate evidence, especially in the historiography, for the continuation of the old cultural symbiosis characteristic of the region and its significant metamorphoses that may have prevailed late into the twentieth century, despite official attempts to replace it with Marxist and Russian ideologies. To the extent that Central Asian historiography reveals the persistence of the traditional urge for inter-ethnic symbiosis, the study will argue that officials with monoethnic preoccupations have failed to overcome the influence of the rich indivisible heritage bolstering the resistance of the cultural elites against persistent manipulation and distortion of the area's history.

Historical precedents

In 1906–7, a Bukharan court chronicler, to avoid royal displeasure, wrote two versions of his chronicle, *The History of the Manghit Rulers*, one for the supposedly God-given Amir and his courtiers, the other, critical of Russians and of abuses under the Manghit dynasts, reserved for private use.[1] In the unauthorised history, he referred to Russian officials stationed in the Amirate following the tsarist conquest in 1868 as 'a small band of vagrants', and for the sorry plight of the Bukharan state he blamed its vicious Amir Muzaffar al-Din (ruled 1860–85) for disregarding 'the justice and equity' of earlier rulers.[2] Notwithstanding his conservatism and limited worldview, the historian distinguished between official hagiography and critical interpretation, thereby setting a precedent for intellectuals in the new era, although the actual content of his history in many passages departed wildly from the factual into the fantastic. Nevertheless, in an important sense, he demonstrated once again that in Central Asia intellectuals have a tendency to counter by evasion rather than confrontation the noxious regulation and ideology imposed by overbearing politicians.

A second local historian writing in the Jadid period, though not a reformist himself, contended directly with the general indifference and ignorance of townspeople about their past and jousted with conservative Muslim theologians of the Russian Governor-Generalship of Turkistan who denounced all history writing as an undertaking contrary to the Muslim religious code (*Shäri'ät*): 'People [generally] hold a unanimous opinion', he wrote, 'concerning the benefit of the field of histories [*'ilm-i tawarikh*] . . . Our Turkistan Sarts [urbanised, Turki-speaking Tajiks and settled tribesmen in the Turkistan Governor-Generalship], giving little importance to history, do not even know [the genealogy of] their forefathers two or three generations back and remain ignorant of the stories and events occurring in their times.'[3]

The Jadids carried their drive for educational and social reform over into the field of history, which they also regarded as essential to the identity and well-being of the community. These reformists wrote about the necessity of educating Central Asians in their own history, calling for communal or Turkistan history,[4] but they seldom, if ever, advocated an orientation that would define the limits of such history in ethnic terms.

Rather, those historians living under Russian rule in the Governor-Generalship of Turkistan advocated the creation of new histories of Turkistan and of Islam; those from Bukhara focused upon the Amirate's former glory and recent difficulties, as with the Khivan and Khokandian chroniclers. The concept of nationality remained absent from the consideration of most Jadids. The identifying frameworks adopted in discussions of history began with the broad compass of Islam, descended to the equally wide scope in Central Asia of the Turkic and Iranian language families, and only after that referred to one or another of the ethnically heterogeneous dynastic states, none of them known at that time by the name of a component ethnic group.[5]

During the Jadid decades (1900–20) the reformists strove for knowledge, using history as an instrument of enlightenment, specifically as a tool to rid the small numbers of educated and semi-educated people of the notions acquired, both verbally and in reading, through folklore, superstition, fanciful stories, legends and unreliable historiography such as that offered by the Bukharan chronicler, Mirza 'Abdal'azim Sami, discussed above. In their educational efforts, reformists tangled with religious ignorance and secular misinformation in equal parts, calling for the writing of clear, new history books that could serve a woefully backward society.

The Jadids gloomily admitted that none of them, even the most erudite, yet possessed the training or ability to write a proper new history. In retrospect, Soviet scholars have judged that 'pre-1917 historians . . . could not give connected, well-proportioned, consistent and deeply scholarly interpretation of the long history of . . . the people of Central Asia'.[6] As a result, the reformists depended upon outsiders, primarily Tatars and Bashkirs, such as Ahmed Zeki Velidi, to publish existing manuscripts or provide the basis for offering a fresh, accurate presentation of Central Asian history, written in alphabets and languages they could understand. At least until 1920, those authors approached the history with a methodology grounded in Turkology rather than in the Islamic framework well known in earlier historiography.[7]

Before long, certain indigenous Central Asian scholars who had begun studying in Russian institutions of higher learning after the turn of the century became the first local historians to emerge under communist auspices. The two histories written by Bolat (sometimes Polat) Saliyif, *A History of Central Asia* (1926) and the continuation that appeared in print in 1929, approached the concept of group identity differently. Without restricting himself to Turkic sources, he regarded general Central Asian history as an inclusive continuum, reaching from ancient to modern times, in which subgroup ethnic identities played only minor roles.[8]

Out of deference to the recently established Uzbek Soviet Socialist Republic he entitled the second volume of his research *A History of Uzbekistan*. In fact, it employed the comprehensive framework of his earlier study. As if in defiance of the nation-centred ideological avalanche grinding downward into the field of history, the author displayed as a frontispiece to his second book a sketch of the infamous Amir Temur (Tamerlaine), anathema to Soviet ideologists in those days.[9] His insistence upon this broad, deep approach to the region's history soon provoked a sharp denunciation by communist ideologists, who described Saliyif's historiography as 'nationalistic and pan-Turkic'. These two pejorative and seemingly contradictory charges were made during a Central Asian Congress of Historians and Scholars held in Samarkand in 1936. The organisers had planned that Congress in order to parcel out and label portions of Central Asian history as 'Kazak', 'Tajik' or 'Uzbek' and so on, but the sessions failed to achieve their goal. Soon afterward, Saliyif's insistence upon scholarly principle led to his execution along with so many other intellectuals purged by the Communist Party in that era.[10]

Saliyif's deliberate conflation of the concept of Uzbekistan with the larger scope of a Turkistan or of all Central Asia reflected the then recent political reality of the three Uzbek tribal dynasties (Manghit, Qonghirat and Ming based in multiethnic Bukhara, Khiva and Khokand) spread across much of southern Central Asia. After 1920, the concept of convergence amongst the identities of Turkistan/Uzbekistan/southern Central Asia had its indigenous historiographical beginnings notably in these two works by Bolat Saliyif. That concept has left a durable legacy in the thinking of urbanites in southern Central Asia.

In Soviet research and writing about Central Asia, however, ideologists banned the name 'Turkistan' from cultural or political usage soon after the dismemberment of the Turkistan Autonomous Soviet Socialist Republic in 1923–4. At about the same time, the authorities placed the reformist movement and the names of Jadid activists and their works on an index of censorship which caused Soviet writers and editors to omit reference to them or left them open to criticism, but not ever to praise. Few living Jadids and none of their senior leaders survived the fatal review of their ideas and writings by ideological critics in the 1930s. The cleansing of un-Marxist concepts outlawed their ideas and essays concerning history and its purposes. This prohibition precluded acceptance of the Jadid idea that the medieval civilisation of Central Asia's foremost centres of learning and arts – Bukhara, Herat, Khiva, Samarkand and others – substantiated the twentieth-century vision of a symbiotic Central Asian culture. That extreme position left Central Asians with little history to write about, other than that of the alleged benefits arising from the nineteenth-century tsarist Russian conquest of the region.

A canon for harmless heroes

Since the end of the 1920s, very few local individuals by themselves have possessed the authority or temerity to issue comprehensive histories of the region, although some Russian scholars have enjoyed greater latitude.[11] In either instance, for at least three decades after the 1930s historiography took a very dim view of nearly everything that had occurred or developed in Central Asia before the time of the Bolshevik coup d'état. To conform to the class-oriented ideology, the treatment of khans and amirs, and the manuscript histories about them and their age, could deal with royalty only negatively, if at all. These restrictions resulted in the creation of histories of rebellions against Central Asia's rulers, but not of rounded histories about those mirzas and sultans.

The dryness of such skeletal works convinced the communist authorities within a few years that they had to institute a change in the rules for historiography. Their solution, worked out tentatively by 1938–9, entailed close supervision through the nomination of an extremely limited set of safe heroes and a careful prior selection of their actions and written works, if any. Thus, these figures would become the pivots around which authors should compose all Central Asian history books, whether for children or adults. A discussion about the particulars of this method follows.

After 1953 brought an end to Stalin's narrow prescriptions for nationality culture, several common traits characterised those sponsored medieval heroes chosen for official canonisation during the final decades of Soviet rule in Central Asia. They had to embody certain Russian values, such as attributing superiority to people who led a settled, rather than a migratory, existence. In addition, to deserve approval,

1. these iconic figures originated within the general area;
2. perforce, such leaders lived mainly a sedentary life;
3. most actively contributed to or patronised arts and culture;
4. they gained renown beyond Central Asia for their scholarship or literature, calligraphy and other arts;
5. all earned fame in the Islamic era, but never exclusively as theologians or religious leaders; and
6. the warriors amongst them vigorously fought against the numerous confederations of surrounding nomads, including Qarakhanids, Seljuqs, Turkmen, Qazaqs (Kazaks), Qalmuqs (Kalmyks) and Uzbeks.
7. Therefore, the prominent nomadic descendants of Chinggis Khan's Qypchaq military empire and other Central Asian forebears failed to receive nomination to the Soviet Asian hall of fame;
8. because, above all, those chosen as cultural heroes and model politicians could not display antagonism towards or make war upon the Russians.

This set of qualifications served to produce what the regime, from its standpoint, and attentive outsiders might call 'harmless heroes', model personages whose biographies presumably would stimulate no urge to resist authority or break convention. The requirements also considerably limited the pool of eligible candidates. Consequently, the communist-approved pleiad prescribed for Central Asians came principally from the Samanid and Temurid eras or dynasties (ninth to sixteenth centuries), and notably featured the non-Uzbeks: Abu Nasr al-Farabi (philosopher, political theorist and musicologist), Rudaki (poet and diplomat of the Tajikistan territory), Abu Raykhan al-Beruniy (astronomer and historian), Abu Ali Ibn Sina (Avicenna) (philosopher and physician), Muhammad ibn Musa al-Khwarazmiy (mathematician and thinker), Mir Ali Shir Nawaiy (poet, moralist and statesman), Mirza Ulugh Beg (astronomer and governor), Sultan Zahiriddin Muhammad Babur (memoirist, poet and dynast) and Magtimguli (eighteenth-century poet of Turkmenistan).[12] The selection committee overlooked a number of settled leaders of renown and erudition – Ubaydullah Khan II of Bukhara (sixteenth century), Abu'l Ghazi Bahadur Khan of Khiva (seventeenth century), a few epic heroes, such as Manas, and others – probably because they demonstrated insufficient timidity or political ineffectiveness to fit the definition of 'harmless'.

Rebellion in the academy

Exasperated by this exclusiveness, a recognised Uzbek scientist/academician undertook to break that restrictive pattern by inserting the name and role of the amir, Temur (Tamerlaine), into Central Asian historiography. During a meeting of the Uzbekistan branch of the USSR's Academy of Sciences in June 1968, he presented a research report entitled 'Amir Temur's Role and Place in Central Asia's History'. Pamphlet versions of his presentation resulting from those discussions came out in Russian and in Uzbek in the same year.[13] After the scholar arranged for republication in 1972 of two works focused upon Temur's principles of governance and upon an official, posthumous history of Temur's military exploits, a political reaction occurred.[14]

A participant in the meeting held in 1968, Muzaffar M. Khayrullaew, later director of the Oriental Institute of Uzbekistan, recorded that Academician Mominaw, intellectually courageous, expected a positive response to his re-evaluation of Temur. Instead, various individuals entered together into a move to oppose these efforts by Mominaw, characterising the booklet as an idealisation of Temur's actions and accusing its author of an unscholarly approach fraught with political-ideological errors. This matter shortly came to the attention of academic institutes in Moscow as well as some members of the Central Committee of the Communist Party of the Soviet Union (CPSU).

The entire incident underlined the seriousness with which cultural managers of the CPSU and the Communist Party of Uzbekistan regarded the prescription of acceptable heroes for Central Asia. The political reality that a Russian scholar cited by Mominaw had in 1946 and again in 1950 published his revised evaluation attributing some positive traits to Temur did not serve as an adequate defence for the Uzbek scholar.[15] This event emphasised that local Central Asian academicians, unlike prominent Russian scholars, lacked the licence to disturb the official historiography. In either instance, this affair also showed the impossibility in those reactionary times, approximately 1970–83, in contrast to the immediate post-Second World War years, of attempting to revise the guidelines established in such matters by the cultural managers. Their list of heroes remained virtually inviolable until the collapse of the USSR.

With the introduction of the standard Marxist interpretation, the historiography produced under these circumstances by Central Asians throughout the middle and later Soviet years, with few exceptions, usually reflected collective efforts at summarising, rather than original research, subject to censorship and controlled through government support of research institutes and publishing houses.[16] Later, historiographers commented that the compilers of the 1950s, for example, using secondary sources, 'launched the writing of summarising surveys [with their] sketchiness [and] shortcomings . . . [introducing] a qualitatively new stage in the study of . . . Tajik history'.[17]

Politicians, dissatisfied too, demanded a strikingly new emphasis in history writing. Party Secretary Sharaf R. Rashidov, at the Second Congress of the Intelligentsia of Uzbekistan in 1959, called for 'major research devoted to the history of the working class and farmers of the republic, [and] . . . the creation of essays about the heroic history of the Communist Party of Turkistan and Uzbekistan'.[18]

Because communist-trained leaders and scholars continue in the 1990s to guide developments in Central Asia, the historiography produced in the post-communist era resembles the Soviet version in most respects, except that a few subjects that were taboo under the Marxist censors – criticism of Russia and mere inclusion or positive treatment of certain earlier rulers and Jadids – now received cautious, selective acceptance. Matters of emphasis and proportion in historical writing very much reflected the ideological tendencies of the leadership. With few exceptions, histories published in the Soviet years had largely avoided detailed discussion of Shaybaniy Khan (d. 1510) and his Uzbek dynasty, and appropriate or favourable treatment of the empires established by Amir Temur (d. 1405) and Chinggis Khan (d. 1227), all three of whom so strongly affected the contemporary and future history of Central Asia.

Owing to its national bias, the current historiography strains to fashion a coherent treatment of the past of heterogeneous Central Asia that will not offend against the restrictions necessarily imposed by ethnic differences. A comparison of several new versions of the history of Central Asia issued since the fall of the Soviet Union makes obvious the traits, limitations and solutions to the ever-present dilemma of finding a suitable framework for preparing historical works that can satisfy the nationalising aspirations of the politicians while remaining true to the awareness of learned men and women about the reality of supranational identities during all but the most recent decades in the history of Central Asia.

As typical examples of post-Soviet historiography from Uzbekistan, readers may first consider volumes I and II in the three-volume *History of the Peoples of Uzbekistan*, edited by Academician Ahmadali Asqaraw for the Academy of Science of his republic. Its lack of originality at once strikes readers who recognise a title that exactly paraphrases the heading applied to volumes issued, but soon withdrawn under ideological criticism, in 1946–50, because they emphasised the role of the nomadic Uzbeks in the medieval and early modern history of Central Asia. The version prepared by Asqaraw resembles the earlier communist-era works in matters of organisation as well as name.

Although the editor describes these parts of the new set as books intended for students in higher educational institutions and for instructors, school teachers and researchers, the work has all the prestige of an official history. The four long chapters preserve much of the structure and terminology of Marxist histories, including the periodisation into 'slave-owning', 'feudal' and 'capitalist' eras, and the emphasis upon 'national liberation movements' and their uprisings against the rulers and colonial governors.

These volumes resemble closely those histories criticised in the 1950s in Tajikistan and Uzbekistan as 'summaries' owing to their lack of original research or methodology. They offer no footnoted authentication for the facts or opinions mentioned, though they have limited bibliographical lists, consisting almost entirely of secondary works, a few earlier local histories and some travelogues. The compilers and editor in this crucial effort to provide a post-communist version of history seem completely unaware of scholarship published outside the former Russian Empire and the Soviet Union, nor do they display any familiarity with the theories that have emerged outside their confines pertaining to cultural, economic, social or political analysis. In a sentence, this new history closely resembles earlier, Soviet-style compilations.[19]

A second, recently published history contrasts in many respects with the foregoing work. *My Beloved History* – first published in Russian in 1990 and in 1992 in Uzbek and written by a single author, the experienced historian, Goga A. Hidoyataw of Tashkent State University's Department of History – draws attention to itself at once in its avoidance of some of the stereotypes seen in the making of the work issued by the Academy of Sciences of Uzbekistan, *A History of the Peoples of Uzbekistan*. Hidoyataw skirts the problems of specifying earlier national identity by his choice of a noncommittal book title and by choosing a chronological form of organisation. A Marxist scholar by training and experience, he too structures his work with reference to various subperiods of 'feudalism'.[20] His well-illustrated book includes several sketch maps and numerous colour photographs. The editors acknowledge the author's often unconventional approach to historiographic problems in Central Asia, announcing at the outset: 'It is possible to debate many of the book's conclusions; several of them demand seeking and locating some new evidence, but the publisher acknowledges the author's right to find new ways to solve historical puzzles.'[21] Hidoyataw, in issuing this somewhat unconventional history, could hardly have demonstrated better timing, for he launched the book at the moment of greatest weakness in the crumbling Soviet regime and immediately before the retrogression and petrification of ideology in the undemocratic, newly independent states of southern Central Asia.

A third new volume of history that has appeared since the break-up of the Soviet Union describes itself as a collection of lectures, prepared by junior scholars under the supervision of the senior professor and doctor of historical sciences, Academician Bori A. Ahmedov, and is entitled *The History and Culture of Uzbekistan*, issued by Tashkent's Educators' Publishing House in 1992. In the introductory discussion, the editors assert that 'in works such as the 1982 version of *The History of the Uzbekistan SSR* (Ozbekistan SSR tarikhi), one constantly senses a spirit peculiar to the period of stagnation [i.e. Brezhnev's stewardship of the USSR]. For that very reason, to this very day there are no lesson books or aids which present the history of the motherland itself in schools and higher institutions that provide precise information concerning the history of the Uzbekistan SSR.'[22] Limited still by the ideological burdens of the past, the bibliographies offered in the early pages of this history remain entirely unemancipated from the Marxist interpretation of Central Asian history, for they list no scholarship originating outside the USSR. Towards the end, however, the authors turn to the daily press, in which they cite not only USSR President Mikhail S. Gorbachev's programmes but also the writings of Kyrgyz author Chinggis Aytmatov and news reports of the latest cultural events in order to capture the sudden changes occurring between 1989 and 1991.

Perhaps the most significant offering in post-communist historiography comes in the form of a thorough, compact guide to a balanced historiography for Central Asia, long needed in institutions of higher learning. Professor of history Torabek S. Saidqulaw's *Pages from the Historiography of the History of the People of Central Asia* (1993) aims to serve serious students of the region's past. Refreshingly presented without reference to the narrowly Marxist frameworks then so recently discarded, the book offers a straightforward chronological inventory and brief evaluations of the numerous main manuscripts and published sources for research and inquiry into developments inside the area and those affecting the region from outside.

Because the author extends his survey from the ancient records up into the early part of the twentieth century, he includes the works not only of Central Asian but of many Russian historians. The guide is organised around the principal periods of Central Asian history, and is embellished with many illustrations taken from important historical manuscripts. Nowhere does Saidqulaw depart from the broad Central Asian framework into an ethnic division of the region's culture.[23] His approach strengthens the trend noticeable amongst students and scholars in other post-Soviet Central Asian states to revive the comprehensive treatment of history in academic research that disintegrated under ideological pressure during the communist period.

Even so, the latest histories have yet to catch up with the great events that are now shaping the configuration of the Central Asian political and cultural landscape. While Central Asia's political leaders grappled with the implications of the USSR's dissolution, they took initiatives to restore, at least superficially, the old symbiosis that had united Central Asia, including Kazakstan, and its economy and culture before the Bolshevik envelopment of Central Asia in 1920 began to orient those processes towards models provided by Moscow.

A striking, though evidently insubstantial, expression of this urge in the direction of a symbolic reunification in Central Asia began soon after the Soviet collapse. This tendency manifested itself in a series of well-publicised meetings, with another planned for Kazakstan in 1997, between the heads of the suddenly independent states of the region as well as those of Azerbaijan and Turkey. Presidents of the Turkic republics held their fourth top-level meeting in Tashkent on 21 October 1996, one that had been preceded by earlier gatherings of the leaders in Ankara, Istanbul and

Bishkek. However, because of the insistent monoethnic nationalism shown by the leaders of these young states of Central Asia, citizens of the region very likely can regard the presidential gestures towards regional unity as moves intended to pre-empt the appearance if not the content of community from the cultural elites without suffering its consequences for republican politicians and their regimes.

Amongst other matters, the six presidents agreed in the Tashkent summit upon measures to promote 'co-operation based on a community of culture, language and spiritual values of the Turkic nations', and to celebrate important dates in the history of Turkic-speaking nations, as well as to enlist UNESCO in an observance of what they called 'the [forthcoming] 1,450th anniversary of the great Turkic Qaghanate'.[24]

Presidential roles

The behaviour of political leaders often reveals more than the image they desire to project or the words of their spokespeople about their real intentions. A government's actions affecting its educated citizens provides a necessary indicator of official attitudes regarding the relationship between cultural elites and the political leaders in the state. That holds true almost everywhere in the Central Asian states, where governments dominate public sources of information.

In the 1990s, the presidents of Kazakstan, Tajikistan, Turkmenistan and Uzbekistan (all former Communist Party first secretaries of their respective republics) increasingly offer themselves, like Stalin before them, as the leading thinkers in their countries, thus attempting to transfuse their politics into the realm of thought. With their multitudes of speeches reproduced in the press and many tracts bearing their names and distributed frequently and without charge, they flood the public with required reading.[25] They are obligatory, because, except for Kazakstan to some extent, these four countries outlaw free press or speech and because people in authoritarian societies must pay attention to the words of the leader or risk costly economic and political reprisals.

Neither aspect of this interrelation linking elites to leadership promises an optimistic future for the opening of society to its own cultural elites. By circumventing the normal function of intellectuals, the authoritarian ruler intends to close the minds of the public and shut down the processes of intellectual innovation. Every culture, polity and society requires the inventiveness of some unruly imagination in order to keep it advancing with the leading civilisations of the world. Now, too much of Central Asia sits beside the great Silk Road of ideas, as before, accepting doctrinaire thinking and avoiding unsettling concepts in favour of selling wares.

If the conditions that briefly obtained during 1989–91 can be taken as a base period of relative permissiveness and openness in Central Asian life, a comparison with subsequent changes in the behaviour of the leadership should serve to give some inkling of the impact and direction of these developments.

In Uzbekistan during the base period, three cultural-political movements, the Unity Popular Movement Birlik, the Freedom Party Erk and the Islamic Renaissance Party, competed more or less openly with the communist oligarchy for support amongst elites and the public at large. As first secretary of Communist Party of Uzbekistan from June 1989, Islam Abduganievich Karimov imitated the fashion set by the USSR's chief executive officer, Mikhail S. Gorbachev in Moscow, by arranging to have himself also named president of the Uzbekistan SSR by that union republic's Supreme Council on 24 March 1990.[26]

In order to manipulate and control the election process set in motion following the declaration of Uzbekistan's independence on 31 August 1991, Karimov disenfranchised the broadly based Islamic Renaissance Party and the Unity Popular Movement Birlik and hamstrung the political efforts by the group of intellectuals forming the Freedom Party Erk. As a result, according to reports, he received 90 per cent of the vote in a fixed election to become the Uzbekistan Republic's first president and (still) head of the former communist oligarchy, renamed the Peoples' Democratic Party of Uzbekistan.

From the earliest months of Islam A. Karimov's tenure as president of the new republic, his speeches and actions have sharply reflected the outlook of an autocrat. In his report to the Supreme Council of the Republic on 3 July 1992, as he warned dissidents against spreading trouble through expressing their opinions, he described himself in his party's press as a 'serious and competent leader'.[27] To a Russian foreign correspondent in early 1993 he rather candidly acknowledged 'signs of authoritarianism' in his actions.[28]

Those signs included suppression of all unofficial press and free assembly, as well as other rights. At the same time, since late 1991 government and party house organs such as *Sawet Ozbekistan* (renamed *Ozbekistan awazi* – Voice of Uzbekistan – from 1 September 1991) have noticeably increased the amount and frequency of front-page space given President Karimov's photograph, decrees and reports of his activities. A selection of four later issues of that house organ of the Peoples' Democratic Party of Uzbekistan circulated in several different months each devotes nearly the entire front page to President Karimov's activities and includes on it no fewer than two large photographs of him in every one of these issues.[29]

The press bulletin of the government's Supreme Council and Council of Ministers', *Khälq sozi*, imitates that presentation of news about President Karimov, whether reporting domestic or foreign affairs. In a sample issue from autumn 1995, seven out of eight front-page articles feature or mention him and two large photos appear, as well.[30] Equally telling in this metamorphosis of the party secretary into dominant ruler stands the documentation compiled by human rights organisations concerning his government's frequent abuse of and violence against opposition politicians, religious leaders, creative writers and performers and other elites.[31] (Specific instances of these abuses appear below, pp. 83–5.)

Saparmirat Niyazov (Turkmenbashy) has declared himself 'the first national hero of Turkmenistan', and has awarded himself his country's first International Prize for establishing Turkmenistan's independence on 27 October 1991. Besides serving as president of the republic, he heads the Democratic Party of Turkmenistan, the renamed Communist Party of Turkmenistan. His supporters proposed in late 1993 to make him president for life, and a referendum held in January 1994 gave him a second term lasting until 2002 as president without the mandated re-election in 1997. According to the Turkmen Press News Agency on 27 September 1995, his Democratic Party would soon debate granting him life tenure as head of the state and the party.[32]

The Turkmenistan president did not stand alone in seeking to prolong his tenure of office. Both President Karimov of Uzbekistan, who organised a referendum in 1995 to extend his term to the year 2000 without bothering with the prescribed statutory elections in 1996, and Kazakstan's President Nazarbaev have done the same.[33] The Kazak leader also made a variety of political moves against the opposition, replacing about one-third of the regional chieftains (*hakimdar*), dismissing the constitutional court, revising the constitution to give him power to dismiss the parliament, securing tight control over the new Observation Council of the State Mass Media and calling parliamentary elections for December 1995 that many opposition groups, including Azat, the Workers' Movement, the Social Democratic Party and members of the Communist Party, and the speaker of the dissolved parliament called illegitimate.[34]

Kyrgyzstan, generally considered, perhaps mistakenly, the paragon of tolerance in Central Asia, has recently experienced unrest over manipulation of election laws by partisans of President Askar Akaev. Opponents charge that the Kyrgyz president, like Uzbekistan's President Karimov, exhibits authoritarian tendencies. In particular, President Akaev and his political advisors received harsh criticism for what adversaries called the unconstitutional extension of the president's term in office. They claim that President Akaev's re-election would constitute a third consecutive term, illegal under the state's constitution. Heavy militia and Interior Ministry special forces (OMON) prevented opposition parties from demonstrating in Bishkek on 28 October 1995 against extension of the president's tenure. Opponents asserted that 'all state media bodies are electioneering in favour of one candidate – Askar Akaev'. They stated further that in Kyrgyzstan the government persecutes freedom of thought, shuts down the opposition press, bars journalists critical of the government from professional activity and instigates physical assaults on opposition members.[35]

The leaders of Central Asia appear more and more to prefer themselves in the role of dynamic strongmen rather than to leave, as their medieval models fervently wished to do, images of themselves as history's esteemed national heroes. Hardy opponents of the government attract persistent, unpleasant attention from the police. The authorities harass Zamira Sydykova for publishing materials critical of President Askar Akaev and have jailed Topchubek Turgunaliev again in a distant village in southern Kyrgyzstan because he refused to cease open political activity against the current regime in Bishkek.[36] The revelations of presidential behaviour in Central Asia suggest one reason for the efforts now underway to sacralise a small set of historical figures in each of the Central Asian republics.

Dissent and leadership

Several years before independence caught the Central Asian ethnore-publics by surprise, clusters of local cultural elites had begun efforts to foster unfettered thinking and activity in their localities. Immediately before the Soviet collapse, such people worked to convince other elites and the literate public that Central Asia required independence from the USSR and from Russia. They actively promoted the enlivening or invent-ing of identifying symbols, especially national languages, alphabets, rituals, religious affiliations and the like. They openly protested police violence against peaceful gatherings of these same groups. When the Moscow government tottered, these new movements continued the drive for independence and swung purposefully in the direction of securing long-denied civil and human rights, emphasising equality and justice as their principles.

Following the disintegration of the CPSU in August 1991, and then the formal dissolution of the USSR in December 1991, that earlier drive for democratic ideals in Central Asia emerged briefly, faltered, then faded away. Before they disappeared as cultural-political movements, those several drives imparted to literate townspeople the idea that the Communist Parties of Tajikistan, Kazakstan and Uzbekistan remained undemocratic, unpopular organisations sustained by police and militia forces. Through publicly articulating such perceptions, shared by many in the population, these feeble, short-lived efforts nevertheless made an impact upon their countries. Their violent suppression by the regimes left as useful reminders new scars upon the psyche of Central Asia's cultural elites. The main ideas advanced by these programmes of dissent in several states between about 1988 and 1992–3 from the first prompted modest but meaningful action.

The Unity Popular Movement Birlik of Uzbekistan as early as July 1989, along with other activities, had organised a special discussion club named Munazara, thus emulating the earlier circles of literary intellectuals mentioned at the outset, this time for debating points of law and politics in the region. Also, the Unity Popular Movement Birlik by January 1990 had set up a Women's National Development Organisation called Tömaris.[37] Registering an awareness of ancient history of Central Asia, they named the group after Tomyris, the valiant woman warrior-general of the Massagetae. According to Herodotus, her forces destroyed Cyrus (d. 529 BC), king of the Medes and Persians, and his armies when they pushed eastward into her territory in a battle foreseen in Cyrus' dream as a conflict between Europe and Asia.[38] Tomyris represented an Asia victorious over Cyrus' version of Europe in that bloody confrontation of the nomadic Massagetae against expansionist, but settled, Persians.

Neither the Soviet-sponsored galaxy nor the post-Soviet sanctioned array of officially designated heroes has put in its top ranks a female personage. In choosing to recognise the historical role of Tomyris, the leaders of the Unity Popular Movement Birlik thus flouted both the rule against local nomination of models for popular recognition and the unstated gender bias. When the government of Uzbekistan suppressed the Unity Popular Movement Birlik, it also nearly stifled the Tömaris Women's National Development Organisation and vetoed the candidacy of a historic woman leader for prominence in Central Asia's approved history. One of the new post-Soviet histories mentions Tomyris in passing only to cast doubt upon the form of her name used in Greek sources.[39]

Deliberate indifference to Tomyris' historic defence of Asia could mean that the authorities chose to avoid popularising dangerous leaders in most instances. But the cultural elites have not forgotten her and people like her. A daring opponent of presidential power in Uzbekistan, the much-persecuted former vice president, Shukrullah Mirsaidov, in 1995 tried to gather representatives of the banned Freedom Party Erk, the Unity Popular Movement Birlik, the Women's Development

Organisation Tömaris, and his own Justice Party (Ädalät-Khäq Yoli), to open a new centre in Tashkent for co-ordinating opposition to the authoritarian regime of the republic.[40]

Another outstanding Central Asian woman, Nadira Khanim (1792–1842), suffered martyrdom at Bukharan hands. Despite her many accomplishments as poet and cultural leader, and her prominent political role at the head of government in the Qoqan (Khokand) Khanate as regent for her young son, Madali Khan, Nadira Khanim, of course, belongs amongst the harmless heroines. She has not merited formal promotion to the higher ranks within the category of Central Asia's official but still tame historical heroes.

Intellectuals openly acknowledged these inequities. The republic's principal local-language cultural newspaper, *Uzbekistan's Literature and Art*, proposed to create a grand memorial to freedom. The memorial would form a round structure that could expand with the growth of time and events, and would stand in the middle of Independence Square in Tashkent so that people could circle around it. Creation of the monument would attract all the gifted people of the republic; there would be no sorts of secret 'closets' where this selecting took place and, when it came time to repair and refurbish, everyone would have to lend a hand. In addition, the project might attract Central Asians abroad. The most interesting aspects of the plan are the heroes it seeks to depict. On seven panels, statues or bas-reliefs would appear, depicting on the first panel Adam and Eve, then events leading up to the invasion of Central Asia by the Arabs (with their sweeping new Islamic ideology); after that, 'ancient Turkic hero Afrasiyab; Padishah Lady Tomyris [not identified as Turkic by most scholars], the bold herdsman Shiraq [legendary Saka opponent of Darius' invading forces], commander Spitamen [who in 329–7 BC roused the Soghdians against the invasion of Alexander the Great] and the like'.[41]

When this visionary proposal appeared only two months after Uzbekistan's Independence Day, it evidently did not receive a significant response, but it displays many remarkable features, including the nomination of Tomyris and other heroic women for first-rank status. For some reason, it completely ignores the rise and envelopment of southern Central Asia by the Uzbeks in the fifteenth century. It also causes some surprise by including numbers of intellectuals martyred by the communist regime and by omitting many Soviet heroes earlier anointed by the local Communist Party as well as by its almost complete silence regarding prize-winning, Soviet-era Uzbek writers of the communist order.

The meaning of the proposal reaches far beyond those rejections or selections, of course, for it represents a thoughtful intellectual's ideas about which events and people have played pivotal parts in the history of his country. In certain panels, it owes a heavy debt to the standard Marxist historiography, understandable in a younger scholar raised entirely in the Soviet system of education. Even so, the proposal offers an interesting contrast to the scheme of heroes chosen by the pre-independence and post-Soviet leaders in the region, a contrast made more glaring with the silence of official Uzbekistan concerning any changes at all – other than the elevation of Amir Temur – to recognition in the array of official heroes inherited from the Soviet regime.

The new meaning of dynasty

For the men at the top of Central Asian politics, that series of choices rather obviously meant to preserve models of arbitrary rule exemplified by the still-intact but renamed Communist Party skeletons of the region. This procedure invoked the region's ancient tradition of dynastic succession,[42] so denigrated in Soviet propaganda but so quickly (re)adopted in practice.

In the case of Tajikistan and Uzbekistan, the application of the medieval Arabic borrowing 'descendant/dynasty' (*sulalä*), ordinarily meant to specify a blood relationship amongst successive rulers, perhaps would better reflect the oligarchy's view of succession as a continuation in power of its strongmen than the contemporary term 'household/dynasty' (*khanädan*) acquired from Persian, as with so many concepts to do with rule. With either terminology, the situation of the cultural elites remained essentially the same. Post-Soviet authoritarianism, regardless of its protestations about progress towards democracy, confined the cultural elites within a prescribed range of thought and expression. This acted much as it had under the iron hands of Temur and his successors in Central Asia, generating panegyrics and insincerity in most public writings.

Following Uzbekistan's declaration of independence on 31 August 1991, the republic's officials chose to resurrect and sacralise the pre-Uzbek conqueror, Amir Temur, in the history of Central Asia's past, and to revise its historiography and identity by association with a renowned Central Asian whose deeds, history and name already have global recognition. Students and other literate Uzbeks can understand the official restoration of Temur to approval as a gesture of independence from Soviet ideologists. By returning Temur affirmatively to the history of Central Asia, the authorities have corrected one of the many communist distortions of the region's history. Citizens of surrounding countries have surely noticed, as well, that restoration of the famous tyrant to favour carries an unsettling innuendo of Central Asian reunification centred around Samarkand as its core.

These motives hardly explain the need for the one-sided, exaggerated admiration for Temur and his dynasty or the fulsome praise attending the current rehabilitation. For balance, Uzbeks need realistically to face the unsavoury aspects in the actions and character of the republic's official heroes, but few have yet done so publicly, reports a witness to the 660th birthday celebrations of Temur in 1996.[43] As a measure of that imbalance, readers in Uzbekistan need only consult a genealogy recently published in Tashkent to see that it devotes twice as much space to Temur and his dynasty as it does to any other set of Central Asian rulers, including those of the genuine Uzbeks, the Shaybanids, who destroyed the Temurids and reigned more than nine decades, or of the Soviet regime, which lasted seventy years and created the outlines for post-Soviet Uzbekistan.[44]

After 1991, two new circumstances changed the thinking of people in the region about the bases for their own group identity, which had long defined itself in good part through reacting to the dominant foreign masters. With the lifting of Moscow's hegemony from Central Asia, the former necessary deference to Russia and Russians suddenly vanished. At the same time, the discrediting of the imposed Marxist ideology created a momentary vacuum that allowed the cultural elites to speak their minds. It also caused the social and cultural managers of the societies to choose between clinging to the old or finding a safe new ideology.

To some degree, the former satraps vacillated between relying intensely upon ethnicity for the new national identity (and ideology) or facing the knowledge that this emphasis could alienate large ethnic minorities, including local Slavs, Germans, Tatars and Koreans, who, with their economically valuable skills and experience, substantially bolstered the economy of their countries. Subsequent developments suggest that Central Asia's thinking people, except in Kyrgyzstan and to some extent in Tajikistan, had failed to provide adequate guidance to their fellow citizens at this crucial moment either in defining the dimensions of community convincingly or in introducing widespread open-mindedness into Central Asia's post-modern cultural and political development.

Why did the cultural elites fail in their defining unofficial function – providing intellectual leadership for the public – at this crucial time and how did the new/old ruling circles behave once they had neutralised the potential leadership of the intellectuals? The intellectuals played an ineffectual part here not only because of an overpowering heritage of the old Soviet politics. Their failure arose from a profound weakness fostered by the absence amongst them of what observers might call customary or sure centrality of elites in the cultural, spiritual or philosophical guidance of the public under the new governments and conditions. Politicians and one-party bureaucrats had yet again usurped the intellectuals' prerogatives.

Though dissent by highly educated people offers little immediate threat to the present police- and militia-reinforced regimes, any disagreement has particularly irked the Central Asian presidents currently enjoying virtual one-man rule. Both local dissenters and human and civil rights organisations outside Central Asia have reported again and again that the newly reinstalled authoritarian leadership carries on with cruel repression of those intellectuals in their societies who fail to conform.

Governmental initiatives

Uzbekistan's government, in 1993, launched a campaign to create what it defined as a suitable ideology for the republic's new-found independence (*milliy istiqlal mäfkuräsi*). At meetings with a group of writers and before the twelfth session of Uzbekistan's Supreme Council, Karimov sketched out his ideas, and advanced the opinion that the country needed an ideology now that Marxism-Leninism had lost authority and favour. That new ideology could not come from abroad, he declared, nor would such an ideology apply universally in the state (sic). In his first address to the General Assembly of the United Nations Organization, President Karimov described an important exception to the reach of ideology: 'First we have proclaimed the priority of economy over politics, [and] de-ideologization of both domestic and external economic relations.'[45]

In the same year, a state publishing house issued a booklet composed of short discussions by various authors about the ideology ostensibly required by the new state. The writers offered interesting proposals devoted mostly to patriotism, political attitudes, socioeconomic imperatives and the like. One of the shortest and most striking contributions came from a senior professor, Matyaqub Qoshjanaw, corresponding member of the Academy of Science of Uzbekistan and doctor of philology, who pointed out that in life no void exists, for something always fills an empty space. Intellectuals must provide a rationale for everyday existence in lieu of discredited communism, or some alien ideology would occupy that place. Thinkers had to introduce an ideology of a new type and direction to fill in such 'emptiness' (*boshliq*). Independence in itself was not an ideology; it was the compass for an ideology. Qoshjanaw argues that 'our society is creating its own ideology', for the outstanding medieval scholars and creative writers of Central Asia – Ahmed Yassawiy

(d. 1166), Alisher Nawaiy (d. 1501) and Abdullah Qadiriy (d. 1938), for example – had created the ideology necessary for the advance of society. 'This [ideology] is truth! This [ideology] is love of mankind! The most important thing is humanism!'[46] His idea may have impressed the politicians.

Uzbekistan's government soon took another initiative to engage the cultural elite in guided endeavour. Just as the Institutes of the Central Asian Academies of Science had for decades routinely assigned to their members the research programs required of them in the years ahead, now the political authorities pre-empted the scholar's plans and moved to mobilise the intellectuals in pursuit of the regime's aims. The country's president on 23 April 1994 decreed the founding of a republican societal centre for 'Spirituality and Enlightenment' (Mä'näwiyät wä Mä'rifät) and the establishment of a new journal of discussion and thought, *Ideas/Reflection* (Täfäkkur). In his message to readers of the journal he expressed the hope that 'the brilliant pens of all our journal's writers will introduce the light of thought [*täfäkkur*] into the heart of every single reader-subscriber and every single household'.[47]

This elegantly produced Uzbek-language journal cannot reach many of the nation's households, because the management publishes only 5,000 copies for the republic's 14.1 million and Tajikistan's 1.2 million Uzbeks (1989).[48] Also, judging by a survey of the first six issues (August 1994 through May 1996), both the abstract content of most articles – usually some sixteen to twenty short selections in each issue – and the journal's erudite style and vocabulary would place it beyond the interests and preparation of ordinary readers. With its maximum length of 128 pages it resembles a 'thick' publication of the Soviet kind devoted to heavy, not popular, material. When the first head of Uzbekistan's new Centre for Spirituality and Enlightenment, Academician Erkin Yusupaw, announced its goals in August 1994, he seemed to aim clearly not at the general public but at a narrower audience, namely the cultural elites and the political decision-takers.

He specified as the Centre's chief obligation its duty 'to serve the progress of the nation and the country by jointly studying the rich cultural and spiritual heritage of our people in connection with Eastern and general human values [*qädriyätlär*]'. Secondly, underscoring the Centre's true purpose, he proposed to draw together the leading ideas useful for the nation's and country's future and then to advance what he called 'the intellectual-creative capacities' of the talented and gifted individuals of the homeland.

The new Centre further would keep in view matters of international amity, concord, peace and quiet in that land and would further the defence, feelings of patriotism, national awareness and the development of new contemporary values of the country. It would make deep and systematic analysis of the values in the national-cultural heritage, in the national awakening and in national independence. And lastly, it would, partly by giving close attention to the positive human qualities of the Centre's personnel, give aid to the country's mass media and public organisations by defining the country's ideology and 'the way to spiritual purity'.[49]

Within two years, the Centre received a different sort of leader, Ne'mat Aminaw, an ideological satirist. Uzbekistan's president began speaking more insistently about the Centre's obligations to society. He demanded, first of all, that it make sure that everyone learned about the newly built museum devoted to Temur and the Temurids and the lessons it taught about power and pride. 'The duty of scholars and writers like you', he told a special meeting of Centre's leadership in September 1996, 'should be made up of ever more deeply implanting, amongst our people and into the heart[s] of our compatriots, [such] momentous dates as the birthday of the one born at the fortunate conjunction of the planets [Temur].'[50] In a new emphasis before that group, he went on to urge that everyone must lovingly train young people in the country's great history.

It seems evident therefore that as late as autumn 1996 Uzbekistan's cultural elites remained unaccustomed to unguided writing if not to undirected thinking, but in their civilisation and tradition they possessed valuable, highly sophisticated models of skill in dissimulation (*taqiyya*) and allegory (*kinayä*).

The intellectuals' response

In nearly every issue, the magazine *Täfäkkur* has revealed the persistent fascination of post-Soviet, Central Asian intellectuals with the Bukharan, Crimean Tatar, Kazak, Khivan and Turkistanian reformists (*Jädid*s) of the century's first two decades. Those brief selections only faintly echoed the enthusiastic embrace of Jadidism by writers more remote from the centre of the elite establishment in the 1980s and 1990s. Such elites published countless articles about and reissued many texts by the Jadid authors – the Bukharan Abdalrauf Fitrat, his mentors, Samarkand's Mahmud Khoja Behbudiy and Hajji Mu'in ibn Shukrullah, Tashkent's Munawwar Qari, Kazakstan's Ahmad Baytursin-ulu and Mir-Jaqib Duwlat-ulu, amongst numerous others.[51]

The attention paid to Fitrat (1886–1938), rightly claimed by both Tajiks and Uzbeks, has increasingly enlivened discussions at meetings and in pages of journals and newspapers of Tajikistan and Uzbekistan.

The reissue of Abdalrauf Fitrat's 1909 fictional allegory, *The Dispute* (Munazira) in the two languages has fuelled closer consideration of his themes. In the original edition, the author caustically dealt with the duties and defaults of educators in Bukharan society. In a surprisingly candid epilogue, he appealed directly to the amir of Bukhara to improve the sorry lot of nearly all Muslims. In particular, he begged the amir to educate and train his own subjects in better schools that he would establish inside the country and in specialised institutions abroad. Fitrat framed this plea within comments regarding a religious contest between modernising Christianity – with its guns, press, trains and steamboats – and backward Islam, a conflict in which he described a besieged Islam overwhelmed by a triumphant, Christian Europe.[52]

This sudden new burst of scholarly and literary scrutiny of Jadidism reflects more than the refreshing novelty introduced by the slackening of Soviet literary censorship and subsequent studied official indifference to Jadid history. Post-Soviet leaders cannot easily suppress that history, though it disseminated many ideas widely, for they know that communist ideologists had banned almost all of the Jadid writings, and, because Revolution despised Reform, violent overthrow had denigrated moderation or erased it from the modern national history of Central Asia. The present political leadership also disregards the rejuvenated spirit of Jadidism, because, with care and Aesopian rhetoric, the Jadids usually avoided insulting the rulers openly.

Instead, the reformists steadily undermined the potentates with ideas of human rights, the emancipation of women and open criticism of history and literature, and of solutions for cultural, social and economic issues known at home and abroad. Had Russia's Bolshevik coup in November 1917 not interrupted that process, the Jadid reform might have transformed most elite thinking and then the understanding of the public from the bottom up throughout all Central Asia – including Bukhara, Kazakstan (then labelled Kirgizstan by Russians), Khiva and Turkistan. That so many intellectuals of the 1990s admire and try to emulate the thinking of Jadids during that semi-permissive period between 1905 and 1920 created by the disintegration of the tsarist regime of course means that the phenomenon must represent something more than mere curiosity.

By giving unusual attention to the reformists of the early decades, and by reprinting their works in Kazak, Russian, Tajik and Uzbek, intellectuals of the 1990s at once speak to the matter of forming a broader group awareness and the concept of a free exchange of ideas and enrichment of education at all levels. In the context of the Jadid period and the new preoccupation with the Jadids and their ideas of society, the contradictory roles of rulers and intellectuals in authoritarian states stand out clearly. Those engaged in rehabilitating the Jadids thereby enlighten the public with attitudes and ideas in strong contrast to the Soviet-style mentality of holdover officials and leaders. At the same time, they sharpen each others' understanding of social as well as aesthetic and intellectual controversies. Autocracy in Jadid times worked as a stimulant to intellectual connivance in a good cause, or, on rare occasions, to defiant intellectual independence. In the post-Soviet era, authoritarian rule probably will do the same. Political independence obviously does not correspond to intellectual independence in Central Asia today, which cannot mean that no independent-minded intellectuals exist there. The painstaking restoration of the Jadid ideal in Kazakstan, Tajikistan and Uzbekistan gives sufficient documentation for that.

Moreover, the Jadid version of group or territorial identity offers a model crucially significant in the current Central Asian search for self-awareness. The Jadids stood for two forms of social and political organisation which so greatly contrast with the arrangements persisting in the 1990s that the reformists' ideas appear almost as recommendations for change in the post-Soviet period.

For the Jadids, the meaningful community of Islam stretched from frontier to frontier across lands combining people of all Central Asian and some foreign varieties, and organised them without reference to singular identities. The Jadids lived and worked in supranational territories bearing non-ethnic group labels, especially in the south, in Bukhara, Khiva and Turkistan. Their writings hardly ever refer to the tensions endemic in later ethnic relations, for they did not aspire to experience life in a nation-state.

Besides confounding partisans of the neo-Soviet status quo in post-communist Central Asia, the Jadid example shows that economic deprivation, maddening bureaucratic suffocation and police state violence against civil and human rights cannot be expected to generate sincere fealty to the strongman and would-be dynast. Stoic tolerance of governmental pressure but inner rejection of official ideology is a more likely response.

In the high drama currently acted out in the region, Central Asia's cultural elite shuns passivity, and in order to outsmart their antagonists – autocrats and strongmen – sometimes have had to find asylum outside Kazakstan, Tajikistan, Turkmenistan or Uzbekistan. Many more turn to the old practice of subterfuge in Uzbekistan or Turkmenistan, and resort to wiles and tricks in Kazakstan, but rouse themselves to unaccustomed assertiveness in Kyrgyzstan.

The cultural elites' indirect methods do provide them some security, but pose dangers to their cause. So long as an authoritarian leader persists in aggressively promoting supra-ethnic symbols for the nation's identity such as the mighty Amir Temur, once master not merely of Transoxiana – partly, the present Uzbekistan – but all southern Central Asia, Afghanistan, the Middle East and India, such tactics may confuse the concept of group consciousness amongst today's elites. It can stymie efforts to formulate and advance a modern, post-Soviet group identity for every nationality within the larger whole, one congruent with the recognised territory of each country but circumscribed by acceptance of community rather than assertive ethnocentrism.

Until politicians restore a defining role to intellectuals, cultural elites may intentionally invoke the ambiguity and obscurity so long practised by poets and writers in the region. In this, they would consciously emulate the Jadids, who followed that famous model for subversion, Abdulqadir Bedil (1644–1721), a Persian mystic poet of Hindustan descended from Central Asians, whose works enjoyed tremendous vogue amongst bilingual reformists and later scholars of southern Central Asia.[53] Threatened by governors of his day, Sufi thinker Bedil taught the future Jadids how to disarm punitive authority through the elaborate use of double meaning and unclarity. In this way, whatever the elites say openly, the government cannot know precisely the attitudes or opinions of the intellectuals. The public, raised in the reading of its society's inexplicit signs, will interpret the elite's communications fairly well.

This old survival technique of intellectuals and underlings, so useful to the early twentieth-century reformists, can gain some flexibility and time for the post-communist intellectuals to proceed with undermining or altering the authoritarian ideas and concepts of imperial nationhood currently advanced by the politicians of Central Asia. Moreover, this phenomenon testifies to the continuing conflict between cultural elites and politicians in Central Asia over the issues of cultural and national group identity and over the issue of cultural symbiosis or separation. The persistent interest amongst literate Central Asians in the Jadids' concept of an ideal Turkistanian, Muslim community suggests that thinking men and women in the region favour ethnocultural symbiosis.

Part II

Ethnopolitics and the construction
of group boundaries

5   Nation re-building and political discourses of identity politics in the Baltic states

> In many cases secession is an attempt to gain independence from a state (in the Soviet case, an empire) that unjustly annexed the territory in question, and annexation is often followed by *colonization*. If the question is whether the group that was wronged ought to be allowed to reclaim its sovereignty, then neither the colonists nor their descendants have any legitimate voice in that decision. They should be disqualified from voting in the referendum. Whether those non-Latvians who played no part in the original injustice should be compensated for their losses if they are expelled from the newly independent Latvia, or whether a condition of permitting secession should be that all who are currently Latvian citizens (Russians included) are accorded full citizenship rights after secession, is a separate matter.
>
> Allen Buchanan, *Secession: The Morality of Political Divorce. From Fort Sumter to Lithuania and Quebec* (Boulder: Westview, 1991), p. 143

> after individuals have entered a certain territory under the justified impression that they will qualify for citizenship, it is unjustified to change these terms retroactively. This is a crucial issue for many republics established after the collapse of the Soviet Union ... While the Estonian rage over the Soviet occupation is understandable, creating another wrong will not right the first one. Estonia and Latvia must face the fact that the injustices inflicted on them have turned them into binational states, and there is no way of turning the clock back.
>
> Yael Tamir, *Liberal Nationalism* (Princeton, NJ: Princeton University Press, 1993), p. 159

The above passages capture a moral predicament that has faced all three Baltic states but which continues to be the subject of much debate in Estonia and Latvia. It raises in particular one of the central issues of post-coloniality: whether those who are labelled the 'colonial other' should enjoy the same entitlements to membership of the citizen-polity as those of the nation who claim a privileged relationship with the sovereign homeland. It in effect represents a tension between universalist and particularist notions of distributive justice. The former hold that, irrespective of ethnic difference, those who reside within the sovereign territory at the moment of the declaration of independence should have a right to membership of that citizen-polity. On this basis, Lithuania, along with most of the other post-Soviet borderland states, can legitimately claim that their citizen-state formations are constructed on the basis of universal principles: all those resident in the national homeland at the moment of the declaration of independent statehood were granted the right to membership of the citizen-polity.[1] In contrast, particularists argue that, while members of the core nation have a special ancestral purchase on the privileges of homeland, the settler communities do not have the same automatic rights to membership. It is this modality of citizenship that has been adopted by Estonia and Latvia. Legitimised on the basis that, like Lithuania, their states were illegally incorporated into the Soviet Union in 1940, both national governments argue that only citizens of the previous inter-war polity and their descendants have an automatic right to membership. Others, primarily Russian-speakers who settled in Estonia and Latvia during the period of Soviet rule, can be admitted to the citizen-polity only upon meeting certain preconditions. These include a residency qualification, calculated from the base year 1990, of two years (now five years) in the case of Estonia and ten years in Latvia, a knowledge of the national language and a declaration that an applicant has 'never served in or was never affiliated with the occupying Soviet forces'.[2] As a result, the social status of a third of the population of Estonia and Latvia, made up more or less exclusively of Russian-speakers of whom the majority have little or no command of the respective state languages,[3] has been redesignated. Their status has been demoted from that of citizens to that of denizens, in which certain privileges not accorded to 'foreigners' exist, but in which those rights enjoyed by the national majority are denied.

Such issues of distributive justice clearly raise important questions concerning the relationship between the politics of national identities and post-colonial democratic state-building. For one school of thought, based upon the premise that democratisation is inherently more difficult in multiethnic polities than in states in which all residents see themselves as members of the same sovereign homeland, competition between political entrepreneurs based upon appeals to national identity has played the crucial role in shaping the nature of these polities. As Adam Przeworski notes more generally: 'Once independence is achieved, political entrepreneurs from each community recognise that the multiethnic coalitions were oversized and surmise that they can defeat the coalition within their own community by advocating extreme positions.'[4] This 'political outbidding', as Metcalf observes, became a central feature of post-independence national politics in Estonia, in which the more radically minded nationalists were able to outmanoeuvre moderate and more ethnically accommodating political elites by advocating a citizen-polity that deprived the Soviet settler communities of membership and that elevated ethnic Estonians as the titular core nation to a central position within the new state institutions of power.[5] Such an analysis can also be applied to Latvia where the demographically larger settler community has been marginalised in a similar way. Thus, as the experiences of such practices elsewhere would suggest, translating the expectation of political dominance of a national group into political practice is likely to so alienate the losers as to induce instability in the regime, if not violence or civil war.[6]

Despite both Estonia and Latvia sacrificing a more representative democracy of the sort that has been established in neighbouring Lithuania by excluding Soviet-era settlers from the citizen-polity, both polities have been characterised by a remarkable degree of social stability, compared to some of the other post-Soviet states. On this basis it can be suggested that Estonia and Latvia have succeeded in securing stability despite having established or even because they have established what the author has referred to elsewhere as ethnic democracies.[7] In other words, while the titular nation has secured a institutionally superior status for itself in part by depriving the settler communities of particular political rights and through the use of draconian language laws, certain universal principles of human rights nevertheless are adhered to, notably within the sphere of civil and collective rights.[8] In this chapter we examine how such an ethnopolitics of exclusion is currently being played out in Estonia and Latvia. First, we explore how differing conceptions of identity politics, as expressed in competing notions of national homeland, are represented in ethnopolitical discourse. Secondly, in focusing on what has become the dominant and official political discourse, based on a specific identity politics of exclusion, we explore how such a discourse is also bound up with a political rationality to nation-rebuilding which, it is suggested, also helps us to understand the popular appeal of such citizenship policies to members of the titular nation. Finally, we turn to consider the identity politics of the settler communities, examining in particular why, despite the persistence of a neo-Soviet conception of homeland amongst elements of the diaspora, such an identity politics has not been sufficiently supported to present a problem to either nationalising regime.

Identity politics and political discourses of homeland

Of all the ethnopolitical codes – that is, the language that certain groups employ to accentuate difference along ethnic lines and that is designed to mobilise constituents and to legitimise the actions of their political elites –

the idea of homeland has emerged as being pivotal. As Michael Billig notes, 'A nation is more than an imagined community of people, for a homeland has also to be imagined.'[9] In the Baltic states, the demarcation, cultivation and transmission of symbols and myths of homeland have emerged as an important means to defining competing representations of national identity. Accordingly, three such positions in the discourse of homeland can be identified and examined, each based on a particular self-defined, normative conception of the nation-state.

First, we can identify a *core nation* discourse. This conception of national identity, which comes closest to that of the official discourse, is associated particularly with the centre-right and with far right-wing nationalist political parties which have dominated much of the political agenda of both countries since 1991.[10] It is based on the idea of nativism, of the state-bearing nation's claim to possessing a special relationship to what is considered to be 'its natural homeland', the place where (in Latvia's case) 'the ancient indigenous nationality in Latvia is the Latvian',[11] and where such natural metaphors as roots, soil, motherland and fatherland are employed to emphasise a sense of genealogical rooted-ness and exclusivity to a place. Having removed itself from Soviet rule, it is contended, the nation can reclaim its historic political homeland, based upon reconnecting with those Western values that it is alleged were also central to the inter-war sovereign homeland, namely, a Western-style democracy, a laissez-faire economy and being part of Europe. By assert-ing that the state that came into existence in 1990 is in effect the legal restoration of the historic homeland,[12] such radical nationalists can claim that only citizens of that inter-war state and their descendants should form the legal foundation of the restored citizen-polity. Thus such accounts in effect blur the differences between the historic and contempo-rary homeland, while the difference between the core nation and the dias-pora is accentuated. Those who settled in the homeland during the Soviet period are therefore represented as 'the colonising other', a remnant of 'a civil garrison of the empire' and potential 'fifth columnists', who threaten the stability if not territorial integrity of the political homeland.

Such a conception of homeland points in particular to the way in which the sheer demographic weight of diasporic intrusion during the Soviet period has transformed Estonia and Latvia from being polities with large national majorities during the inter-war years, in which the titular nation made up 90 per cent and 75 per cent respectively of their total populations, to their present demographic status as multiethnic states, in which their core nations compose only 55 per cent and 65 per cent of their political homelands. As a consequence, core nation-statists claim that the national language and culture are under threat from such externally imposed immigration. At one extreme are proponents of a conception of national identity who would dearly wish to see the outright removal of 'the other' from the homeland; supporters of the more moderate form advocate policies that encourage resettler migration, and expect those who enter the citizen-body to become part of what in Latvia has been termed the 'one community nation-state', that is, one in which the cultural and linguistic attributes of the core nation become those of its citizenry.[13]

While also acknowledging the special historical relationship that the core nation has with its political homeland, the second conception of identity politics, which we can label *multiculturalist*, accepts that the Baltic states are the homelands of a variety of minority groups, including the Russian diaspora, who it is noted can legitimately claim to have a relationship with the region that stretches back centuries. It is thus a conception of homeland which plays down ethnic difference and which holds that all residents who live and work within the homeland should have a right to membership of the citizen-polity. Its supporters therefore emphasise a political concept of the nation (a political homeland for all) rather than one based on an ethnic designation. Indeed, during the struggle for independent statehood in 1988–91, many within the nationalist movements of both Estonia and Latvia adhered to such a vision of statehood, which was also supported by many of the Russian diaspora, including Soviet-era settlers. Hence in the 1990 referenda on home rule, a third of all Russian-speakers in both Estonia and Latvia, by supporting independent statehood, no doubt held a vision of sovereignty in which a sovereign Estonia or Latvia was envisaged as a guarantor of their future cultural freedoms as well as providing the prospects for a level of material well-being that membership of the Soviet Union could not ensure.[14] The other, the common enemy, was not equated with a people or a homeland but with a particular ideology and sociopolitical system, Stalinism. Thus in contrast to core nation-statists, who see the core nation as the main victim of Soviet rule in the region, multiculturalists interpret the Soviet era as one in which ethnic groups constituted a common 'community of fate' who suffered equally at the hands of a totalitarian regime. Consequently, the diaspora should therefore not be judged as responsible for the misdeeds of Soviet rule. However, like core nation-statists, multiculturalists see the Western-inspired economic and political modernisation of the inter-war state as both a national symbol and political strategy for the present. They particularly note the virtues of connecting with a tradition of tolerance and multiculturalism that was characteristic of both polities during the 1920s but which during the second decade of the inter-war period was abandoned with the establishment in all three Baltic states of authoritarian-nationalist regimes. While sharing a vision of their homelands within Europe, multiculturalists are in addition keen to rebuild economic and political links with their powerful eastern neighbour.

Finally, there exists what can be labelled a *neo-Soviet* discourse of self-identification in which a sense of homeland derives mainly from the Soviet period. This category of identity includes those who took for granted the political and socioeconomic institutions and ways of life of Soviet times. At one extreme it is bound up with the irredentist goal of securing reunification with co-nationals in one larger 'Soviet' or 'Russian' homeland, but it is also associated with those for whom the loss of 'the big homeland' and what it stood for has had a deeply disturbing impact. Aspects of this orientation include a nostalgia for such socialist values as the extensive welfare state and a suspicion of the benefits of, if not downright hostility towards, privatisation and European reintegration. Support for this sense of self-identification comes primarily from Soviet-era settlers who have little or no knowledge of the state language and who are amongst the 250,000 residents of Estonia and Latvia who, since 1991, have opted to take advantage of the Russian Federation's policy of offering extra-territorial citizenship to those who were once members of the Soviet homeland. Needless to say, the neo-Soviet type is pro-CIS in political and economic orientation and is happy to ascribe to Russia the role of ethnic patron, and thus of protector and guarantor of their people's diasporic rights.

The 'rationality' of nationalising regimes

If we are to understand the success of the core nation discourse as a form of identity politics, then what might be more important than is invariably given credit for is that such nationalising regimes and the actions that their political elites take with regard to exclusionary citizenship policies are inextricably bound up with a political rationality, however immoral or distasteful some may find it. In other words, as Claus Offe notes with regard to post-communist regimes more generally, ethnopolitical elites have shown a propensity to make rational political choices (however short-sighted, local or unrealistic they may be) by selecting a course of action with a particular political outcome in mind.[15] Thus political rationality is served if nationalising elites secure political power positions by mobilising their constituents along ethnic lines through convincing them of the costs and benefits that will accrue from taking certain political actions. Under such circumstances, ethnopolitical codes can be used, adapted and invented by nationalising elites in order to secure those political outcomes that are considered beneficial to the titular nation.

In relation to the Baltic states, we can suggest that five perspectives have become especially important to the core nation discourse of the citizen-homeland and to shaping and legitimising the boundaries of inclusion and exclusion: titular nation status, de-Sovietisation, the standardising state, protection of the historic homeland's culture, and the return to Europe.

Core nation status

Members of the titular nation have a vested interest in the institutionalisation and reproduction of ethnic and linguistic difference that are provided by their respective laws on citizenship. Thus, if titular nation members can secure over-representation in national and local government, central administration, the courts, media, schools and universities, such an outcome implies a virtually exclusive domination over the state's major institutions and considerable benefits for those who are members of this new political class. As Anton Steen observes, one of the main reasons why Estonia and Latvia adopted such an ethnocratic line on citizenship was

that after the breakdown of the totalitarian system when Russians were expelled from higher positions, the indigenous elites not only safeguarded national independence and cultural awakening, they also opened up career opportunities for a new, young and ambitious political class. National ethnic rhetoric, which is a basic element in building any new independent nation, also became a platform for recruitment and power consolidation of indigenous elites. Since higher positions are few and a source of personal prestige and income, the national elites will see Russians as unwanted challengers to such limited resources.[16]

Thus as a result of the first post-independence national elections in Estonia in 1992, all 101 members of the parliament were ethnic Estonian. Following Latvia's 1993 national elections, only seven out of the hundred deputies elected to parliament were ethnic Russians, while seventy-eight deputies were ethnic Latvian. However, despite a marginal increase in the representation of Russians following the 1995 parliamentary elections in Estonia,[17] the new political class in both countries is still reluctant to adapt citizenship policies to meet the linguistic and cultural demands of Russian representatives. This is due in part to the challenge that such a change would pose not only to the self-preservation of their national cultures but also to the security that an ethnic democracy provides for those who benefit from status positions associated with preserving the near-monopoly that members of the core nation have now secured over the country's political, cultural and administrative professions.

A similar logic operates with regard to securing the conditions for the reproduction of titular nation interests in relation to property rights. By limiting the rights of the diaspora to participate in the privatisation process, considerable material benefits have accrued to members of the core nation. This has been secured in two ways. First, all three Baltic states adopted a policy of restoring property to those inter-war citizens and their descendants whose homes, farms and companies were expropriated during Soviet rule. Coded in terms of redistributive justice, this has resulted in the emergence of a small-scale class of property owners, made up almost entirely of members of the titular nation.[18] Secondly, a voucher programme distributed, within most public spheres, only to citizens, but also linked to the number of years a resident has worked within the homeland, has ensured that the titular nations were the main beneficiaries in the sale of property and in the allocation of shares in their place of work.[19] However, non-citizens are allowed to purchase property, despite opposition in both countries from the nationalist far right. Yet what has emerged as a major tension concerning economic liberalisation is that – in part due to the limited career horizons open to Russians within the public sector and the delay concerning legislation on whether non-citizens should be permitted the right to own property – the settler communities have come to occupy important niches within the non-property-owning business sector, including the growing black economy. An emerging 'ethnic division of labour', to rephrase Michael Hechter's term,[20] can therefore be detected, in which Russians dominate certain niches within the emerging capitalist economy, while Estonians and Latvians have a near-monopoly within the political and bureaucratic structures of government. Consequently, there is an increasing sense amongst some members of the titular nations that they are no longer in control of their national economies, a situation which is ready ammunition for radical nationalists to argue the case for the adoption of more stringent economic laws concerning the rights of the diaspora.[21]

De-Sovietisation

The nationalising policies of Estonia and Latvia are based on the rationality of political decolonisation, on the argument that their political homelands will be fully secure only if they are purged of the individuals, institutions and organisations that were responsible for their people's oppression in the first place. Thus one of the first steps in de-Sovietisation that these states embarked upon was to outlaw those sociopolitical organisations, notably the Communist Party, which had been the mainstay of Soviet rule in the region. Moreover, on a number of occasions, the centre-right within the governing coalitions of both countries has declined to support particular issues or elections to cabinet or premier offices because of an individual's past association with the Communist Party. Indeed, it is especially for those political elites who had a strong association with the past regime that public claims of disassociation with the Soviet regime can be seen as a way of symbolising their homeland patriotism by attempting to convince their supporters of their anti-Soviet credentials. Thus, for instance, many political elites in Estonia and Latvia who took a multiculturalist stance on citizenship during the late 1980s became amongst the most ardent in their opposition to automatically granting citizenship to the settler community once independence was secured. This included, most notably, Latvia's first post-independence prime minister, Anatol Gorbunovs.[22]

In these circumstances, the use of ethnic codes by such political elites, of associating in the mindset of their peoples a symbiotic relationship between 'the colonising other' with the institutions and organisations associated with Soviet rule, provides a way of demonstrating loyalty to the new polity as well as legitimising the outlawing of such organisations and institutions. Moreover, in their political discourse of outbidding to the nationalist right, the centre-right also capitalised upon the previous relationship that some of the leaders of the post-independence and newly formed centre-left opposition parties had with the Communist Party. By accusing the leaders of Latvia's parliamentary faction Harmony and the Equal Rights Faction – who have supported a more inclusionary citizenship policy – of having links with the former Communist Party, the centre-right has been able to capitalise on fears amongst the electorate that the sovereign homeland is still not fully secure from the legacy of Soviet rule. Indeed, such bracketing did not even exclude members of the centre-right governments. In one of the most controversial cases, Latvia's foreign minister, Janis Jurkans, was accused of 'lobbying in favour of Russia' following a speech which questioned the merits of adopting an exclusionary citizenship for securing both internal social stability and a favourable foreign policy with Russia and the West.[23] As a consequence he was forced to resign.

De-Sovietisation is also seen as politically rational from the standpoint of securing the territorial integrity of the homeland, notably from any secessionist challenge that may emerge from the eastern and predominantly Russian enclaves of north-east Estonia and south-east Latvia (known as Latgallia). In 1993, local diasporic elites in north-east Estonia began lobbying for greater cultural, economic and territorial autonomy in their region. Such lobbying was precipitated in part by a proposed aliens law which threatened the rights of residency and employment of non-citizens. A local referendum was therefore called by the north-east's political elites on the region's future. As a consequence, over four-fifths of those who voted in the referendum favoured some form of regional political autonomy.[24] However, despite the fact that the referendum was an attempt not so much to secede from Estonia as to exert pressure on the central government to modify its policies towards the settler community, the government interpreted the situation differently: the north-east, because of the language of ethnic and class politics that was employed, was not only interpreted as attempting to re-Sovietise the region but also as making a direct challenge to the territorial integrity of the fledgling state. For Premier Maart Laar, such events were precipitated by 'former communist functionaries' who feared 'losing their current power at the forthcoming local administrations' elections'.[25] In representing such political elites as posing a potential threat to the territorial security of Estonia, and by downplaying the genuine concern that the local urban communities had about their future security following the introduction of the aliens law, the Estonian government was able to legitimise the removal from power of the cities' municipal representatives and further to justify a law that barred 'aliens' from standing for local government office.

De-Sovietisation is also linked to distancing the Baltic states from the chaos and uncertainty that have flowed from 'the East' based on the claim that, by regulating and monitoring the flow of goods and people across its borders, there is a greater likelihood of ensuring the building blocks of economic modernisation and geopolitical security of their political home-lands. This monitoring has included protecting their previously porous borders from the inflow of a whole variety of transnational problems such as migrant surplus populations, refugees and alien elements, administrative chaos and illegal goods. As the president of Estonia, Lennart Meri, put it in a speech commemorating Estonia's Independence Day in February 1993, 'It is precisely in the name of European values that Estonia needs a secure border . . . Our border is the border of European values.'[26] The introduction of the aliens law in Estonia a few months later, coded as being in 'the national interest', was part of such a political and economic rationality of protecting Estonia's eastern border. It insists that those who arrived in Estonia before July 1990 and who wish to remain in the country, including those who wish to exercise the right to move across the country's border, have to register as 'aliens' within two years (later extended to four years), apply for citizenship or leave the country. It has also meant the phasing out of the so-called red passports (the old Soviet passports) which will no longer be valid for cross-border travel.[27] Accordingly, nearly 330,000 largely Soviet-era settlers who have been issued with residence permits have been reclassified as 'aliens'.[28] This enables the Estonian state not only to ensure the more effective surveillance of its residents, but also to monitor transfrontier movement with greater effectiveness, especially important in north-east Estonia where Russian settlers commute regularly to see family members and friends in neighbouring towns and cities in Russia. Moreover, it also helps the state cope with the growth in the transfrontier black economy, which because it is part of 'the unregistered economy' deprives the government of an important part of its tax revenue. By labelling Soviet-era settlers in pejorative terms as 'alien', a sense of 'them' and 'us' is reinforced which unscrupulous xenophobes can use to their advantage by earmarking this group as responsible for the country's escalating crime and corruption.[29] In contrast, in Latvia non-citizens have been issued 'identity cards'. Although similar to Estonia in the rights and status accorded to their holders, in some respects Latvia's legislation is more restrictive, notably in not granting non-citizens the right to participate in local elections.[30] None the less, as in Estonia, the far right in Latvia has opposed some of the privileges that go with identity card status, arguing that the government has been far too complacent, especially in relation to rights of both residency and movement.[31]

The standardising state

The notion that cultural standardisation facilitates the economic and political modernisation of the state is based on the claim that historically the success of west European nation-state building is based on making the nation and state spatially congruent and that linguistic and educational standardisation is therefore commensurate with the running of a more efficient national economy and 'scientific' state bureaucracy, and with creating a more harmonious and loyal citizen-polity.[32] This is in effect what is implied when the Latvian state declares its aim of aspiring to the idea of the 'one nation-state community', one in which all residents are expected to speak the same language and in which the national culture will therefore be secure throughout the political homeland. In addition to the adoption of language laws in 1988–9 which made the respective core nation language the official state language and which signalled the beginning of an end to Soviet rule by putting the Russian language in a subordinate position, further language laws in Latvia (May 1992) and in Estonia (June 1993 and March 1995) have completed the process of de-Russification by stipulating that anyone applying for employment in public or private sector organisations needs to prove a command of the state language. Moreover, it is envisaged that, with regard to national education, the long-term goal is to have only titular-language secondary schools, originally envisaged by Estonia to be in place by the year 2000, although this timetable is now acknowledged to be unrealistic.[33]

In the efficient and effective running of the public sector, certain employees need to demonstrate higher levels of competence in the state language in order to carry out particular jobs, notably within the medical and teaching professions, the police force and the state bureaucracy. Dismissals have therefore followed within the state sector, especially within central administration, and particularly in organisations which at one time supported a large number of employees superfluous to need. Some Russian-speaking employees have been dismissed due to inadequate language skills, whereas others have felt their position so intolerable due to an insufficient knowledge of the state language that they have left voluntarily. Such 'nationalising policies' can also be used as an instrument to prevent members of the diaspora from entering certain niches within the labour market. This can be particularly important in relation to unscrupulous town councils and employers who can fulfil their xenophobic desires, while at the same time justifying economic rationalisation based on the need for cost efficiency in their plant or municipality. This seems to be particularly so in the small private sector where companies use the language requirement as a means of discharging superfluous workers from middle-tier management. State sector urban industrial workers have, however, been less affected, in part because language is not so crucial to carrying out the everyday activities of their employment, although, with the transition to a market economy and given the over-representation of Russians in the least competitive state industries compared to members of the core nations, diasporic unemployment is now far higher than amongst the titular nations, particularly in the Russian urban–industrial enclaves of north-east Estonia, Latgallia and Riga.

Such standardising practices and preconditions for both citizenship and continuing membership of the labour market have meant that those who administer the naturalisation process have the power to act as 'citizen gatekeepers', in which they have some leeway in interpreting and executing the law. Many have little vested interest in effecting or incentive to effect the transition to making citizenship commensurate with all members of the political homeland, especially as their continuing employment prospects depend on a restricted labour market. Additionally, within state bureaucracies that have to cope with the sheer scale of applications for citizenship and for residence permits, there is considerable individual scope to initiate the slowing down or rejection of particular applications. Bureaucrats routinely complain that they have neither the resources nor the civil servants to process applications. In particular Latvia's Department of Citizenship and Immigration has come in for specific criticism in its handling of applications; it has been accused of manipulating the registration of non-citizens, thus making it impossible for applicants to receive some of the benefits of denizenship, notably welfare benefits, the right to set up a business or to receive medical assistance.[34] According to one source, the underlying viewpoint amongst some Latvian officials towards the settler community is summed up in the statement: 'It is not so much the case that we need you to possess a knowledge of the language but that you need to know your place.'[35]

Protecting the culture of the historic homeland

Cultural self-preservation, according to communitarians, is 'a social good', and by pursuing policies commensurate with this claim, such as protecting the language and culture of the homeland, it is claimed that the social and cultural well-being of those who share this common culture is more likely to be secured. Estonian and Latvian core nation-statists therefore argue that, after decades of facing 'near cultural genocide', they have a right to protect their national cultures based on such a claim to national self-determination. Expected benefits will also follow for those who are included within the titular nation.

Besides a language policy that promotes the titular tongue, more controversial means of achieving this end stage have been considered and implemented, most notably the introduction of a quota system in Latvia designed to regulate the number of people who are to be naturalised each year. The exact composition of this group depends on age and place of birth, with those born outside Latvia not being able to apply for citizenship until 2003.[36] Thus in June 1994 parliament decreed that an amount equivalent to 0.1 per cent of Latvian citizens (or around 2,000 people) should be naturalised each year based on the claim that it was essential to regulate numbers in order to safeguard the national culture and its language. This was inextricably linked to the claim that Latvia was not out of line with other small and culturally more vulnerable European states, like Switzerland, which also operate a strict policy on citizenship quotas. Moreover, such arguments were also bound up with a homeland discourse that links cultural survival to the core nation's level of natural population increase,[37] in which it has been noted that, because Latvia had the lowest birth rate in Europe and one of the highest death rates, it would be difficult for the titular nation to sustain itself at around the mid-1990s level of 55 per cent of the country's population.[38] Indeed, the main political parties that compose the far right opposition, namely the Latvian National Independence Party and Fatherland and Freedom Party, want to go further, arguing that the quota system should be designed so as to secure the 75 per cent of ethnic Latvians in Latvia characteristic of the inter-war years, and that any quota system should go hand in hand with encouraging the repatriation of the settler communities.[39] Such views were even more succinctly put by other far right-wing movements, The 18 November Society and the Republican Party, which advocated the 'Three D's – deoccupation, de-Bolshevization and decolonisation'.[40] A similar logic is also supported in Estonia, as reflected in the establishment in February 1993 of the Decolonisation Foundation. Opposed to the Estonian government's plans to give legal alien status to the settler communities, this movement, which receives support from a number of centre-right and far right political parties, is fearful that the adoption of such a law will mean 'the voluntary Russification of the country'. It has called for 'a velvet re-emigration', thus ensuring that the Estonian titular nation would increase its share of the state population from the present 63.5 per cent to an 'optimal' 80 per cent.[41]

Although a tension exists in both Estonia and Latvia between the far right, which focuses on 'decolonisation', and the centre-right governments, which advocate 'integration of the immigrants', none the less the idea of decolonisation, repackaged as 'repatriation', has also received official governmental backing.[42] As part of this scheme, Soviet-era settlers are provided with some financial support to emigrate. In addition to facilitating a return to Russia, bilateral citizenship agreements have also been signed with the other two main Slavic countries, Ukraine and Belarus, from which a large number of Soviet-era settlers also originated.[43] Emphasis is placed on what one centre-right politician claims is the wish amongst many Russians 'to go back to Russia' and that the only obstacle to the state facilitating such 'return migration' is limited financial resources which, it is suggested, could come from the West.[44] Indeed, if it were not for the national economies of Estonia and Latvia being so dependent on a Russian industrial labour force, official government support for emigration might have been far more enthusiastic. Instead, the number of Russians who have emigrated since 1991 is relatively small, at under 10 per cent of the total Russian population of both polities, reaching a height in the immediate aftermath of statehood (see figure 5.1).

Officially it is also contended that, in engaging in such political practices, the core nation is not exploiting a right to cultural protection to the detriment of the liberties of others, based on the 'restored state' logic that such practices are the legitimate outcome of the electoral consent of the citizen-community. The counter-communitarian argument, that those who are not part of 'the historic homeland' but who reside within the polity should also be consulted over such decisions, is also rejected on

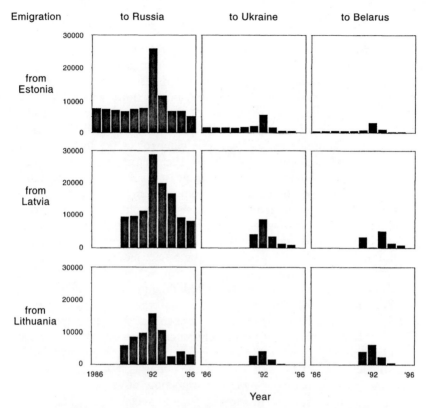

Figure 5.1. Emigration from the Baltic states to Russia, Ukraine and Belarus, 1986–1996
Source: Citizenship and Immigration Departments of the respective Baltic States (Tallinn, 1997; Riga, 1997; and Vilnius, 1996); Goskomstat (Moscow, 1996; and 1997)

familiar nationalist grounds that the political homeland is the only territory where the core nation has a historical homeland, in contrast to Russians who have their own homeland elsewhere.[45] Moreover, both national governments legitimately argue that multicultural rights for the citizen-polity are anyway guaranteed by their 1991 (Latvia) and 1993 (Estonia) laws on cultural autonomy, including the right of citizens to acquire a foreign-language education and representation in local government, both of which it is claimed are wholly consistent with laws on multiculturalism that existed during the inter-war period.

The return to Europe

The idea of 'rejoining Europe', which figures prominently within the
political rhetoric of Baltic modernisers and nationalists alike, is held up as
a key means to ensuring their countries' economic modernisation, geopolitical security and general social well-being. Both the inter-war and
post-Cold War political homeland are coded as being inextricably part of
Europe and its dominant cultural values, punctuated only by 'the recent
dark past of communism', which it is claimed artificially severed the
Baltic peoples from what is considered 'their natural European home'.
Thus within the economic sphere, although it is acknowledged that there
are short-term costs to economic decolonisation and to not becoming
part of a Russian-dominated CIS, these are judged to be more than com-
pensated for by the longer-term economic benefits of being part of
Europe. Indeed core nation-statists make great play of the fact that the
economic benefits of membership of the Soviet federation were limited
anyway, given that throughout most of the Soviet era all three Baltic
republics were net contributors to the federal budget and that if they had
not been incorporated into the USSR in 1940 they would now be enjoying living standards comparable to their Scandinavian neighbours.[46]
Thus for Baltic nationalists, far from independence being seen as an irra-
tional obstacle to their modernity, statehood was judged and presented as
the only feasible way forward. Indeed, the remarkable speed at which the
Baltic states have made the economic transition into a European trading
system and their success in moving from a socialist to a laissez-faire
economy while keeping both inflation and unemployment low are held up
as testimony to the already tangible benefits of again being part of
Europe.[47]

Rejoining Europe is, however, also bound up with a recognition that
security against the East also necessitates becoming embedded as rapidly
as possible within the West's military and political institutional architecture, notably the European Union, NATO and the Council of Europe.
The Balts have therefore been keen to demonstrate their European credentials and to be seen to be willing, when necessary, to abide by 'modern
European conditions' in terms of international legal codes of conduct.
Unwilling to jeopardise their future security in Europe, they have shown
when pushed a preparedness to moderate their citizenship laws whenever
their European credentials are seen to be in question. Indeed, there is an
element of truth in the claim that 'the major factor preventing the Baltic
states from slipping down the road towards authoritarian rule . . . is the
effort towards "Europeanisation"'.[48] Thus, when Latvia's parliament in

1993 came under criticism from both the Council (now Organisation) for Security and Co-operation in Europe (OSCE) and the Council of Europe over the proposed adoption of stringent naturalisation quotas that threatened to jeopardise Latvia's successful application to join the Council of Europe, the country's president, Gunter Ulmanis, intervened by returning the law for reconsideration to parliament. As a consequence, Latvia followed the other two Baltic states in being admitted into the Council of Europe in 1995. Similarly, the proposed adoption by the Estonian parliament on 21 June 1993 of a more restrictive aliens law than was eventually implemented also received widespread criticism from the OSCE, resulting in Estonia's president, Lennart Meri, also returning the proposed legislation to parliament for reconsideration. In both cases, the outcome was the enactment of more moderate legislation, illustrating that, when the nationalist right is confronted with the requirements of Europe, there are limits to their attempts at political outbidding.

Throughout, both Estonia's and Latvia's positions on citizenship have been justified on the grounds that not only are they abiding by European standards, but also that their stance on naturalisation and residency requirements is amongst 'the most liberal in Europe'. Thus the Estonian prime minister, Maart Laar, following criticism by a number of European human rights organisations, noted that 'there is no reason to say that the [Estonian local] elections are unfair . . . Are foreign citizens [sic] allowed to vote in the Western countries of Europe and America?'[49] In a similar vein, one of the architects of an early draft version of Latvia's citizenship law, Juris Bojars, noted that, just as Western countries do not automatically open their doors to third-world immigrants because they prefer these countries to their own,[50] so Latvia is justified in following a similar policy with regard to its non-citizen minorities.

For its part, Europe has been willing to accommodate the Baltic states in welcoming them into European organisations, which in turn has added further legitimacy to an exclusionary stance on citizenship. Thus, as a result of modifying its 1993 aliens law, the Swedish prime minister, Carl Bildt, acknowledged that 'Estonia has secured its ties with the values and institutions of Western democracies. It is highly regarded by all who consider Estonia as a secure and well-off European country.'[51] That the West is willing to accommodate such nationalising states is in part linked to geoeconomic and geopolitical interests, but it is also bound up with the Baltic states having found a convenient loophole in international law in which a Western community had never accepted their *de jure* incorporation into the USSR, and therefore logically has had to acknowledge their new status as 'restored citizen-polities'.

The ethnopolitics of 'the other'

How then have the Russian diaspora and especially those who are not citizens of the polity reacted to their newly found position within such
nationalising regimes? Most theories of collective action would predict
that, under circumstances of political exclusion, ethnic relations would
become so strained as to cause the marginalised to become frustrated or
discontented, leading to their alienation. That such a sense of alienation
exists amongst the diaspora has already been established by a number of
public opinion surveys conducted in the period from 1993 to 1997.[52]
Thus, in a 1993 survey, it was found that well over four-fifths of the diaspora in both Estonia and Latvia felt that the requirements for citizenship
were unjust. This contrasted with only one-fifth in Lithuania where
citizenship was granted automatically to all those resident there in 1990.
These findings are also comparable to the results of a survey undertaken
later that year, which revealed that, when asked if the government treats
Russians fairly, 61 per cent of Russians in Estonia disagreed or strongly
disagreed with the statement, compared with 54 per cent in Latvia and 17
per cent in Lithuania.[53] Just over half of the diaspora in Estonia and
Latvia did feel, however, that a residency requirement was fair, no doubt
reflecting that for most length of residency was no longer a major impedi-
ment to membership of the citizen-polity.[54] Amongst those members of
the diaspora most concerned with the citizenship legislation in Estonia
there is a high correlation between different legally codified groups (citizens, aliens, Russian citizens) and sense of alienation[55] (see also table
5.1). Such differentiated attitudes also correspond with similar findings
in Latvia.[56] Thus a sense of alienation is especially high amongst the
113,000 residents of Estonia and the 65,182 in Latvia[57] who have opted
to take up Russia's offer of extra-territorial citizenship for former citizens
of the Soviet Union, and whose rights are the least safeguarded by the
state. Especially notable amongst this group of Russian citizens is that,
when asked in a 1996 survey if they preferred life under the Soviet period
to the present day, a very high proportion, over two-thirds in Estonia,
opted for the Soviet period.[58]

So, although a sense of grievance is not as high amongst some sections of
the diaspora as might be expected, none the less it is still very evident. Yet it
would seem that alienation is not a sufficient condition to produce a mass
politics of collective action. Indeed, the majority of Russians in both states
responded negatively when asked if they would demonstrate in the streets
over who should be a citizen.[59] Although Russian-based social and cultural organisations do exist, their membership, duration and effectiveness
have also been limited and their organisational reach highly localised.

Table 5.1 *Attitudes of non-Estonians towards citizenship and related questions, 1996 (per cent of respondents)*

	Citizenship of Estonia	Those without citizenship	Russian citizenship
Born in Estonia	63	43	15
Those under forty years of age	64	65	27
Those with higher education	34	18	16
Speak Estonian fluently or well	37	8	1
Consider Russia 'a safe neighbour'	34	42	53
Support dual citizenship	54	71	83
Prefer life in Soviet Estonia to now	42	48	70
Believe that non-possession of Estonian citizenship makes life difficult	—	73	53
Favour Estonia joining the EU	60	53	43

Source: Tartu Ulikooli Turu-uurimisruhm (Tartu, 1997).

Competitive assimilation

According to one school of thought, the main reason for the remarkable stability is that, although there is a sense of alienation amongst particular elements of the diaspora, most have none the less acknowledged the reality of their situation and have opted to integrate themselves into the ideal nation-state as espoused by the core nations' political entrepreneurs. This has given rise to what Laitin calls 'competitive assimilation'.[60] Based upon the politics of rational choice and focusing on the importance of language as a determinant of Russian-speakers entering the citizen-polity, it is hypothesised that the migrant nationality will wish to ensure that their offspring receive rapid training in the titular nation language in order to secure a place in the upwardly mobile employment market. Accordingly, it also follows that it would then be rational for any parent to do this, that all parents will think that other parents will be likely to do it and that therefore they should see to it that their children gain competence in the language of their new society (i.e. move towards linguistic assimilation) before the middle-class job market is saturated.[61] The only likely brake to this trend towards competitive assimilation is when cultural entrepreneurs within the settler community can successfully raise the status of people who refuse to give up their cultures, a trend which has not been sufficient to secure a reversal of fortune in any of the Baltic states. So according to this thesis, within the all-important social arena of language, rational individuals will accept 'the nationalising state' and its rules, provided that they can see the longer-term economic and social benefits of going through such hurdles to become members of the citizen-polity.

The growth in attendance amongst Russian-speakers at Estonian and Latvian language schools, for instance, indicates that many Russians are keen to exploit the avenues that exist to becoming citizens.[62] This is particularly so for the younger generation who indicate a greater willingness both to learn the state language and to become members of the citizen-polity.[63] In addition, because the state is keeping open the prospects of the diaspora as individuals becoming members of the citizen-polity, thus offering the possibility of improving personal social and economic status, the short-term costs of being a non-citizen are weighed against the longer-term benefits of membership of the citizen-polity. This may also explain why many individuals chose to invest their time and resources in qualifying for citizenship rather than engaging in collective action.

Yet, while it is the case that large numbers of the diaspora have recognised the success of the nationalising state programmes and have adapted to or are in the process of developing a facility to speak the state language, this thesis assumes that the initially excluded will prove more malleable than they have so far been in practice. For one thing, the numbers engaged in language learning may not be as high as this thesis would suggest.[64] Furthermore, the problem of language learning is compounded by a shortage of teaching resources, especially in the Russian-speaking enclaves of north-east Estonia and Latgallia. For another, while most non-citizens accept that a knowledge of the titular nation language is fully justifiable in particular spheres of public sector employment, notably within the professions, language as a universal criterion of citizenship is considered very differently. Three-quarters of the diaspora surveyed in both Estonia and Latvia 'completely disagreed' with the contention that knowledge of the titular nation language should be a condition of citizenship, a position not shared by respondents in Lithuania, where only one-third held this view.[65] Moreover, in essentialising language as the criterion for breaking down ethnic markers, this thesis is too ready to assume, contrary to the evidence from other multiethnic polities (e.g. Belgium, Spain, Canada), that a growth in bilingualism amongst minorities necessarily goes hand in hand with the depoliticisation of ethnic identities.

The regulatory role of the state

What, however, is also likely to be important in explaining the low level of collective action is the regulatory role that the state has played in setting out a diasporic politics of the permissible. As Sidney Tarrow notes, 'collective action increases when people gain the resources to escape their habitual passivity and find the opportunities to use them'.[66] Thus the political opportunities created by the state and its political system can provide both incentives and disincentives for people to undertake collective action. In particular, one important opportunity dimension – the degree of formal access to the political-administrative and electoral system – is, according to Tarrow, likely to act as a brake, as individual incentives to engage in collective action are linked to judgements about the prospect of success. In the case of Estonia and Latvia, how the state has structured the citizen-polity and its political system is therefore of crucial importance, for it enables the state to define and regulate channels of access which are as likely to demobilise the diaspora into collective action as to mobilise them into it.

Thus, the state has played an important part in regulating collective action by limiting and manipulating access to institutional politics. By codifying membership of the citizen-polity on non-ethnic criteria – that is, based on the idea of the restorationist state rather than on ethnicity – both states are in effect practising what can be crudely referred to as a strategy of 'divide and rule', a policy which has also operated in tandem with a practice of co-optation, whereby those non-citizens who are deemed to have provided 'special services' to the state have been rewarded with citizenship.[67] Consequently, the state has helped to create 'insiders' and 'outsiders' amongst the diaspora and, in the process, weakened any social base for mass-based collective action. Such a policy has therefore facilitated political factionalism within the diaspora, between so-called integrationists, who have chosen institutional politics as the arena to champion the idea of a more multicultural homeland, and an increasingly smaller and largely ineffective diasporic group, who by and large operate outside the system of political parties and institutional politics and who look towards their ethnic patron, Russia, for their political supports.[68] Thus, recent attempts by the Russian diaspora in both states to co-ordinate diasporic movements on both the national and transnational scales have been limited not only by their failure to define a common political agenda but also by a regulatory state that does not recognise the right of non-citizens to form social movements that have political objectives. This is notably the case in Latvia with the League of Apatrides, set up in January 1994 and intended by its membership to perform the same co-ordinating role as its counterpart in Estonia, the Democratic Representative Assembly. While its leadership made clear the movement's commitment to the Latvian state and declared that its aim was to facilitate a dialogue between non-citizens and the state, its application in April 1994 for registration as a social organisation was rejected on the grounds that only citizens should participate in political movements.[69]

Thus political opportunities to effect change are limited to particular areas of institutional politics. Consequently, such political opportunities have the potential to provide a source of institutional capacity because they provide a set of levers and political access that make group mobilisation more likely. In the first place, electoral opportunities which potentially can facilitate collective action exist at the scale of local municipal government. While only citizens can stand for election at the municipal level, non-citizens have the right to vote in elections in Estonia (although not in Latvia). In those municipalities where Russian-speakers constitute a clear demographic majority, as in north-east Estonia, local government therefore provides an opportunity to put diasporic issues on to the local urban agenda. Since 1993, however, following the first post-independence local elections in both polities, local diasporic communities have had to rely on citizens to represent their interests. Such incumbents have tended to play the role of urban gatekeepers by redefining and moderating what appears on the local political agenda. Although primarily concerned with local community interests that transcend citizen/non-citizen divides, most notably with issues that focus on creating the conditions for local economic growth and better employment opportunities within the municipality, elected representatives have also come to play an important part in articulating 'a rights-based urban politics', a practice which is also evident in a number of other cities where there is a large Russian population, including Tallinn and Riga. Such a rights-based politics, however, rather than directly challenging the central state and the political status quo, focuses primarily on calling for more resources in order to ease the plight of non-citizens and to facilitate their integration into the larger political community, such as making available more facilities for the learning of the state language and of providing housing for those who have been uprooted as a consequence of state policy on property restitution.

Secondly, political opportunities also exist for the formation of diasporic political parties amongst the citizenry. While both polities have witnessed the transition from the initial emergence of a large number of small and highly localised and ineffective Russian social movements to the formation of national political parties, it is only in Estonia that such political parties have succeeded in gaining parliamentary representation. Thus at the 1995 national elections in Estonia, three Russian political parties making up the political faction Our Home Is Estonia (Mei Kodu On Eestimaa) gained 6 of the 101 parliamentary seats (5.9 per cent of the popular vote).[70] In Latvia, however, no political party representing exclusively Russian interests was elected in the country's 1995 national elections, although the political faction Harmony for Latvia, whose main political platform is based on reconciling differences between Latvians and the diaspora, secured 6 out of the 100 seats in parliament (or 5.6 per cent of the vote). Although voting at national elections remains more ethnically partisan in Estonia than in Latvia, in part due to a historically less-rooted Russian community, Estonia's Russian political parties remain heavily factionalised around the personalities of their leaders. Consequently, their effectiveness to speak with one voice in parliament and to champion their declared commitment to a sovereign but multiculturalist Estonia in which Russians would participate more fully in government is limited.[71]

Finally, each regime has set up a non-legislative extra-parliamentary body to discuss minority issues, the so-called Estonian Round Table, which was established in 1993, and its counterpart in Latvia, the Minorities Consultative Council, set up three years later. Established to provide an unofficial dialogue between members of the titular nation and the minorities, their multiethnic membership also includes non-citizens, although Russian citizens are excluded from representation.[72] As the more established of the two bodies, the Estonian Round Table has displayed a remarkable consensus between its ethnic representatives over a wide range of issues that are of everyday concern to its minorities.[73] However, it remains only an advisory body with limited influence and effectiveness and which has little or no legitimacy amongst non-Russians who remain unrepresented.[74]

Political resources and the politics of collective action

It is not just the structures of political opportunity that are important in determining the form and limited scale of collective action but also, as resource mobilisation theorists would note,[75] the extent to which political resources are available for the marginalised to draw upon. Forming a post-colonial sense of identity, forging a new politics of communalism as a political resource for collective action, is made difficult by a variety of cross-cutting boundary markers that heterogenise any sense of communality and that therefore weaken the prospects for diasporic mobilisation. These discourses include social divisions based on codification by legal status (citizens, non-citizens and Russian citizens), the extent of geographical rootedness (recent settlers and historic communities), language (monolingual and bilingual speakers) and religion/secular faith (there has been a revival of Russian Orthodoxy amongst the diaspora, but the consequences of five decades of an official secular

faith have weakened the institutional mobilising potential of the Church).
Moreover, occupational and geographical displacement, especially within
those urban communities most affected by the transition from public to
private sector employment, has also had a fragmenting effect. While
growing unemployment or downturns in the performance of the national
economies have the potential to be seized upon and 'ethnicised' as a political resource within such urban communities, they are unlikely to result in
wholesale mobilisation. For those who have moved into the private sector,
considerable benefits from market reform have followed, while others
have been swept along by the prospects of a likely improvement in their
material well-being. However, it is precisely in those communities of
north-east Estonia and Latgallia in which the benefits of marketisation
have been least evident and in which many of its inhabitants face the
prospects of long-term unemployment that the idea of a 'Soviet homeland' and its public sector supports remains attractive, albeit not
sufficient in itself to facilitate an engagement in collective action.

Not only are such communal boundary markers not that clear-cut or
encompassing, but the diaspora also lack a substantive political or cultural elite who are willing and able to champion ethnic grievances. As
experiences elsewhere show, for ethnic and nationalist movements to
succeed, such a codifying and mobilising role usually involves a cultural
intelligentsia who also have a particular stake in protecting and ensuring
the reproduction of cultural difference. As a social stratum, however, the
diaspora's cultural intelligentsia is demographically small and largely
ineffective, even more so since 1991, given that those amongst the diaspora who have returned to Russia are disproportionately drawn from this
social stratum.[76]

Finally, there is the political resource of the diaspora's ethnic patron,
Russia, in influencing the nature and scale of collective action. Even for
that part of the diaspora whose associational ties with Russia are confined
primarily to a cultural identity, the extent to which there exists a politics
of support from 'back home' is still likely to be of interest. If only as insur-
ance against a worsening situation, the diaspora are therefore likely to
take more than a passing interest in the sorts of political supports that
Russia may or may not provide. Thus the type and scale of institutional
and financial support that Russia is willing and able to provide have no
doubt had some reassuring consequences for the diaspora. Most notably,
Russia's policy of extra-territorial citizenship provides the diaspora with a
sense that they have not been abandoned and that institutionally they are
still bound to those amongst their number who regard Russia as their
homeland.[77] In addition, Russia has also provided financial support for its
diasporic citizens through the Russian Citizens Fund, set up by a 1996
presidential decree. The sums involved, however, are limited, while the

aims of a Fund earmarked for 'humanitarian programmes' remain ambiguous.[78]

Indeed, the leverage and capacity of Russia to influence political events in both Estonia and Latvia are more limited than is often generally supposed.[79] While Russia possesses considerable geopolitical leverage to secure its interests in what it codifies as 'the near abroad', the completion of the negotiated withdrawal of Russian troops from the Baltic states in August 1994 has weakened its capacity for leverage over these states. In both Estonia and Latvia there is a sense amongst elements of the diaspora that, despite Moscow's relentless rhetoric of accusing both governments of practising 'social apartheid' and 'ethnic cleansing',[80] Russia has in effect turned its back on them, even though, it is argued, more pressure could have been exerted in linking troop withdrawals to its declared aim of standing up for 'human rights abuses'. Although Russia has since the mid-1990s stepped up its criticism of Estonia's policy towards the diaspora and has continued to threaten the republic with a variety of economic sanctions, including trade embargoes, its room for economic leverage has been much weakened by the success of both countries in reorienting their economies away from the East.

Similarly, the role played by diasporic nationalist organisations in Russia and their support-based linkages within the Baltic states have not evolved fully. For one thing, given that the exit of 'returnees' from the Baltic states has been limited and those who have left have not got involved in diasporic politics, there has been little pressure from such returnees within Russia to do something about the plight of their co-nationals. However, while some contact exists between nationalist far right movements in Russia and the diaspora in Estonia and Latvia (notably through the Moscow-based Congress of Russian Communities and Vladimir Zhirinovsky's Liberal Democratic Party), the extent and scale of such linkages appear to be poorly developed.[81] What are more important, however, are the linkages between the Communist Party of the Russian Federation and Russian citizens in the Baltic states. In the Russian presidential elections of 1996, in both Estonia and Latvia, Russian citizens voted overwhelmingly for the Communist Party candidate, Gennady Zyuganov, rather than the centre-right (Boris Yeltsin) or the extreme nationalist right (Alexander Lebed or Vladimir Zhirinovsky). However, with the Communist Party banned in both polities, the Russian Communist Party has neither the organisational reach nor, it would seem, the financial resources to lend support to its diaspora. Furthermore, the ambiguity of its policies concerning the nature of the resurrection of the Soviet homeland also provides little sense of direction for those who still identify with the values and security of such a vanished homeplace.[82]

Conclusions

Conflicting representations of homeland therefore occupy an important part in the political identities of the peoples of Estonia and Latvia. Of the three discourses that we have explored, the most successful has been a core nation discourse that envisages a polity in which nation and state should ideally be socially and spatially congruent. We have also noted that, in relation to defining the boundaries of citizenship, such a nation-state discourse is not simply non-instrumentalist: both regimes have adopted exclusionary policies that reflect considerable benefits for those who are members of the core nation. Despite the exclusion of the majority from membership of the citizen-polity, the diaspora have displayed a remarkable tenacity to comply with the new political order. It would therefore seem that, for most of the diaspora, notwithstanding benefits to the individual from assimilating into such nationalising regimes, identities are still in a state of flux and are not as yet being produced anew through transformation, as is the case amongst well-established diaspora in many Western countries.[83] For others, especially Russian citizens, a neo-Soviet homeland remains virtually the only category thought capable of providing a sense of who they are, but it is limited to a nostalgia for how things were rather than providing a programme for mobilisation and political resistance. However, it may well be that, as a result of the actions of the Estonian and Latvian governments in creating the conditions whereby large numbers of the diaspora have not secured citizenship of the states in which they reside and who have therefore opted for the security of Russian citizenship, a more empire-minded patron has at its disposal a pretext, if it wishes to use it, for coming to the aid of its citizens abroad.

6 Redefining ethnic and linguistic boundaries in Ukraine: indigenes, settlers and Russophone Ukrainians

This chapter focuses on the politics of symbolic and cultural representation between (and within) three key groups of roughly equal size in Ukraine: Ukrainophone Ukrainians, Russophone Ukrainians and ethnic Russians. The threefold division is a simplification, but a useful one. It helps to explain why the titular nationality in Ukraine is divided within itself and has been unable to impose a nationalising agenda in the manner of Estonia and Latvia, or even some of the Central Asian states. It also helps to shift analysis away from ethnicity as the sole factor of importance in Ukrainian society and to focus attention on Russophone Ukrainians as a vital swing group. On the other hand, this chapter also seeks to deconstruct such categories by analysing the three groups as social constructs. It is not argued that they have immutable essences and boundaries.

According to Soviet census methodology (there has been no national census in Ukraine since independence in 1991; the first is scheduled for 1999), 64 per cent of the population of Ukraine in 1989 were classed as 'native tongue' Ukrainians, 9 per cent as ethnic Ukrainians who identified Russian as their 'native tongue' and 22 per cent were 'Russian' in terms of both ethnicity and language. The use of the term 'native tongue' in Soviet censuses (*ridna mova* in Ukrainian, *rodnoi iazyk* in Russian), however, was highly ambiguous. It tended to be interpreted in ancestral terms and therefore overlapped with ethnicity to an exaggerated extent. Moreover, ethnicity was further reified by the refusal to allow respondents to classify themselves by using multiple or (surprisingly) Soviet identities, by the practice of encoding father's ethnicity in ambiguous cases, and, by fixing ethnicity in passports, hindering the possibility of ethnic re-identification.

In Ukraine, however, ethnic and linguistic boundaries are exceptionally fluid. The raw figures of the 1989 census obscured the extent of Russian-language penetration of everyday life, and were unable to express the complicated and contested nature of the Ukrainian–Russian cultural 'border'. More recent studies have attempted to address realities of day-to-day language use in Ukraine by asking Ukrainian citizens about their language of *preference* in sociological surveys conducted by bilingual interviewers. According to these, approximately 40 per cent of the population are Ukrainophone Ukrainians, 33–4 per cent Russophone Ukrainians and 20–1 per cent ethnic Russians.[1] However, although the latter approach is clearly more in line with observed reality in Ukraine, it can be readily accepted that as sociological categories the three 'groups' are currently highly amorphous entities for which clear-cut bounded identities and even agreed definitions do not yet exist. What, for example, is one to make of individuals who can move between Ukrainian and Russian at ease, those who speak the Ukrainian/Russian mixture known as *surzhyk* or those who are perfectly happy with a situational or mixed identity, all of whom are common identity types in Ukraine?[2]

It is the contested nature of identities in modern Ukraine which are their most interesting characteristic. We therefore take a different approach by concentrating on *discourse* as a constitutive feature of emerging group identities. Our argument is that it is precisely the processes through which each 'group' represents the other that are likely to define group boundaries and shape inter-group relations in the future. Identity formation and the creation and maintenance of group boundaries are very much ongoing processes. Both are inherently social phenomena, in which 'identity formation and self/other relations' are best explained 'in terms of *different* discourse practices'.[3] Each group, or more exactly the ethnic entrepreneurs who claim to speak for the group, operates within a given field of discourse in which a variety of different elements are combined, but where there is also a characteristic core of ethnopolitical concepts which attempt to define the supposed essence of both the 'self' and the 'other'. Moreover, the structure of intra-group discourse helps to determine the status claims made by each group for itself and, correspondingly, the status it would apply to others. Negative stereotyping serves to reinforce differences and promote policies of exclusion, while a more open-ended discourse helps to prevent group polarisation.

However, once again, although each 'group' tends to reify the other, it should be stressed that 'groups' are socially constructed entities. The boundaries constructed by ethnic entrepreneurs are not immutable in reality. Indeed, in the Ukrainian case they are particularly fluid, and political entrepreneurs opposed to ethnic categorisations have sought to keep them so. Each side's attempts to refute the characterisations of the other are overlain by voices that deny the significance of ethnic or linguistic boundaries at all. Nevertheless, it is also characteristic of ethnopolitical discourse to ignore such fluidity and assert that rival groups are always and everywhere 'other' and even alien.

This chapter seeks to examine the different discourse practices constructed by Ukrainophone Ukrainian, Russophone Ukrainian and Russian ethnic entrepreneurs, and also by those who deny the importance of ethnolinguistic identities in Ukraine. Ukrainophone Ukrainians have a characteristic ethnopolitical discourse that focuses on their unique rights as an 'indigenous' people or 'core nation', and correspondingly depicts ethnic Russians as outsiders, even as 'immigrants' or 'settlers', thereby potentially delegitimating their long-term moral claim to the rights which the Ukrainian state has granted them since 1991. Ukrainophones characteristically also have a dismissive attitude to Russophone Ukrainian culture, wishing away its long history as the result of forcible 'Russification'.

Ethnic Russians on the other hand use totally different concepts in their characteristic cultural and political discourse. To a much greater extent than Russians in the Baltic states or Central Asia (Kazakstan excepted), it can be claimed that Russians are also an indigenous people in Ukraine, especially in designated territories in the east and south. They should therefore enjoy the same rights as Ukrainians, including the right to the public use of the Russian language and to be left undisturbed in traditional cultural patterns. In fact some Russians go further and attempt to paint nationalist Ukrainophones as the 'aliens', the product of Habsburg, Polish or German 'intrigue' and an artificial implant into the Ukrainian body politic preventing Ukrainians and Russians from living in their natural state of fraternal harmony.

The third group, Russophone Ukrainians, are the crucial swing group. Although they share some of the same symbolic concepts as their Ukrainophone siblings, they deny the Ukrainophone nationalist assertion that cultural and linguistic crossover into the Russian space is the result of forcible 'Russification' alone, and claim that their own tradition has always existed in parallel with the nationalist vision of the Ukrainian 'self'. Again, Russophone Ukrainians assert that theirs is also a genuine indigenous tradition with deep historical roots.

Finally, attempts by ethnic entrepreneurs to reify the boundaries of the three groups are offset by a broad set of discourse practices that depict cultural and linguistic crossover as historical and natural (as with Russophone Ukrainians) and seek to avoid unnecessary group polarisation.

Our key argument is therefore that questions of national identity in Ukraine cannot be understood via a crude contrast between 'Ukrainians' as the eponymous state-bearing nation and 'Russians' as a diaspora group of the Russian Federation, but only through an examination of the complex interrelationships between the three 'groups' outlined above.

Although Ukraine is often presented as a model civic state, this study will demonstrate how underlying tensions between the three groups are likely to shape the future Ukrainian polity and the possibilities for ethnolinguistic accord.

Ethnic Ukrainians: the discourse of indigenous rights

The key concepts structuring Ukrainophone identity and Ukrainophone attitudes towards the other two groups are indigenousness, colonialism and Russification.[4] Together they form a classic nationalist argument for the privileged rights of the titular people. In addition, when speaking on behalf of all Ukrainians, Ukrainophones assume that their 'European' past distinguishes them from Russians. A final factor to be considered is the tension between historical-political and linguistic conceptions of the Ukrainian 'national idea', that is, of national identity.

The Ukrainians as an indigenous people

Ukraine is not an 'ethnic democracy'. It has not attempted to confine political rights to the titular nation. In sharp contrast to Estonia and Latvia, the citizenship issue was largely defused in the immediate aftermath of independence. The Law on Citizenship passed by the Ukrainian parliament in October 1991 granted citizenship to all those then resident in Ukraine, and this open-ended commitment has since been reinforced by Ukraine's accession to a series of international treaties and organisations, such as the Council of Europe in 1995 (paradoxically many members of the Ukrainian left welcomed this particular step as a means of increasing third-party leverage over 'minority rights' issues in Ukraine).[5]

In practice, however, political debate has continued around questions of group identity and group rights. In the early phase of 'national revival', most 'national-democratic' groups consciously avoided explicitly ethnic appeals and promoted the concept of a 'Ukrainian political nation', a 'single socium' of all Ukraine's various ethnic and linguistic groups.[6] However, on closer examination this was never a purely civic concept. Ukrainian national-democrats have always said at the same time that the 'core of this union is the Ukrainian people'.[7] Significantly, when it came to adopting a new Ukrainian constitution in the early 1990s, they attempted to insist that it define sovereign power as residing with the 'Ukrainian people [*ukraïns′kyi narod*]', with the clear understanding that this means – as, in essence, in Latvia and Estonia – the titular nationality alone.[8] The same elision is evident in such alternative formulae as 'we, the

Ukrainian people – the union [*sukupnist'*] of citizens of Ukraine of all nationalities, the basis of which is formed by the Ukrainian nation'.[9]

Many national-democrats have demanded more straightforwardly that 'the constitution should fix that the Ukrainian state is established on the basis of the sovereign self-determination of the Ukrainian nation', that Ukrainians should be the 'leading element' in the state, and that 'the national character of Ukrainian statehood', 'a state of the indigenous Ukrainian people', should be recognised.[10]

Their position therefore crosses over to opinions held on the political fringes, where radical Ukrainophones have had no qualms in referring specifically and frequently to the need to create a 'national state', and have attacked the idea of building a community based on 'cosmopolitanism or false internationalism'.[11] They have argued that 'by means of [such] perfidious formula[e] the Ukrainian people, an indigenous [*korinnyi*] people on their ancestral territory, are deprived of the right to create their own state . . . a right that is given over to national minorities . . . to create a cosmopolitan state [with the assistance of] outside forces'.[12] Radical nationalists have talked instead of a state tailored 'to the customs and tastes' of Ukrainians,[13] and have revived the slogans popular in western Ukraine in the 1920s and 1930s of a 'national dictatorship [*natsiokratiia*]',[14] and 'Ukraine for the Ukrainians'.[15] (The idea of a *natsiokratiia* is a state in the service of the nation, 'understood as an ethnos, building its own statehood, with power over itself and over national minorities'.)[16]

Moreover, since 1990 the dynamics of political competition within the Ukrainophone camp have encouraged outbidding to the nationalist right.[17] All elections since 1990 have shown that Ukrainophone nationalists could make only limited inroads into the Russophone electorate (that is, neither to ethnic Russians *nor* to Russophone Ukrainians). In core support areas of western and central Ukraine, national-democrats have therefore had to compete with the radical right rather than risk appealing across linguistic boundaries, and the discourse of a 'Ukrainian political nation' has gradually been superseded by the rhetoric of ethnic revival.[18]

However, it should not be assumed that all Ukrainophones are nationalists. Many have continued in the attempt to define ethnicity out of the political equation by promoting the idea of the 'people of Ukraine' (*narod Ukraïny*), as in Lithuania, where sovereignty is vested in a political abstract, the 'nation of Lithuania' rather than the 'Lithuanian nation',[19] or have preferred to use the explicitly multiethnic concept 'the peoples of Ukraine'.[20] Both formulations, however, are anathema to Ukrainophone nationalists: the former because it threatens to dissolve the Ukrainian nation into a new and 'artificial' imagined community, the latter because it contradicts the fundamental nationalist belief that only the Ukrainians (and Crimean Tatars and Karaïm) are real indigenous peoples *of* Ukraine – other minorities simply live *in* Ukraine. They have 'homelands' elsewhere.

The 1996 constitution compromised by adopting the formula, 'we, the Ukrainian people – citizens of Ukraine of all nationalities', a rather awkward combination of a singular (though collective) noun with a liberal policy commitment.[21] It also defined the 'right to self-determination' as somehow belonging jointly to 'the existing Ukrainian nation, all the Ukrainian people'.[22] In contrast, a draft Law on Indigenous Peoples prepared in 1996 promised to grant certain rights to groups such as the Crimean Tatars, whilst at the same time promoting 'the renewal and free development of the *dominant nation*'.[23]

Ukrainophone nationalists have not, therefore, been able to impose a narrow nationalising agenda on Ukrainian politics. In part this is because they have to share power with ethnic Russians and/or Russophones. In fact, the latter are arguably dominant in government. Without the support of at least Russophone Ukrainians, Ukrainophones do not have a sufficient critical mass to enforce a wholesale Ukrainianisation policy. Ukraine is therefore not a paradigmatic 'nationalising state' in its political practice, although this does not mean that many nationalist Ukrainophones would not like it to be so.[24]

Colonialism

Ukrainophone attitudes towards the rights of ethnic Russians in Ukraine are also coloured by the assumption, hotly disputed by most Russians, that the Treaty of Pereiaslav in 1654 began a process of Russian 'colonisation' of Ukraine (see also chapter 2).[25] The 'natural' order of affairs in Ukraine has therefore supposedly been turned upside down by the experience of empire, and Russians continue to enjoy the rights that ought to be reserved for the titular nation. As with Estonian or Latvian nationalism, the Russian presence on the national 'homeland' is delegitimised by characterising it as the result of imperial policy rather than voluntary migration. Formal legal equality for Ukrainians and Russians is therefore desirable on an abstract level, but it should not be allowed to perpetuate an unnatural situation brought about by force.

Moreover, many Ukrainophones would argue that quasi-colonial conditions still pertain in Ukraine, or at least that Ukraine still has to live with the consequences of the colonial experience that has turned Ukrainians into a minority in their own country, particularly in the east and south. According to one of the leaders of the Congress of Ukrainian Nationalists, for example, 'today in the large towns of the east and south of Ukraine we still see the unnatural, artificial . . . priority and privileges created by Russian tsarism and Bolshevik Moscow for the Russian ethnic minority, most of whom [arrived as] parasites in the state-bureaucratic structure and security apparatus created by the empire, [or occupied] colonial functions in the sphere of production and spiritual culture and participated in well-known policies of Russification [*rosiishchennia* – see below, pp. 127–8] and brutal repression of the Ukrainian word, the Ukrainian individual'.[26]

More moderate Ukrainophones are prepared to accept that Russians, having lived in Ukraine for centuries, are in some sense also 'rooted', but they would still deny that the Russians are truly indigenous: Russians do not live in Ukraine *as a nation* in the same manner as they do in their own homeland.[27] In a standard formula, Ukrainophone nationalists tend to confine the promise of 'national-cultural autonomy to those national minorities who do not have their own state beyond the borders of Ukraine' (i.e. excluding Russians).[28]

Discourses of Europe

To Ukrainophone nationalists, the presence of Russians in Ukraine also means the presence of 'Asia' in 'Europe'. As with many other east European peoples (see also chapter 5), Ukrainians conceive of themselves as an *Antemurale*, an outpost of European civilisation against both Islam and 'Asia'.[29] In this respect, it is Russia which is 'Asia' and therefore radically 'other',[30] while 'Europe', albeit mediated largely through Poland, was supposedly historically always a part of Ukrainian life until the imposition of Russian influence in 1654, 1793–5 or 1945.[31]

The consequences for perceptions of national identity are clear. The myth of Europe versus Asia places a very clear boundary marker between Ukrainians and Russians, widening an otherwise relatively narrow cultural gap. It also explains why the most common Ukrainian name for 'Russian' uses a place-name – *Moskaly* (a pejorative version of 'Muscovite'). The other side of the coin, however, is that a geographical definition of 'otherness' would also allow local Russians in Ukraine to be 'European', although for many nationalist Ukrainophones 'Asia' is a cultural phenomenon that affects all Russians alike.[32]

Russophone Ukrainians, on the other hand, should obviously also be 'European'. Hence Ukrainophone nationalists' incomprehension and anger when they prefer to assert the cultural solidarity of the eastern

Slavs, often against a common European or Atlantic 'other'. Ethnic Russians, presented with the equation of 'Europe' and 'Ukraine', may well reject both, or promote the idea of a 'Eurasian', pan-Slavic Ukraine, cleansed of its Galician 'Europeans'.

The 'national idea'

The Ukrainophone assumption that Russophone Ukrainians must lie on the same side of the cultural divide is a result of their essentially linguistic conception of the 'national idea'. Roman Szporluk has argued that the founding fathers of the Ukrainian national revival in the late eighteenth and early nineteenth centuries originally framed Russian–Ukrainian difference in terms of rival myths of descent and of national 'character', and that the revival of this concept by Ukrainian dissidents in the 1960s helped establish a modern Ukrainian civic nationalism.[33] National identity was therefore essentially framed by a historical-political conception. However, during the nineteenth century, the Herderian equation of language and ethnicity also entered nationalist discourse.[34] Ukrainians did not, after all, then enjoy statehood. Nor were the territories they inhabited clearly bounded by administrative divisions, and they were often far removed from the key historical Ukrainian homelands of the Kievan and Cossack periods. It was therefore to an extent predictable that the founders of Ukrainian political geography used language as the primary determinant of ethnicity,[35] and by equating the two felt able to assert the existential unity of all Ukrainians. Moreover, in the multilingual states of eastern Europe, retention of one's 'native' language has always been a key status issue, and assimilation implies a loss of 'authenticity'.

Most contemporary Ukrainophone nationalists simply assume that ethnicity and language naturally coincide. Even those who are committed to the idea of a 'civic nation' would build it around their own ethnolinguistic 'core', and language revival is always to the forefront of their programmes.[36] In part, following Herder, this is conceptual: 'language', they argue, 'is the main sign of the ethnos . . . the genetic code of the nation',[37] but it is also due to the historical argument that Ukrainians who speak Russian do so only as a result of forcible Russification (see below, pp. 127–8).

Ukrainophone activists tend to assume that mobilisation strategies which rely on the myths and symbols of the Ukrainian-language group can in fact appeal to *all* ethnic Ukrainians. However, in practice their conceptual framework makes unwarranted assumptions about Russophone Ukrainian identity, which is much more of a mélange of ethnic, linguistic, cultural and historical influences.[38]

Russification

Ukrainophone Ukrainians tend to deny that Russophone Ukrainians, unlike ethnic Russians, are in any real sense 'other', and that any departure from this situation must be the result of artificial 'Russification', itself a product of Ukraine's past colonial status. Ukrainophones argue that the sheer depth of penetration of the Russian language in Ukraine, and the unnatural division 'between Russian Ukraine and Ukrainian Ukraine',[39] can be explained only as a consequence of forcible administrative pressure, rather than in terms of natural cultural affinity or free choice. The only point of dispute is whether the normal Ukrainian term for 'Russification', *rusyfikatsiia*, is capable of giving full expression to this phenomenon. Radicals have argued that it should be replaced by *rosiishchennia* or *Moskovshchennia*, as *rusyfikatsiia* is supposedly a Germanism derived from the malapropism Rus´, actually the name of the medieval (for nationalists proto-Ukrainian) Kievan state, whereas the real historical agent of enforced acculturation has been the modern Russian state (*Rosiia* or *Rossiia*), or, more succinctly, Moscow. Moreover, the broader terms help to emphasise aspects of acculturation beyond the mere loss of language.[40] On the other hand, the term 'Sovietisation', which would arguably provide a more accurate insight into the nature of Russophone Ukrainian identity, is rarely used.

The proliferation of terms indicates a certain confusion as to the exact identity of Ukraine's 'other'. Nevertheless, in all variants it is assumed that a genuine Ukrainian identity existed in the past before it was 'Russified'. It can therefore be restored. Because it is assumed that Russophone Ukrainians are simply 'denationalised [*vynarodovlenni*] Ukrainians' or 'cultural hermaphrodites',[41] the hapless victims of 'Russification', Russian-speaking culture is not regarded by Ukrainophone nationalists as having a legitimate historical foundation in Ukraine (indeed, it is denied that it is a *culture* as such), which cannot but cast doubt on the solidity of legal guarantees on language rights, however generous. The formal position of legal tolerance has to be set against the nationalist desire to 'unite a disjoined [*rozporoshenyi*] people into a single national organism',[42] that is, the hope that in the long term the historical tendency of Ukrainians to assimilate to Russian language and culture will be reversed.

Despite such statements as 'for us nothing would be sweeter than the national enlightenment of the Russian population of Ukraine',[43] 'national revival' is in fact targeted in the first instance at Russophone Ukrainians and is predicated on the assumption that they will automatically respond to any Ukrainianisation campaign,[44] as indicated by the demand that 'the percentage of Russian-language schools in Ukraine should be reduced [from just under 50 per cent] to the percentage of Russians in the population – 20 per cent [sic]'.[45] This, however, assumes a community of identity and interest that is not necessarily present. As Ukrainophone nationalists reject the historical foundations of the (putative) Russophone Ukrainian identity out of hand (see below, p. 133), they fail to grasp the true significance of potential boundary markers between the two groups.

The assault on 'Little Russianism'

The conceptual and historical framework of Ukrainophone nationalists has resulted in a long tradition of disdain for the local 'Little Russian' complex allegedly possessed by many Russophone Ukrainians and by the Ukrainian intelligentsia in general. Dmytro Dontsov, the ideological mentor of west Ukrainian nationalism between the two world wars, argued that the 'Russian complex', 'spiritual lameness', 'provincialism' and 'Moscowphilia' of the Ukrainian intelligentsia was the key reason for the relative weakness of the Ukrainian national movement.[46] Significantly, his views were echoed in the 1920s by the Soviet Ukrainian writer Mykola Khvyl'ovyi, who also attacked the 'psychological servility' and 'cultural epigonism' of the Russophone Ukrainian intelligentsia, who 'could not imagine themselves without the Russian conductor', because they were 'unable to defeat within [themselves] the slavish nature which has always worshipped the northern culture'.[47]

This theme was further developed by the émigré author Ievhen Malaniuk, who viewed 'Little Russianism' as a 'national disease' with 'pathological characteristics', a form of 'national defeatism . . . capitulation before the battle', creating 'a nationally defective type, maimed psychologically and spiritually, and – in consequence – even racially'.[48] 'Little Russianism' was therefore seen mainly as the product of weakness of character. Unlike political Austrianism under the Habsburg Empire, it did not result from rational calculation and free choice, but was a 'brutal, mass-mechanical fabrication', the product of 'the terrorist-police machine of a totalitarian state'.[49] Unlike Austria, Russia was incapable of creating a true synthesis of identities, only of 'tearing up the living organisms of the conquered and powerless nations'. It was Ukraine's misfortune that not only the peasant 'dark masses' but also the 'semi-intelligentsia and intelligentsia' were so 'denationalised', depriving the nation of its 'brain centre'.[50]

The theme of betrayal by one's own brethren has often crowded out a more honest analysis of the deep-seated historical reasons for the bifurcation of ethnic Ukrainian culture. Even after independence in 1991, and especially after the election of Leonid Kuchma as Ukrainian president in 1994, many nationalist Ukrainophones have argued that state power was being hijacked by slavish Russophiles.[51] The October 1995 'Manifesto of the Ukrainian Intelligentsia', for example, attacked the 'higher echelons of power' in Ukraine, 'vulgar cosmopolitans',[52] who were accused of 'turning on orphan [*bezridnykh*] lumpen elements, who are indifferent to who feeds them or controls their national riches', to conduct a *de facto* 'Russian nationalist' policy of 'turning their native land into a colony of Russia'. 'The majority of politicians speak the language of a foreign country', it continued, and had allowed what was 'in essence ethnic cleansing to be conducted against Ukrainians in Ukraine'.[53]

Ethnic Russians: a diaspora in the making?

Ethnic Russians have lived in Ukraine for centuries. On the other hand, they have never really developed a fully formed identity attuned to the circumstances of being 'Russians-in-Ukraine'. Nevertheless, they also have a characteristic political discourse relating to their history and perceived status, directed in particular at two of the key fundamentals of the Ukrainophone nationalist worldview, 'colonialism' and 'indigenousness'.

Firstly, in contrast to the Ukrainophone view of history, ethnic Russians tend to argue that local population movements have been voluntary and multidirectional, and that the gradual influx of ethnic Russians to the south-east of Ukraine represented a process of peaceful settlement rather than colonial 'occupation'. Secondly, ethnic Russians would therefore also claim that they are no less 'indigenous' than Ukrainians in large areas of eastern and southern Ukraine.[54] They should certainly not be classed as a 'national minority' (in Soviet times 'national minorities' came low in the ethnic pecking order, below the titular nationalities of the fifteen union republics and twenty autonomous republics).[55]

For example, the Crimean 'Congress of the Russian People' declared in 1996 that 'the Russian people [*Russkii Narod*] has lived continuously [*izdrevle*] on the territory of the modern state of Ukraine and in Crimea [sic] since the time of Kievan Rus´, and cannot consider itself a newcomer or an occupying people, as some historians and politicians are trying to depict them . . . [The latter are in fact] representatives of other ethnic groups that arrived and formed themselves on the territory of Crimea and other regions of the state of Ukraine much later than the Russians, [although they] are now trying to claim exclusive national rights and priorities.'[56]

A draft law on the use of the Russian language in Ukraine prepared by the Congress of Russian Organisations of Ukraine and Civic Congress of Ukraine in 1996 began with the following demand: 'considering the deep historical roots of Russians in Ukraine, their special role in the expansion and opening up of Ukrainian lands, and also their immense importance in the modern life of Ukraine, in agreement with Articles 10 and 11 of the Constitution of Ukraine, [we call on the Ukrainian authorities] to recognise Russians alongside Ukrainians as an indigenous people of Ukraine'.[57]

According to one survey undertaken in 1991, 90 per cent of the Russian inhabitants of Crimea and 89 per cent of Russians in eastern Ukraine agreed with the statement, 'I do not consider myself a foreigner [chuzim] on the territory of this republic.'[58] 'Rootedness' has its consequences, however. In regions such as the Donbas it has supposedly meant the development of both a 'borderland'[59] and a 'melting-pot' identity,[60] shared with many ethnic Ukrainians. It is often argued that local Russians are therefore different from 'Muscovites' (Moskaly), because they 'have taken on certain local values and attitudes, which have created clear differences between them and Russians in Russia'.[61] Russians in Crimea might speak 'Moscow' Russian and could be compared to 'true Russians, but their language is fundamentally different from the Russian–Ukrainian mixture of the south-eastern tracts [smuhy] of Ukraine . . . for the inhabitants of the Donbas the [mixed] language of Kiev or neighbouring Rostov is closer than Crimean-Russian'.[62] In so far as this is a point sometimes made by Ukrainophones, it undermines the radical othering of 'colonial' Russians that is otherwise characteristic of Ukrainophone discourse.

On the other hand, this possible 'southern Russian' identity has yet to be properly articulated at an elite level. In the past Russian elites in Ukraine tended to think in all-Russian terms. Indeed, many were violent Ukrainophobes, such as Vasilii Shul'gin, editor of the main Kiev daily Kievlianin before the 1917 revolution, or the author Mikhail Bulgakov, who grew up in Kiev.[63] Before 1914 Ukraine was a strong centre of Russian nationalist activity.[64] Local Ukrainophobe discourse, however, has been mainly negative. The claims of Ukrainophiles have traditionally been refuted on all-Russian grounds, with little sense as yet of building up a positive understanding of what it means to be a Russian in Ukraine. Ukrainian independence therefore suddenly cut local Russians off from their traditional source of myths and symbols, and without an obvious identity map political mobilisation has been surprisingly difficult.[65] Moreover, like Russophone Ukrainians, Russians in Ukraine do not have an influential culture-forming intelligentsia. There was a Russian intelligentsia in cities such as Kiev, Kharkiv and Odesa before the revolution, but it did not survive Soviet rule.

Ethnic Russians in Ukraine therefore have an ambiguous notion of 'homeland', located partly in Ukraine, partly in the Russian Federation and partly in both at the same time. Russians in Ukraine do not yet define themselves as a 'diaspora', in terms of an irredenta of a broader homeland. Many are as confused by the appearance of the Russian Federation as they are by the emergence of an independent Ukraine. Most would define not only themselves, but also all their fellow eastern Slavs, as part of 'Eurasia'.[66] The logic of the Russian position therefore drives them towards support for the restoration of some kind of overarching political unity between Ukraine and Russia, rather than towards local separatism (Crimea excepted).

However, identity politics amongst Russians in Ukraine also depends in turn on the discourse and policies adopted by official and unofficial actors in the Russian Federation. In the immediate aftermath of the Soviet break-up Russia has lacked the resources to make a serious bid for the identity and loyalty of Russians abroad. This is a political fact in itself, encouraging such Russians towards strategies of accommodation with the new host states. However, there remains considerable cultural capital in Ukraine on which Russian nationalist political entrepreneurs, either from Russia or in Ukraine itself, could draw in the event of worsening confrontation between the two states, especially if Ukrainophone nationalist discourse serves to 'other' and to alienate local Russians, or even Russophones en masse.

Russophone Ukrainians: two Ukraines?

The Ukrainophone nationalist position is that Russophone Ukrainians are simply denationalised or déraciné Ukrainians. It can certainly be accepted that, of the three 'groups', it is most difficult to speak of a fully bounded identity in the case of Russophone Ukrainians. A Russophone Ukrainian is still a Ukrainian, but is nevertheless a Ukrainian of a specific type – or perhaps several types, as there are many ways in which the consequences of speaking Russian or adopting Russian culture can impact on identity. Russophone Ukrainians therefore possess sufficient elements of a separate identity, historically that of the 'Little Russian' (*maloros*), to justify their separate treatment.[67] On the other hand, this identity has meant different things at different times and in different places, in circumstances very different to the conditions prevailing in the post-Soviet period.

Originally, 'Little Russianism' developed as an identity for *all* Ukrainians, when, as most of Ukraine became a part of imperial Russia between 1654 and 1795, it defined a combination of loyalty to the tsar with continued localist sentiments.[68] By the nineteenth century, however, it came to refer to those Ukrainians who had been progressively absorbed into the Russian cultural sphere (as, to a degree, with 'Anglo-Scots').[69] It followed from Ukrainian activists' own essentially linguistic definition of national identity that Ukrainian *malorosy* such as the playwright Mykola Gogol who consciously rejected the Ukrainian for the Russian language were somehow 'less Ukrainian'. However, as many Ukrainians in the nineteenth century identified with Russian culture *tout court*, 'Little Russian' still implied a certain residual loyalty to a local Ukrainian identity. Gogol himself wrote in an identifiably Ukrainian cultural milieu. Moreover, the 'Russia' with which many Ukrainians linked their identity was *rossiiskii* not *russkii*, implying a broader identity which could somehow accommodate both Russians and Ukrainians.

This historical model is less appropriate to the circumstances in which Russophone Ukrainians find themselves at the turn of the millennium. The *maloros* has never before had to consider the possibility of a permanent political division between Russia and Ukraine. Moreover, in so far as 'Little Russianism' was an *instrumental* identity, a rational calculation of the greater practical and symbolic benefits of Russian culture, it may be losing its appeal (for the philosopher V''iacheslav Lypyns'kyi, Little Russianism was specifically a 'disease of statelessness').[70] The imperial centre that provided such a pole of attraction in the past is no longer capable of drawing Ukrainians into its service bureaucracy, although it may continue to exercise a certain cultural pull. English-language 'global culture' may increasingly provide an alternative escape route for those who continue to seek an identity capable of transcending Ukrainian 'provincialism', although indirect access to global culture is often still through Russian, despite Ukrainophile attempts to create a 'unified information space'.[71]

On the other hand, some aspects of Russophone Ukrainian identity may be valued in themselves; it should not be too readily assumed that 'Little Russianism' must now wither away as political boundaries begin to firm up and kick over the traces of past patterns of cultural interaction. Russophone Ukrainians have an existential interest in contesting Ukrainophone stereotypes on at least two points. There is no logical need for Russophone Ukrainians to care about Ukrainophone attitudes to 'indigenousness', as the claim applies to all Ukrainians. However, Russophone Ukrainians are likely to challenge the discourse of 'colonialism' and 'Russification' and to resist attempts to characterise past (and future) relations with Russia in purely negative terms, as, in order to assert their own identity, it is important to stress that their crossover into Russian cultural space has been voluntary. The Ukrainophone nationalist

equation of ethnicity and language as joint determinants of national identity is therefore also likely to be rejected.

Ukrainophone historiography that excludes Russians and Russian-
speakers from its narrative also has little appeal to Russophone Ukrainians
(see chapter 2). Their view of Ukrainian–Russian relations requires a
more catholic historical myth. For prominent Russophone Ukrainians,
such as the former deputy chairman of the Ukrainian parliament and
leader of the Interregional Block for Reforms Volodymyr Hryn´ov,[72] 'on
the majority of what is now Ukrainian territory', centuries of history have
been marked by 'the common development of two peoples close in language, culture and historical past – Ukrainians and Russians'.[73] The two
languages in fact were like 'a pair of boots [sapogi], one the "left" and the
other the "right"',[74] the two cultures sufficiently intertwined to be considered a 'broad transitional stratum [shyrokyi marginal´nyi shar]'.[75] There
was therefore no historical basis to consider that 'Ukraine was ever a
Russian colony, the Ukrainian people the people of a colonised country or
that the Russian people were ever the "conquerors" of Ukraine'.[76] Rather,
the common 'Eurasian space' inhabited by both Ukrainians and Russians
has always possessed a 'special cultural value', above all the harmonious
unity of the east Slavic peoples.[77] If Russia is claimed to be Ukraine's
'natural' partner and Russia is in 'Eurasia' or both Europe and Eurasia,
then so is Ukraine, making it difficult for Ukraine to adopt an unambigu-
ous trajectory towards Europe. Even those who embrace 'European
values' argue that Ukraine and Russia ought to proceed towards Europe in
tandem, or that Ukraine should revert to its seventeenth/eighteenth
century role as a bridge to Europe for the whole Russophone world.[78]

The philosopher Myroslav Popovych has pointed out that there was no
real 'ethnic division of labour' in Ukraine under the USSR. Russians and
Ukrainians worked side by side; the so-called '"colonisers" [never]
created separate social-cultural enclaves'.[79] There has always been a voluntary crossover between what were never in any case completely separate cultural spheres. The present language situation in Ukraine cannot
therefore be explained solely in terms of the actions of 'zealous
Russifiers'.[80] A greater cultural gap in fact supposedly exists between the
common diapason of Dnieper Ukraine and the nationalist west. Artificial
Ukrainian–Russian hostility supposedly resulted from the atypical
environment of 'underdeveloped' western Ukraine.[81] Myths of common
Russo-Ukrainian struggle against enemies such as Nazi Germany remain
strong.[82]

Resistance to an enforced choice between 'Ukrainian' and 'Russian'
cultural spheres that many Russophone Ukrainians regard as in any case

only partially distinct remains a defining feature of the Russophone Ukrainian identity. In the words of one (Russian) activist, 'in terms of national-cultural identification we belong to a single Russian–Ukrainian cultural space', and should not therefore be forced artificially 'to chose between a mono- and polycultural' identity.[83] According to one survey in the Donbas in September 1992, only 12 per cent of the local sample (18 per cent of Ukrainians, 11 per cent of Russians) agreed with the Ukrainophone nationalist view that 'the population of the Donbas is in the main Ukrainians who have acquired specific characteristics because of the particularities of their living conditions' (that is, they have been 'Russified'). On the other hand, 49 per cent (48 per cent of Ukrainians, 49 per cent of Russians) agreed that 'a special community has been created in the Donbas, linked equally with both Ukraine and Russia'. Moreover, 58 per cent (55 per cent of Ukrainians, 61 per cent of Russians) expected that situation to continue.[84] Historical intermingling and high levels of mixed marriage in eastern and southern Ukraine mean that 'passport' ethnicity is often fairly meaningless.[85]

The Party of Slavonic Unity of Ukraine has attempted to provide an alternative identity for *all* Russophones in Ukraine (Russians and Ukrainians) by attempting to revive the term 'Rusichi' for individuals with a mixed east Slavic parentage, arguing that they have been developing as a 'nation' since the seventeenth century and now number some 127 million throughout the former USSR. The party argues that between nineteen and twenty million such 'Rusichi' live in Ukraine, making up the majority population in border regions of the south and east, and in neighbouring oblasts in Russia, where there has been a constant 'exchange of populations' since the time of the Cossacks.[86] In so far as the term 'Little Russian' (or indeed 'Rusich') identifies a real historical phenomenon, several Russophone activists have argued that 'there is nothing belittling in the word' and it should continue to be used.[87]

Nevertheless, it can be accepted that both historical 'Little Russianism' and the idea of a new 'Rusich' nation are largely theories about the *origins* of Russophone Ukrainian culture, or about orientations to state formations that have disappeared. They are less well attuned to providing a coherent *future* identity for Russophone Ukrainians. Indeed, opinion polls indicate that their political attitudes have lagged behind developments. Significantly, it is disproportionately Russophones (ethnic Russians *and* Russophone Ukrainians) who cling to a vanishing 'Soviet' identity,[88] and who have also expressed nostalgia for some form of overarching political union between Ukraine and Russia.[89]

An additional problem for Russophone Ukrainians is the lack of an obvious ideologue to give moral and historical support to their position.

Possible mentors, such as Mykola Kostomarov and Panteleimon Kulish, nineteenth-century Ukrainian writers who argued that Ukrainian and Russian culture could coexist, have been co-opted by contemporary Ukrainian nationalists as prophets of national revival.[90] Bohdan Khmelnyts'kyi, revered by many Russophones for uniting Russians and Ukrainians against the oppression of 'Poles and Lithuanians',[91] remains an ambiguous figure, as he also led the Ukrainian 'national uprising' of 1648. Moreover, Russophile Ukrainians, such as (in his later years) Iakiv Holovats'kyi in western Ukraine or Volodymyr Vernads'kyi, Iurii Kotsiubyns'kyi and Maksym Kovalevs'kyi in the east,[92] do not receive the prominence in recent histories that they deserve (as is also true of the powerful Russophile movement in Galicia before 1914).[93] Even Gogol, perhaps the best example of the mutual influence of Ukrainian and Russian culture, has been shifted more into the Ukrainian camp.[94] Without a culture-forming intelligentsia, however, Russophone Ukrainian identity is likely to remain amorphous and vulnerable to assimilation at either extreme.

The great paradox for Russophone Ukrainians is that, while their numbers are much larger than has traditionally been assumed, organised collective action in defence of their interests has been less frequent and less formidable than might have been predicted from strength of numbers alone. Moreover, without a clear-cut sense of identity this situation is likely to persist. Significantly, both ethnic Russians and Russophone Ukrainians have had difficulty in forming social movements and political parties without the relative advantages of the symbolic and institutional resources enjoyed by Ukrainophones.[95]

Deconstructing boundaries: alternative narratives of identity

Not all political leaders in Ukraine can be classed as ethnic entrepreneurs. Many politicians, including some of those already mentioned above, have used explicitly non-ethnic or pan-ethnic mobilisational strategies, or, if they accept that there is no natural 'ethnopolitical unity' in Ukrainian society,[96] have argued that different ethnic and language groups must enjoy equal status, as 'the interests, rights and specific traits and language of one nation' (i.e. Ukrainians) must not be placed 'above those of other nations and nationalities'.[97] As in Estonia and Latvia, pressure from international organisations such as the Council of Europe and OSCE has also worked against the reification of identities. Moreover, although 'civic' ideals command less of a consensus in Ukraine than they did in 1990–1, moderate voices are over-represented in government, while nationalist entrepreneurs of whatever hue are confined to the wings.

Many elites, including many liberal Ukrainophones, have continued to promote the idea of subsuming all ethnic and linguistic differences in Ukraine into a single 'Ukrainian political nation'. The Donbas-based Liberal Party of Ukraine, for example, has called for 'international and interconfessional accord as the basis for forming the citizens of Ukraine into a Ukrainian political nation',[98] the Socialist Party of Ukraine for a new political culture anchored in a 'mass consciousness based on the ideas of internationalism'.[99] In another favourite formula of the parties of the left, it is argued that 'Russians and Ukrainians are two branches of the one people of Ukraine.'[100] President Kuchma and others have consistently defended the virtues of a multiethnic society (it helps that Kuchma is, in his background at least, an archetypal Russophone Ukrainian).[101] Others have talked of the simultaneous consolidation of a 'Ukrainian nation (ethnosocial definition)', that is, of disparate regional identities and ethnographic subgroups (Lemkos, Rusyns, etc.) within the ethnic Ukrainian group, and of a 'Ukrainian nation (ethnopolitical definition)', that is, all those subjectively oriented towards the Ukrainian state.[102]

A second political strategy open to those on the left is to continue to locate this pan-ethnic ideal in a still extant 'Soviet' identity. Mention has already been made of the persistence of 'Soviet' identity on a mass level, particularly in parts of eastern and southern Ukraine. It is tempting to classify this a generational phenomenon that will fade away in time but, as it also expresses the desire to maintain some form of overarching identity between Ukraine and Russia, it may prove surprisingly persistent. In regions such as the Donbas the percentage defining themselves as 'Soviet' has declined only slowly in the immediate post-independence period.[103] Many on the left continue to talk as if the 'Soviet people' still existed and remained an active social group.[104]

Advocates of the primacy of regional identities have also adopted pan-ethnic strategies on a smaller scale. The Crimean constitution adopted in September 1992 spoke of sovereign power resting with 'citizens of the republic of Crimea of all nationalities, who make up the people of Crimea [*narod Kryma*]'.[105] Similarly, political entrepreneurs in the Donbas have continued to argue for the primacy of a local (*Donchanin*) identity, as have some in Odesa (*Odessiti* or *Chornomortsi*), Kharkiv (*Slobozhani*) and elsewhere.[106]

An alternative strategy has been the attempt to mobilise all Russophones (ethnic Russians and Russophone Ukrainians) together against the 'nationalising' strategies of Ukrainophones, given the fact that 'almost half the population of Ukraine considers it [Russian] their native language'.[107] To this end, Russophone activists have argued that 'there is a division *within* the Ukrainian ethnos' which is 'historical-cultural' rather than ethnic, between 'those who consider that Ukraine is a part of the general Russian ethnos . . . and those who think that Ukraine and Russia are different states and different cultures which are fundamentally opposed to one another'.[108] In part, this divide is held to overlap with that between the Uniate Catholic west and the Orthodox majority, although at the same time the common Orthodoxy shared by most Ukrainians and Russians has tended to diminish the salience of religious identity markers in Ukraine.[109]

Significantly, the founding father of the Ukrainian national movement, the historian Mykhailo Hrushevs'kyi, himself warned in 1906 (when Ukrainian territories were still divided between the Habsburg and Romanov Empires) that there was a danger of the Ukrainians, like 'the Serbs and the Croats' forming 'two nationalities on one ethnographic base'.[110] Modern Russophone activists have therefore often argued that Ukrainians in Dnieper Ukraine should make common cause with ethnic Russians against nationalist Ukrainophones in the west, thereby turning the Galicians with their peculiar history into the 'other'. 'Urban Galicians', according to the Party of Slavonic Unity of Ukraine, 'are a nation formed out of passive Slavdom, a national-aggressive type of world Jewry, relics and ethnically embedded Armenians, Germans, Hungarians, Tatars, Poles, Lemkos, Boikos and others, mixed together after the Austrian revolution of 1848–9' (see also chapter 2).[111] They, not Russians, are the true 'fifth column' in Ukraine.[112]

Although this 'historical-cultural' divide is not itself linguistic, it can interact with linguistic divisions, as in the 1994 presidential election, when anti-Ukrainophile activists successfully appealed for a common front of all Russophones against the incumbent president Leonid Kravchuk (who was supported on this occasion by both western Ukraine and the Right Bank of central Ukraine).[113]

Significantly, the Congress of 'Russian' (*Russkikh*) Organisations of Ukraine founded in March 1996 did not narrow its target constituency to ethnic Russians alone. It variously defined itself as 'a movement of citizens of Russian culture of all nationalities',[114] and of those who 'recognise the Russian language and culture as their own, alongside any other language and culture'.[115] Its leader (*starosta*), Aleksandr Baziliuk (also head of the Civic Congress of Ukraine), talked at various times of 'defending the rights of Russian-speaking [*russkoiazychnye*] citizens . . . of all citizens who consider Russia their homeland' (a Russia with 'a thousand-year history' from the time of Kievan Rus') and even of 'citizens of Russian culture'.[116] The Congress talked of uniting Ukraine's 'twelve million ethnic Russians and thirty million Russian-speakers [sic]'.[117]

Conclusions

The range of identity options in Ukraine is clearly wider than in many other post-communist states, despite the best efforts of ethnic entrepreneurs both to reify their own group and to firm up its boundaries by 'othering' outsiders. Significantly, survey evidence (from 1993–4) indicates that some 25–6 per cent of the population of Ukraine continue to think of themselves as somehow *both* Ukrainian and Russian.[118] (In a 1997 survey, 14.4 per cent saw themselves as both Ukrainian and Russian, 5.2 per cent as 'more Russian than Ukrainian' and 9.9 per cent as 'more Ukrainian than Russian'.)[119] Moreover, the boundary between the Russian and Russophone Ukrainian 'groups' is as fluid as that between Ukrainophones and Russophone Ukrainians. Indeed, when questions of language are to the forefront in the determination of identity it makes more sense to consider all Russophones together.

Ukraine may in the long run succeed in building a more culturally homogeneous society.[120] The political realities of independence are likely to shape identities to an extent. On the other hand, cultural groupings, especially those with such large critical masses (using the survey evidence cited above, there are something like 21 million Ukrainophone Ukrainians, 17 million Russophone Ukrainians and 11 million Russians), have often shown extraordinary resilience. Many other culturally divided societies, such as Canada and Belgium, have retained internal distinctions, despite periodic 'nationalising' pressures emanating from the centre.

In Ukraine therefore 'in'- and 'out'-group boundaries are likely to remain contested, with the efforts of ethnic entrepreneurs to promote the identity of their own group and to identify targets for assimilation opposed by those who would rather see boundaries remain fluid.

7 The Central Asian states as nationalising regimes

In firmly linking nationality to the notion of ethnic homeland, the practitioners of Soviet ideology generated a belief system which held that each titular nation is indivisibly connected through its putative history to a particular territory that is the natural patrimony of that nation. As in the other post-Soviet successor states, the collapse of the USSR has allowed political entrepreneurs in Central Asia to link the cultures of the titular nations even more closely to state structures and to further secure their political pre-eminence within the new citizen-polities.

This chapter explores the nationalising state, which Rogers Brubaker has defined as the polities *of* and *for* particular core nations,[1] as a plausible and useful model to describe the new states of Kazakstan, Kyrgyzstan, Uzbekistan and Turkmenistan.[2] The study is in two parts. The first part discusses the social, demographic and political forces both inducing and constraining nationalisation processes in those states, and the second part examines and compares specific nation-building practices as well as the implications that follow for the large Russian diasporas in the region.

The titular nation as primus inter pares

In addition to drawing on Soviet bureaucratic structures and institutions, the Central Asian states have underpinned their independence by elaborating nationalising policies and practices that seek to assert the hegemony of their respective titular nations. Despite formulations in the constitutions and other legislative acts guaranteeing the equality of all citizens, nationalising policies and practices are manifest in, *inter alia*, the iconography of the new regimes, the privileged status accorded to the local languages, newly revised histories and the exclusion of members of non-eponymous groups from the echelons of power.

This study categorises and examines nationalising policies and practices which are carried out *at the state level*, promulgated and implemented by titular national elites. Although the nation-builder must take into account the interests of both titular and non-titular groups in formulating policy (depending on demographic as well as other factors), it is a principal assumption of the present investigation that state actors in the newly independent Central Asian states have been influenced first and foremost by the non-Russified segments of the indigenous intelligentsias,[3] who have come to be regarded as the guardians and protectors of national culture.

According to a typology formulated by two Kazakstani[4] academicians, members of the Kazak intelligentsia can be divided into three primary categories with regard to their viewpoint on the construction of the 'ethnocratic' state.[5] The first and most numerous group comprises rural members of the educated classes, born mainly in Kazak towns and villages with a traditional-patriarchal structure. Having been educated in Kazak schools, they tend to perceive Russian culture as alien. Members of this group who have become fully integrated into urban life none the less retain their traditional worldview, which sets them in natural opposition to a linguistically and otherwise Russified urban culture. The second and least numerous group encompasses the urban Kazak intelligentsia, who are not only linguistically Russified but also estranged from Kazak culture and regard Russo-European culture as their own. Members of the third group have assimilated both Kazak and Russian cultures to a nearly equal degree (being generally of rural origin but having been educated in Russian-language primary and secondary schools) and are therefore characterised by an 'ethnocultural and linguistic dualism'.

Broadly speaking, this classification of the indigenous intelligentsia, which follows an urban–rural dividing line and emphasises educational environment, can be successfully extrapolated on to the native intelligentsias of the other Central Asian states. In crafting nationalising policies, contemporary Central Asian leaders are guided principally by the members of the first group as well as certain members of the third group (depending on the degree to which identity has been informed by Russian culture and language) in the typology described above. It is they who fill the ranks of the state apparatus, championing the notion of a strong national state. Carrying with them the memory of past injustices, they seek to redress those grievances in the form of new nation-building measures. The primary targets of their nationalising measures are not only ethnic Russians but also their Russified co-ethnics (*Mankurty*),[6] whom they regard as having betrayed the national cause.

Even though Slavic-based organisations in Central Asia have failed to formulate clear agendas and mobilise support effectively (or have been shut down altogether in the case of Uzbekistan and Turkmenistan), the interests of the settler communities within the new citizen-polities none the less act as constraints on the nationalising tendencies of the titular elites, especially in states lacking clear-cut ethnic cores. Kazakstan and – to a lesser degree – Kyrgyzstan are ethnically bifurcated societies, while the Slavic diasporas in Uzbekistan and Turkmenistan do not significantly impair the cultural unity of those states.[7] Hence, the question of granting an elevated status to the titular nationality and redressing past injustices assumes a special urgency in the former two countries, each of which still lacks a single hegemonic ethnic group. In Kazakstan, certain nationalising policies have at their core the fear of secession of the country's Russian-dominated northern and eastern regions (e.g. the transfer of the country's capital to Aqmola, the state-sponsored resettlement of ethnic Kazaks in the country's northern regions and the harsh treatment accorded to certain Russian groups; see below, pp. 156–60).

However real or likely the threat to the country's territorial integrity, the spectre of secession and possible annexation to Russia remains an ever-present factor shaping Kazakstani state policy and its nationalising practices in particular.

In general, the less ethnically homogeneous the population of a Central Asian state and the less authoritarian its system of rule, the greater the controversy engendered by its nationalising policies. While the Uzbekistani and Turkmenistani parliaments act as rubber stamps for the executive branch, usually passing new legislation after the first reading, in Kazakstan the adoption of laws with an ethnic dimension has precipitated intense public debate. The more open nature of Kyrgyzstani society, in particular, coupled with its heterogeneous demographic composition, has allowed ethnic divisions to come to the fore in that country. As a consequence, there has been an ethnic component to virtually every major sphere of state activity, ranging from the adoption of the constitution and the establishment of foreign policy priorities to the introduction of a national currency.[8] In addition to a successor state's ethnic composition and form of rule, its relationship with the Russian Federation as well as Russian foreign policy initiatives can act as important constraints on the nationalising process.[9]

Titular elites in Central Asia have engaged in nation-building not only as a response to pressure exerted 'from below' by the indigenous intelligentsias, but also as a means of fortifying the integrity of the titular nations themselves, which has been undermined to a certain extent by subethnic ties and loyalties. The promulgation of a national unifying policy becomes all the more urgent when one considers that many members of the titular nations regard their region, extended family or neighbourhood as their principal attachment. To cite but one example of a subnational loyalty, the *mahalla* (neighbourhood community, quarter) system in Uzbekistan, which is indigenous to the region and present in both rural and urban communities, is the primary institution of local self-government as well as the main regulator of social behaviour. The *mahallas*, headed by committees, have traditionally regulated the unofficial taxation of their members and the disbursement of funds to local mosques. With a view to exerting partial government control over this time-honoured institution, which is believed to provide an ideal environment for the formation of ethnoreligious identity, the Uzbekistani leadership has given the *mahalla* committees the official status of 'organs of local self-government' as set down in the constitution and a 1993 law. Slavs and other linguistically Russified groups tend to remain outside these closely knit community structures and consequently do not receive the social benefits that accompany membership.

Nationalisation by stealth

Although Russians and other non-titular groups have been granted an automatic right to membership of the citizen-polity, in contrast to non-titulars in Estonia and Latvia, the Central Asian states are not true civic states in that ethnicity can often be used to political and (sometimes economic) advantage. Certain nationalising measures intended to secure the cultural and political resurgence of the titular nation have been openly promoted (e.g. the upgrading of the local language, the re-invention of putative national holidays), while others have been 'tacit', informal practices carried out in accordance with the unwritten rules of the game.

A prime example of a tacit nationalising policy is the steady displacement and exclusion of the non-eponymous nationalities from the public sector. 'Nationalisation by stealth' is particularly rife in the civil service and social services spheres, where 'covert' nationalisation methods have been utilised in the employment, firing and promotion of personnel. General lay-offs have taken place, after which many of the same positions were restored and priority was given to titular nationals during the re-hiring process. Another common practice used by ministries and state-run organisations has been the issuance of official memorandums specifying that a knowledge of the state language is required in order to qualify for employment or promotion, thereby effectively eliminating the overwhelming majority of Slavs and other Russophones from consideration (see below, p. 154). Similarly, perquisites have been given to those who do possess a knowledge of the state language: in 1996 in Kazakstan's Semipalatinsk region (which was merged with East Kazakstan region in May 1997) – where ethnic Russians constituted approximately one-third of the population – government employees who had passed the Kazak language test received an automatic pay increase of 15 per cent.[10]

To be sure, such positive discrimination or 'affirmative action' practices have been in existence in Central Asia since the very early days of Soviet rule. The origins of the policy of *korenizatsiia* or nativisation can be traced back as far as 1923, when the Central Committee of the RCP(b) in Moscow adopted a program of measures to, *inter alia*, increase the political representation of the non-Russian nationalities and train managers and civil servants from amongst their ranks.[11] By the 1960s *korenizatsiia* had attained a momentum of its own as well-placed titular nationals accorded preferential treatment to their ethnic brethren in regard to job opportunities at the upper levels and access to higher education. As the indigenous population of the Central Asian republics began to increase at an especially rapid rate and titular nationals assumed more and more of the responsible positions in the economy and administration, actual Russian dominance began to erode. Competition between titular and non-titular groups for jobs in the cultural, educational, health care, service and other sectors intensified; and by the end of the 1970s the Central Asian republics were registering a net outflow of Russians and other Russophones. These trends, already in place well before the advent of *perestroika*, dramatically accelerated in 1989 with the passage of new language laws. With the advent of independence, the process of the concentration of power into the hands of the titular nations gained even greater momentum as positions of authority in government and state administration, law enforcement agencies and banking and court systems moved over to members of the titular nations.

The problem of opposing perceptions

While nationalising policies tend to be felt by all non-titular groups, they have been a greater source of psychological dislocation for the Russian diaspora in particular since its members are closely associated in the popular mindset with the tsarist and Soviet empires and, hence, are often regarded as erstwhile 'colonisers'. Many Russians themselves have facilitated such associations by continuing to regard either Russia or the now defunct Soviet Union as their homeland and lending support to the idea of a revived USSR.[12] A major study undertaken by the Moscow Institute of Strategic Studies in Kazakstan in 1995 found that every second Russian surveyed who was resident in an urban area of that country named the former Soviet Union as his or her homeland.[13]

Accustomed to their position as the 'leading nationality' during Soviet rule, many Russians are now acutely aware of their new status as minorities and are consequently especially prone to regard themselves as victims of discrimination, often experiencing an exaggerated sense of threat. Other linguistically Russified groups – whether Tatar, German or

Jew – have had several decades to acclimatise to their position as minority groups and are therefore less inclined to regard themselves as the direct victims of nationalising policies. Although many Russians look with understanding on the efforts of the titular nations to regain aspects of their cultural heritage, others consider it a violation of their human rights that they do not enjoy the same cultural advantages as their co-ethnics in Russia and that they must now learn Uzbek or Kazak – widely regarded as underdeveloped languages – in order to keep their jobs in the public sector. This sense of grievance is heightened by the perception that the titular nations have shown insufficient appreciation for the Russian contribution to Central Asian development. Taught by the Soviet system that their forefathers had played a crucial part in enlightening and educating the Central Asians following the annexation of the territory to Russia, members of the Russian diaspora have frequently expressed their outrage that their 'civilising role' in the region has now been forgotten.[14]

Mark Beissinger has asked: 'How does one explain the gulf between the self-perceptions of Russians and the perceptions of Russian actions by others?'[15] And has the post-independence era given rise to policies of discrimination or natural justice? Owing to the 'opposing perceptions' dilemma, the answer to these questions would appear to lie in the eye of the beholder. Whereas a Cossack might regard the Kazakstani state as promoting a policy of 'genocide against the Russian population',[16] a radical Kazak nationalist is bound to regard current nationalising measures as insufficient to rectify historical injustices. Perhaps of greater importance to the nation-building process, as Brubaker has pointed out, is the fact that 'events, officials, organisations, even "the state" as a whole are *perceived* as nationalising by representatives of the national minority' and therefore exercise a real effect on relations between titular and non-titular groups.[17]

Nationalising policies and practices

State semiotics: recovering the past

To create unified and distinctive nations and impart a sense of common destiny to their members, nation-builders unearth, appropriate and exploit the ethnosymbolic resources at their disposal (e.g. customs, toponyms and ethnonyms, heroes, myths, state iconography). All ruling elites in Central Asia accord great meaning to the ideology of unity of the titular ethnic group and the fortification of this group identity by the introduction and liberal use of official symbols that draw on the culture of the titular nation.

The new state flags of the Central Asian states contain carefully selected symbols specific to the titular nation's culture: both the Turkmenistani and Uzbekistani flags display crescent moons – prominent symbols of Islam – while those of the less ethnically homogeneous states of Kazakstan and Kyrgyzstan do not. The Turkmenistani flag depicts five carpet *guls* (a design used in producing rugs), each of which is associated with a different tribe.[18] The Kyrgyzstani flag also utilises the tribal motif in the form of a sun with forty rays representing the forty Kyrgyz tribes; additionally, in the centre of the sun is a stylised representation of the roof of the traditional Kyrgyz yurt. The Kazakstani flag is perhaps the least nationalistic, containing only a fairly neutral 'national ornamentation' on the hoist side.

The image of Manas (the legendary warrior and the hero of the Kyrgyz epic poem) on a rearing horse has become ubiquitous in post-Soviet Kyrgyzstan. In Turkmenistan, President Saparmirat Niyazov himself has become the country's most prominent national symbol, and many aspects of nation-building have been condensed into the distorted embodiment of the nation in the form of its leader. Referred to as 'Turkmenbashy' (meaning the 'chief of all Turkmen'), Niyazov has stated that this title symbolises the nation's unity and cohesion at a time of trial. The new state hymn of Turkmenistan begins with the words: 'The great creation of Turkmenbashy – our native state of Turkmenistan'.[19] Signs proclaiming 'Nation, Homeland, Turkmenbashy' (*Halq, Vatan, Turkmenbashy*) are omnipresent, as is Turkmenbashy's portrait, which can even be found on the new national banknotes. His name or title of Turkmenbashy has been given to over 1,000 objects in the country.

Of the Central Asian states, it is also Turkmenistan that has placed the greatest emphasis on the revival of national customs. Niyazov sought to re-invent tradition even during his reorganisation of Turkmenistan's political structures in May and June of 1992. At that time he created what is probably Central Asia's most unusual ruling organ, the Halq Maslakhaty (People's Council), a body which is intended to hark back to the Turkmen 'national tradition' of holding tribal assemblies to solve the most pressing problems.[20] More than fifteen new national holidays have been created in Turkmenistan since 1991, many of which pay homage to an object or custom closely associated with Turkmen culture, such as Turkmen Racehorse Day and Turkmen Carpet Day. Turkmenbashy also imparted national meaning to melon when he proclaimed the second Sunday in August Turkmen Melon Day, remarking that 'all measures should be taken to rehabilitate the bygone glory of the melon, which is inseparably linked to the fate of the Turkmen people'.[21]

Focusing somewhat less than the Turkmen on the reinvention of tradition, the Uzbeks and the Kazaks have placed greater emphasis on affirming the historical existence of the nation by ensuring continuity between the modern nation and the older ethnic communities from which they believe they stem.[22] Uzbekistani president Karimov has chosen the medieval ruler Temur (Tamerlaine – whose ancestry goes back to the Chinggisid Mongols, not the early Uzbeks)[23] as Uzbekistan's primary political icon, glorifying the warlord by erecting a total of eleven monuments to him throughout the country, including a large equestrian statue in central Tashkent.[24] The year 1996 was declared the year of Amir Temur, to celebrate the 650th anniversary of his birth, and a museum dedicated to the Temurid dynasty was opened in Tashkent.[25] The deliberate linking of the Temurid period with present-day Uzbekistan seeks to prove false all assertions that the Uzbek nation is an artificial construct of the Leninist–Stalinist period. Moreover, the selective emphasis on the Temurid period also invokes an historical 'Golden Age' and a state of greatness that could, perhaps, be achieved once again. In glorifying Temur, President Karimov may also be attempting to enhance his own prestige and authority by likening himself to the legendary ruler.

Contemporary Kazak historiographers have underscored the idea of 'historical continuity', which is to serve as the cornerstone for a renewed historical consciousness. The officially outlined 'Conception of the Establishment of an Historical Consciousness in the Republic of Kazakstan', which was approved by the President's National Council on State Policy in June 1995, stresses that the Kazaks are autochthonous on the territory of modern-day Kazakstan. 'The statehood of the Kazaks', asserts the document, '*is the continuation of the statehood* [emphasis added] of the major nomadic empires and individual khanates which have existed on the territory of Kazakstan since antiquity.' Further underlining the antiquity of the nation, the Conception goes on to state that 'the genealogical chain of kinship, the commonality of origin of the peoples can be traced continuously from the modern Kazaks to the Sacae, the Usuns, the Kangli and further to the tribes of the Andronov culture [Bronze Age]'. Thus, state policy has mandated the primordial and perennial bond of the Kazaks to the territory of the state, with the implicit assumption that they should occupy a pre-eminent status therein.[26]

The replacement of Russian and Soviet toponyms by indigenous ones has been an important way both to recover the past and to graphically symbolise a change in the ownership of the land. A multitude of regions, cities, streets, squares, collective farms – and even settlements founded by Russians during their colonisation of the region – have been renamed or are scheduled to be renamed. In other instances, when the original place-names were clearly associated with tsarist rule, the Soviet-era toponyms have remained; hence, the name of the Kazakstani capital, Almaty, was not changed (other than its spelling) as its pre-Soviet name, Verniy, smacked of Russian colonialism.

Uzbekistan has been the most overtly anti-Russian of the Central Asian states in its toponymic overhaul, attempting to eliminate that language from public view as much as possible. Noting that 'the names of objects that serve the old order and communist ideology deflect the people from the concept of independence', President Karimov signed a resolution in June 1996 on the renaming of designated administrative-territorial and other objects by September 1 (Independence Day); the decree also states that the new names should take into account 'historical and national features'.[27]

Nor have Soviet-era monuments escaped the national revival process: amongst the most prominent to have been removed were the towering statues of Lenin in central Tashkent and Almaty; Turkmenbashy has opted to erect a statue of himself as a Muslim pilgrim at Ashgabat's train station, in addition to many others throughout the country.

Constitutions

In addition to acting as primary symbols of newly acquired sovereignty, an unwritten premise of the constitutions of the Central Asian states is to ensure the political pre-eminence of the titular nations and provide special protection for their cultures. This unwritten premise is manifest in certain formulations that set apart the titular nation from the citizenry at large.

To underscore the unique connection of the Kazak nation to the territory of the present-day state, the preamble to the revised constitution of Kazakstan, adopted after a referendum on 30 August 1995, reads: 'We, the people of Kazakstan . . . create a state on primordial Kazak land' (the first Kazakstani constitution, adopted in January 1993, used the less emphatic 'ancient' in place of 'primordial'). However, the 1995 Kazakstani constitution eliminated the controversial passage present in the first constitution which had declared that 'the Republic of Kazakstan as a state system is self-determined by the Kazak nation', perforce relegating all non-Kazaks to an inferior position within the state.

The preamble to the constitution of the Kyrgyz Republic, adopted on 5 May 1993 after lengthy parliamentary debates, begins by proclaiming the importance of 'providing for the national renaissance of the Kyrgyz'. In second position and of apparently lesser importance is 'the protection and development of the interests of the members of all nationalities who, together with the Kyrgyz, form the people of Kyrgyzstan'. The preamble also asserts that: 'We, the people of Kyrgyzstan, affirm our adherence to human rights and to the idea of a national [*natsional'naia*] state.' In addition, the 1993 constitution changed the country's name from the 'Republic of Kyrgyzstan' to the more ethnically charged 'Kyrgyz Republic'. Together with a litany of democratic affirmations, the preamble to the Uzbekistani constitution, adopted in December 1992, states that the people of Uzbekistan 'are guided by historical experience in developing Uzbek statehood'.

The right of the titular nationality to occupy a pre-eminent position in the multiethnic state is personified in the figure of the highest-ranking political leader, who is to be chosen from amongst the titular nation's members. This tacit rule was effectively demonstrated during the landmark Almaty (then Alma-Ata) riots of December 1986, which were precipitated by the appointment of an ethnic Russian to replace the ethnic Kazak republican Communist Party first secretary. In the era of independence, constitutional provisions stipulating that the country's president must be a member of the titular nation or at least have a command of the state language have proved to be of great symbolic importance in the newly independent Central Asian states. Article 55 of the Turkmenistani constitution states clearly that the president must be a citizen 'from amongst the Turkmen'. Although the original version of the Kyrgyzstani constitution put forward by parliament declared that the president of the country must be an ethnic Kyrgyz,[28] Kyrgyzstani president Askar Akaev successfully fought to eliminate this stipulation from the final version, which states simply that the president must 'have a command of the state language'.[29] Article 90 of the Uzbekistani constitution stipulates only that the president must 'have a fluent command of the state language'. According to the Kazakstani constitution, the president and the chairmen of both houses of parliament must be fluent in the state language.

The process of privatisation

The historical narratives currently under construction by nation-builders in Central Asia, which seek to link modern nations firmly to the territories of present-day states, carry the subtextual implication that the members of the titular nation are the 'real' owners of the land. The tacit belief in the exclusive ownership rights of the titular group has at times been a source of conflict during the privatisation process, especially when attempts have been made by members of the titular group to enshrine this belief in legislation.

Such was the case with the land law adopted by the Kyrgyzstani parliament in May 1991, which declared that the land and natural resources were the property (*dostoianie*) of the ethnic Kyrgyz. In a small, mountainous country where land is at a premium, the formulation threatened to aggravate already strained relations with the Uzbek population and possibly even reopen the conflict between Kyrgyz and Uzbeks in Kyrgyzstan's Osh region,[30] where Uzbeks constituted nearly 30 per cent of the population and have traditionally been employed in agriculture.[31] Akaev vetoed the offending article and put forward the alternative formulation 'the land is the property of all the peoples of Kyrgyzstan', which was accepted by the Kyrgyzstani parliament in September 1991. In February 1992, when nationalist feeling was still running high in Kyrgyzstan, a National Land Fund was established by presidential decree, which envisaged the distribution of 50 per cent of the country's land to ethnic Kyrgyz during the process of privatisation in order to encourage farming amongst them.[32] Although heavily promoted by nationalists and nationalist-minded parliamentary deputies during the initial stages, the idea of creating a national land fund was later indefinitely shelved.

These struggles over the role of ethnicity in land ownership had their antecedents in the events of May 1989, when young Kyrgyz students in Frunze (today Bishkek) began spontaneously to seize parcels of public land on the capital's outskirts in order to build homes for themselves. City officials, recognising that a solution to the housing crisis could not be found in the near term, allowed the squatters to keep the plots. The builders – over 98 per cent of whom were Kyrgyz[33] – formed themselves into an organisation, Ashar, which was officially recognised and permitted to decide questions pertaining to the supply of building materials and the construction of private homes. Much of the capital's non-titular population regarded the stance taken by the authorities to the crisis as nothing short of capitulation to nationalistic demands and the *de facto* legitimation of illegal land seizures by and for ethnic Kyrgyz.

In Kazakstan, many titular nationals feared that the outright privatisation of state property in Kazakstan would have put the Kazaks at a disadvantage, given that non-Kazaks preponderate in the cities and would therefore have received wealth out of proportion to their political weight. Kazakstani president Nursultan Nazarbaev's regime was unwilling to cede control to industrial managers – the vast majority of whom were Russian – by granting them *de facto* ownership privileges over enterprises still belonging to the state; in the event, the authorities opted to issue vouchers to all citizens (independent of age or work record), thereby giving the Kazak nomenklatura an edge in the privatisation process.[34] Moreover, it is a widely held belief that the Kazakstani authorities have deliberately driven certain Slavic enterprises and collective farms to the verge of bankruptcy in order to enable Kazak-controlled investment groups to privatise them at low prices.[35]

Language laws

Replete with symbolic meaning, the adoption of language laws granting sole state status to the titular languages was a high priority for the Central Asian republics, all of which passed such legislation in 1989 (in 1990 in Turkmenistan).[36] As a result, language – widely regarded as a primary marker of national identity – became the first major issue to pit ethnic communities against each other in parliament and other fora.

As the euphoria of independence has passed, however, all of the ruling regimes have come to the realisation that the full implementation of the 1989 laws within the established deadlines would be not only unfeasible but also undesirable in view of the panoply of material and organisational constraints facing them.[37] Efforts to introduce legislation have met squarely with such obstacles as a lack of standardised terminologies, shortages of qualified teachers and textbooks, and resistance on the part of the Russophone population to learning what are widely regarded as 'inferior' languages.[38] Such resistance is not surprising given that Russians in Central Asia have displayed the lowest levels of linguistic assimilation of all the post-Soviet successor states, according to official Soviet census data. In 1989 a mere 0.9 per cent of all ethnic Russians in Kazakstan claimed knowledge of Kazak, while only 1.2 per cent of ethnic Russians in Kyrgyzstan were fluent in Kyrgyz (compared with 33.5 per cent of Lithuania's Russian population who spoke Lithuanian, for example). The highest rate of linguistic assimilation in Central Asia was in Uzbekistan, where 4.6 per cent of all ethnic Russians claimed a good command of Uzbek; in Turkmenistan, the corresponding figure was 2.5 per cent.

Although all of the original language laws granted Russian a special status as the language of 'inter-ethnic communication', the post-independence trend has been to downgrade its *normative* status in Uzbekistan, upgrade it in ethnically divided Kazakstan and Kyrgyzstan and retain more or less the status quo in Turkmenistan. Hence, turning a blind eye to the Soviet legacy of linguistic Russification, a revised edition of Uzbekistan's language law, adopted in December 1995, removed Russian's normative status as the language of inter-ethnic communication in that state.[39] Nor does the Uzbekistani constitution provide the Russian language with any special protection. The 1992 Turkmenistani constitution also failed to grant Russian any protected status, as President Niyazov has argued that such a move is unnecessary since Russian's status as the medium of inter-ethnic communication is spelled out in that country's law on languages.

In Kazakstan, by contrast, where Russian is still the *de facto* lingua franca in all spheres of public life, the 1995 constitution upgraded the status of Russian from the 'language of inter-ethnic communication' to an official language. The new-found equilibrium was disturbed not long thereafter, however, when in November 1996 the lower house of the Kazakstani parliament passed a draft revision of the language law requiring the executive branch to draw up a list of state sector posts for which a working knowledge of Kazak would be obligatory. The draft further stipulated that this provision would go into effect in the year 2006 for non-Kazaks while Kazaks would have only until the year 2001 to acquire a facility in the state language.[40] The Senate (the upper house of parliament) rejected the bill, however, sending it back to the lower house for revision. The final version of the law adopted by both houses of parliament in July 1997 set no deadline for the full switch to Kazak in public administration. In line with the Kazakstani constitution, the new language law states that 'Russian is used on a par with the Kazak language in state organisations and organs of local self-government.'

Debates concerning the normative status of Russian in Kyrgyzstan have been even more protracted. In June 1994, President Akaev signed a decree making Russian an official language in predominantly Russian-speaking areas as well as in 'vital areas of the national economy'; the decree also declared the intention of the government to correct the imbalances in personnel indigenisation practices.[41] (Article 5 of the 1993 Kyrgyzstani constitution had given Kyrgyz sole state language status while guaranteeing 'equal rights' for Russian and all other languages used by the republic's population.) The June decree, entitled 'On Measures to Regulate Migrational Processes in the Kyrgyz Republic', was an official acknowledgement by Kyrgyzstani authorities – in contrast to other Central Asian governments – of the primary importance of social and political factors in inducing the out-migration of the non-titular population. Since 1996 Akaev has repeatedly attempted to push through a constitutional amendment that would elevate the position of Russian still further by giving it the role of 'official' language. However, although the proposed amendment was approved by the Constitutional Court in late 1996, in June 1997 the Kyrgyzstani parliament failed to pass it.[42]

The indigenisation of power

A key component of the nationalisation process in post-Soviet Central Asia has been the steady displacement of the Slavic population and other linguistically Russified groups from leading positions in the public sector.

Having circumscribed their social mobility and participation in political life, the practice of concentrating power in the hands of the titular nationality has been a greater source of resentment for the settler communities than perhaps any other aspect of nationalisation, with the possible exception of language indigenisation.

The 'squeezing out' of non-titular nationals from leading positions to make room for members of the titular nationality was the main device for distributing political and economic power well before the advent of independence. To be sure, the creation of a class of native elites was amongst the most important goals of Soviet nationalities policy. Taking Kyrgyzstan as an example, Russians constituted only 10.5 per cent of the labour force in that republic in the 1920s, although they accounted for over half of all teachers, doctors and lawyers and nearly 70 per cent of all scientists and artists. By the 1980s, however, ethnic Kyrgyz were better represented amongst the scientific and creative intelligentsia than were their ethnic Russian counterparts.[43]

Yet it was not until the collapse of the USSR and the achievement of independence that the practice, albeit tacit, of according preferential treatment to the titular nation was fully legitimated in the eyes of most titular nationals. The practice of indigenising power has been highly visible in the legislatures of the Central Asian states, where the ethnic composition of the parliaments is heavily weighted in favour of the titular nationality. The first parliamentary elections in independent Turkmenistan took place in December 1994, when fifty candidates stood unopposed for fifty seats in the unicameral legislature, the Mejlis. Of those, forty-five were Turkmen, three were Uzbek and two were Russian.[44] Kyrgyz are over-represented in the Kyrgyzstani parliament, the Zhogorku Kenesh, which was elected in February 1995: of a total of 105 seats, 85 (81 per cent) went to Kyrgyz, 8 to Uzbeks and 6 to Slavs,[45] although Kyrgyz made up only some 60 per cent of the country's total population (see table 7.1). More than two-thirds of the seats in the upper house of the Kazakstani parliament, the Senat, elected in late 1995 and early 1996, are occupied by Kazaks (thirty-two of forty-seven), while Russians hold less than one-third (thirteen seats). Similarly, Russians hold only 28 per cent of all seats in the lower house, the Majlis, while Kazaks hold 65 per cent (although they made up only 46 per cent of the population in 1995).[46] An overwhelming majority of the members of Uzbekistan's parliament are Uzbek, including the Aliy Mäjlis' chairman, two of its four deputy chairmen, and all the chairmen of its twelve committees.[47]

The commanding heights of executive as well as legislative power have been indigenised. The vast majority of senior presidential staff, ministers

Table 7.1 *Ethnic composition of Kazakstan, Kyrgyzstan, Turkmenistan and Uzbekistan*

Kazakstan (1997)[1]	Kazaks	50.6%	8,033,400
	Russians	32.2%	5,104,600
	Ukrainians	4.5%	720, 300
	Uzbeks	2.3%	358,700
	Germans	1.9%	303,600
	Tatars	1.8%	277,600
	Others	6.7%	1,062,500
Kyrgyzstan (1997)[2]	Kyrgyz	60.8%	2,781,100
	Russians	15.3%	698,100
	Uzbeks	14.3%	653,300
	Ukrainians	1.6%	70,900
	Tatars	1.2%	53,200
	Kazaks	0.9%	42,400
	Tajiks	0.8%	38,800
	Germans	0.4%	17,300
	Others	4.7%	219,000
Turkmenistan (1995)[3]	Turkmen	77.0%	3,452,000
	Uzbeks	9.2%	412,000
	Russians	6.7%	300,000
	Kazaks	2.0%	90,000
	Armenians	0.8%	36,000
	Azerbaijanis	0.8%	36,000
	Baluchis	0.8%	36,000
	Tatars	0.8%	36,000
	Others	1.9%	85,000
Uzbekistan (1993)[4]	Uzbeks	74.5%	16,540,000
	Russians	6.9%	1,530,000
	Tajiks[5]	4.8%	1,107, 000
	Kazaks	4.1%	910,000
	Tatars	2.6%	577, 000
	Kyrgyz	0.9%	200,000
	Germans	0.1%	20,000
	Jews	0.1%	20,000
	Others	6.0%	1,332,000

Notes and sources:
[1] *Statisticheskoe obozrenie Kazakhstana*, Natsional'noe statisticheskoe agentstvo Ministerstva ekonomiki i torgovli Respubliki Kazakhstana, Almaty, No. 1, 1997, p. 3.
[2] *Natsional'nyi sostav naseleniia Kyrgyzstana*, Informatsionno-issledovatel'skii tsentr, Assamblei naroda Kyrgyzstana, Bishkek, April 1997, p. 5.
[3] The Turkmenistani government carried out a census in January 1995, although the results were not announced until the following year: *Neitral'nyi Turkmenistan*, Ashgabat, 28 and 29 February 1996.
[4] *Uzbekistan: otchet po chelovecheskomu razvitiiu 1995* (UNDP: Tashkent, 1995).
[5] Tajiks accounted for 4.8 per cent of the population of Uzbekistan in 1993 according to official statistics, although the actual figure was much higher. For fuller information, see chapter 9 in this volume.

and deputy ministers are members of the titular nation. The non-titular population is also under-represented at the lower levels of power: in Kazakstan, for example, regional administrations have been 'Kazakified' even in many northern regions where Russians form a majority.[48] Likewise, key posts in other areas of the power structure (e.g. the justice system, law enforcement agencies) are filled by members of the dominant ethnic group. The process of personnel indigenisation has also made considerable inroads into other areas of the public sector, such as the state-run media, hospitals and academic institutions, where titular nationals generally hold the senior positions.

As has already been noted, the indigenisation of the public sector is often carried out using 'covert' nationalisation methods, such as the practice of issuing official instructions concerning the hiring, firing and promotion of personnel. At an executive meeting of the Ministry of Internal Affairs of Kazakstan in August 1992, for example, a directive was passed concerning the advancement and hiring of employees with regard to their knowledge of the state language. An excerpt of the resolution stated: 'In the promotion of personnel and the conferral of titles upon employees, the attitude of the employee in question towards the study of the Kazak language shall be taken into consideration.'[49] Likewise, in accordance with a directive issued by the board of directors of a music school in the southern city of Shymkent, several teachers were fired for 'failing to observe the law on the state language'.[50] Russians in Uzbekistan have pointed to indigenising methods that 'leave no paper trail' and are therefore entirely subjective, such as their claim that the criminal justice system is weighted against non-Uzbeks, with the result that judges and law enforcement officials are inclined to treat them more harshly.[51] The 'opposing perceptions' dilemma discussed above makes it virtually impossible to substantiate such accusations, but the perception of their reality has none the less served to further entrench the boundary markers between eponymous and non-eponymous groups.

Passport ethnicity

As Brubaker has noted, the Soviet system institutionalised nationality and nationhood on the substate level by classifying them as social categories wholly separate from those of state and citizenship.[52] The most conspicuous manifestation of the institutionalisation of nationality was the infamous 'fifth column' (*piataia grafa*) in USSR internal passports which denoted a citizen's ethnic nationality (Kyrgyz, Russian, Jew, etc.) as distinct from his citizenship (Soviet). Ethnic nationality was transmitted by descent, irrespective of place of residence, and citizens did not have the right to change it. Furthermore, it could play a role in either helping or hindering a citizen's chances of gaining employment or admission to institutes of higher learning.

Whether or not to retain the line denoting ethnicity in the new passport was a subject of intense debate in Kyrgyzstan. Initially, a landmark decision to eliminate it was taken in February 1996, which made Kyrgyzstan the first and only Central Asian state to embark on such a move. According to the decision, the line indicating ethnic nationality was to be replaced by one which read simply 'citizen of the Kyrgyz Republic'.[53] However, the decision prompted a backlash of protests, primarily by more nationally minded Kyrgyz, in which the proponents of the measure were accused of 'betraying national interests'.[54] As a result, the 'fifth column' was restored a few months later by an edict of Prime Minister Jumagulov.

Kazakstani, Uzbekistani and Kyrgyzstani authorities have found innovative ways to keep the 'fifth column' as an ethnic marker in the new passports by retaining it on the page intended for 'internal consumption' (written in the Cyrillic script) while eliminating it on the page intended for 'external consumption' (written in English), thereby averting potential accusations of ethnocratic behaviour from abroad.[55] Both the Kazakstani and the Uzbekistani passports contain a line denoting ethnic nationality on the first page, which is written in the state language and in Russian. The second page, however, which is written in English and in the state language (and in Russian, in the Kazakstani case) omits all reference to ethnicity, replacing it instead with a line indicating citizenship. Thus, the line for citizenship on page 2 indicates either 'Kazakstan' or 'Uzbekistan', regardless of one's ethnic origin; while the line denoting ethnicity on page 1 indicates *Russkii* for ethnic Russians, *Kazak* for ethnic Kazaks, *Ozbek* for ethnic Uzbeks, etc. At least one citizen of Kazakstan, resident in Shymkent, has attempted to have 'Kazakstani' (*Kazakstanets*) written next to the line for ethnic nationality; he was allowed to do so only after special consultation with authorities in Almaty.[56] Kyrgyzstani authorities have followed essentially the same model, the only substantial difference being that the Kyrgyzstani passport devotes a separate page each to Kyrgyz-, Russian- and English-language versions. Ethnicity only is indicated in the Kyrgyz and Russian texts (*ulutu* and *natsional'nost'*, respectively), while citizenship only ('Kyrgyz Republic') is indicated on the page with English-language text.

As far as the Uzbekistani passport is concerned, a further source of confusion is the usage of the same term in Uzbek to denote both ethnic nationality and citizenship (*milläti*), even though a separate term in the Uzbek language to denote citizenship (*fuqäraligi*) theoretically could have been employed; in the event, only the response -- *Ozbek* as opposed to 'Uzbekistan' - makes it clear which concept is implied. Only in the

Kazakstani passport are distinct terms used in Russian as well as in Kazak to distinguish ethnicity from citizenship (*natsional'nost'* and *ülti* versus *grazhdanstvo* and *azamattïghï*, respectively).

The move to Aqmola: anchoring the northern regions

In November 1997 opening ceremonies were held to mark the transfer of the Kazakstani state capital from Almaty to Aqmola (meaning 'white grave'), a city in the country's northern steppe with some 300,000 inhabitants, of which approximately only a third are ethnic Kazaks. In justifying the move, Kazakstani officials have put forth, *inter alia*, the following arguments, none of which alludes to an ethnic dimension: the city of Almaty has nearly exhausted its potential for growth; it is far removed from the country's industrial and geographical centre due to its location in Kazakstan's extreme south-eastern corner; it lies in an earthquake zone and is plagued by air pollution.[57]

The long list of official reasons notwithstanding, the planned move to Aqmola is widely regarded as a means to consolidate the titular nation's hold on the state by 'diluting' the Russian-dominated northern regions through the migration of Kazaks from the south. Ethnic Russians constituted a majority of the population in three of Kazakstan's northern regions in 1994 (63.6 per cent in East Kazakstan region, 61.7 per cent in North Kazakstan region and 52.8 per cent in Karaganda region) and more than a third of the population in five others (46.5 per cent in Aqmola region, 39.3 per cent in Kokshetau region, 47.3 per cent in Kustanai region, 44.5 per cent in Pavlodar region and 33.9 per cent in Semipalatinsk region). In addition, they composed more than half the residents of Almaty.[58] It is hoped that the proposed change of capital will firmly anchor and integrate the northern part of the state, thereby foiling any Russian claims to the region. However, the grandiose project is beset by problems: although the new capital officially opened in late 1997, authorities have still not managed to find the bulk of the money needed to finance the transfer (and this amid record labour protests over the government's failure to pay wage arrears), and the construction of new ministries has barely begun. Moreover, Aqmola's freezing winter temperatures have provided a disincentive to government employees to make the transfer.

The 'in-gathering' of the nation

In the case of Kazakstan, certain nationalising polices have been justified by invoking the argument that the ethnic Kazaks have become a minority in the land of their ancestors through no fault of their own and, hence, should be accorded a special status within 'their' modern-day state. Such was the rationale behind granting ethnic Kazaks living abroad the right to possess citizenship of the Republic of Kazakstan together with the citizenship of other states, provided the laws of those states allowed it. This right was spelt out in Article 3 of the law on citizenship,[59] adopted on 20 December 1991, as well as in Article 4 of Kazakstan's first constitution. However, the revised constitution of 1995 omitted this provision, which was also eliminated from the country's citizenship law in October 1995.

By permitting dual citizenship for ethnic Kazaks living in other states, the Kazakstani leadership hoped to encourage their migration to their newly independent 'historic homeland'. This intention was made clear in the final paragraph of Article 3 of the law on citizenship[60] (which was retained in the revised 1995 law) as well as in immigration laws that provided financial support for this effort. Since 1992, Almaty has actively pursued the resettlement in Kazakstan of the nearly three million ethnic Kazaks who live abroad, primarily in China (1,200,000), Mongolia (150,000), Russia (600,000), Uzbekistan (830,000) and Turkmenistan (90,000).[61] Proponents of this measure have argued that it was needed to facilitate the process of rehabilitation, since Kazaks were forced to leave their native land and resettle elsewhere in the aftermath of the 1917 revolution and during the years of Stalinist repressions and forced collectivisation. Sceptics have countered that the measure is part of a larger government scheme to raise the share of the ethnic Kazaks in the country's overall population and 'squeeze out' the non-Kazaks, particularly in light of the fact that most Kazak in-migrants have been resettled in eastern and northern Kazakstan where the Russian population predominates.

As a means to achieve the 'in-gathering' of the nation, in September 1992 the Kazakstani government convened a Qazaq Qurultay in Almaty, to which members of the Kazak diaspora from all over the world were invited. The Qurultay adopted a resolution which appealed to all Kazaks to unite on the territory of their historic homeland and also declared that any ethnic Kazak who had left Kazakstan, for any reason, was to be granted automatic refugee status and its concomitant privileges.[62] According to President Nazarbaev, more than 200,000 Kazaks have resettled in Kazakstan in the last several years.[63] Many have come from Mongolia (more than 60,000),[64] although smaller numbers have come from Iran, Turkey and Uzbekistan. Few members of the large Kazak diaspora in China have chosen to resettle in Kazakstan, which is a reflection of the Chinese government's negative attitude towards the emigration of its national minorities.[65] However, the government programme to resettle ethnic Kazaks in Kazakstan has been encountering serious obstacles, largely as a result of the state's inability to provide many in-migrants with employment and adequate housing (especially in rural regions, where most are sent). In-migrants have also complained of serious cultural and lifestyle differences between themselves and the local Kazaks. Consequently, the number of in-migrants has fallen sharply in recent years; moreover, many emigrants to Kazakstan, particularly from Mongolia, have decided to return to their countries of origin.[66]

The treatment of Russian-based organisations

Although Kazakstani authorities dare not discuss it openly, their fear of the threat of secession of the country's northern regions – periodically inflamed by the statements of Aleksandr Solzhenitsyn and others concerning the reintegration of Russia, Ukraine, Belarus and northern Kazakstan – is palpable. The advocating of separatism or irredentism is strictly prohibited in the constitution and other laws, and the Russian newspaper *Komsomol'skaia pravda*, which enjoys widespread popular support in Kazakstan, was even outlawed there for several months in 1996 following the publication of an article in which Solzhenitsyn outlined his views on the re-creation of a 'greater Russia'. Article 5 of the Kazakstani constitution expressly prohibits the creation of social organisations whose aim it is 'to violate the integrity of the country', and this now well-known constitutional clause has frequently been used to circumscribe the activities of Russian nationalists.

Relations between Russian-based organisations and government officials in Kazakstan have visibly deteriorated in recent years. The escalation of anxiety over separatist sentiments has translated into harsher sanctions: the activities of some regional branches of the Slavic movement Lad, the Society for Slavic Culture and the Russian Community, have been banned; high-profile Russian activists have been arrested on charges of, *inter alia*, 'inciting inter-ethnic hatred' and 'insulting persons in authority';[67] and correspondents of the Moscow media have been subject to harrassment.[68] Cossack organisations have been singled out for particularly harsh treatment.[69]

Authorities in Uzbekistan and Turkmenistan have adopted an exceptionally hostile stance towards 'unofficial' social or political groupings in general and towards those with ethnic or religious affiliations in particular. All initiatives on the part of the Russian populations in those two countries to form social organisations have been quashed. The group Russian Society in Turkmenistan was refused permission to register in May 1992. After only a brief existence, the International Union of the Peoples of Uzbekistan (Intersoiuz), a group of Russians and other non-

Uzbeks formed in 1989 in reaction to the indigenisation of leadership and managerial posts in Uzbekistan,[70] was shut down by the authorities on charges of 'inciting inter-ethnic hatred'. And it was not until January 1994 that the Russian community in Uzbekistan was finally permitted to establish its own cultural centre[71] (a privilege that had been accorded to other non-Uzbek ethnic communities long before); however, the centre's newspaper, *Vestnik kul'tury*, was closed by Uzbekistani authorities following the publication of the newspaper's first issue.[72]

In contrast to the three Central Asian states discussed above, Russian-based organisations in Kyrgyzstan operate with relative freedom. The Slavic Foundation of Kyrgyzstan is officially registered with the Ministry of Justice, produces its own newspaper (*Slavianskie vesti*), has freely carried out surveys of the country's Slavic population (in conjunction with the Russian Academy of Sciences) and publishes critical reports in the local press.[73]

Anti-Russian rhetoric

Anti-Russian rhetoric, often criticising some aspect of the colonial past or present-day Russian hegemonic behaviour, appeared most frequently in the Central Asian media in the years immediately leading up to and following independence. A notable example was the declaration in 1992 by the Asaba Party of National Revival in Kyrgyzstan that 'in the nineteenth century the Russians occupied our land . . . During the bloody genocide of 1916 half of the innocent nation, including women, children and old people, were brutally slaughtered.' Asaba went on to assert that the entity 'the People of Kyrgyzstan' was a fiction, and that the country's land should be the exclusive property of the ethnic Kyrgyz. These assertions, printed in several newspapers, engendered a number of protests from the Russian community, prompting an official statement from the Ministry of Justice that Asaba's claims were historically false and legally unfounded.[74] Since 1994–5, however, following a marked improvement in relations between Kyrgyzstan's Russian and Kyrgyz communities, anti-Russian rhetoric in that state has been on the decline.

In Uzbekistan, on the other hand, rhetoric directed against Russia (and implicitly against Uzbekistan's Russian population) was stepped up after Russia imposed onerous conditions on ruble-zone members in 1993,[75] and also after the decision taken by the Russian State Duma in March 1996 to declare the abolition of the Soviet Union null and void. The Russian newspaper *Pravda* has described the heightened anti-Russian sentiment in Uzbekistan as an 'unprecedented and all-encompassing ideological campaign' which is becoming 'anti-Russian in its essence'.

Remarking on the regular references to Russian 'imperialist ambitions' in the Uzbekistani press, *Pravda* noted that the Uzbekistani paper *Khälq sozi* even went so far as to accuse the Russian television news programme *Vremia* of colonialist tendencies in that it has continued to give weather forecasts for the former Soviet republics in addition to the Russian regions.[76] Whether or not such accusations contain substance, official statements directed against the Russian Federation are none the less a source of psychological discomfort for many members of Uzbekistan's Russian community, who fear that they may come to be regarded as a fifth column for Uzbekistan's powerful northern neighbour.

Anti-colonial discourse in Kazakstan, while extant, has been less prominent than in Uzbekistan. An important historiographical turning point for the new state was the beginning of the discussion of the suffering endured by the Kazaks during the Stalinist collectivisation–sedentarisation campaigns.[77] Yet Kazakstani authorities realise that they can ill afford to engage in, or allow nationalist groups to engage in, openly anti-Russian rhetoric, given that the forging of closer ties between Russia and Kazakstan may be the best means of placating the disgruntlement among some members of the latter's large non-Kazak population.

Revival of Islamic symbols

Since the Soviet period, the distinction between religious and 'national' rituals has become increasingly blurred in Central Asia as the titular nations have come to regard the Islamic legacy as part of their national heritages.[78] As a result, the leaderships of all four Central Asian states under discussion have taken care to cultivate Islamic symbols (albeit to different degrees), sanctioning in particular the rapid construction of mosques, the refurbishment of holy places and the restoration of Islamic holidays. Presidents Karimov and Niyazov improved their respective Islamic credentials soon after achieving independence by making the pilgrimage to Mecca, earning themselves the title of *hajji* in the process, while Presidents Karimov and Akaev both swore their presidential oaths of office on the Qur'an in addition to their respective constitutions.

Kazakstani president Nazarbaev has preferred to promote the concept of Eurasia rather than use the Islamic card, given that only some 50 per cent of his country's population is Muslim. The Uzbekistani and Turkmenistani leaderships have endorsed the revival of certain Islamic practices while striving to keep religion within strictly controlled official boundaries. The Committee for Religious Affairs attached to the Uzbekistani Cabinet of Ministers maintains firm control over that country's religious institutions. A council for religious affairs, the

Gengesh, was created within Turkmenistan's presidential apparatus in April 1994. Its members included Turkmenistan's highest religious authority, Kazi Nasrullah ibn Ibadullah, who acts as chairman; the head of the Orthodox Church in Turkmenistan, who acts as co-chairman; and state officials, who 'ensure the observance of the law'.[79] Additionally, the *kaziat* appoints Islamic clerics in all rural areas, thereby allowing the state to exert control over religious affairs down to the village level.

Although elites have stressed the secular nature of their states, their use of Islam as a means of proclaiming their identities has none the less heightened fears amongst the region's non-Muslim population (although not as much as the general Islamic resurgence in the region), deepening the perceived divide between 'Asian' and 'European' cultures.

Citizenship

Citizenship and voting rights in the Central Asian states are based on the 'zero-option' principle, having been automatically extended to permanent residents at the time the laws on citizenship went into effect in the early 1990s.[80]

Although the citizenship laws of the Russian Federation have made it relatively easy for most former Soviet citizens to acquire citizenship rights in that state,[81] few Russians in Central Asia have opted to do so. Exchanging local for Russian citizenship not only disenfranchises a Central Asian resident, possibly limiting his rights to certain social benefits, but can also create suspicions of disloyalty in the eyes of Central Asian authorities. Moreover, since permanent residents of Central Asia were automatically conferred with the citizenship of their host state, they must undergo the formal bureaucratic procedure of *renouncing* that citizenship before they can receive a Russian passport.[82] Consequently, owing to both pragmatic and bureaucratic considerations, the vast majority of Russians in Central Asia have in essence accepted local rather than Russian citizenship by default.[83]

Still reluctant to permanently throw in their lot with the Central Asians and sever their ties to their 'historic homeland', most Russians in Central Asia have supported the institution of dual citizenship agreements with the Russian Federation. The Russian leadership has fully supported the idea of dual citizenship with the successor states, regarding it as its most reliable instrument for defending the rights of 'compatriots' in the near abroad and curbing the large flow of migrants to Russia.[84]

Despite Russian promotion of the idea at the highest state levels, Turkmenistan and Tajikistan[85] are thus far the only Soviet successor states to have concluded agreements on dual citizenship with Russia.

Presidents Niyazov and Yeltsin signed such an agreement in December 1993, at which time Niyazov symbolically issued Yeltsin with a new Turkmen passport, declaring him an honorary Turkmen. The agreement was ratified by the Russian State Duma nearly a year later, in October 1994. In the absence of a common border with Russia and having only a relatively small Russian diaspora, the Turkmenistani leadership apparently hoped that the agreement would fortify its relationship with Russia while helping to slow the exodus of its Russophone population. Of particular importance to many Turkmenistani Russians, the accord enables them to use the Russian health care system and study in Russian higher educational institutions as citizens of Russia rather than as foreigners.[86]

The leaderships of Uzbekistan, Kazakstan and Kyrgyzstan have rejected the institution of dual citizenship in their states, arguing that it would result in divided loyalties amongst their respective Russian populations. After initially advocating the idea of dual citizenship,[87] Kyrgyzstani president Akaev later reversed his stance on the issue, succumbing to the stronger nationalist-minded forces in the country who vehemently opposed the measure. The Nazarbaev government has also rejected the idea of dual citizenship, perhaps fearing that its introduction would blur the border separating Kazakstan's northern and eastern regions from the Russian Federation, and possibly even stimulate revanchist sentiment.

In lieu of concluding an agreement on dual citizenship, Kazakstani and Russian authorities have signed an agreement on the simplified acquisition of citizenship by citizens of one country who are permanently resident in the other (although the agreement came into effect only in August 1997).[88] Furthermore, a treaty on the legal status of citizens of either country who permanently reside on the other's territory grants Russian citizens in Kazakstan more rights than those enjoyed by other foreigners living there (and vice versa), such as the right to hold managerial posts in governmental and other agencies, to own property and participate in the privatisation process.[89] Although it is not as far reaching as the Kazakstani agreement, Kyrgyzstani authorities also concluded an agreement with Russian authorities in April 1996 on the simplified acquisition of citizenship by citizens of the Kyrgyz Republic who are permanently resident in Russia and by citizens of Russia who are permanently resident in Kyrgyzstan.

Of all the Central Asian states, the Uzbekistani leadership has been the most resolute in its rejection of dual citizenship, calling it the 'soft option' of preparing for eventual emigration to Russia and arguing that it would put Uzbekistan's non-indigenous population in a privileged position, thereby reducing their 'patriotic fervour'. 'Dual citizenship is impermissible', President Karimov has stated. 'Why should some [nationalities] be protected by two laws and have a "reserve airport", if you like, while others are not? And how can you demand love, selflessness and self-sacrifice for the motherland from a person with two citizenships?'[90] Unlike the other countries in the region, Uzbekistan has not signed agreements with Russia regulating migratory processes and the status of Russian citizens living permanently in Uzbekistan.[91]

None of the laws on citizenship of the Central Asian states make any mention of ethnicity (the provision in the Kazakstani law allowing ethnic Kazaks living in other states to hold dual citizenship having been eliminated in October 1995; see above, pp. 156–7); consequently, these laws do not facilitate the nationalisation process as such. Moreover, it is difficult to regard the refusal of most successor states to allow dual citizenship as an infringement of human rights, given that a number of democratic countries restrict or prohibit the practice. None the less, many ethnic Russians in particular have come to regard dual citizenship as their right, given that the country to which they once belonged no longer exists and the countries in which they have found themselves resident are, in their view, culturally and technically regressive states.

Conclusions

As nationalising regimes, the Central Asian states have accorded a higher status to their respective titular nations – which remain sharply distinguished from the citizenry of the state as a whole – that has legitimised the adoption of policies and practices that aim to promote the specific interests of those nations. Recalling Russian administrative and linguistic domination under Soviet rule, Central Asian national elites have contended that constitutions and other acts of legislation should legitimise and secure the political and cultural resurgence of the eponymous group, particularly in the initial stages of nation-building. Yet, the laws promulgated by the ruling regimes have, in most instances, simultaneously upheld the principle that the state should be based on an undifferentiated concept of citizenship. As a result, 'hidden', informal practices and the 'unwritten rules' of nationalisation often contradict – and in certain instances directly contravene – the civic principles enshrined in constitutions and other normative acts. Rather than viewing this phenomenon as a product of the post-independence period, such 'nationalisation by stealth' is more properly regarded as the logical, if unintended, outcome of Leninist indigenisation (*korenizatsiia*) policies.

Just as the nation-building process carries a greater sense of urgency in demographically divided societies, it inevitably engenders greater controversy there as well. It is also a process subject to revision, as attested to by the protracted debates in Kyrgyzstan and Kazakstan over the normative status of the Russian language. Material and organisational constraints can also frustrate ethnocultural nationalisation as governments come to terms with the enormity of the challenges posed by national revival. Yet, despite the obstacles, the nationally minded wings of the titular intelligentsias have continued to exert pressure 'from below' in pursuance of the national state models outlined in the preambles of their respective constitutions, thereby ensuring that the nation-building process has a momentum of its own.

Part III

Language and nation-building

8   Language myths and the discourse of
nation-building in Georgia

Language issues have played a large part in the nationalist discourse and in the shaping of new and transformed national identities in the post-Soviet states: witness the requirement to learn Estonian built into the citizenship legislation of Estonia and the return to the Latin script in the Central Asian states.[1] Cases such as these could be subsumed under the heading of language planning, whether in the form of attempts to purge the language of foreign elements or of legislation on language use. No less significant is what has been described as the 'impromptu linguistics' of politicians and civil servants.[2] Although the tenets of this form of linguistics bear only a passing resemblance to those of contemporary linguistic scholarship, their consequences are vastly more significant than those of the beliefs held by linguistics professionals. Implicitly or explicitly, they underlie irredentism, ethnic conflict, mass migration and ethnic cleansing, and the redrawing of national and regional boundaries. A key element in such politicised linguistics and the discourse of nation-building in many of the post-Soviet states is myths about language. Since the publication of Anthony D. Smith's *The Ethnic Revival* (1981) and Benedict Anderson's *Imagined Communities* (1983), to name but two of the most distinguished contributions to the subject, the importance of myth, belief and self-image in the formation of group identity has been acknowledged to be a crucial factor in the emergence of many nationalisms.[3] In charting these beliefs, scholars have tended to focus on myths relating to ethnohistory and homeland; language myths have barely been touched upon. Why is this? Several factors are at work: the inaccessibility of source material;[4] the lack of the specialised linguistic knowledge required to interpret and evaluate language myths; the absence of a theoretical framework within which to situate the myths; and a pervasive tendency amongst social scientists to reduce language and language issues to questions of communication and language planning.[5] It is the purpose of this chapter to set out some basic concepts relating to language myths, to provide a taxonomy of the commonest myths and to investigate their historical antecedents and their use in the construction and redefinition of

Georgian identity. We shall thereby shed light upon an important component of Georgian nationalism in particular,[6] and take a first step towards the integration of language myths in general into current scholarship on the discourse of nation-building.[7]

Language in Georgia

Any visitor to Georgia is immediately struck by the centrality of the Georgian language, both in everyday functions and in cultural contexts. Georgians are deeply proud of their language and literature. Until recently, every well-born Georgian girl was expected to have memorised great chunks of Shota Rustaveli's late twelfth-century epic, *The Knight in the Panther's Skin*, before marriage, and it forms part of the heritage of educated Georgians to this day in much the same way that Shakespeare and the King James version of the Bible were the common heritage of all educated English-speaking people until the present generation. The revered writers of the nineteenth century – Ilia Chavchavadze, Nikoloz Baratashvili, Vazha-Pshavela – are still widely quoted. And, as one Tbilisi resident remarked, 'We have many more poets in Georgia than we need: almost every "mountain person" is a poet.'

Oral communication plays a more ritualised role in the functioning of society than in contemporary English-speaking countries. Georgians – middle-aged professors as much as love-struck teenagers – expect to initiate and receive large numbers of social telephone calls, maintaining contact on a daily basis with a wide network of relatives, friends and acquaintances. Academic and business visitors from abroad find that they are expected to make an ever-increasing number of social visits, simply for the purpose of phatic communion – keeping the lines of communication open – to such an extent that the time-pressed Westerner despairs of ever getting down to work. His Georgian host, meanwhile, arrives at work the next day bleary-eyed and out of pocket, but with a sense of a social obligation duly fulfilled. Most conspicuously institutionalised is the traditional role of the *t'amada*, the toastmaster, whose job it is at formal dinners to pace the drinking and entertain the company with his eloquent words – and not in a single speech, but in a rich and variegated series of discourses. The holy places of Georgia, the visitor from afar, the parents who gave us birth, our revered teachers, the state of the nation and so on and so forth – each topic provides the occasion for a lengthy display of verbal virtuosity. No *t'amada* would ever dream of using notes.[8] Even the folk music is predominantly vocal: Georgians speak with pride about their rich repertoire of polyphonic song, but seldom mention traditional instruments such as the *salamuri*, the *duduki* and the *p'anduri*.

Equally, Georgian newspapers not infrequently carry articles with a bearing on language. In England, language is seldom deemed to be newsworthy. When it is, it is in one of two contexts: language choice, as in the debate over what variety of English Jamaican children should be taught at school; and grammar, as in the recent controversy over the use of 'they' as an impersonal pronoun. Both issues belong, broadly speaking, to the domain of language planning. But in Georgian newspapers, particularly between 1989 and 1993, one encountered articles on a huge range of language-related subjects, from the origin of the alphabet to the purchase of Georgian typewriters by the independent government of 1918. In part this is a consequence of differing journalistic traditions: recent academic books and monographs are far more likely to be reviewed or summarised in popularising newspaper articles than is the case in Britain.[9] Indeed, the *State Programme for the Georgian Language* (1989)[10] included amongst its numerous measures to promote the use of Georgian the publication of newspaper articles on the history of the Georgian language, its function in contemporary life and the defence of the purity of the written language. Theories about language and ethnohistory thus tend to receive wide public exposure in Georgia, arousing energetic, often acrimonious debate, and assuring their authors a degree of fame (or notoriety) rarely achieved by British scholars in comparable areas. On another level, odes to the Georgian language continue to form, if not an obligatory part of a poet's oeuvre, at any rate a not uncommon element in it.[11]

Georgia could thus be characterised as a highly language-conscious society. As regards the current language situation, the state of Georgia is very far from linguistically homogeneous: over a dozen languages are spoken on its territory. Georgian itself, the titular language and the first language of over half the population, is a member of the Kartvelian (South Caucasian) branch of the Ibero-Caucasian family, which, although it is geographically situated amidst languages belonging to the Indo-European (Armenian, Ossetic, Russian) and Turkic (Azeri, Turkish) families, is not related to either group. The more distant affiliations of the Ibero-Caucasian family remain unclear, although suggestions of remote kinship with Basque and Sumerian, now generally advanced on typological rather than genetic grounds, are still current. Establishing how many people are native speakers of Georgian is not as easy as it might appear, in that speakers of other Kartvelian languages may sometimes have recorded themselves as Georgian-speakers. Of the 3.78 million 'Georgians' recorded in the 1989 census (70 per cent of the population), it is estimated that 'about one million people' are speakers of the closely related Mingrelian language.[12] The next largest minority language is Armenian, spoken by approximately 437,000 people (8 per cent of the population). Other languages, such as Azeri, Ossetic, Svan, Laz, Abkhaz, Bats, Russian and Ukrainian, are spoken by much smaller percentages of the population.

The first references to the language situation in this region underline its complexity: late in the first century BC Strabo remarked that three hundred languages could be heard in Dioscurias, on the Black Sea coast of Georgia, a comment echoed two generations later by Pliny the Elder.[13] The eleventh-century historian Leonti Mroveli, in *K'art'lis tskhovreba* (Life of Georgia), says that several languages were in use in K'art'li (central Georgia) in the reign of King P'arnavaz (third century BC), but that P'arnavaz 'extended Georgian, and no other language than Georgian was spoken in K'art'li'.[14] Later sources, notably the edition of *K'art'lis tskhovreba* by Vakhushti Bagrationi (1696–1757), provide more detailed accounts of the language situation. Vakhushti's description evokes a picture of a dialectically differentiated use of Georgian across a large part of the territory under Georgian sovereignty, but of a restricted degree of bilingualism in certain areas (notably Chaneti (Lazistan)), while in Mingrelia and Abkhazia only the elite are reported as knowing Georgian.[15]

Georgian writers attached, and continue to attach, great importance to the use of Georgian as the common language of scholarship, culture, religion, law and inter-ethnic communication, allegedly from the time of King P'arnavaz on.[16] But with the annexation of much of Georgia by the Russian Empire in 1801, Russian replaced Georgian as the official language of administration and of the Church. A policy of Russification was carried out through the nineteenth century at the expense of Georgian, and attempts were made to foster minority languages through the creation of alphabets for and the preparation of elementary textbooks in Mingrelian, Abkhaz and Svan.[17] The policy of fostering minority languages would have obviated any need for the use of Georgian by their speakers, leading to the replacement of Georgian by Russian as the vehicle of high culture, and the grooming of the newly created written forms of the minority languages to take over from Georgian as the vehicle of everyday literacy. Georgians, not surprisingly, regarded this policy as a deliberate attempt to weaken the status of Georgian, a prelude to the splitting of the country.[18] During the brief period of Georgian independence (1918–21) before incorporation into the Soviet Union, a policy of Georgianisation was introduced in an attempt to reverse the effects of a century of Russification: Georgian was specified as the sole official language of the republic, and Tbilisi State University was founded as a Georgian-medium institution of higher education (1918). Indeed, so high a priority was attached to the reinstatement of the Georgian language that N. Chkheidze, the chairman of the National Council, wrote to the Georgian Technical Society on 31 May 1918, just five days after Georgia declared independence, to ask for assistance in organising the mass conversion of Russian typewriters to a Georgian font as quickly as possible.[19] Attempts after 1921 to reintroduce Russian were resisted by Georgian communists as well as by the intelligentsia, to the point where Sergo Orzhonikidze, first secretary of the Georgian Communist Party, had to remind Georgians that Russian was not 'the language of oppression', but 'the language of the October Revolution'.

The policy of *korenizatsiia* promoted the development of a new type of nationalism with the effect of furthering the appointment of ethnic Georgians to important positions at the expense of the minorities. In the 1920s Georgian was introduced throughout the education system. Dissertations could be written and defended in either Georgian or Russian, rather than in Russian alone, and higher degrees were awarded for several decades without consulting authorities in Moscow. During the 1930s, under Beria (himself a Mingrelian from Abkhazia) and Stalin, there was a revival of Georgianisation, with native-language schools in Abkhazia (which acquired the status of an autonomous republic in 1931) and Ossetia (an autonomous region from 1922) forced to close, a script based on Georgian being introduced for Abkhaz and Ossetic in 1938, and minorities generally coming under pressure.[20]

A reaction took place after the death of Stalin, when the position of minority languages was strengthened at the expense of Georgian. Thus, in 1954 a Cyrillic alphabet was reintroduced for Abkhaz and Ossetic, and in the same year new teacher-training courses in 'Abkhaz language and literature and Russian language and literature' and in 'Russian language and literature and Ossetic language and literature' were created in the Sukhumi Pedagogical Institute and in the South Ossetian Pedagogical Institute respectively.[21] Similar courses in Russian and Armenian and Russian and Azeri were also introduced.[22] These measures simultaneously enhanced the status of selected minority languages and Russian, and downgraded Georgian in the autonomous regions and other areas with a significant minority population. Attempts to promote the teaching of Russian throughout the USSR during the 1970s created increasing resentment in Georgia (as elsewhere).[23] Ethnic conflict and complaints of linguistic discrimination recurred in the 1970s, when Eduard Shevardnadze was first secretary of the Communist Party in Georgia. When, early in 1978, the central government in Moscow attempted to compel the Transcaucasian republics to drop the clause guaranteeing the position of the titular language as the state language from their respective constitutions, a huge demonstration in Tbilisi resulted in the withdrawal of the measure.[24]

Continued anxiety over the centre's intentions reinforced Georgian suspicion *vis-à-vis* both Russians and the minorities such that the *State Programme for the Georgian Language*, published in December 1988 and officially adopted in revised form in August 1989, contained a large number of measures designed specifically to enhance the position of Georgian, such as furthering the teaching of Georgian to non-native speakers resident in Georgia (I 6), introducing compulsory examinations in Georgian for students of art, theatre, music and technology (III 9), creating courses in Georgian stylistics and the history of Georgian literature for students in the non-Georgian sectors of the philological faculties (III 15) and the establishment of a Georgian Language Day (I 7).[25] It may be, however, that these provisions contributed to the increasing polarisation and mutual suspicion[26] which, exacerbated by the extreme nationalist policies of the government of Zviad Gamsakhurdia, resulted in ethnic conflict in South Ossetia and, under Eduard Shevardnadze, in Abkhazia, and tension in the area of language policy.[27] Significantly, an unsigned editorial in the May 1997 issue of *Burji erovnebisa*, a popular monthly devoted to language, literature and religion, laments the fact that the programme was never implemented and calls for its revival and implementation.[28] In an interview in the same issue the director of the A. Chikobava Institute of Linguistics of the Georgian Academy of Sciences, Gucha Kvaratskhelia, announces 'the project of the revitalisation of the Programme' as one of the goals of the standing State Commission on the Georgian Language (of which Shevardnadze is the chairman).[29]

Language relations in Georgia since 1801 have thus been far from straightforward. The respective attitudes of Georgians and ethnic minorities to each other's languages are often ambivalent or downright contradictory. The relationship obtaining between Georgian and Russian in the post-Soviet period appears to be changing swiftly. A major component in it is a fear that the Georgian language and, with it, the Georgian identity are still under threat from Russia. Andrei Sakharov's now ubiquitous model of Georgia as a 'little empire' captures another aspect: even as Russia once rode roughshod over Georgian aspirations and rights, so Georgians are now perceived as behaving similarly towards the minorities within their state. But Georgian fears and suspicions *vis-à-vis* the Russians are by far the most significant factor underlying their current attitudes, and their minority policy often represents a response to perceived Russian intentions as much as it reflects Georgian sentiments towards the minorities themselves. The tempestuous recent history of language relations is one manifestation, and a highly visible and significant one, of Georgian nationalism engaged in a process of self-definition ostensibly *vis-à-vis*, and often at the expense of, minority nationalisms, but with ever anxious glances over the shoulder in the direction of Russia. It is against this backdrop that we should consider the myths about the Georgian language current amongst Georgian-speakers, to which we shall now turn.

Language myths

Language myths are widely held beliefs about the origins, history and qualities of a language, whether one's own or a foreign language. The use of the word 'myth' does not necessarily imply that these beliefs are false. In some instances, popular belief and current scholarly orthodoxy may coincide; in others, they may be at loggerheads. Often, the matters at issue have long ceased to interest orthodox linguists, being regarded as 'non-issues', questions not susceptible to scholarly investigation or just plain uninteresting. 'Myth' is the term used in current academic discourse to denote such beliefs.

As we shall see, many language myths are extraordinarily resilient, emerging in near-identical form in one *ethnie* after another, generation after generation. A number of those found today are attested already in the sixteenth century, in the discourse of the emerging nationalisms of early modern Europe. But there is at least one significant difference between their status amongst early modern intellectuals, and the standing of their contemporary manifestations in the post-Soviet states. In the sixteenth and seventeenth centuries, and to a large extent in the eighteenth, language myths constituted an element of linguistic orthodoxy. The most highly regarded scholars of their day contributed to their formation and elaboration. Certainly, scholars clashed over individual myths: even his fellow-countrymen regarded J. Goropius Becanus' claim that Dutch/Flemish was the *Ursprache*, the primeval language of mankind, with scepticism. But by and large such myths were accepted by the entire educated community, and all its members could legitimately contribute to their refinement, from country parsons to scions of the aristocracy. Early in the nineteenth century, however, this academic eclecticism vanished. The reform of the university system carried out in Prussia by the scholar-diplomat Wilhelm von Humboldt (1767–1835), imitated throughout Europe, created an acknowledged path of training in all academic disciplines, including linguistics, and this training became the indispensable badge of the Establishment scholar; those without it were henceforth stigmatised as amateurs, fringe writers, eccentrics.

Concurrently, the locus of research shifted to the universities, making it difficult for those without an institutional affiliation to achieve recognition for their ideas, not least because of the control over the recognised channels of dissemination – academic journals and monograph series – exercised by members of universities and research institutes.

Thus, the notion of professionalism took root in linguistics as in other disciplines, and the consequence was the creation of two distinct groups of people writing about language: the professionals, a self-defined and self-regulating group characterised by a common path of training (with local and temporal variations) and shared notions of scientific method; and the non-professionals, fringe linguists who might themselves be professionals in a related sphere – theology, literature, journalism – but whose lack of the common training and outlook results in non-recognition by the linguistics professionals. Thus, in historical terms we can observe a shift from the position in the sixteenth and seventeenth centuries, when these myths were an element of linguistic orthodoxy, through the eighteenth and earlier nineteenth centuries, when they underwent a process of refinement and testing, to a point in the middle third of the nineteenth century when they were rejected by orthodox linguists, and the previous situation was reversed: beliefs that were previously constitutive of linguistic orthodoxy now became a badge of heterodoxy.[30]

Today this dichotomy exists as much in the post-Soviet states as in the West.[31] Just as in Britain it is the educated layperson, and not the professional linguist, who worries about the decline in standards in English usage and takes pride in the extensive vocabulary of English, the largest, s/he firmly believes, of any language in the world, so too in Georgia it is artists, journalists and teachers who most energetically propound comparable myths and attitudes. Georgian professionals – university teachers of linguistics and researchers in the A. Chikobava Institute of Linguistics of the Georgian Academy of Sciences – would disavow most, if not all, of these beliefs, and indeed some of this writer's Georgian professional contacts were deeply embarrassed that a foreigner had encountered such 'unscientific' views. For our purposes, the scientificity of these myths is not at issue; they are incontestably a reality at one highly significant level, namely, in the mental universe of a number of educated, articulate and influential Georgians who are actively engaged in examining and reconstructing their national and ethnic identity, and in formulating policy in all spheres from education to ethnic relations. That alone justifies taking language myths seriously.

Language-extrinsic and language-intrinsic myths

Language myths may be divided into two broad groups: those that emphasise *language-extrinsic* features such as the origin and destiny of a language, and those that focus on *language-intrinsic* features such as purity, elegance and lexical resources. Many of the myths occur repeatedly in different language communities, often redeployed with the express intention of demonstrating that *my* language is every bit as good as *yours*; some, however, are language- or culture-specific. It does not necessarily follow that it is the language-specific myths which are the most resonant or effective; as we shall see, the very fact that a popular myth is perceived as having enhanced the status of a rival language in the past may make it all the more effective as a tool to enhance the status of one's own language. Thus, A. D. Smith's comment about cultural symbols in general – 'it is the *specific* doctrines and ideas that provide the symbolism and ceremonial that arouse the deepest popular emotions and aspirations'[32] – is true only in a restricted sphere, that of *visual* symbols, where by the nature of the thing linguistic symbols have to be chosen from amongst material realisations of language with clear ethnic associations: a monument to a celebrated writer, an ancient inscription or a medieval manuscript, the signature of a famous author, the title page of a work with powerful emotional resonances. At the conceptual level, the *recycled myth* may contribute as much as more specific myths (or indeed more) to the legitimation of a sense of linguistic identity which is under siege or as yet weakly established. Some may be deployed absolutely ('our language is better than any other'), others relationally ('our language is better than yours').

Language-extrinsic myths

Those beliefs which focus on the external history and context of a language – its origins and antiquity, its genetic affiliations, its destiny, its perfect match to its speakers or to Nature – constitute the repertoire of *language-extrinsic myths*. To a large extent, language-extrinsic myths are intertwined with ethnic myths – myths of origin, of descent, of homeland and so forth – and are founded upon the identification of the language and its speakers. This equation is as old as the Bible, an enduring theme in the history of both linguistic and ethnological thought.[33] Not only is the language = *ethnie* equation widespread, but many of the specific arguments used to bolster the status of one language also reappear across the frontier, pressed into the service of a rival language. At times it may suit the shapers of nation-building discourse better to transfer the language =

ethnie equation on to the diachronic plane, substituting language history for ethnohistory. (See further pp. 192–4 below.)

Language-extrinsic myths may intersect with religious traditions, notably in myths about the chosen language or about the language spoken by Adam in the Garden of Eden ('the Adamic language'). They may ultimately be calqued upon the doctrine of linguistics professionals, albeit with divergent content, as in the many metamorphoses of the myth of the parent language or *Ursprache*. Alternatively, they may be related only indirectly to religious or mainstream academic doctrine, reflecting instead an amalgam of aspirations and self-image: witness the myths of conformity to Nature, of conformity to national character and of foreign approbation.

1. Myth of primordiality

- Myth of the parent language: 'our language is the parent of all related languages'.
- Myth of the *Ursprache*: 'our language is the original language of mankind'.
- Myth of the Adamic language: 'our language is the language spoken in Paradise by Adam and Eve'.

The three variants of this myth, although in principle distinct, shade over into one another with such facility that they are best discussed as facets of one and the same myth.

In the Middle Ages, it was accepted universally throughout the West and in much of the East that Hebrew was the Adamic language and the parent of all existing languages. Only in the Renaissance, with the growth of interest and pride in the national vernaculars, did scholars begin to investigate alternative scenarios. Speakers of Romance languages tried to legitimate their vernaculars by tracing their pedigree back to one or another of the *tres linguae sacrae*, the 'three sacred languages', Latin, Greek and Hebrew. The Italians traced their language back through Greek and Etruscan to Hebrew; the French, anxious to avoid giving ground to their cultural and political rivals in Italy, looked not to Latin but to Greek (via the Gauls, who according to Caesar used the Greek alphabet). Speakers of German and Dutch, uncomfortably aware that any attempt on their part to do likewise would meet with derision, adopted an alternative strategy: they claimed that their language was independent of any other. Indeed, one patriotic citizen of Antwerp, Johannes Goropius Becanus, redeployed the arguments commonly used to demonstrate Hebrew's status as the *Ursprache* to show that his native Flemish had a better claim to that status.[34] Celtic, favoured by British antiquaries, was a later contender. Shortly after 1800, the integration of

Sanskrit, the ancient literary and liturgical language of India, into the mainstream of Western linguistic thinking resulted in a brief burst of claims that *it* was the parent language, if not of all the languages in the world, then at least of most of the languages of Europe. Soon Sanskrit was displaced, far less romantically, by constructs such as 'the lost Indo-European parent language', 'proto-Indo-European' and analogous formations, up to 'Nostratic' and 'proto-World'. Fringe attempts to demonstrate the identity of the parent language with some existing language, and to bring an ever wider circle of languages into a genetic relationship with it, proliferated through the later nineteenth century and into the twentieth.[35]

In early twentieth-century Georgia, the fixation of Western scholars with the Indo-European family of languages was a source of no little resentment. This attitude marginalised the non-Indo-European Georgian and its relatives and, to the considerable chagrin of Georgian linguists, exalted both Russian and the neighbouring Armenian to what they regarded as a totally unmerited position of superiority. It was partly in reaction to this that Georgia's most celebrated linguist, Nikolai Marr (1864/5–1934), formulated the Japhetic hypothesis. Marr's relationship to the academic community of his day was complex. Marr himself, the offspring of a Scottish father and a Georgian mother, was never regarded as properly Georgian by his fellow-countrymen: they thought he was 'an English prince'. Within his own country he fell out with much of the academic establishment, a break underlined by Ivane Javakhishvili's refusal to give him the coveted post at the newly founded Tbilisi State University. (Javakhishvili later reconsidered his decision, but it was too late: Marr remained embittered.) Nor were his relations with Western scholars entirely easy. On the other hand, he rose to positions of great eminence within the Soviet scholarly establishment, becoming vice president of the Soviet Academy of Sciences (1930) and a member of the Order of Lenin (1933), and having the Institute of Language and Thought named after him (1933).

Marr postulated a Japhetic family of languages, of which Georgian and other Ibero-Caucasian languages were the initial 'core' members. It gradually expanded to take in all the languages of the Mediterranean, including Basque, Etruscan and Pelasgian, and a great many others besides. In a later form of the theory Georgian–Sumerian kinship was advanced, possibly via Sumerian as the link between the Basque, Caucasian and Mongolian languages. By 1928 Marr had succeeded in establishing to his own satisfaction a relationship not only between Indo-European and Semitic, but also with Turkic, Chinese, African, Oceanic, Australian and Amerindian languages via his Japhetic root-language, and in due course he announced that Indo-European was simply a later, imperialistic, stage of Japhetic. Although Marr's ideas were denounced in 1950 by a number of prominent linguists, including the Georgian scholar Arnold Chikobava (the probable ghost-writer of Stalin's celebrated speech on linguistics), they lived on in the popular consciousness; indeed, whereas the Institute of Linguistics of the Georgian Academy of Sciences (named after Chikobava) espoused Chikobava's repudiation of Marr, Tbilisi State University supported his ideas, and the division is said to live on to this day.[36]

'Japhetic' swiftly became part of educated Georgian common knowledge. On the first page of *Sak´art´velos istoria* (History of Georgia),[37] S. R. Gorgadze outlined the place of Georgian amongst the world's languages as follows:

There was a time when human beings all spoke one language; but when they multiplied and moved away from one another, the language gradually became differentiated: many languages arose in the place of the single one. Scholars today divide these languages into a number of families. For us the following three families are of the greatest significance: Semitic, Japhetic and Indo-European or Aryan. Each family has its own branches and dialects . . . The Japhetic family has the following branches: Elamite, Primitive Local 'Armenian', Georgian, Chan-Mingrelian and Svan.

Semitic and Indo-European are allocated two lines each, whilst the Japhetic family occupies some twenty-one lines. Whereas Gorgadze's wording implies that there are other language families besides those named, his formulation passed into popular consciousness without the qualifying rider. Several educated Georgians have informed this author that there are three 'root-languages' in the world, which invariably turn out to be the three listed by Gorgadze. An indication of the extent to which this myth is an unexamined item of belief is that, asked where Chinese fits in this scheme, all these individuals immediately concluded that the 'fact' cannot, after all, have been meant to be all encompassing; instead of defending it, they abandon it.[38]

Marr's ideas, with their pronounced anti-Indo-European (and therefore both anti-Russian and, when expedient, anti-Armenian) colouring, provided a convenient linguistic and ethnolinguistic underpinning for the ethnic nationalism propounded by Zviad Gamsakhurdia, president of Georgia from October 1990, when he took power in Georgia's first democratic elections since the arrival of the Bolsheviks, to his overthrow in January 1992. Gamsakhurdia, an expert on American literature and on the medieval Georgian epic *The Knight in the Panther's Skin*, took up Marr's ideas and popularised them in, amongst other writings, his address 'The Spiritual Mission of Georgia' (1990) and his article on

Ioane Zosime's *Praise and Glorification of the Georgian Language*.[39] Gamsakhurdia cites Marr and Wilhelm von Humboldt for the notion that the Sumerians, Pelasgians, Etruscans and others were all connected with the proto-Iberians,[40] and Marr for the statement that 'the proto-Georgian [*proto-k'art'uli*] or Japhetic root-language is a unique language-generating phenomenon, the common root of every language originating from it by a process of differentiation'.[41]

Whereas Marr had been anxious to enhance the status of the Japhetic languages generally (and the Ibero-Caucasian languages in particular), and not exclusively that of Georgian (which sank, in the course of his career, from being 'one of the best-preserved Japhetic languages and one with the least admixture'[42] to being a 'hybrid language'), his more extreme followers amongst Georgian nationalists have preferred to ignore that aspect of his work, equating Japhetic with proto-Georgian. Thus, one Tbilisi researcher, an English teacher by profession, is currently engaged upon a huge project aimed at demonstrating that all Indo-European languages are descended from Georgian and other Ibero-Caucasian languages, beginning with the most ancient toponyms in the British Isles as proof to support the thesis.[43]

Overall, it is plain that the *Ursprache* myth has proved to be remarkably successful in contemporary Georgia. The Japhetic hypothesis advanced by Marr and his immediate followers served throughout the Soviet era to enhance the self-esteem of the Georgians in the face of the overwhelming might of the Indo-Europeans, represented for Georgia by the Russians. Zviad Gamsakhurdia combined the Japhetic hypothesis with Zosime's messianic hints (see pp. 180–2 below) to create a myth of salvation for the language, and hence for the nation as well. Meanwhile, others continue to seek linguistic ways of gaining recognition in the world for Georgian and its speakers – by seeking the origins of Indo-European lexical stock in it, so reducing the conquerors' much vaunted parent-language to a mere Johnny-come-lately offshoot of the despised Japhetic languages, or by tracing back the oldest known writing systems – Phoenician (the acknowledged ancestor of all Graeco-Roman scripts, including Cyrillic), Egyptian and 'Sumerian' – to one or another of the Georgian scripts.[44]

The *Ursprache* myth has played a role in the nation-building activities of other nationalities, during and since the Soviet period. Another case from the Caucasus is reported from Ossetia by Suzanne Goldenberg.[45] The *-don* morpheme in *London* and *Croydon* is identified with the *-don* ending of many Ossetian place-names and adduced as evidence for an ancient Ossetian empire spreading across Europe to include Britain. Beyond the Caucasus, a striking example comes from the mid-century Lithuanian diaspora. In a pamphlet reprinting a portion of the introduction to his *Comparative Philology and an Outline of Lithuanian Grammar*, volume II, Theodore S. Thurston[46] rewrites a celebrated paragraph known to all Indo-Europeanists, the account of the relationship of Sanskrit to Latin and Greek from Sir William Jones' *Third Anniversary Discourse* (1786), placing Lithuanian in the position Jones gave to Sanskrit:

The Lithuanian language, whatever its antiquity, is of a wonderful structure, more perfect than either Sanskrit or Greek, more copious than Latin, and more exquisitely refined than any of these three. Yet, Lithuanian bears to all three of them a stronger affinity than could have been produced by nature, not only in the roots of verbs, but also in forms of grammatical structure and the morphological construction of words. So strong is this affinity that any philologist can see very clearly that Sanskrit, Greek, and Latin must have sprung from a common source, Lithuanian.

There is a similar reason for supposing that the Heruli, Rugians, Goths, Old Prussians, and Latvians, and their language, had the same origin, for they were ancient Lithuanian people.[47]

Lithuanian thus becomes the Indo-European *Ursprache*. Thurston goes on to claim: 'Renowned philologists have agree[d] that the Lithuanian language is not only the oldest language in the world today, but the language used by Aryans before the invention of evolution of Sanskrit.' Such argumentation is intended to create respect for the language, and with it the people, leading inexorably to a call for Lithuanian independence: 'the world today would be greatly enriched with an independent Lithuania and with its ancient and important language in the field of linguistic science'. The device of ignoring or overturning generally accepted scholarly views of language relationships for political ends is very much alive in the contemporary Baltic republics, where the long-established orthodox notion of a Balto-Slavonic subgroup of Indo-European languages, comprising the Baltic languages – Latvian, Lithuanian and Old Prussian – alongside Russian, Polish and the other Slavonic languages, has been rejected in favour of a Balto-Germanic subgroup. Far harder to substantiate on purely linguistic grounds, this theory owes its existence to the desire to create linguistic independence from Russian in order to provide a further justification, using the language = *ethnie* equation, for political independence.[48]

> *2. Myth of the chosen language: 'our language has been singled out above all others for a special destiny'.*

The archetypal 'chosen' or 'sacred' language is Hebrew, *leshon ha-qodesh*, in transparent parallelism with the proclaimed destiny of the Jewish people.[49] From Bishop Isidore of Seville (d. 636) on, medieval Christendom expanded this notion of a 'chosen' or 'sacred' language to accommodate the liturgical languages of the Church, Greek and Latin alongside Hebrew. The resulting myth of the 'three sacred languages', *tres linguae sacrae*, created a linguistic dualism which mirrored the widespread medieval social practice of a ruling elite of one ethnic stock presiding over a populace of another. The European vernaculars were on an equal footing – all alike inferior, a curse brought upon mankind by the presumptuous building of the Tower of Babel. The *tres linguae sacrae* alone stood outside the ebb and flow of time, the perpetual flux to which all other languages had been condemned. Only the *tres linguae sacrae* were capable of being reduced to rule, of being described in grammars; only they could guarantee intelligibility across great tracts of time and space; only they were worthy of study.

In the Orthodox East a less pessimistic view was adopted. Išoʻdad of Merv (c. 850) tells us that God created linguistic diversity 'in order to instruct, develop and exercise the intelligence and lead to the growth of wisdom'.[50] In contrast to the Church of Rome, which imposed Latin upon its converts, the Greek Church adopted a policy of translation, creating an alphabet where none existed, and encouraging the translation of the Bible and exegetical writings into the local language. Thus, Syriac, Armenian, Georgian, Gothic and Old Church Slavonic all became the vehicle of high culture long before this could be said of any Western vernacular (with the partial exception of Old Irish). It was in this climate of linguistic tolerance that the first text in defence of the Georgian language was written in the tenth century, *Praise and Glorification of the Georgian Language*, by the hymnographer Ioane Zosime. Enigmatic in the extreme to modern eyes, it begins:

> Buried is the Georgian language
> As a martyr until the day of the Messiah's second coming,
> So that God may look at every language
> Through this language.
> And so the language
> Is sleeping to this day.

Later we read:

> Every secret is buried in this language . . .
> And this language
> Beautified and blessed by the name of the Lord,
> Humble and afflicted,
> Awaits the day of the second coming of the Lord.[51]

Praise and Glorification is unique, not only in Georgia, but in Europe as a whole, at this early date. Not until the late fifteenth century did writing in praise and defence of the vernacular commence in the West. Leaving aside the many questions which surround the origins and *raison d'être* of this text, however, we should note that it has become a potent symbol of Georgian linguistic nationalism in the twentieth century. Amongst the many scholars to have attempted to unravel its numerous obscurities is the former president, Zviad Gamsakhurdia. Gamsakhurdia's reading united the destinies of language and people, seeing both the Georgians and their language as humiliated and pushed into obscurity by the Indo-Europeans, but predicting their ultimate resurrection and elevation to the spiritual leadership of mankind.[52] This messianic interpretation was eagerly taken up by Gamsakhurdia's supporters – it is significant that the article was placed first in his collected works – and Zosime's text, a symbol of the transcendence of the Georgian language, became a leitmotiv of nationalist discourse. Thus, two articles published in nationalist newspapers on the occasion of Georgian Language Day, 14 April 1993, invoke the *Praise and Glorification* with specific reference to Gamsakhurdia, one concluding with a few sentences from his essay,[53] and the other juxtaposing the complete text with a photograph of Gamsakhurdia and a facsimile of a few lines from the autograph manuscript of his essay, with the title page of the first school textbook in the Georgian language, Iakob Gogebashvili's *Deda ena*.[54] The Georgian language, represented by *Deda ena*, is linked visually with the deposed leader and conceptually, via Zosime's *Praise and Glorification*, with the message of resurrection: the political overtones are transparent.

An interest in *Praise and Glorification of the Georgian Language* thus links both official academic culture and the fringe discourse of nationalism. The professionals, in this case philologists and medievalists, publish their theories in specialist journals, focusing on the work as a historical document to be interpreted with respect to its tenth-century context, whereas the fringe professionals and nationalists deploy it as a symbol to reinforce their existing concerns, exploiting its mythopoeic potential. Zviad Gamsakhurdia, as a scholar turned politician, was a member of both groups, but from 1990 on his role not only as the spokesman of Georgian nationalism but also as the political leader of Georgia increasingly dominated his scholarly persona. Despite numerous attempts to claim the text for nationalist ends, Georgian medievalists have continued to grapple with the very real interpretive difficulties posed by every line.

3. Myth of conformity to Nature: 'our language has a deep inner connection with extralinguistic reality, mirroring the world directly in its sounds, letters and vocabulary'.

Of all the language myths this one is the most diverse in its manifestations and the most pervasive. At some level we all sympathise with the English-speaker who exclaimed: 'Isn't "cow" a wonderfully cowlike word!' As native speakers, we have instilled into us from earliest childhood the feeling that the words of our language are the only possible way to express our emotions and describe the outer world. As we grow in linguistic sophistication, we come to realise that speakers of other languages hold the same view of their languages; and we may well encounter the dogma formulated first by Aristotle but given its most celebrated articulation by Saussure: 'l'arbitraire du signe'. And yet the poet in us maintains a covert sympathy for the unorthodox view, the view which finds in Tennyson's 'murmuring of immemorial elms' a clear case of sound echoing sense.[55]

During the Middle Ages the search for extra-linguistic correlations to linguistic phenomena was underpinned by a serious theoretical motivation. Scholars trained in the Judaeo-Christian tradition deeply regretted the existence of linguistic diversity, believing as they did that it was a punishment visited upon Man for his arrogance in attempting to build the Tower of Babel. As a result, the harmony and mutual understanding which had prevailed while all human beings shared the Adamic language was lost. Nevertheless, the three sacred languages – Latin, Greek and Hebrew – were held to be in some way superior to the rest, and to be to some extent immune to the consequences of the 'fall' of language. Scholars embarked upon a lengthy quest to identify features of these languages which still retained some element of their original 'rightness', revealing an intrinsic connection with extra-linguistic reality. Thus, Latin was said to have five vowels because man has five senses, while the seven vowels of Greek correspond to the seven planets. Instances of such correlative thinking are frequent throughout the Middle Ages in both the Byzantine and the Roman cultural spheres, and likewise in Jewish writing.[56] With the Renaissance discovery of the vernaculars, the locus for extra-linguistic correlations was transferred from the *tres linguae sacrae* to the vernacular. Concurrently the rationale behind the search shifted too: no longer was it a matter of seeking redemption from the 'fall' of language by focusing on a small group of 'superior' languages and ignoring the rest; rather, successful demonstration of a close correlation between one's own language and extra-linguistic reality could be used not only to enhance the prestige of one's own language, but even to buttress its claim to be the Adamic language.

Conformity to nature was sought in all aspects of language, but four domains stand out: sounds, vocabulary, sentence structure and letter forms. Sounds and sentence structure, frequently invoked by early modern Western writers, have not been invoked in recent Georgian nationalist discourse to demonstrate the superior 'naturalness' of their language, and they will therefore not be discussed here.

Vocabulary

One lexical item advanced in support of the 'naturalness' of Georgian is the verb *dzgers*, meaning 'beat', allegedly used exclusively of the heart. Particular significance is claimed for this on account of the great attachment Georgians feel for the notion of the heart, *guli*; it follows that there should be a special word for the beating of the heart. This claim is problematical, however, in that *dzgers* can also be used of a throbbing finger or a twitching eyelid, and indeed the author who reports this claim distances herself from it by attributing it by name to another authority, Guram Petriashvili (formerly a member of Round Table, Gamsakhurdia's party[57]).

Letter forms

The possibility that the shapes of the letters might reflect something beyond themselves, whether material or spiritual, has been discussed since antiquity. Perhaps the clearest statement of 'graphemic Platonism' comes from an artist who has taken a deep, often polemically articulated interest in the sources of the Georgian alphabet, Zurab K'ap'ianidze. On his poster about the Old Georgian *asomt'avruli* script he declares: 'I consider an alphabet meaningless when it has no other significance, either numerical or astronomical, except the meaning of a letter-symbol.' Western scholars of the eighth and ninth centuries saw typological and allegorical significance in the letters – the Trinity in the three strokes of the letter A, the Old and New Testaments in the two bows of the letter B and so on. The natural philosophers of fourteenth-century Oxford tried to trace a correlation between the shapes of the letters and the type of motion carried out by the articulatory organs, foreshadowing numerous later attempts to demonstrate a correlation between the position of the organs of the vocal tract and the letter forms. J. P. Ericus (1686), in a veritable *tour de force*, traced the Greek vowel signs back to the planetary symbols and the consonants to drawings of various animals and objects.[58] In the post-Soviet context, Georgian offers fertile material to thinkers of a like turn of mind, in that it has an alphabet of considerable antiquity associated primarily[59] with the titular language. Let us take two examples. Alina Chaganava, the author of one of the articles commemorating Georgian Language Day 1993 mentioned above (p. 182) remarks that the name Jesus (*Ieso*) 'represented in Georgian letters takes the form of a cross: იესო.' (This observation is not common knowledge amongst Georgians: several of this writer's Georgian acquaintances have expressed surprise on having this pointed out to them.) Perhaps the most remarkable manifestation of 'graphemic Platonism' in Georgia, however, is K'ap'ianidze's research on the origins of the earliest Georgian alphabet, the *asomt'avruli* script. In a book bearing the (translated) title *The First*

Alphabet of the Human Race (1990) and an associated poster K′ap′ianidze set out to demonstrate that the forms of the *asomt′avruli* letters reflect cosmic astronomical phenomena. Thus, the first letter, *ani*, represents the waning moon, the most auspicious season for any undertaking. Placing a moon symbol at the start of the alphabet points to the fact that the lunar calendar is encoded in the alphabet, and that it should ultimately be possible to discover the cosmic-astronomical significance of every letter. Likewise, each letter possesses religious or mythological significance, again transparently exemplified in the first letter: the Sumerians, we are told, called their moon deity *An*.[60]

As might be expected, K′ap′ianidze's ideas have not been taken seriously by the Georgian academic establishment. The extent of the union between K′ap′ianidze's cosmic-astronomical interpretation of the alphabet and Georgian nationalism emerges from his attack on a bastion of the academic establishment in Georgia, T′amaz Gamqrelidze (Gamkrelidze). Gamqrelidze, whose credentials include the directorship of the Oriental Institute of the Georgian Academy of Sciences, membership of the Soviet Academy of Sciences and recognition by numerous learned societies abroad, including the British Academy and the Linguistic Society of America, accorded for his work in Indo-European linguistics, published a book on the origins of the Georgian alphabet in 1990.[61] His conclusion, that the Old Georgian script was founded upon Greek rather than directly upon earlier forms of the Semitic alphabet, surprised no one in the West, but aroused great ire in Georgia. K′ap′ianidze's vitriolic response,[62] full of personal abuse, accuses Gamqrelidze of playing into Russian hands, joining the ranks of those traitorous Georgian scholars who assist the Russians in suppressing Georgian history. Such an attack makes vividly clear the extent to which research into Georgian linguistic history is bound up with nationalism amongst fringe linguists.[63] Likewise, Ayvazian's claim that the Armenians invented the first alphabet, as reported in chapter 3 (p. 51 above), is intended to reinforce Armenian claims to primordiality.

> *4. Myth of conformity to national character: 'our language reflects the character of its speakers not only in the sentiments expressed through it, but in its very sounds, vocabulary and structure'.*

In the early modern period, circular arguments about the relationship of language to national character were rife, as exemplified in the celebrated characterisation of European languages by William Camden:[64] 'Our *English* tongue is (I will not say as sacred as the *Hebrew*, or as learned as the *Greeke*,) but as fluent as the *Latine*, as courteous as the *Spanish*, as courtlike as the French, and as amorous as the *Italian*.' Needless to say, here and in many other such characterisations the conventionally acknowledged qualities of the literature (in the case of dead languages) – the Hebrew Bible, Platonic and Aristotelian philosophy, Ciceronian oratory and so forth – and the stereotype characteristics of the speakers of living languages are being projected on to the associated languages. Of course, every language boasts its own special term for a dispositional quality allegedly foreign to other speech-communities: German *Gemütlichkeit*, Portuguese *saudades* and English *fairness* are well-known examples. Chaganava provides a striking development of this in the Georgian context:[65]

The Georgian language has the character of the Georgian man. Both are tolerant by nature, and in this there is a divine element. 'He killed the man unintentionally', the Georgian says, and thereby tries to justify that weightiest of all sins – the killing of one man by another: 'It is a mistake', he says. In so saying he seeks the reason for the mistake elsewhere than in the individual.

To a Western reader, this seems a truly remarkable example of tolerance – an attempt to explain away a homicide; other examples offered by Georgian-speakers include *puri shemomech'ama*, 'I unintentionally ate up all the bread' and *bavshvi shemomelakha*, which can be paraphrased as 'I didn't mean to hit my child, but did so through a momentary loss of control.'[66] This passage stands out for its use of another item of belief prominent in Georgian nationalism, both Zviadist and post-Zviadist: the stress upon the traditional tolerance of the Georgians. Thus, in the words of a booklet produced by the Georgian government, 'under the influence of specific historical conditions and due to their nature the Georgians have developed a high degree of national and religious tolerance'.[67] This too could be classed as a perennial myth spontaneously generated amongst one people after another.

5. Myth of foreign approbation: 'our language possesses such unique qualities that foreigners come from far and wide to study it'.

That a language's potential or actual interest to foreign scholars should be advanced as a matter of national pride is itself indicative of the way in which the discourse of nation-building is so often reliant upon external vindication. External scholarly interest is a claim that has been possible only since the advent of the serious academic study of languages for languages' sake. As long as languages were studied purely as a means to an end – an entrée to a prestigious foreign culture, as in the case of Ancient Greek since the Renaissance, or because of their relevance to one's own culture and contemporary concerns, as in the case of Anglo-Saxon in the theological controversies of sixteenth- and seventeenth-century England – the preconditions for this belief were lacking.[68] Consequently, this myth is not attested in early modern Europe; effectively, it is found only in the twentieth century (although in principle one might expect to find it in the latter part of the nineteenth as well). Thus, the Georgian diaspora scholar Kita Tschenkéli devotes five pages of the introduction to his Georgian grammar to a section headed 'Importance of the Study of Georgian' (Bedeutung des Studiums des Georgischen, pp. xxiii–xxvii), composed largely of extensive quotations from scholars from A. Dirr (1904) to V. Polák (1950) testifying to the philological interest of Georgian.[69] G. I. Tsibakhishvili's elementary grammar of Georgian (in Russian) is a more striking example; the work is prefaced with a series of quotations testifying to the qualities of the language drawn from four authorities, each with his credentials and nationality: N. Ia. Marr, academician; D. Allen, professor (England); R. Meckelein, professor (Germany); I. Marschev, professor (Switzerland). The introduction, by academician Sh. V. Dzidziguri, devotes several paragraphs to evidence of foreign interest, listing the countries in which Georgian culture and Georgian language were arousing interest, and naming foreign Kartvelologists.[70] Likewise, on a poster about the Georgian alphabet published c. 1990 the English scholar W. E. D. Allen is quoted in praise of the perfectly phonemic nature of the alphabet, uniquely amongst the writing systems of the world. Such testimonials are, needless to say, absent from grammars by Western writers.

Chaganava, in the article already cited,[71] makes the point explicitly, albeit in more general terms: 'See what riches, what a unique linguistic phenomenon we Georgians have at our disposal! Scholars from various countries have studied and are studying our exceedingly ancient language in order to obtain the valuable textual and grammatical data preserved in it.' Chaganava, writing in 1993, two years after Georgia gained internationally recognised independence, has little call to develop the possible political implications of linguistic uniqueness. Theodore S. Thurston, the Lithuanian diaspora writer already quoted, demonstrates the logical endpoint of such argumentation, a consequence documented time and again since the era of Fichte and Herder.[72] Passages testifying to the antiquity and intrinsic worth of Lithuanian are quoted from the writings of the British ethnologist Robert G. Latham (1812–88), the American educationalist Benjamin W. Dwight (1816–89), the French geographer Elisée Reclus (1830–1905), the English archaeologist and philologist Isaac Taylor (1829–1901) and the philosopher Immanuel Kant (1724–1804), prefaced by the apparently anodyne formulation, 'The following fragmentary quotations from eminent linguistic scholars will show the value and importance of the Lithuanian language to the culture of the world.' At the end, the real motivation is revealed: 'The above quotations from the renowned linguistic scholars of the 19th century substantiates [sic] the fact that the world today would be greatly enriched with an independent Lithuania and with its ancient and important language in the field of linguistic science.'[73] These renowned long-departed scholars are thus made to lend their authority to the cause of Lithuanian independence: because they have recognised the unique worth of the language, the argument goes, the world should recognise the uniqueness and independence of its speakers. Quite why Thurston should draw attention to the fact that his authorities all belong to the last century – a factor that would lessen his authority in the eyes of contemporary academics – is unclear: the 'oldest is best' mentality which often prevails amongst amateur scholars? The use of such outdated testimonials was no doubt forced upon Thurston by the fact that such sweeping value judgements would have been hard to find in more recent linguistic scholarship.

The last word on the consequences of the judgements of outsiders belongs to a small ethnic group in Dagestan. On learning from the anthropologist Robert Chenciner that so far as was known their language was related to no other, the people responded: 'Very well. In that case, we have two questions. First, does this mean that we are descended from monkeys? And secondly, should we declare independence?'[74]

Language-intrinsic myths

Claims centring on the perceived – or desired – characteristics of a language – its purity, its euphoniousness, the size of its vocabulary, its expressiveness and so forth – constitute the *language-intrinsic myths*. The basic repertoire of language-intrinsic myths remains strikingly constant from one nation to another, and indeed myths of this kind are if anything more readily transferable than language-extrinsic myths. Certain language-intrinsic myths are mutually exclusive, in competition, as it were; thus, a writer who boasts of the purity of his language will probably not also vaunt the copiousness of its vocabulary, nor will the myth of monosyllabicity be invoked in the same breath as that of elegance. The particular myths selected tend to mirror current cultural and linguistic rivalries.[75] Although such myths still bulk large in popular consciousness, they tend to be invoked less in the discourse of contemporary nation-building in eastern Europe and the former Soviet Union than language-extrinsic myths, where the language = *ethnie* equation is more apparent, an issue we shall return to below. A second factor which may be contributing to their relegation to the sidelines is the ever wider awareness of the doctrine of linguistic relativity. Up to the end of the eighteenth century it was accepted that some languages (notably Greek and Latin) were intrinsically superior to others, and much energy was devoted to rescuing 'inferior' languages, either by demonstrating that they too possessed the prized features of the superior languages, or alternatively by redefining the shibboleths of superiority. With the advent of Romanticism, linguistic and cultural diversity were celebrated as manifestations of the diverse

Volksgeister, and gradually, in a process extending well into the twentieth century, scholars learnt to think of languages as different but equal. The equality of languages is one of the fundamental tenets of contemporary linguistics, such that people with even minimal exposure to the beliefs of linguistics professionals are likely to share it, and consequently to disavow language-intrinsic myths and any claims founded upon them to a far greater extent than is the case with language-extrinsic myths.

1. Myth of euphoniousness: 'our language is more harmonious than others'.

Like most of the language-intrinsic myths, the myth of euphoniousness plays only a minor part in the discourse of Georgian linguistic nationalism. Even Chaganava restricts her comments on 'harmony' to the forms of the letters.[76] Might this reflect some unwritten item of popular belief about the harshness of Georgian? With its abundant repertoire of ejectives, affricates and fricatives, and its frequent complex consonant clusters, Georgian presents an initially formidable aspect to speakers of many other languages, although the difficulties are more apparent than real. Kita Tschenkéli, the Georgian diaspora scholar already mentioned (p. 186 above), seeks euphoniousness not in the phonemic inventory but in the intonation pattern, quoting two earlier philologists, the Russian scholar A. Dirr and the German scholar Hugo Schuchardt: 'Georgian speech runs along like murmuring water' (Dirr) and 'the accentuation is like the sea after a storm' (Schuchardt).[77]

2. Myth of unique expressiveness and untranslatability: 'our language is capable of expressing all concepts, even the most technical, whereas other languages cannot adequately translate from ours'.

Perhaps the most drastic version of this claim is exemplified in Georg Philipp Harsdörffer's challenge (1644) to speakers of foreign languages to translate a series of German verses describing animal cries:

> Die Lerche tirieret ihr tiretilier,
> Es binken die Finken den Buhlen allhier,
> Die Frösche koachsen und wachsen in Lachen,
> Reckrecken und strecken sich lustig zu machen.[78]

Given that even Lewis Carroll's 'Jabberwocky', not to mention the writings of James Joyce, has been translated effectively into a great range of other languages, the claim of untranslatability nowadays finds short shrift. Somewhat more persuasive is the subtler approach of Cooper (1685):

Those matters which are written wittily and succinctly in our language are to be translated into other languages with considerable difficulty, and it is scarcely possible to avoid weakening their style and vigour of wit, whereas matters written in other languages may be translated into our language much more easily, with the same elegance and the same degree of vigour of wit.[79]

A short passage from one of Marr's writings quoted by Chaganava runs as follows:

The Georgian language is able to transmit the concepts of abstract thought fully and without distortion. The entire output of both Asian and European culture can easily be translated into Georgian . . . Georgian readily appropriates the thought of neighbouring and foreign peoples and renders their expressions. Georgian is one of the world's most developed languages.

Although Marr does not say outright that other languages are unable to do this, the implication is clear, and is driven home in the final sentence. Marr provides one of the mottoes for Tsibakhashvili's grammar of Georgian:

Everything that can be expressed in any language on Earth is expressed in Georgian . . .
   Georgian embodies every thought highly artistically, without distortion or misrepresentation . . .
   Georgian is so rich that it is a language of world significance in its inner nature.[80]

The first and last sentences had already figured as the motto of Sh. V. Dzidziguri's little book about Georgian,[81] and no doubt in countless other works besides. Lurking unstated behind such claims is an assumption of superiority: 'Whereas the other perceives and expresses reality only partially, we can do so perfectly.' This almost instinctive feeling has lost a lot of ground amongst the educated as the notion of linguistic equality has become ever more widespread.

3. Myth of lexical copiousness: 'our language has a larger vocabulary than others'.

Renaissance scholars marvelled at the wealth of vocabulary they found in Latin and Greek, and compared it ruefully with what they regarded as the lamentably underdeveloped vocabularies of their own vernaculars. Heartened by Cicero's story of how Latin lacked philosophical terminology when he began to write, but (thanks to his attention) became as rich and expressive a medium for philosophical reflection as Greek, sixteenth-century scholars vied for the title of the 'Cicero' of their respective languages, creating new terms for technical and literary domains alike. It became a common complaint in sixteenth- and early seventeenth-century England, for instance, that ordinary citizens could no longer understand literature in their own language on account of the ubiquitous latinate neologisms. The myth persists to this day, in that many an educated

English-speaker 'knows' that English has the largest vocabulary of any language in the world, even though s/he also knows that by no means all these words are available to all speakers.[82] Equally, the English and their neighbours have been aware ever since the sixteenth century that this rich vocabulary has been built up at the expense of lexical purity: English has borrowed extensively from the numerous languages its speakers have encountered in the course of their history. Stigmatised as a 'gallimaufrey', a 'mingle-mangle' and 'the scum of languages', English has patently not been able to lay claim to linguistic purity in the same way as some of its neighbours. Georgian writers, although they revel in the expressiveness and untranslatability of their language, do not single out lexical copiousness as a prized feature of their language. Is this on account of its incompatibility with the myth of purity, or because of a competing and dominant myth about the superior lexical copiousness of Russian? Declarations concerning the wealth of the Russian vocabulary are not far to seek.[83]

> 4. *Myth of purity: 'our language has maintained its original vocabulary and grammar as handed down by our ancestors, pure and uncontaminated by outside influences'.*

The only language which in sixteenth-century eyes could claim true purity was Hebrew, the sole language to have escaped the consequences of the confusion of tongues at the Tower of Babel (or so it was argued). Even Latin, revered though it was as the language of scholarship, contained a number of transparent borrowings from Greek; and as for the vernaculars, most were acknowledged to be swarming with loanwords reflecting their tumultuous histories. English, for instance, was, in the words of the Swiss doctor and polymath Conrad Gesner, 'the most mixed and corrupt of all present-day languages; for initially the ancient British language [i.e. a Celtic dialect] was partly obliterated by the rule of the Saxons, partly corrupted; and then it borrowed large numbers of words from French'.[84] Apart from the antiquaries, scholars concerned with ancient texts who looked back nostalgically to an age when their languages were pure and 'unmixed', it was only German- and Dutch-speakers who made great play of the status of their language as 'a pure untouched virgin'.

Interestingly, in the light of the obvious ethnic overtones of all such argumentation, Georgian writers remain silent on this issue. A certain degree of purism, and a strong awareness of the status of loanwords versus calques was a conspicuous element in Soviet language planning.[85] Around 1990 there was a move to replace some Russian loanwords with coinages of Georgian stock, a common corollary of nationalist movements.[86] Significantly, the account of the activities of the Department for the Cultivation of Georgian Speech (*k'art'uli metqvelebis kulturis ganqop'ileba*) of the A. Chikobava Institute of Linguistics of the Georgian Academy of Sciences published in 1991 in honour of the Institute's fiftieth anniversary does not so much as mention the Russian language, although 'purification' (*sits'minde*) of Georgian is alluded to. It may be that the reprinting in the same issue of an old article by V. T'op'uria on the extirpation of a Russian syntactic construction from Georgian is an oblique indication of the sympathies of the Institute.

Anecdotal confirmation of the strength of popular belief in a largely 'pure' Georgian vocabulary comes from a scholar involved in the compilation of the eight-volume *Ganmartebit'i lek'sikoni*: 'One could never indicate *all* the borrowings from foreign sources because people would get too angry.' Thus, the widely held popular etymology of Georgian *t'avaziani*, 'polite', from Georgian *t'avi*, 'self', serves to confirm the Georgian self-perception as an intrinsically courteous people, the notion of selfhood being built into the very word for 'polite'. Its actual derivation (from Arabic) would be 'unacceptable'. At an early editorial meeting attended by A. Chikobava, G. Tsereteli and other highly regarded philologists it was decided not to mention the presumed foreign origin of such long-naturalised words as *puri*, 'bread', and *lukma*, 'bit, piece, crumb', partly because their immediate provenance was unknown, and partly in order not to anger people unnecessarily.

Elsewhere in the post-Soviet states, notably in Ukraine, movements to purify the language of Russian elements have made considerable headway. At the Second International Conference of Ukrainianists in L'viv (1993) a purist attack on the allegedly Russian preposition *po* aroused angry interventions from the audience. In general, linguistic purism is a perennial concomitant of nationalism, and particularly of nationalisms with a pronounced ethnic component. Even in present-day Belarus, as elsewhere in the post-Soviet states, the issue of Russification is a subject of concern. In a little book by S. Stankevich, the history of the process in Belarusian is traced in detail, and Russicisms in morphology, syntax, idiom and vocabulary (including some involving the preposition *po/pa*) are catalogued. The state of the language today is contrasted with its historical status as the official language of the Grand Duchy of Lithuania – thereby extending across a huge tract of eastern Europe – in the early modern period.[87]

Conclusion

Why are language myths so important in the discourse of Georgian nationalism? As we saw at the outset, oral components play a large part in Georgian culture, but this would seem to be a precondition for developing a language-oriented form of national consciousness, context rather than cause. The answer has much to do with divergent perceptions of language history and ethnohistory. As a good many Georgians will readily acknowledge in conversation, and occasionally in print, apart from a brief Golden Age in the twelfth century their ethnohistory does not provide a satisfactory self-image, whether one focuses on the past – subjugation by Arabs, Mongols, Turks, Persians, Russians – or on the present – civil and inter-ethnic conflict. Furthermore, the creation of rival ethnohistories by scholars seeking to strengthen Ossetian and Abkhaz claims to statehood[88] has had the effect of narrowing the scope of the term 'Georgian', a process hastened by the Zviadist slogan, 'Georgia for the Georgians'. From meaning 'all who live under Georgian sovereignty', approximately in the way that 'Russian' was used to mean 'Soviet citizen' in the West before the break-up of the USSR, the term *k'art'velebi*, 'Georgians', is increasingly being used in the restricted sense of 'ethnic Georgians'. The extreme nationalist claim to exclusive rights to a Georgian identity is now backfiring as the marginalised minorities create new identities for themselves and secessionist movements arise (with or without Russian assistance). If, as many Western observers predict, the Mingrelians travel the same path, that will be a worse blow to Georgian identity than any previously suffered. Only brief glimpses of a glorious past remain – a successful challenge to the might of the Roman Empire under Parsman II in the second century, the Golden Age under David the Builder and T'amar in the twelfth and thirteenth centuries. Attempts to boost morale by focusing on these episodes, frequent during the first few years of independence, now tend to meet at best with scepticism, at worst with derision.

It is in this climate that language history finds a role, functioning as a substitute for an unsatisfactory ethnohistory. The new and hotly contested picture of distinct ethnic identities stretching back millennia, united only fitfully and under compulsion, gives way to the cherished image of harmonious voluntary coexistence in the common heritage at once symbolised and created by the Georgian language. The most prized aspect of Georgian national character, according to the national self-image – tolerance – is transferred from ethnic relations, where it is patently at variance with recent history, to linguistic relations. In one sphere after another, language history permits the construction of a more favourable picture of the past than ethnohistory:

- Millennia of subjugation by foreign powers are replaced by a lengthy history of linguistic independence, beginning with the earliest written monuments at the very latest in the fifth century AD, a good two centuries earlier than the earliest texts in English (or for that matter in French or German), as

Georgians take pleasure in pointing out. Other readings take the history of written Georgian back to the third century BC, to the era of the mythical creation of the Georgian alphabet by King P´arnavaz; more extreme readings still would see in the Georgian alphabet the ancestor of the Egyptian or Phoenician scripts, or even of all alphabetic writing systems.

- Even if the Georgians themselves have been downtrodden and subjugated, they can comfort themselves with the thought that their language was once dominant throughout Europe, older than and therefore superior to the languages of the imperialistic Indo-Europeans, and will one day again be triumphant: a messianic, teleological view of ethnohistory replaces widespread feelings of despair. As the poet Vakhtang Gorganeli put it, 'Is not our Georgian language / A monument of our refusal to yield?'[89]
- The language is seen to reflect back the most highly prized character trait of the Georgians, tolerance. Extremists would argue that the very forms of the Georgian letters encapsulate cosmic-astronomical verities long since lost to other scripts. Both readings support the view that Georgian is in some sense more 'natural' than other languages.
- The picture of foreign interest in the language balances the feelings of abandonment and despair which arise out of their recent history. Many Georgians believe that at the Malta summit of 1991 the then US president, George Bush, conceded Georgia to Russia's sphere of influence, and in this way they rationalise what they regard as the otherwise inexplicable Western failure to intervene or even speak out in the face of clear evidence of Russian involvement in Abkhazia. Interest in their language on the part of foreign philologists serves to counteract this sense of abandonment, although it may also raise unrealistic expectations based upon an exaggerated view of the political influence of Western scholars.

Georgia is thus a case of an *ethnie* looking to its language for an alternative history and source of symbols at a time when ethnohistory fails to provide them or, rather, provides the 'wrong' story.

This account raises several issues, some specific to the Georgian case, others of a more general theoretical nature. For one thing, the materials on which this article is based are largely from nationalist sources from shortly before, during and after Zviad Gamsakhurdia's period in power. To what extent is linguistic nationalism a feature of nationalist discourse amongst followers of Shevardnadze? Have they managed to appropriate it, or is it perceived as being too closely linked with the deposed president?[90] Secondly, although it would be easy to recast Georgian linguistic history with Georgian in the role of aggressor, this possibility has apparently not entered into the consciousness of those who have cultivated linguistic nationalism. One would predict that, if such a version of Georgian-language history entered circulation, linguistic nationalism would be downplayed. More broadly, one might predict that, where linguistic nationalism is prominent, there is a strong likelihood that language history and ethnohistory are tacitly perceived as being at variance, and that the myths provided by language history are considered to conform more closely to the image of the *ethnie* which the purveyors of nation-building discourse are seeking to reinforce.

Transcending all these possibilities is the greater issue of the nature of the nationalism which prevails in a given area. It could be argued that there is a correlation between the type of nationalism and the kind of language myth favoured. Broadly speaking, the Georgian examples considered here emphasise language-extrinsic myths; language-intrinsic ones, in contrast, play only a minor role. In recent Western history the reverse is true. To take one instance, the preferred language myths in the discourse of nation-building in Ireland in the latter part of the nineteenth century singled out language-intrinsic features such as euphony, expressiveness and logical structure. Language-extrinsic myths, frequent up until around 1800, had disappeared almost totally from view by the middle of the century.[91] Two factors are no doubt at work in this. One, and a very powerful one, is the spread of linguistic orthodoxy in the form of comparative philology, with its emphasis upon the Indo-European family of languages and the position of Irish Gaelic as one of the daughter languages of Indo-European. The widespread currency of this tenet of linguistic orthodoxy thus served to undermine those language-extrinsic myths which sought to affirm the historical uniqueness of Gaelic as the language of Adam and Eve.

Secondly, however, the relatively inclusive type of nationalism adopted in western Europe ruled out the language-extrinsic myths with their implicit language = *ethnie* equation. Ireland, of all countries, many of its patriots English-speakers who knew no Gaelic, could not afford an exclusive brand of linguistic nationalism. Only the language-intrinsic myths, which could be claimed indifferently by any of the speakers of the language in question, regardless of their ethnic origin, lent themselves to use in this context. In eastern Europe and the former Soviet Union, where an exclusive, largely ethnic form of nationalism tends to prevail, it is to be expected that language-extrinsic myths will be favoured in order, via the language = *ethnie* equation, to strengthen the self-image of the *ethnie*. As the type of nationalism changes, veering from relatively inclusive to rela-

tively exclusive, or vice versa, the type of language myth selected to reinforce the sense of identity will change too.

INCLUSIVE NATIONALISM ↔ *LANGUAGE-INTRINSIC MYTHS*
↕   ↕
EXCLUSIVE NATIONALISM↔*LANGUAGE-EXTRINSIC MYTHS*

Thus, in the middle of the twentieth century it suited the shapers of identity in both the Soviet Union and the British Commonwealth of Nations
to emphasise the intrinsic virtues of Russian and English respectively, the
common heritage and bond of a multitude of different *ethnies*. In present-
day Georgia, however, a disjunction manifestly exists between two forms
of discourse. On the one hand, government sources and the Tbilisi intelligentsia continue to perpetuate the inclusive historical myth of the
Georgians as a tolerant people and of the traditional ethnic harmony of
the country as a whole; but at the same time the language-extrinsic myths
are being deployed to create an image of Georgian identity which is exclusive rather than inclusive in nature. The attitudes implicit in the language-
extrinsic myths are thus at variance with the official statements about
tolerance, harmony and so forth. To say that such statements are untrue
would hardly be fair: many very sincere Georgians believe them utterly
and do their best to live by them. But precisely because the type of nationalism encoded in language myths is covert rather than overt, they are a
better indicator of the views which prevail amongst the shapers of the
national self-image and should be given more attention than they have
been hitherto by students of nationalism and the discourse of nation-
building.

9 Language policy and ethnic relations in Uzbekistan

As elsewhere in the Soviet borderland states, an important watershed in the nation-building process in Uzbekistan was the adoption in October 1989 of the law 'On the State Language', which granted Uzbek the status of the sole state language within the Uzbek Soviet Socialist Republic. Lying at the heart of the new language politics were issues of power and status rather than communication, for, as Donald Horowitz has pointed out, language is a potent symbol of both new-found group dignity and status.[1] Although the new law made Russian the 'language of inter-ethnic communication', it also required employees in the state sector as well as those serving the population to command enough Uzbek for the fulfilment of job responsibilities. Owing to material and organisational constraints, however, the pace of implementation of language legislation inevitably slowed. In December 1995, more than six years after the passage of the original legislation, a revised version of the Law on the State Language was adopted. The revised edition no longer made knowledge of Uzbek compulsory for public sector employees, yet it also abolished Russian's special status, putting that medium on a par with all other 'foreign' languages.

This chapter examines language policy in Uzbekistan and assesses how legislation has reconstituted ethnic relations between the titular group and key non-titular minorities. The first part outlines the general evolution of language policy in Uzbekistan since 1989, comparing the significant ways in which the first edition of the language law diverges from the revised edition. The second part analyses the responses of the Russian and Tajik communities to their redefined positions within Uzbekistan and the extent to which they have integrated themselves into the nationalising state. The third part examines the attitudes of the three communities towards specific provisions of the language law on the basis of results from a public opinion survey carried out by the author in conjunction with a Tashkent sociological centre amongst roughly equal groups of Uzbeks, Russians and Tajiks in June 1996.

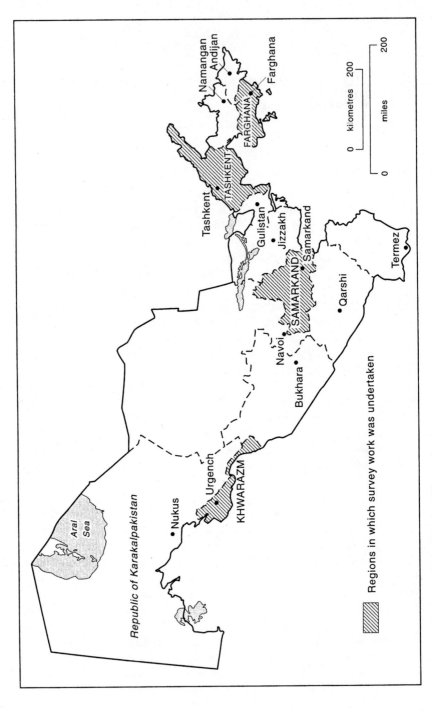

Figure 9.1. Uzbekistan and its regions

Language legislation

As the primary purpose of the first edition of Uzbekistan's Law on the State Language was to raise the status of the titular group, its provisions primarily addressed issues of language function (delimiting spheres of use) rather than language structure (standardization, development of the lexicon, etc.). In addition to widening the role played by Uzbek in society, other central aims of the 1989 legislation were to utilise the state language as a means of cultivating national consciousness and developing national culture; to 'de-Russify' those Uzbek elites with a weak knowledge of their 'native' language; and to promote the state language as a prominent symbol of republican sovereignty.

Although the Soviet constitution did not accord official or state status to any language,[2] Russian had been given a *de facto* pre-eminent position within the USSR to aid the creation of a universal Soviet culture and facilitate intra-union affairs. More than just the 'language of inter-ethnic communication', it was the medium of success through which one could attain a high level of education in the greatest amount of subjects and secure the greatest degree of social and professional mobility. Uzbek, on the other hand, while a fully functional language, took a clear second place to Russian in public life. The new legislation was in part a reaction to Russification and in part an indictment of the Soviet past; hence, assertive efforts to legislate the use of the Uzbek language in the public sector were viewed as necessary in the early years of independence in order to compensate for past injustices. Uzbek activists and cultural elites were the original and most fervent proponents of a new law that would raise the status of Uzbek – as well as the status of the group that spoke it – and make its use compulsory in the state sector.[3] A renaissance of the Uzbek language was therefore viewed by those groups as perhaps the best means of redistributing both cultural and political power in the republic.

Many ethnic Uzbeks also pointed to the fact that only a very small percentage of the Russian population in Uzbekistan had learned the local language as evidence of the latter's colonial attitude. Particularly from the 1930s onwards, Soviet authorities had promoted a policy of 'bilingualism', which in essence meant that non-Russians were encouraged to learn Russian while most Russians remained monolingual speakers of Russian.[4] Consequently, only 4.6 per cent of Uzbekistani Russians claimed fluency in the vernacular as a second language in 1989, the year of the final Soviet census, despite the fact that many had lived in Uzbekistan for decades. Linguistic inequality had persisted despite clear Uzbek demographic superiority: although Uzbeks had always been the dominant ethnic group in Uzbekistan, by 1989 they constituted 71.4 per cent of Uzbekistan's population, the vast majority of whom regarded Uzbek as their primary language. Russians, on the other hand, accounted for only 8.3 per cent of the country's population in that same year.

For their part, 22.3 per cent of Uzbeks had claimed fluency in Russian as a second language in 1989. However, Soviet census data on fluency in a second language (a vaguely defined concept in itself) should be treated with caution as they are particularly susceptible to manipulation. Figures from the 1979 census, for example, indicated that 49.3 per cent of Uzbeks had a fluent knowledge of Russian, although the corresponding figure in 1970 had been only 14.5 per cent. This astonishing jump in knowledge of Russian amongst Uzbeks – much larger than those reported in any other republics of the USSR – was in fact most likely due to strategic over-reporting and considerations of political expediency on the part of Uzbekistani officials rather than to improved Russian skills.

The second edition of the Law on the State Language

The majority of the articles contained in the second edition of the Law on the State Language, adopted in December 1995, provide for the use of Uzbek in state administration, education, the justice system, the mass media and other spheres of public life, although care has been taken in most instances to allow for the use of 'other languages' as well.[5] As with the first edition, the second is concerned primarily with issues of language function and the tasks it should carry out rather than making changes to the language itself (status vs corpus planning). Yet, the 1995 edition of the law differs from the 1989 edition in at least three noteworthy respects:

The status of Russian While the 1989 edition of the Uzbekistani language law accorded Russian a secondary but protected status, the 1995 edition puts it on a par with all languages other than Uzbek, despite the fact that Russian remains the language of convenience for the majority of the country's non-titular population as well as a significant proportion of ethnic Uzbek elites. As Asqar Khalmuradav, the chairman of the parliamentary committee responsible for overseeing the implementation of the law, has remarked, 'The first edition gave Russian a special significance, but now this language will be used in the same way as the languages of the other nations and peoples living in Uzbekistan.'[6]

From the point of view of linguistic reform, Uzbekistan is unique amongst the Central Asian states in that neither its constitution nor its revised language law makes any special provision for the Russian language whatsoever, either as an official language or as the language of inter-ethnic communication. By contrast, in Kazakhstan, where non-titulars account for a greater share of the population, the trend since 1995 has been to upgrade the status of Russian by enshrining it as an official language in the new constitution. In Kyrgyzstan, President Akaev and his supporters have been heavily promoting a similar constitutional amendment, although the parliament has thus far failed to pass it. However, Akaev signed a decree in June 1994 that made Russian an official language in predominantly Russian-speaking areas as well as in 'vital areas of the national economy', and the country's language law also accords Russian the status of the language of 'inter-ethnic communication'.[7]

The elimination of any status for Russian in the new edition stands in sharp contrast to the original law, which had granted wide-reaching powers to that language and expressly guaranteed the 'development and free usage of Russian as the language of inter-ethnic communication of the peoples of the USSR'. As a consequence, Russian figured prominently in the text of the 1989 law, warranting mention either directly or in its capacity as the language of inter-ethnic communication no fewer than thirty-two times.[8] By contrast, the revised text mentions the Russian language only once in a relatively insignificant provision, noting that citizens are able to receive notarised documents in that language by special request (Article 12). Furthermore, whereas the 1989 edition did not specify that state sector employees were required to know Russian in its capacity as the language of inter-ethnic communication (although Article 27 prohibited 'responsible officials' from refusing citizens' petitions, complaints and suggestions on the grounds that they did not know the state language or Russian), the revised law leaves no doubt that monolingual Uzbek-speakers do not need to learn a second language.

Deregulation The second edition of the Law on the State Language is markedly more compact than the first edition, having eliminated Russian's role as the medium of inter-ethnic communication and further entrenched the hegemony of the Uzbek language within the state. Furthermore, the revised text seeks to deregulate the use of language in Uzbekistan to a significant degree by removing many of the specific provisions included in the 1989 law. Perhaps most notably, the new version discarded the controversial Article 4, which had required managers (and workers, according to the Russian text) employed in the state sector as well as those serving the population to command enough Uzbek for the fulfilment of job responsibilities. Similarly, managers of state and other organisations no longer 'carry personal responsibility' for the observance of the requirements of the language law within their areas of competence, as stipulated under Article 28 of the old law.[9]

In another instance of streamlining, the new law covers the issue of education in one article (Article 6), whereas the first edition had devoted six articles to language-related issues within the educational system (e.g.

the language of instruction at various levels, Uzbek and Russian as compulsory subjects, the presentation and defence of dissertations, etc.). Unlike the first, the second edition makes no provision for the study of the Arabic-based script, which was in use throughout the region until the late 1920s and is still regarded as a potent symbol of Islam. The removal of this article was particularly logical in light of the decision taken by Uzbekistani authorities in September 1993 to replace the Soviet-era Cyrillic script by the Latin (in 1928–9 the Arabic script was replaced by the Latin script, which was in turn replaced by the Cyrillic script in 1939–40).

Slowdown in implementation As in other post-Soviet Central Asian states, the sobering economic and social concomitants of independence have required officials in Uzbekistan to back-pedal on the implementation of language legislation. Originally, all provisions of the language law – including those relating to statistical and financial documentation and knowledge of Uzbek by employees in the state sector – were to have been fully introduced by the end of 1997. The revised law, however, stipulates that Articles 9 and 10, which concern the use of the state language for the work of state and administrative organs and for office work and statistical and financial documentation, respectively, are to go into full effect only from September 2005, to coincide with the deadline established for the completion of the transition to the Latin script. Uzbekistani officials have also been forced to re-think the original timetable set out for the introduction of the new script: according to the 1993 law, the Latin script was to be phased in gradually over a seven-year period, with work being completed by September 2000, at which time the republican law of 1940 decreeing the switch from the Latin to the Cyrillic script was to be rendered null and void.[10] In June 1995, however, a parliamentary resolution pushed the deadline back five years to September 2005 on the grounds that the necessary preparatory measures for the switch had not been completed within the established time period.[11]

Aside from the fact that changes in patterns of language use are not easily legislated and require a significant number of years to accomplish, the Uzbekistani government has been limited in its ability to implement linguistic reform owing to a panoply of organisational and material constraints, such as a shortage of qualified Uzbek teaching staff and equipment, the lack of a modernised terminology and inadequate translations of scientific and technical literature.[12] Khalmuradav has admitted that the state has thus far been unable to work out quick and effective methods of teaching Uzbek as a foreign language.[13] The lack of standardisation in Uzbek may also have been a factor slowing down implementation, for, as with the first edition, the revised text expressly stipulates that the 'scientific rules and norms' governing the use of literary Uzbek must be observed (Article 7). (Despite the promotion of a standard written and spoken Uzbek language over the last seventy years, there are still many dialects in use throughout the country.)[14] Finally, as Russian remains the lingua franca for many Uzbekistani elites, particularly in business, science and the professions, a more rapid pace of implementation would undoubtedly have given rise to disruptions in the work of the state and concomitant negative economic consequences. As William Fierman has observed, problems in implementing linguistic reform have led the regime to give precedence to 'symbolic' over 'substantive' measures.[15] As a result, like the early Soviet regime, the Karimov government has been zealous in its efforts to overhaul the country's toponymy and eliminate the Russian language from public view.

The politics of linguistic reform

In a move which vividly illustrated the growing authoritarianism of the current Uzbekistani regime, the draft of the new edition of the law was not published or laid open to public discussion before its adoption by the parliament in December 1995. In 1989, by contrast, the presidium of the Uzbek SSR Supreme Soviet had passed a decree several months before the law's adoption requiring the publication of the draft bill as a means of setting in motion a republic-wide discussion.[16] The draft bill proved highly controversial, and the ensuing passionate public debate played a crucial role in the decision ultimately to adopt a stronger language law that considerably reduced the role of Russian in comparison with the draft.[17]

Noting that 1989 was a year of growing Uzbek nationalism and violent inter-ethnic conflict (in May of that year rioting had broken out between Uzbeks and the local Meskhetian Turk population, resulting in more than 100 deaths), Uzbekistani president Karimov stated in 1996 that the regime had adopted the first language law under duress, with the consequence that it had 'in fact infringed the rights of part of the population, especially those of Russian-speakers'.[18] Similarly, William Fierman has argued that it was a sense of *Realpolitik* rather than conviction that prompted President Karimov to lend his support in 1989 to the stronger version of the language law that downgraded Russian's status.[19] Whatever his true convictions at the time, there can be little doubt that the fully revised 1995 edition – which eliminates any special status for Russian whatsoever rather than simply reducing its role – fully bears Karimov's imprint and unqualified stamp of approval. Hence, despite Karimov's protestations to the contrary, with hindsight it appears more likely that he was in fact genuine in his support of the stronger version of the bill advocated in 1989 by the nationally minded cultural elite in so far as he viewed it as a means of proving his newly found nationalist credentials.

The second edition of the language law was adopted a full six years and two months after the passage of Uzbekistan's first one, although the newly independent regime had originally planned to revise the law in 1992.[20] Official statements have not gone far towards explaining this delay: according to Khalmuradav, the first law was revised because it contained out-of-date phrases, such as the 'Uzbek SSR' and 'the Russian language – the language of inter-ethnic communication', as well as phrases that smacked of communist ideology.[21] President Karimov's explanation that it was only 'the change in the attitudes of the people' that enabled the Uzbekistani parliament to amend the law appears particularly disingenuous in light of the authoritarian methods his regime has been employing with particular vigour, beginning with the crackdown on the political opposition in 1992.[22] Although only speculative, a probable explanation for the delay is that ruling elites wanted to achieve a certain distance from authorities in Moscow before eliminating the *de jure* position of the Russian language in the country, which, if removed earlier, could have been interpreted as an undisguised affront on Uzbekistani–Russian relations. As such, the demoted status of Russian reflects Uzbekistan's heightened independent stance in regard to the Russian Federation and CIS structures. Moreover, the premature downgrading of Russian might have hastened the departure from the country of skilled Russophone specialists, who were already emigrating at a rapid rate.

Uzbekistan's original language law was adopted when that republic's leadership still envisaged itself as part of a revamped union. In the context of independence and economic crisis, however, the systematic implementation of language legislation has naturally become less of a priority. This approach is all the more understandable given that demographic momentum, current educational trends and the passage of time are all bound to further entrench the pre-eminent position of the state language within Uzbekistan.

Ethnic minority responses to language reform and the nationalising state

Russian responses: collective action, exit or integration?

Transformed from elder brother to erstwhile coloniser, Uzbekistani Russians have been experiencing an especially acute sense of psychological unease as a result of the collapse of the Soviet empire, for it was their language that had been the tongue of progress and social mobility and their culture that had formed the basis of Soviet society.

This is all the more true in Uzbekistan where, despite significant back-tracking in the pace of implementation, the shift to the titular language has been faster and fuller than elsewhere in Central Asia. This can be par-tially attributed to the fact that, even before the collapse of the USSR, Uzbek was the dominant language in the republic's press and mass media, and the majority of the republic's children were studying in schools with Uzbek as the medium of tuition.[23] While less prevalent in higher education, Uzbek was still in greater use than the titular languages of the other Central Asian republics within their respective higher educa-tional systems.[24] Consequently, whereas Russian is the first language of nearly two-thirds of urban Kazaks,[25] a clear majority of urban Uzbeks have either an excellent or good command of Uzbek. As already noted, demographic trends are only fortifying Uzbek's position.

None the less, the Russian language still acts as a unifying force between disparate cultures in Uzbekistan, as in the rest of Central Asia. The diminution of its status, however, has brought differences between indigenous and settler cultures into sharp relief. As is explored below, the responses of Uzbekistani Russians in the face of the political and social vicissitudes that have accompanied the collapse of empire have not neces-sarily broken down into the all too neat categories of 'exit, voice and loyalty'.[26]

Collective action While language and other nationalising policies have created a sense of grievance amongst Uzbekistan's Russian popula-tion, as will be discussed below, it has not been a sufficient condition to spur a politics of reaction in defence of minority interests. According to resource mobilisation theory, would-be activists require, *inter alia*, polit-ical opportunity and material resources in order to facilitate political mobilisation.[27] Uzbekistan is in effect an authoritarian state and, as such, has placed severe restrictions on the ability of ethnic minorities to successfully launch collective action. Despite constitutional guarantees, Uzbekistani citizens are in fact unable to exercise a number of basic civil rights, such as freedom of speech, association, assembly and political participation. As a consequence, Russians and other minorities who may harbour a sense of deprivation are unable to express it, much less mobilise in order to achieve collective rights.

Given the prevailing repressive political backdrop coupled with the over-arching demographic superiority of the Uzbeks, it is not surprising that the Russian community in Uzbekistan has failed to put forward political

Table 9.1 *Net out-migration of Russians from Central Asia to the Russian Federation (1989–1996)*

	Total number of Russians at beginning of 1989 (× 1,000)	1989	1990	1991	1992	1993	1994	1995	1996	Total number of Russians at beginning of 1997 (× 1,000)[1]	Net Russian out-migration 1989–1996 (× 1,000)	Percentage by which Russian population decreased 1989–1996
Tajikistan	388		382.6	350.9	336.5	289.6	248.7	222.9	200.5	185.4		
Decrease by		5.4	31.7	14.4	46.9	40.9	25.8	22.4	15.1		202.6	
% of Russian population	1.4%		8.3%	4.1%	13.9%	14.1%	10.4%	10.0%	7.5%			52.2%
Uzbekistan	1653		1635.3	1595.1	1567.3	1502.7	1452.0	1358.5	1294.3	1271.3		
Decrease by		17.7	40.2	27.8	64.6	50.7	93.5	64.2	23.0		381.7	
% of Russian population	1.1%		2.5%	1.7%	4.1%	3.4%	6.4%	4.7%	1.8%			23.1%
Kyrgyzstan	917		913.2	897.1	881.7	840.2	773.7	730.8	717.4	710.1		
Decrease by		3.8	16.1	15.4	41.5	66.5	42.9	13.4	7.3		206.9	
% of Russian population	0.4%		1.8%	1.7%	4.7%	7.9%	5.5%	1.9%	1.0%			22.6%
Turkmenistan	334		331.1	326.7	322.0	311.2	304.5	291.5	279.3	265.3		
Decrease by		2.9	4.4	4.7	10.8	6.7	13.0	12.2	14.0		68.7	
% of Russian population	0.9%		1.3%	1.4%	3.4%	2.2%	4.3%	4.2%	5.0%			20.6%
Kazakstan	6228		6202.1	6165.9	6140.3	6058.0	5953.6	5719.3	5575.5	5477.3		
Decrease by		25.9	36.2	25.6	82.3	104.4	234.3	143.8	98.2		750.7	
% of Russian population	0.4%		0.6%	0.4%	1.3%	1.7%	3.9%	2.5%	1.8%			12.1%

Notes:

Calculations are based on the 1989 census and data provided by State Committee on Statistics of the Russian Federation.

[1] Russian population figures after 1989 do not take into account natural population increase.

demands to the state or even press for greater cultural autonomy. There are no Russian-based political parties in Uzbekistan, and Uzbekistani Russians were permitted to establish their own cultural centre only long after other ethnic minorities had already done so; two years later, the centre had still not managed to begin publishing its own newspaper.[28] A dearth of leadership skills, organisational structures and experience in forming social movements are other possible reasons for the low level of political activity on the part of Uzbekistani Russians.

Migration Faced with growing economic and social pressures, migration to Russia has been the response of choice for a significant number of Central Asian Russians. Since the collapse of the USSR (1992–6), 59 per cent of all net migration to Russia from the former Soviet republics has been from the Central Asian states; of that, 25 per cent has come from Uzbekistan in particular.[29] Ethnic Russians constituted approximately 70 per cent of all migrants from the Central Asian region to Russia between 1989 and 1996, while Tatars, Ukrainians, Belarusians, Germans and Jews accounted for most of the remainder. The net population transfer of ethnic Russians from Central Asia to Russia during that same period was equal to over 17 per cent (1.6 million people) of the ethnic Russians permanently resident in the region in 1989, the year of the final Soviet census.[30] Uzbekistan registered a net loss of 381,400 ethnic Russians from 1989 to 1996, or 23.1 per cent of the Russian population resident in that republic in 1989 (table 9.1).

While language policy has been but one factor inducing the large-scale out-migration of ethnic Russians from Central Asia,[31] it would appear to have had a significant influence on the timing and volume of the outflow. While all of the countries in the Central Asian region had been experiencing positive net out-migration rates with the Russian Federation (a greater number leaving for the Russian Federation than arriving from that country) since the second half of the 1970s, the outflow of Russians and other non-titular groups began to accelerate rapidly in the late 1980s. The migrational boom commenced just after the adoption of language laws in all of the Central Asian republics in 1989 (save Turkmenistan, which passed its language law in May 1990). If net out-migration levels in 1989 were comparable to those in 1988, in 1990 they rose by more than 80 per cent. The outbreak of inter-ethnic violence and, in particular, the conflicts between Uzbeks and Meskhetian Turks in the Farghana valley in 1989 and between Uzbeks and Kyrgyz in 1990 were perhaps an even more important factor in spurring the exodus of Russians and other non-titulars from the region at that time. Although Russians have not been the targets of inter-ethnic violence in Central Asia, the nearness of Tajikistan for Uzbekistani and Kyrgyzstani Russians, the proximity of Afghanistan and the constant tension on the southern border has engendered a feeling of vulnerability amongst them. Other oft-cited reasons by Russian out-migrants for their departure have been economic decline and severe dis-locations in the workforce, fear for their children's future, manifestations of nationalism, growing indigenisation and cultural differences. A certain amount of migration was to have been expected in any event, given that less than one-half of Russians resident in Central Asia in 1989 were born there and were therefore lacking firm roots in the region.[32] Finally, it is worth bearing in mind that the set of factors inducing an individual to emigrate can rarely be reduced to only one or two variables.

Debates concerning the underlying causes of the outflow of Russians and other non-titular groups from the region have tended to pit those who argue that the emigration has been economically determined against those who contend that ethnopolitical and ethnosocial factors have played a more important role. The former point of view has been advo-cated most strongly by leading members of the ruling regimes of the Central Asian states (Kyrgyzstan and Tajikistan excepted), who have pointed to the relatively low levels of net out-migration of Russians from the more prosperous Baltic states – despite the introduction of exclusion-ary citizenship laws there – as evidence to support their argument. At the other end of the continuum, nationalist-minded Russian groups as well as some titular elites have asserted that the exodus of the non-titular popula-tion is the direct consequence of the discriminatory policies being carried out by the Central Asian leaderships.

Such a polarised debate underemphasises the *interplay* of economic and ethnopolitical factors, and, in particular, the ways in which national-ising policies can directly impinge on perceptions of wage expectations and economic security. Certainly a young, skilled Uzbekistani Russian who believes his or her chances for professional advancement are limited by virtue of ethnicity rather than ability is unlikely to place great store in a future in that state. Moreover, while economic arguments may take precedence in spurring migration from poorer to wealthier countries (as in the case of the ethnic Germans leaving Central Asia for Germany), the ethnocratic impulses of newly independent states would appear to play a crucial if not primary role in determining out-migration trends when (a) the country of destination of the disaffected minority is only margin-ally more prosperous (or less prosperous) than the country of origin and (b) the dominant culture of the nationalising state is apprehended by the ethnic minority as an alien and 'backward' one.

Particularly since 1996, however, the stream of migrants from all the Central Asian states except Turkmenistan has decreased substantially, as

Central Asian Russians have become fully aware of the hardships that await them in their 'historic homeland'. Many emigrants have resettled in neglected rural areas of Russia, where conditions have proved particularly inhospitable for these former urban professionals. New arrivals have been known to wait months to receive housing, employment and social services. Moreover, emigrants have reported being labelled as outsiders by locals, who 'exclude them from the common ethnic and thus civic community'.[33] Indeed, Russians in Central Asia have frequently described themselves and the particular values they hold (e.g. drinking less, working harder, stronger family orientation) as 'different' from those held by their co-ethnics in Russia. In certain regions of Russia, especially those with labour surpluses, the newcomers have been regarded as intruders and have been particularly vulnerable targets of criminal activity.[34] Perhaps an even more logical explanation for the recent drop in out-migration from Central Asia is simply that the most mobile and skilled Russians for whom emigration has posed the fewest difficulties and the greatest benefits have already left the region.[35] Tatiana Regent, the head of the Russian Federal Migration Service, has noted that Russia's economic problems and the war in Chechnya have also contributed to the decline.[36] Yet, despite the reduction in numbers, a certain proportion of Central Asia's non-titular population is likely to continue its exit from the region into the next millennium, albeit on a much smaller scale.

Assimilation While the Central Asian states have registered unprecedented net outflows of Russians and other Russophone minorities in recent years, the stream of out-migrants has still been smaller than many observers had initially anticipated. As migrational flows have dropped off, particularly beginning in 1995–6, it has become clear that the majority of Russians resident in Central Asia in 1989 would remain in that region, at least for the time being. The decision to stay, however, is not necessarily a portent of assimilation, which David Laitin has defined as 'the process of adoption of the ever-changing cultural practices of dominant society with the goal of crossing a fluid cultural boundary separating [minorities] from dominant society'.[37]

Separated by a cultural and religious chasm, the Uzbek and Russian communities of Uzbekistan have traditionally lived in relative isolation from each other. The majority of Uzbekistani Russians migrated to the region during Soviet rule, where they by and large settled in urban areas and undertook the industrialisation of the republic. The indigenous population remained concentrated in agriculture in the rural regions, retaining a traditional way of life; consequently, a society bifurcated along ethnic lines evolved. Everyday contact and communication between the two groups remained limited even in Tashkent, where Uzbeks constituted only 44 per cent of the population in 1989.

A circumstance which has particularly militated and continues to militate against the assimilation or even integration of Russians into the dominant Uzbek society has been a striking lack of fluency in the local language. Widely regarding Uzbek as a medium less advanced than their own, the majority of Russians have been disinclined to trade what they believe is a wealthier linguistic heritage for a poorer one. As with the Bengalis in Assam, the Chinese in Malaysia and the Kewri in Mauritania upon being required to work and study in the language of a 'backward' group,[38] Russians in Uzbekistan have pointed to the inadequacy of Uzbek as a medium in scientific and technical fields and its overall 'inferiority' to Russian as disincentives to learn the local language.

The decisions that Uzbekistani Russians make in regard to their children's education will be an important factor determining the degree of language shift that is to occur in this group, if any. According to Laitin's theory of 'competitive assimilation', a non-titular resident of a given state is likely to feel compelled to enrol his child in a school with the titular language as the medium of instruction in order to increase his child's upward mobility potential, especially in so far as he anticipates that other non-titulars will also place their children in titular-language schools. Such a pattern is likely to occur, it is argued, if 'the expected lifetime earnings of a young person are substantially greater when that person is fluent in the language of the state in which the family now resides'.[39] While this hypothesis might hold true for Yiddish-speaking migrant families in New York or for Castilian-speaking migrant families in Catalonia (to cite Laitin's examples),[40] it is problematic when applied to Russians in post-Soviet Uzbekistan. First, it is widely believed by non-Uzbeks (and many Uzbeks, too) that schools with Uzbek as the language of tuition offer a lower standard of education than that provided by Russian-language schools in Uzbekistan. Hence, Uzbekistani Russians are unlikely to encourage the linguistic assimilation of their children at the expense of what is believed to be a superior education. Secondly, many Russian parents are determined to preserve or even maximise their children's chances to seek a higher education or employment *outside* Uzbekistan, and in Russia proper in particular, and are therefore likely to continue to send them to Russian-language schools.

Adaptation without assimilation: a fourth alternative? As we have already noted, the decision to remain in Uzbekistan does not necessarily presage assimilation or even integration in so far as many Uzbekistani Russians have stayed – at least for the present – owing only to a lack of opportunity to leave. Still others, particularly those who are gainfully employed, have determined that their prospects for the future are better in Uzbekistan than elsewhere. Although acknowledging the pre-eminence of the Uzbek nation within the state, many of these Russians intend to preserve their cultural self-identification in the post-independence era in much the same ways as they did during Soviet rule. Encouraged by the slackened pace of language law implementation, they hope to be able to continue to rely on Russian in their professional and personal lives while adjusting to possible losses in economic and social status. Furthermore, these Russians can underpin their hopes with the experience of other former 'colonies', such as India, in which the language of the colonists has continued to be used in an official capacity. Yet, even Russians who are willing to learn Uzbek are unlikely to attempt to cross the high cultural barriers that stand in the way of full assimilation, since most tend to regard traditional Uzbek culture as a regressive link to the third world rather than a bridge to the more 'civilised' states of Europe and the West.

Tajik responses

While language legislation has fortified Russian–Uzbek group boundary markers, the bulk of the Tajik minority in Uzbekistan has responded to the new laws with relative equanimity. Several factors appear to have underpinned this reaction. First, although the Uzbekistani Tajiks overwhelmingly regard Tajik as their native language, a far greater number of them have acquired a facility in Uzbek in comparison to Uzbekistani Russians. Secondly, already accustomed to minority status, the Tajiks do not regard the laws as having either diminished or elevated their standing in relation to other groups. Given that language legislation has been primarily concerned with reducing the spheres of use for Russian while expanding the use of Uzbek, most Tajiks have not been inclined to view the policy as an exclusionary one.

Thirdly, although some ethnic entrepreneurs claiming to speak for the two groups have emphasised group differences, Tajik–Uzbek group boundaries are still fluid and imprecise. Indeed, as the civil war in Tajikistan has dramatically illustrated, the Tajik nation is far from consolidated, and, as Muriel Atkin has argued, 'the very notion of who is a Tajik contains ambiguity'.[41] While the valley Tajiks share a common material culture, social structure, cultural heritage and historical memory with the Uzbeks, they regard themselves as having little in common with the 'peripheral Tajik' – namely the Pamirian peoples, mountain Tajiks and Yagnobis of Tajikistan. Similarly, the valley Uzbeks differ less from the Tajiks in terms of culture than from the Lokais, who comprise nearly one-third of all Uzbeks in Tajikistan. Despite the institutionalisation of nationality under the Soviet regime, different forms of self-identification, whether based on region, neighbourhood or extended family, still exist in contemporary Uzbekistan. In carrying out field work in the Tajik-dominated city of Samarkand, two researchers of Moscow's Institute of Ethnology and Anthropology found that some Uzbeks and Tajiks understood the term 'our nationality' to refer to the region's indigenous population rather than to any particular ethnic group. Moreover, many Tajiks in particular were reported to have 'spontaneously referred to themselves sometimes as Uzbeks, sometimes as Tajiks, *without seeing any contradiction in this* [emphasis added]'.[42]

To be sure, before the advent of Soviet rule Uzbeks and Tajiks were not conscious of forming nations distinct from each other, as the urban communities in the heart of Central Asia had shared a common culture at least since the fifteenth century that employed three literary languages: Turki (Chaghatay),[43] Farsi (Persian) and Arabic (for the educated classes), all of which were written in the Arabic script although they belonged to unrelated language groups. Just as the concepts of 'nation', 'nationality' or 'ethnicity' held little meaning, the notion that the various peoples inhabiting the region should be distinguished by their language was an alien one, particularly given the long prevailing tradition of multilingualism in the region.[44] Rather, since the most salient distinction was between sedentary oasis dwellers and pastoral nomads, the term 'Sart', which referred to the region's sedentary population (whether speaking a Turkic or Iranian tongue), was widely used to distinguish it from the nomadic Turks. However, language became the guiding principle of the Soviet regime during the National Delimitation of the Central Asian republics of 1924. Following the National Delimitation, the category 'Sart' was eliminated and census-takers in 1926 were instructed to interpret that response to the question on *narodnost'* (people) as 'Uzbek (Sart)'.[45] Thus, sedentary peoples who lived in essentially the same way but spoke a Turkic or Iranian language found themselves identified as either 'Tajiks' or 'Uzbeks'.

As in pre-Soviet times, many if not most Tajiks would still find it difficult to differentiate Uzbek oasis culture from 'their own'. High levels of mixed marriage between Tajiks and Uzbeks have made group entities all the more amorphous, rendering official nationality irrelevant in many instances. Moreover, the concept of 'official nationality' is particularly suspect when applied to Uzbekistani Tajiks, given that local Soviet authorities in the 1920s recorded much of the Tajik-speaking populations of Samarkand, Bukhara, Shahr-i Sabz and other cities as Uzbeks in their passports in order to make the divisions between the new administrative units neater.[46] 'Passport Uzbekisation', which often facilitated professional advancement, continued under the Soviet regime. As a result of all these factors, it is impossible to determine with any degree of certainty the number of individuals who consider themselves members of the Tajik ethnic group in Uzbekistan, particularly given that some original Tajik-speakers were linguistically Turkicised long ago. While Tajiks officially accounted for only 4.8 per cent of Uzbekistan's population in 1993, the actual proportion of Tajik-speakers was undoubtedly much larger (some Tajiks put the figure as high as 25–30 per cent).[47] As a further indicator of the inaccuracy of official statistics in regard to Uzbekistan's Tajik population, Soviet census data indicated that the number of Tajiks in Samarkand region had ostensibly grown by more than 140 per cent between 1979 and 1989, while the number of Uzbeks in that region had grown by only 26 per cent during that same period.[48]

Particularly in Samarkand and Bukhara, which are ancient bastions of Persian–Tajik culture, 'Tajik' and 'Uzbek' are neither clear-cut nor immutably bounded identities. Yet, as national consciousness strengthened during the decades of Soviet rule, ethnic entrepreneurs sought both to manufacture differences and to magnify relative ones in an effort to solidify group boundaries. Wary of Uzbek hegemonic aspirations in the region and the promotion of Turkic pride, Tajik elites have argued that the Uzbeks are Turkicised Iranians while some Uzbek elites, for their part, have maintained that the Tajiks are simply Turks who have forgotten their original language.[49] Tensions have centred on two primary points: accusations by each side that the other has arrogated unto itself various aspects of the common Central Asian cultural heritage, and the dearth of cultural and educational facilities (e.g. Tajik-language schools, publications and broadcasts) for Uzbekistani Tajiks. Shortly before the collapse of the USSR, Tajiks in Samarkand and Bukhara began a hunger strike to protest against their 'Uzbekisation', after which authorities allowed the demonstrators to change the nationality registered in their passports from Uzbek to Tajik.[50] As with other forms of independent political activity, however, since 1991 Tajik activists pressing for greater cultural autonomy and an official status for the Tajik language have been systematically suppressed.[51]

While some ethnic entrepreneurs may regard current language legislation as a continuation of a decades-long policy of forced assimilation, it is difficult to determine the degree to which that sentiment finds resonance amongst Uzbekistani Tajiks as a whole. To be sure, Tajik culture has not flourished in Uzbekistan under either Soviet or independent Uzbekistani rule;[52] yet it would appear that most Tajiks do not regard their language and culture – which has managed to endure in the region despite many centuries of Turkic rule – as under any particular threat.

Table 9.2 *Comparison of 1989 census data and survey sample in Uzbekistan*

	Uzbeks		Russians		Tajiks	
	Census 1989	Survey 1996	Census 1989	Survey 1996	Census 1989	Survey 1996
Urban	30%	45%	95%	82%	32%	37%
Rural	70%	55%	5%	18%	68%	63%
Male	50%	54%	45%	54%	50%	58%
Female	50%	46%	55%	46%	50%	42%
Age 16–29	27%	32%	21%	32%	27%	30%
Age 30–9	11%	27%	17%	23%	11%	22%
Age 40–9	5%	23%	11%	18%	5%	24%
Age 50–9	5%	13%	11%	16%	6%	17%
Age 60+	5%	5%	13%	11%	6%	8%
Higher education	4%	26%	12%	16%	4%	19%
Secondary education	25%	39%	19%	22%	26%	29%
Unfinished secondary	11%	11%	14%	11.5%	11%	7.5%
Tashkent	7.6%	31%	19.0%	61%	9.6%	6%
Farghana	12.3%	26%	7.5%	25%	12.3%	12%
Samarkand	12.5%	10%	6.9%	4%	22.4%	81%
Khwarazm	6.8%	33%	0.9%	10%	0.0%	1%

Attitudes towards language legislation

In order to examine the views of Uzbekistan's largest ethnic groups on language legislation, a public opinion survey of roughly equal groups of Uzbeks, Russians and Tajiks was undertaken by the author in conjunction with a Tashkent sociological centre in June 1996 in four regions (*vilayätlär*) of the country (Tashkent, Farghana, Samarkand and Khwarazm).[53] The survey was based on 600 structured interviews conducted in one of the three relevant languages with interrelated controls for several major indicators in addition to self-ascribed ethnic nationality:[54] urban/rural settlement type, gender, age, level of education and region (table 9.2). Members of linguistically Russified non-titular minorities that are not indigenous to the Central Asian region composed 10 per cent of the total sample (referred to hereafter as 'Russophone minorities').[55]

It should be borne in mind that survey work carried out in Uzbekistan is likely to be a less precise indicator of public opinion than in other, less authoritarian political regimes. To enhance the willingness of respondents to answer freely and without regard to political considerations, interviews were conducted in the language of convenience of the respondent by local survey-takers rather than 'outsiders'. The revised edition of the Law on the State Language had been adopted only six months before the survey was carried out; consequently, language-related discussions which had appeared regularly in the press and other media during the months leading up to the survey were still relatively fresh in the minds of the respondents.

As could be expected, there was a strong correlation between level of knowledge of Uzbek and support (or lack thereof) for the language law. In order to determine levels of language knowledge with greater precision, in addition to indicating their native language all respondents were asked in separate questions to name their language of primary use both at home and at work and to evaluate their facility in Uzbek, Russian and Tajik (tables 9.3 and 9.4). (Particularly in the Soviet and post-Soviet context, the term 'native language' (*rodnoi iazyk*) can be an ambiguous one that may serve more as a measure of ethnic group attachment than as an indicator of linguistic ability.)

Generally speaking, there is an inverse relationship between the number of Russians living in a given region in Uzbekistan and that group's facility in the Uzbek language. In 1989, there were fewer Russians in Khwarazm region than in any other region in Uzbekistan; accordingly, nearly one-quarter of all Russians resident there claimed to have a fluent command of Uzbek compared to 4.6 per cent for the republic as a whole, according to 1989 census data. Likewise, according to our 1996 survey results, more than a third of Russians in Khwarazm claimed an excellent or good command of Uzbek, while only 7 per cent of Russians in Tashkent did the same.[56] Over 90 per cent of all Tajiks surveyed claimed either an excellent or a good facility in Uzbek.

In examining attitudes towards specific provisions of the language law, a divergence of views arose between 'indigenes' (Uzbeks and Tajiks) on the one hand and the 'settler' communities (Russians and Russophone minorities) on the other. Despite categorical assertions by Uzbekistani authorities that the new edition of the law had removed all trace of discrimination,[57] three out of five Russians surveyed believed that the granting of sole state language status to Uzbek infringes the constitutional rights of minorities living in Uzbekistan. The vast majority of Uzbeks and Tajiks, however, were united in the opinion that Uzbek's status as the sole state language does not constitute a violation of minority rights (figure 9.2). Similarly, although President Karimov has stated that 'there is not and cannot be discrimination on the basis of ethnic affiliation or religion in Uzbekistan',[58] the majority of Russians (58 per cent) maintained that certain ethnic groups in that state, and Uzbeks in particular, enjoy greater

Table 9.3 Native language and primary language at home and at work by ethnic group (survey sample) in Uzbekistan

	Native language				Primary language at home				Primary language at work			
	Uzbek	Russian	Tajik	Other	Uzbek	Russian	Tajik	Other	Uzbek	Russian	Tajik	Other
Uzbeks	96.5%	3%	0.5%	0%	92%	5%	3%	0%	85%	13%	2%	0%
Russians	0.5%	96.5%	0%	3%	1%	99%	0%	0%	3.5%	96.5%	0%	0%
Tajiks	5%	0%	94.5%	0.5%	5%	2%	93%	0%	24%	9%	67%	0%
Tatars	0%	48%	0%	52%	4%	84%	0%	12%	32%	68%	0%	0%
Koreans	0%	87.5%	0%	12.5%	0%	94%	0%	6%	10%	90%	0%	0%

Table 9.4 Knowledge of state language and Russian by ethnic group and region (survey sample) in Uzbekistan

	Uzbek (facility claimed by respondent)					Russians (facility claimed by respondent)				
	Excellent	Good	Average	Poor	None	Excellent	Good	Average	Poor	None
Uzbeks										
(total)	73%	24%	3%	0%	0%	18%	25.5%	44%	8%	4.5%
Tashkent	73%	20%	7%	0%	0%	30%	27%	40%	1.5%	1.5%
Farghana	80%	20%	0%	0%	0%	4%	26%	50%	10%	10%
Samarkand	75%	20%	5%	0%	0%	20%	50%	20%	10%	0%
Khwarazm	66%	31%	3%	0%	0%	17%	17%	51%	11%	4%
Russians										
(total)	2%	9%	28%	39%	22%	78%	21.5%	0%	0%	0.5%
Tashkent	0%	7%	28%	40%	25%	80%	19%	0%	0%	1%
Farghana	4%	7%	32%	39%	18%	84%	16%	0%	0%	0%
Samarkand	0%	14%	0%	57%	29%	100%	0%	0%	0%	0%
Khwarazm	6%	29.5%	29%	29.5%	6%	90%	10%	0%	0%	0%
Tajiks										
(total)	27%	66.5%	6%	0.5%	0%	8%	46%	32%	9%	5%
Tashkent	40%	60%	0%	0%	0%	0%	70%	30%	0%	0%
Farghana	20%	80%	0%	0%	0%	0%	45%	35%	0%	15%
Samarkand	28%	65%	6%	1%	0%	9%	45%	31.5%	5%	4.5%
Khwarazm	0%	0%	100%	0%	0%	100%	0%	0%	10%	0%
Russophone minorities										
(total)	3%	27%	40%	25%	5%	52%	45%	1.5%	1.5%	0%
Tashkent	4%	13%	50%	29%	4%	54%	42%	4%	0%	0%
Farghana	17%	0%	50%	33%	0%	67%	33%	0%	0%	0%
Samarkand	0%	0%	0%	67%	33%	100%	0%	0%	0%	0%
Khwarazm	0%	48%	33%	15%	4%	41%	57%	0%	2%	0%

Did the conferral of state status on the Uzbek language infringe the constitutional rights of non-Uzbeks living in Uzbekistan? (responses as a percentage)

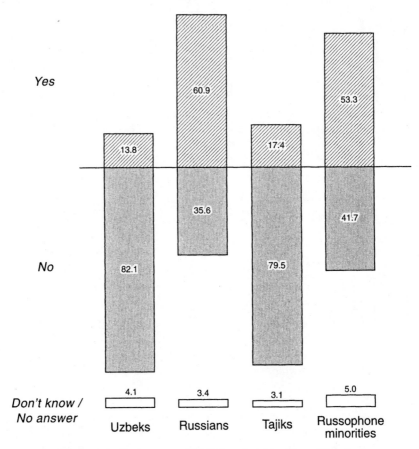

Figure 9.2. State status of Uzbek and rights of non-Uzbeks

rights than others in spite of constitutional guarantees. This view was par-ticularly prevalent amongst Russians in Samarkand and Farghana, whereas the majority of Russians in ethnically homogeneous Khwarazm (59 per cent) held that no single ethnic group enjoys more rights than any other.

Russian and Russophone minority groups had particularly strong views concerning the normative status of the Russian language in Uzbekistan. The overwhelming majority of those two groups (96 per cent

*Which language or languages, if any, should have state status
in addition to Uzbek in Uzbekistan?
(multiple responses allowed, responses as a percentage)*

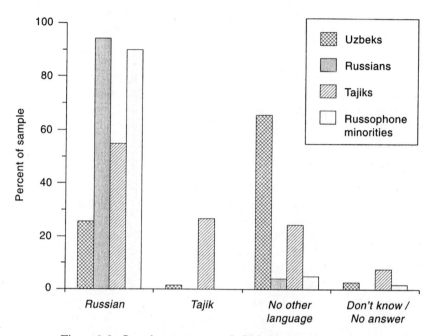

Figure 9.3. State language status in Uzbekistan

and 93 per cent, respectively) believed that Russian should be accorded
state status in addition to Uzbek, while only 32 per cent of Uzbeks had the
same opinion (figure 9.3). (As expected, all Uzbeks whose primary language of use at home was Russian felt that that language should also be
given state status, while only a minority of Uzbeks whose primary language at home was Uzbek had the same opinion.) Uncharacteristically,
the largest group of Tajiks (39 per cent) concurred with the Russians
rather than the Uzbeks on this issue, maintaining that both Uzbek and
Russian should have state status in Uzbekistan; 15 per cent of Tajiks
believed that Uzbek, Russian and Tajik should all have state status, and
only 11 per cent of Tajiks were of the opinion that Tajik and Uzbek should
be the two state languages of the country. Even in the Tajik-speaking
stronghold of Samarkand, only one in four Tajiks wanted Tajik to have
state language standing together with Uzbek, while twice as many
believed that Russian should have that status in addition to Uzbek.

However, in regard to the question of re-establishing Russian's official status as the 'language of inter-ethnic communication' (as stipulated in the 1989 edition of the language law but eliminated in the 1995 edition), Tajiks and Uzbeks once again took the same stance, with a clear majority of both groups holding the view that *no* language should carry that status. Whereas only one in three Uzbeks in Samarkand and Farghana was against the designation of an official language of inter-ethnic communication, however, three out of four Tashkenti Uzbeks held that opinion. Amongst the Uzbeks and Tajiks who were in favour of re-implementing an official medium of inter-ethnic communication, Russian was the language of choice. Keen to ensure that the Russian language would continue to play a role in the new political order, three-quarters of the Russian and Russophone minority groups supported the restoration of that language's former status as the official language of inter-ethnic communication.

This same polarity of views between settlers and indigenes was also in evidence with respect to the use of the state language for statistical and financial documentation and for office work. Over 80 per cent of all Uzbeks and Tajiks approved of this provision of the language law, although the Uzbeks were stronger in their support of it, particularly in Tashkent (most Uzbeks responded 'agree completely' while most Tajiks responded 'rather agree'). Predictably, 80 per cent of all Russians disagreed with the shift to Uzbek for office work and financial documentation. Whereas the renaming of administrative-territorial units, squares, streets and other geographical objects – a process that has been more visible in Uzbekistan than elsewhere in Central Asia – was supported by the overwhelming majority of Uzbeks and three-quarters of Tajiks, the Russians were divided into equal groups over the replacement of Russian and Soviet toponyms by indigenous ones. Regional differences amongst them were pronounced: three-quarters of Russians in Khwarazm were in favour of toponymical changes compared to 57 per cent of Samarkandi Russians, 54 per cent of Tashkenti Russians and only 25 per cent of Russians in Farghana.

When asked what effect, if any, language legislation had had on their professional lives, nearly 60 per cent of Uzbeks and Russians stated that the law had had no impact whatsoever (table 9.5). An even greater number of Tajiks had been unaffected professionally by the language law (83 per cent). This circumstance was most likely a result in part of the slackened pace of implementation and in part of the jaundiced view that many Uzbekistanis appear to have taken of the law's all-encompassing promises and legalistic guarantees. However, one-third of Uzbeks believed that the law had had a positive effect on their professional lives,

Table 9.5 *Effect of language legislation on professional and other spheres of life in Uzbekistan*

Effect of language legislation on professional life

	None	Positive	Negative	Don't know/ No answer
Uzbeks	59.5%	32.8%	4.6%	3.1%
Russians	57.5%	0.0%	40.8%	1.7%
Tajiks	82.6%	9.3%	6.2%	1.9%
Russophone minorities	65.0%	0.0%	33.4%	1.6%

Effect of language legislation on other spheres of life

	None	Positive	Negative	Don't know/ No answer
Uzbeks	67.2%	30.3%	1.5%	1.0%
Russians	54.0%	0.6%	44.3%	1.1%
Tajiks	88.8%	4.3%	3.1%	3.7%
Russophone minorities	73.3%	0.0%	26.7%	0.0%

primarily in terms of expanding their educational opportunities and possible choice of professions. By contrast, not a single Russian or member of a Russophone minority group had been positively affected by the law in the workplace. Amongst the 41 per cent of Russians who had been negatively affected, decreased job security was cited as the most common adverse consequence of language legislation in the professional sphere. A larger proportion of Russians in Samarkand and Farghana had been negatively affected than Russians elsewhere, which was most likely a reflection of the relatively faster rate of implementation of the language law in those two regions. Just as inside the workplace, outside the workplace a majority of all respondents had also remained unaffected by language legislation. Russians who had felt the impact of the law, however, primarily complained that communication with state governmental organs had become more difficult for them.

More than half of all respondents were of the opinion that language legislation had had some impact on ethnic relations, whether positive or negative (figure 9.4). Not surprisingly, more than half of Uzbeks and nearly one-third of Tajiks believed that the law had had a positive or somewhat positive influence, while half of Russians and nearly two-thirds of Russophone minority group members believed its effect had been neg-

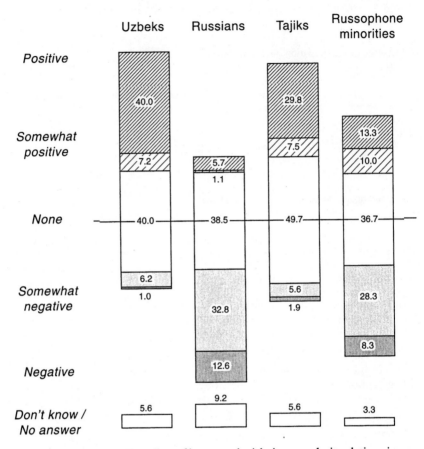

(responses as a percentage)

Figure 9.4. The effect of language legislation on ethnic relations in Uzbekistan

ative or somewhat negative. Amongst the Russians, recent settlers – whose Uzbek skills were the weakest – were inclined to regard the law's impact on ethnic relations as particularly negative. Conversely, those Russians with the strongest Uzbek skills viewed the law's impact on ethnic relations as minimal.

Although the revised edition of the language law adopted in 1995 no longer made knowledge of Uzbek a precondition for employment in state organisations and in the service sector, nearly half of the Russian and lin-guistically Russified groups none the less believed that language legislation had made their position in the republic more tenuous. Yet, despite this vulnerability, *70 per cent of Russians with poor or non-existent Uzbek skills had no intention of learning that language.* While there were no marked regional differences, Russians who had moved to Uzbekistan within the last twenty-five years showed a greater willingness to learn Uzbek than those who had lived there for longer periods of time. This unwillingness to learn the state language was no doubt strengthened by the belief amongst the vast majority of them that Uzbek was a less advanced (*razvitii*) language than Russian.

Conclusions

As with so many laws promulgated in the post-Soviet states, language legislation in Uzbekistan proclaims to fulfil two competing objectives: it seeks to entrench the hegemony of the language of the titular nation on the one hand while claiming to safeguard the rights of non-titular minorities on the other. In so far as a substantial proportion of the country's Russian population has come to view it as a hallmark of the nationalising state, language legislation has served to rigidify Uzbek–Russian group divisions. However, it has had little, if any, impact on Uzbek–Tajik group boundaries, which are remarkable for their high degree of fluidity. Although Tajik (and Uzbek) ethnic entrepreneurs have promoted the principle that ethnicity and language must coincide, in regions where concentrated groups of Tajiks and Uzbeks live side by side most are still able to regard themselves as united by a common culture and religion, thereby signifying that language need not always serve as the primary marker of ethnicity. Likewise, groups whose languages differ only slightly can regard themselves as distinct ethnic communities, a case in point being the Bosnians, Serbs and Croats.

Despite a slackening in the pace of implementation of the more substantive provisions as well as the elimination of certain controversial ones, Uzbekistani Russians and other Russophones do not find the revised 1995 edition of the language law an improvement over the first edition in so far as it gives no normative status to the Russian language, which, they argue, is still the medium of convenience of millions of former Soviet citizens. Legislation aside, however, the higher birthrates amongst the indigenous population coupled with the migration of part of the non-titular population will leave only a relatively small Russophone minority in Uzbekistan, virtually guaranteeing that linguistic 'Uzbekisation' will proceed of its own accord.

Notes

1 POST-COLONIALISM AND BORDERLAND IDENTITIES

1 For the purposes of this book, the fourteen borderland states include the Baltic states of Estonia, Latvia and Lithuania, the south-western borderland republics of Ukraine, Belarus and Moldova, the Transcaucasian republics of Georgia, Armenia and Azerbaijan, and the Central Asian states of Kyrgyzstan, Kazakstan, Tajikistan, Turkmenistan and Uzbekistan.

2 Simon During, 'Postmodernism or Post-Colonialism Today', in Bill Ashcroft et al., *The Post-Colonial Studies Reader* (London: Routledge, 1996), p. 125.

3 Rogers Brubaker, *Nationalism Reframed* (Cambridge: Cambridge University Press, 1996), p. 63.

4 Julie Mostov, 'Democracy and the Politics of National Identity', *Studies in East European Thought*, vol. 46, 1994, pp. 9–31. See also Dominique Arel, 'Ukraine: The Temptation of the Nationalising State', in Vladimir Tismaneanu (ed.), *Political Culture and Civil Society in Russia and the New States of Eurasia* (New York: M. E. Sharpe, 1995), pp. 157–88.

5 Roxanne Doty, 'Sovereignty and the Nation: Constructing the Boundaries of National Identity', in Thomas Biersteker and Cynthia Weber (eds.), *State Sovereignty as Social Construct* (Cambridge: Cambridge University Press, 1996), p. 123.

6 Ronald Suny, 'Ambiguous Categories: States, Empires and Nations', *Post-Soviet Affairs*, vol. 11 (2), 1995, p. 187.

7 Bruce Parrot, 'Analysing the Transformation of the Soviet Union in Comparative Perspective', in Karen Dawisha and Bruce Parrot (eds.), *The End of Empire? The Transformation of the USSR in Comparative Perspective* (New York and London: M. E. Sharpe, 1997), p. 3. See also Karen Barkey and Mark von Hagen (eds.), *Imperial Collapse: Causes and Consequences* (Boulder: Westview, 1997).

8 See, for example, Suny, 'Ambiguous Categories'; Alexander Motyl (ed.), *The Post-Soviet Nations: Perspectives on the Demise of the USSR* (New York: Columbia University Press, 1992); Graham Smith, 'The Soviet Federation: From Corporatist to Crisis Politics', in M. Chisholm and D. Smith (eds.), *Shared Space, Divided Space: Essays on Conflict and Territorial Organisation* (London: Unwin Hyman, 1990), pp. 84–105.

9 Graham Smith, 'Federation, Defederation and Refederation: From the Soviet Union to Russian Statehood', in Graham Smith (ed.), *Federalism: The Multiethnic Challenge* (London: Longman, 1995), pp. 157–79.

10 Isabelle Kriendler, 'Soviet Muslims: Gains and Losses as a Result of Soviet Language Planning', in Yaacov Ro´i (ed.), *Muslim Eurasia: Conflicting Legacies* (London: Frank Cass, 1995), pp. 187–203.

11 Brubaker, *Nationalism Reframed*; Suny, 'Ambiguous Categories'; Graham Smith, 'Ethnic Nationalism in the Soviet Union: Territory, Cleavage and Control', *Environment and Planning. C. Government and Policy*, vol. 3, 1995, pp. 49–73.

12 Shirin Akiner, 'Melting Pot, Salad Bowl – Cauldron? Manipulation and Mobilisation of Ethnic and Religious Identities in Central Asia', *Ethnic and Racial Studies*, vol. 20 (2), 1997, pp. 362–98.

13 Roman Szporluk, 'Statehood and Nationbuilding in Post-Soviet Space', in Szporluk (ed.), *National Identity and Ethnicity in the New States of Eurasia* (London: M. E. Sharpe, 1994), p. 6.

14 Graham Smith, *The Nationalities Question in the Post-Soviet States* (London: Longman, 1996), p. 10.

15 John Dunlop, 'Russia: In Search of an Identity?', in Ian Bremmer and Ray Taras (eds.), *New States, New Politics: Building the Post-Soviet Nations* (Cambridge: Cambridge University Press, 1997), p. 29.

16 Donna Barry, *Outside Moscow: Power, Politics and Budgetary Policy in the Soviet Republics* (New York: Columbia University Press, 1988).

17 See David Laitin, 'The National Uprisings in the Soviet Union', *World Politics*, vol. 44 (1), 1991, pp. 134–77, and Graham Smith, 'The State, Nationalism and the Nationalities Question in the Soviet Republics', in Catherine Merridale and Chris Ward (eds.), *Perestroika: The Historical Perspective* (London: Edward Arnold, 1991), pp. 202–16.

18 Mark Beissinger, 'The Persisting Ambiguity of Empire', *Post-Soviet Affairs*, vol. 11 (2), 1995, pp. 149–84.

19 Pierre Bourdieu, *The Logic of Practice* (Stanford, CA: Stanford University Press, 1990).

20 Jorge Klor De Alva, 'Postcolonisation of the (Latin) American Experience: A Reconsideration of "Colonialism", "Postcolonialism" and "Mestizaje"', in Gyan Prakash (ed.), *After Colonialism: Imperial Histories and Postcolonial Displacements* (Princeton, NJ: Princeton University Press, 1995), p. 345.

21 Dominic Lieven, 'The Russian Empire and the Soviet Union as Imperial Polities', *Journal of Contemporary History*, vol. 30, 1995, p. 615.

22 For consideration of such questions in relation to the Russian Empire, see Geoffrey Hosking, *Russia: People and Empire, 1552–1917* (London: Harper Collins, 1997).

23 For a full account of Russia's legal position on offering citizenship to Russians living outside the Russian Federation, see *Rossiiskaia gazeta*, 22 January 1994, p. 4, and 23 September 1995, p. 4.

24 For a fuller discussion of the role of the Communist Party in Russia since 1991, see Joan Barth Urban and Valerii Solovei (eds.), *Russia's Communists at the Crossroads* (Boulder: Westview, 1997).

25 Gennadii Zyuganov (ed.), *Sovremennaia russkaia ideia i gosudarstvo* (Moscow: RAU, 1995).

26 *Pravda*, 23 August 1993.

27 *Pravda*, 25 June 1994.

28 Michael Bakhtin, 'Discourse in the Novel', in Michael Holquist (ed.), *The Dialogic Imagination* (Austin: University of Texas Press, 1981), p. 360.

29 Quoted in Beissinger, 'The Persisting Ambiguity of Empire', p. 165, from *Nezavisimaia gazeta*, 12 January 1994, p. 4.

30 Graham Smith, 'The Ethnic Democracy Thesis and the Citizenship Question in the Baltic States of Estonia and Latvia', *Nationalities Papers*, vol. 24 (2), 1996, pp. 199–216. See in particular the interview with the chair of the Commission on Citizenship issues to the President of Russia concerning Russia's official view on why the exclusion of Russian speakers from automatic citizenship can be considered as synonymous with the violation of human rights: *Nezavisimaia gazeta*, 21 January 1994, p. 2.

31 *Segodnia*, 12 July 1994.

32 See, for example, Boris Yeltsin's speech in which he made it clear that 'twenty-five million of our compatriots in these countries must not be forgotten', a clear numerical reference to the Russian diaspora: *Nezavisimaia gazeta*, 1 January 1994. For a fuller discussion of what is encoded in the notion of 'compatriots abroad', see the interview with Konstantin Zatulin, chair of the State Duma Committee on CIS Affairs and Relations with Compatriots, *Delovoi mir*, 2 December 1995, p. 6.

33 Igor Zevelev, 'Russia and the Russian Diasporas', *Post-Soviet Affairs*, vol. 12 (3), 1996, pp. 265–84.

34 Suny, 'Ambiguous Categories'.

35 D. Morley and K. Robins, 'No Place like Heimat: Images of Homeland in European Culture', in E. Carter et al. (eds.), *Space and Place: Theories of Identity and Location* (London: Lawrence and Wishart, 1993), p. 8.

36 Anssi Paasi, 'Inclusion, Exclusion and Territorial Identities', *Nordisk Samhallsgeografik Tidskrift*, no. 23, October 1996, p. 10.

37 Michael Billig, *Banal Nationalism* (London: Sage, 1995).

38 Anthony Smith, 'Culture, Community and Territory: The Politics of Ethnicity and Nationalism', *International Affairs*, vol. 72 (3), 1996, p. 450.

39 Ann Maria Alonso, 'The Politics of Space, Time and Substance: State Formation, Nationalism and Ethnicity', *Annual Review of Anthropology*, vol. 23, 1994, pp. 379–405.

40 Bakhtin, 'Discourse in the Novel', p. 13.

41 Alonso, 'The Politics of Space, Time and Substance', p. 383.

42 During, 'Postmodernism or Post-Colonialism Today', pp. 125–6.

43 David Laitin, 'Language and Nationalism in the Post-Soviet Republics', *Post-Soviet Affairs*, vol. 12 (1), 1996, pp. 4–24.

44 During, 'Postmodernism or Post-Colonialism Today', p. 125.

45 This particular way of differentiating between national minority groupings is an expanded and refocused version of Offe's categories. See Claus Offe, *Varieties of Transitions: The East European and East German Experience* (Oxford: Polity Press, 1996).

46 Graham Smith and Andrew Wilson, 'Rethinking Russia's Post-Soviet Diaspora: The Potential for Political Mobilisation in Eastern Ukraine and North-East Estonia', *Europe–Asia Studies*, vol. 49 (5), July 1997, pp. 845–64.

47 Philip Roeder, 'Post-Soviet Institutions and Ethnopolitics', paper presented

at the annual meeting of the American Political Science Association, New York, September 1994.

48 David M. Crowe, *A History of the Gypsies of Eastern Europe and Russia* (London: I. B. Tauris, 1995).

2 NATIONAL HISTORY AND NATIONAL IDENTITY IN UKRAINE AND BELARUS

1 'Myth' is here used in the original Greek sense. 'Mythos' is a narrative, neither necessarily true nor necessarily false.

2 The terms are used without any pejorative overtones, and in order to avoid labelling any version of history as more 'nationalist'. It is not argued that the work of every historian in Ukraine, Russia or Belarus conforms to the ideal-types described, although it can certainly be argued that more pluralist and multilayered approaches are in danger of being squeezed out by the extremes.

3 See also Andrew Wilson, 'Myths of National History in Belarus and Ukraine', in George Schöpflin and Geoffrey Hosking (eds.), *Myths and Nationhood* (London: Hurst, 1997), pp. 182–97, which concentrates mainly on the relative weakness of Belarusian historiographical mythology.

4 See also Anthony D. Smith, 'National Identity and Myths of Ethnic Descent', *Research in Social Movement, Conflict and Change*, vol. 7, 1994, pp. 95–130.

5 This chapter is unable to assess the extent of popular belief in the various myths – a task to be undertaken in a further stage of research.

6 Soviet theories of 'ethnogenesis', and the teleological fallacy that current ethnic boundaries can be used to delineate historical subjects in an unbroken chain of development, are still a powerful influence on local historians and archaeologists.

7 The author is grateful to Vera Rich for making this point.

8 On the importance of boundary markers, see Fredrik Barth (ed.), *Ethnic Groups and Boundaries: The Social Organisation of Culture Difference* (London: George Allen and Unwin, 1969).

9 In the nineteenth century Belarusian historiography was limited to occasional works of *landespatriotismus*. See Aliaksandr Ts´vikevich, *'Zapadno-russizm': narysy z historyi hramadzkai mys´li na Belarusi ŭ XIX i pachatku XX v.* (Minsk: Navuka i tekhnika, 1993), a reprint of a work first published in 1929.

10 Vatslaŭ Lastoŭski, *Karotkaia historyia Belarusi* (Minsk: Universitetskae, 1993), a reprint of the original 1910 edition; and Usevalad Ihnatoŭski, *Karotki narys historyi Belarusi* (Minsk: Belarus´, 1991), from the 1926 edition. See also M. V. Doŭnar-Zapol´ski, *Historyia Belarusi* (Minsk: Belaruskaia entsyklapedyia imia Petrusia Broŭki, 1994), from a manuscript withdrawn from publication in 1926, and Svetlana Sel´verstova-Kul´, 'Istoriografiia politiki tsarizma v belorussii i natsional´noe vozrozhdenie belorusov', *Slavianovedenie*, no. 5, 1996, pp. 3–17.

11 Aleh Suvalaŭ, 'Idealohiia i historyia: pra adnosiny idealohii da belaruskai

histarychnai navuki z 1917 da kantsa 40-kh hadoŭ', *Belaruskaia minuŭshchyna*, no. 2, 1994, pp. 3–6.

12 See the two in-depth surveys of Ukrainian historiography by Stephen Velychenko, *National History as Cultural Process: The Interpretation of Ukraine's Past in Polish, Ukrainian and Russian Historiography* (Edmonton: Canadian Institute of Ukrainian Studies (CIUS), 1992), and *Shaping Identity in Eastern Europe and Russia: Soviet and Polish Accounts of Ukrainian History, 1914–1991* (New York: St Martin's Press, 1993). Also useful are Orest Subtelny, 'The Current State of Ukrainian Historiography', *Journal of Ukrainian Studies*, vol. 18 (1–2), Summer–Winter 1993, pp. 33–54; and the survey of the various schools of Ukrainian history in V. F. Soldatenko and Iu. A. Levenets', 'Vstup: istoriohrafichni notatky', in Soldatenko, Volodymyr Kryzhanivs'kyi, Iurii Levenets' et al. (eds.), *Ukraïns'ka ideia: istorychnyi narys* (Kiev: Naukova dumka, 1995), pp. 3–16.

13 Mykola Kostomarov, *Dve russkie narodnosti* (Kiev: Maidan, 1991), a reprint of the original 1861 edition.

14 Hrushevs'kyi's eleven-volume magnum opus, *Istoriia Ukraïny–Rusy*, is being reprinted by Naukova dumka in Kiev with assistance from the CIUS. Volume V appeared in 1995. For some analyses of Hrushevs'kyi's schema, see Thomas M. Prymak, *Mykhailo Hrushevsky: The Politics of National Culture* (Toronto: University of Toronto Press, 1987); Lubomyr R. Wynar, *Mykhailo Hrushevs'kyi: Ukrainian–Russian Confrontation in Historiography* (Toronto: Ukrainian Historical Association, 1988); and O. L. Kopylenko, *'Ukraïns'ka ideia' M. Hrushevs'koho: istoriia i suchasnist'* (Kiev: Lybid', 1991).

15 Author's interview with Petro Tolochko, 24 June 1997. See also Natalia Iakovenko, 'Mizh pravdoiu ta slavoiu', *Suchasnist'*, no. 12 (December), 1995, pp. 68–76.

16 Volodymyr Kyrychuk, 'Istorychni koreni ukraïns'koho narodu: do pytannia etnohenezu ukraïntsiv', *Heneza*, no. 1, 1994, pp. 142–9, at p. 143. See also V. P. Petrov, *Pokhodzhennia ukraïns'koho narodu* (Kiev: Feniks, 1992); Leonid Zalizniak, *Narysy starodavn'oï istoriï Ukraïny* (Kiev: Abrys, 1994); Halyna Lozko, 'Etnohenetychni protsesy v Ukraïni', in her *Ukraïns'ke narodoznavstvo* (Kiev: Zodiak-EKO, 1995), pp. 9–27; O. M. Motsia, 'Starodavnia doba', in V. A. Smolii (ed.), *Istoriia Ukraïny: nove bachennia*, vol. I (Kiev: Ukraïna, 1995), pp. 5–39; and Volodymyr Borysenko, 'Anty. Rusy. Ukraïntsi', *Viche*, no. 7 (July), 1993, pp. 138–48. For a more balanced treatment, see Iurii Pavlenko, *Peredistoriia davnikh rusiv u svitovomu konteksti* (Kiev: Feniks, 1994), and (to an extent) Iaroslav Isaievych, 'Problema pokhodzhennia ukraïns'koho narodu: istoriohrafichnyi i politychnyi aspekt', in Isaievych, *Ukraïna: davna i nova* (L'viv: Kryp''iakevych Institute, 1996), pp. 22–43.

17 Victor Shnirelman, 'From Internationalism to Nationalism: Forgotten Pages of Soviet Archaeology in the 1930s and 1940s', in Phillip L. Kohl and Clare Fawcett (eds.), *Nationalism, Politics and the Practice of Archaeology* (Cambridge: Cambridge University Press, 1995), pp. 120–38. Soviet historians and archaeologists supported the 'autochthonous' theory in order to

reject rival 'migrationist' theories that supposedly served German interests by seeking to paint the eastern Slavs as marginal peoples.

18 Kyrychuk, 'Istorychni koreni', p. 143.

19 Ibid., pp. 145 and 144.

20 Iurii Shylov, *Prarodina ar'ev* (Kiev: SINTO, 1995). See also the interview with Shylov in *Samostiina Ukraïna*, no. 7 (March), 1994.

21 The 'Indo-European' theory is associated above all with the émigré author Lev Sylenko. See his *Maha vira* (Spring Glen, NY: Society of the Ukrainian Native Faith, Oriana, 1979), quotes from pp. 59, 116 and 323. For other versions of the 'Indo-European' theory, see Iurii Shylov, *Brama bezsmertia* (Kiev: Ukraïns'kyi svit, 1994), and Iurii Kanyhin, *Shliakh ariïv: Ukraïna v dukhovnii istoriï liudstva*, 2nd edn (Kiev: Ukraïna, 1996).

22 See the claim by Serhii Plachynda, leader of the Peasant-Democratic Party of Ukraine, that 'Ukrainian mythology is the oldest in the world. It became the basis for all Indo-European mythologies, just as the ancient Ukrainian language – Sanskrit [sic] – became the basis [*pramatir''ia*] for all the Indo-European languages': *Slovnyk davn'o-ukraïns'koï mifolohiï* (Kiev: Ukraïns'kyi pys'mennyk, 1993), p. 6.

23 See also Siân Jones, *The Archaeology of Ethnicity: Constructing Identities in the Past and Present* (London: Routledge, 1997), ch. 2.

24 Rolle Renate, *The Scythians* (New York, 1989); and Tadeusz Sulimirski and Timothy Taylor, 'The Scythians', in *The Cambridge Ancient History*, 2nd edn, vol. III, part 2 (Cambridge: Cambridge University Press, 1992), pp. 547–90. See also Pavel M. Dolukhanov, *The Early Slavs: Eastern Europe from the Initial Settlement to the Kievan Rus* (London: Longman, 1996).

25 Anatolii Ponomar'ov, 'Pokhodzhennia ta etnichna istoriia ukraïntsiv', *Ukraïns'ka etnohrafiia* (Kiev: Lybid', 1994), pp. 96–111. For a similar Russian point of view, see Boris Rybakov, *Iazychestvo drevnikh slavian*, 2nd edn (Moscow: Nauka, 1994), and his *Nachal'nye veka russkoi istorii* (Moscow: Shik, 1995), the first volume in the series *Istoriia Rossii*.

26 Oleksander Montsibovych (ed.), *Herodot pro Skytiv* (Adelaide: Knyha, 1986), p. 9. Herodotus actually depicted the Scythians as a savage race of itinerant horsemen.

27 Isaievych, *Ukraïna: davna i nova*, p. 35.

28 Compare Tadeusz Sulimirski, *The Sarmatians* (London: Thames and Hudson, 1970).

29 Kyrychuk, 'Istorychni koreni', pp. 146 and 147.

30 V. F. Soldatenko and Iu. V. Syvolob, 'Vytoky i peredvisnyky ukraïns'koï ideï', in Soldatenko, Syvolob and I. F. Kuras (eds.), *Ukraïns'ka ideia: pershi rechnyky* (Kiev: Znannia, 1994), pp. 5–25, at p. 11.

31 Volodymyr Païk (an émigré Ukrainian), '"Velyka Skytiia" – Velyka Skolotiia', *Derzhavnist'*, nos. 1 and 2, 1992.

32 V. F. Soldatenko and Iu. V. Syvolob, 'Vytoky i peredvisnyky ukraïns'koï ideï', p. 8.

33 Iaroslav Dashkevych, 'Osnovi etnichnoï istoriï ukraïns'koï natsiï: mifolohizatsiia ta demifolohizatsiia', *Ratusha*, 4–5 September 1991.

34 Aliaksandar Miadz'vedzeŭ, 'Nasel'nitstva Belarusi ŭ zhaleznym veku (VIII

st. da n. e. – VIII st. n. e.)', *Belaruski histarychny ahliad*, vol. 1 (1), November 1994, pp. 15–37, at p. 37. See also Liudmila Duchyts, 'Bal'ty i slaviane na terytoryi Belarusi ŭ pachatku II tysiachahodz'dzia', *Belaruski histarychny ahliad*, vol. 2 (1), October 1995, pp. 15–30, and Aliaksei Mikulin, 'Etnahenez belarusaŭ – pohliad antrapolaha', *Litaratura i mastatstva*, no. 22, 2 June 1995. The Russian archaeologist Valentin Sedov has expressed similar views in his *Slaviane v drevnosti* (Moscow: Fond arkheologii, 1994).

35 Victor A. Shnirelman, 'The Faces of Nationalist Archaeology in Russia', in Margarita Díaz Andreu and Timothy Champion (eds.), *Nationalism and Archaeology in Europe* (London: University College Press, 1996), pp. 218–42, at p. 229.

36 Heorhi Shtykhaŭ, *Kryvichy: pa materyialakh raskopak kurhanoŭ u Paŭnochnaŭ Belarusi* (Minsk: Navuka i tekhnika, 1992); and 'Vytoki belaruskai narodnastsi (IX–XIII stst.)', *Belaruskaia minuŭshchyna*, no. 2, 1993, pp. 5–8. See also Leanid Lych, *Nazvy ziamli belaruskai* (Minsk: Universitetskae, 1994).

37 See also the excellent summary by Viktor Shnirelman, 'Natsionalisticheskii mif: osnovnye kharakteristiki (na primere etnogeneticheskikh versii vostochnoslavianskykh narodov)', *Slavianovedenie*, no. 6, 1995, pp. 3–13.

38 The text can be found in Paul Robert Magocsi, *A History of Ukraine* (Toronto: University of Toronto Press, 1996), p. 673.

39 Significantly, even Petro Tolochko argues against the Normanist theory. See his *Kyïvs'ka Rus'* (Kiev: Abrys, 1996), pp. 39–49. Although the 'St Petersburg' school of archaeologists in Russia was able to embrace many elements of the Normanist theory in the 1970s and 1980s, the issue is of greater existential importance to modern Ukraine. Cf. the more balanced survey by A. A. Hors'kyi, 'Shche raz pro rol' normanniv u formuvanni Kyïvs'koï Rusi', *Ukraïns'kyi istorychnyi zhurnal*, no. 1, 1994, pp. 3–9.

40 Raïsa Ivanchenko, *Kyïvs'ka Rus'. Pochatky Ukraïns'koï derzhavy: posibnyk z istoriï* (Kiev: Prosvita, 1995); Oleksa Novak, 'Derzhava Ukraïntsiv – Kyïvs'ka Rus'', *Klych*, nos. 6 and 7 (June), 1993; and Iaroslav Dashkevych, 'Natsiia i utvorennia Kyïvs'koï Rusi', *Ratusha*, 9 September 1993.

41 Petro Kononenko, *Ukraïnoznavstvo* (Kiev: Lybid', 1996), p. 222.

42 Or possibly two, as Ukrainian and Belarusian were not yet properly differentiated. On the timing of linguistic differentiation, see Kononenko, *Ukraïnoznavstvo*, pp. 125–9.

43 Andrii Buriachok, 'A naspravdi bulo tak . . . movna sytuatsiia v Kyïvs'kii Rusi', *Literaturna Ukraïna*, 13 October 1994.

44 Vasyl' Levchenko, 'Razom z imperiieiu vmyraiut' fal'shyvi teoriï ta mify', *Klych*, nos. 2 and 3 (April), 1993. See Ivan L. Rudnytsky, 'Franciszek Duchinski and His Impact on Ukrainian Political Thought', in his *Essays in Modern Ukrainian History* (Edmonton: CIUS, 1987), pp. 187–202, for the origins of this idea in the nineteenth century.

45 Mykola Sytalo, 'Rozvidka pro utvorennia rosiis'koho narodu-natsiï v etnichnykh mezhakh', *Respublika*, no. 2, 1995, pp. 40–5.

46 Kost' Huslystyi was able to express this idea in Soviet times. See his *Do pytannia pro utvorennia ukraïns'koï natsiï* (Kiev, 1967).

47 Petro Tolochko, for example, attacks the 'tendency to limit the under-

standing of "Kievan Rus'" solely to the territory of modern Ukraine' and
continues to argue that between 'the ninth and thirteenth centuries a relatively united eastern Slavic community was founded, which continued to
exist even after the destruction of Rus' by the Mongol-Tatars': *Kyïvs'ka Rus'*,
pp. 7 and 255.

48 O. P. Motsia, 'Kyïvs'ka Rus': rezul'taty ta perspektyvy doslidzhen'',
Ukraïns'kyi istorychnyi zhurnal, no. 4, 1996, pp. 41–9, at p. 48.

49 S. V. Tarasaŭ, 'Polatskae kniastva ŭ XI st.', in Mikalai Kryval'tsevich et al.
(eds.), *Staronki historyi Belarusi* (Minsk: Navuka i tekhnika, 1992), pp.
37–47, at p. 39.

50 Mikhas' Chapniaŭski, 'Iakiia belaruskiia dziarzhavy byli ŭ starazhytnastsi?',
in Z'mitser San'ko, *100 pytanniaŭ i adkazaŭ z historyi Belarusi* (Minsk:
Zviazda, 1993), pp. 3–4. See also Mikola Ermalovich, *Starazhytnaia
Belarus': polatski i novaharodski peryiady* (Minsk: Mastatskaia litaratura,
1990).

51 Chapniaŭski, 'Iakiia belaruskiia dziarzhavy byli ŭ starazhytnastsi?'

52 Siarhei Tarasaŭ, 'Kali pryishlo na Belarus' khrystsiianstva?', in San'ko, *100
pytanniaŭ i adkazaŭ z historyi Belarusi*, pp. 4–5.

53 Uladzimir Arloŭ, *Eŭfrasinnia poltskaia* (Minsk: Mastatskaia litaratura,
1992).

54 Compare for example Iaroslav Malyk, Borys Vol and Vasyl' Chupryna,
Istoriia ukraïns'koï derzhavnosti (L'viv: Svit, 1995), which has chapters on all
eras from the time of the Antes, and Mikhas' Bich, 'Dziarzhaŭnasts'
Belarusi: stanaŭlenne, strata, barats'ba za adnaŭlenne (IX st. – 1918 hod)',
Belaruskaia minuŭshchyna, no. 5–6, 1993, pp. 3–7 and 21, and Radzim
Haretski, 'Dziarzhaŭnasts' na Belarusi mae bol'sh chym tysiachahadovuiu
historiiu', *Belaruskaia minuŭshchyna*, no. 1, 1994, pp. 4–6. See also
Uladzimir Arloŭ, *Taiamnitsy polatskai historyi* (Minsk: Belarus', 1994).

55 Leonid Kravchuk in *Komsomol'skoe znamia*, 4 September 1991.

56 Soldatenko and Syvolob, 'Vytoky i peredvisnyky ukraïns'koï ideï', pp. 10–11.

57 R. D. Liakh and N. R. Temirova, 'Halyts'ko-Volyns'ka derzhava', in Liakh
and Temirova, *Istoriia Ukraïny: z naidavnishykh chasiv do seredyny XIV stolittia* (Kiev: Heneza, 1995), pp. 79–83, at p. 79; Iaroslav Isaievych, 'Halyts'ko-
Volyns'ka derzhava', in Smolii, *Istoriia Ukraïny: nove bachennia*, vol. I, pp.
95–112. At its height the western kingdom supposedly ruled over '90 per
cent of the then population' of Ukraine; Soldatenko and Syvolov, 'Vytoky i
peredvisnyky ukraïns'koï ideï', p. 15.

58 V. I. Naulko, 'Formuvannia ukraïns'koï narodnosti i natsiï', in Naulko et al.
(eds.), *Kul'tura i pobut naselennia Ukraïny* (Kiev: Lybid', 1991), pp. 13–21, at
p. 16. See also O. V. Rusyna et al., *Na perelomi: druha polovyna XV – persha
polovyna XVI st.* (Kiev: Ukraïna, 1994).

59 See M. F. Kotliar, 'Davn'orus'ki poperednyky kozatstva', in the round-table
discussion in *Ukraïns'kyi istorychnyi zhurnal*, no. 12, 1990, 'Ukraïns'ke
kozatstvo: suchasnyi stan ta perspektyvy doslidzhennia problemy. (Materialy
"kruhloho stolu")', pp. 12–29, at pp. 15–18. Natalia Iakovenko, in 'Rodova
elita – nosii "kontynuïtetu realii" mizh kniazhoiu Russiu i kozats'koiu
Ukraïnoiu', *Suchasnist'*, no. 1 (January), 1994, argues that continuity
between the two periods was provided by the local Orthodox nobility. For an

interesting commentary on these two claims, see Stepan Horoshko, 'Lakovanyi obraz Bohdana', *Politolohichni chytannia*, no. 1, 1992, pp. 250–69.

60 Naulko, 'Formuvannia ukraïns'koï narodnosti i natsiï', p. 18. See also Valerii Smolii and Valerii Stepankov, *Bohdan Khmel'nyts'kyi: sotsial'no-politychnyi portret*, 2nd edn (Kiev: Lybid', 1995); Leonid Mel'nyk, *Borot'ba za ukraïns'ku derzhavnist' (XVII st.)* (Kiev: Osvita, 1995); and the special issue of *Ukraïns'kyi istorychnyi zhurnal*, no. 4, 1995, on Khmel'nyts'kyi.

61 Valerii Shevchuk, *Kozats'ka derzhava* (Kiev: Abrys, 1995); Valerii Smolii, 'Ukraïns'ka kozats'ka derzhava', *Ukraïns'kyi istorychnyi zhurnal*, no. 4, 1991, pp. 5–19; 'Ukraïns'ke kozatstvo: suchasnyi stan ta perspectyvy doslidzhennia problemy. (Materialy "kruhloho stolu")', *Ukraïns'kyi istorychnyi zhurnal*, no. 12, 1990, pp. 12–29; V. S. Stepankov, 'Bohdan Khmel'nyts'kyi i problemy derzhavnosti Ukraïny', *Ukraïns'kyi istorychnyi zhurnal*, nos. 9 and 11, 1991, pp. 127–39; and V. A. Smolii et al., *Ukraïns'ka kozats'ka derzhava: vytoky ta shliakhy istorychnoho rozvytku (Materialy Chetvertykh Vseukraïns'kykh istorychnykh chytan')* (Kiev and Cherkasy: Instytut istoriï, 1994), esp. pp. 15–29 and 57–66.

62 I. Svarnyk, 'Natsional'no-vyzvol'ni rukhy u XVIII st.', in Iurii Zaitsev et al., *Istoriia Ukraïny* (L'viv: Svit, 1996), pp. 141–51; and the chapters on Ivan Mazepa and Pylyp Orlyk in Soldatenko et al., *Ukraïns'ka ideia: pershi rechnyky*, pp. 47–80; and Volodymyr Kryzhanivs'kyi and L. P. Nahorna, 'Samoutverdzhennia Ukraïny: politychni idealy, vtracheni iliuziï', in Soldatenko et al., *Ukraïns'ka ideia: istorychnyi narys*, pp. 33–62.

63 Ukrainian president Leonid Kravchuk nevertheless accepted a symbolic handover of authority from the government of the UNR in exile in 1992; see the commemorations in the special issue of *Rozbudova derzhavy*, no. 3 (August), 1992.

64 'Ukraïns'ka natsional'no-demokratychna revoliutsiia', and 'Ukraïna v borot'bi za zberezhennia derzhavnoï nezalezhnosti (1918–1920 rr.)', in the tenth-grade textbook by F. H. Turchenko, *Novitnia istoriia Ukraïny: chastyna persha (1917–1945 rr.)* (Kiev: Heneza, 1994), pp. 6–167; Mykola Lytvyn, 'Vyzvol'ni zmahannia 1914–1920 rr.', in Zaitsev et al., *Istoriia Ukraïny*, pp. 213–51; Mykola Lytvyn and Kim Haumenko, *Istoriia ZUNR* (L'viv: Olip, 1995).

65 Iurii Badz'o, 'Ukraïna: chetverta sproba, abo chy vyzhyvut' ukraïntsi?', *Rozbudova derzhavy*, no. 9 (September), 1995, p. 10.

66 'Zaiava URP do 75-i richnytsi utvorennia Tsentral'noï Rady', *Samostiina Ukraïna*, no. 14 (March), 1992. Cf. Mykola Lytvyn, 'Tut vyrishuiet'sia dolia derzhavy', *Samostiina Ukraïna*, no. 29 (August), 1994.

67 S. V. Kul'chyts'kyi, 'Ukraïns'ka Derzhava chasiv Het'manshchyna', *Ukraïns'kyi istorychnyi zhurnal*, no. 7–8, 1992, pp. 60–79, at p. 79, also denies that Skoropads'kyi's 'administration was at heart a puppet, collaborationist government' (of the occupying German army).

68 See for example the pedagogical guide published in early 1993, Mikhas' Bich, 'Ab natsyianal'nai kantseptsyi historyi i histarychnai adukatsyi ŭ respublitsy Belarus', *Belaruski histarychny chasopis*, no. 1, 1993, pp. 15–24; and Anatol' Hrytskevich's introduction to Ihnatoŭski, *Karotki narys historyi*

Belarusi, pp. 9–17. Also author's interviews with the historians Adam Mal'dzis, 31 August 1995, Anatol' Hrytskevich and Valentin Hrytskevich, 2 September 1995, and Uladzimir Arloŭ, 1 September 1995. Leanid Loika, 'Respublika i iae epokh', *Belaruskaia minuŭshchyna*, no. 6, 1995, pp. 4–6, divides the Polatsk period in two: before 1132 when it was part of the 'east Slav federation', and true independence thereafter. Much of the material for the sections on Belarusian national historiography was derived from the two popular works, Z'mitser San'ko (ed.), *100 pytanniaŭ i adkazaŭ z historyi Belarusi*, and V. F. Holubeŭ, U. P. Kruk and P. A. Loika, *Tsi vedaetse vy historyiu svaëi krainy?*, 2nd edn (Minsk: Narodnaia asveta, 1995).

69 *Kanstytutsyia respubliki Belarus'* (Minsk: Belarus', 1994), p. 66.

70 Aleksandr Rogalev, *Belaia Rus' i belorusy: v poiskakh istokov* (Homel': Belorusskoe agentstvo nauchno-tekhnicheskoi i delovoi informatsii, 1994).

71 Mikola Ermalovich, *Starazhytnaia Belarus': vilenski peryiad* (Minsk: Bats'kaŭshchyna/Besiadz', 1994); Ivan Saverchanka, 'Vialikae kniastva Litŭskae: utvarenne dziarzhavy', *Belaruski histarychny chasopis*, no. 2, 1993, pp. 11–17; Viachaslaŭ Nasevich, *Pachatki Vialikaha kniastva Litoŭskaha: padzei i asoby* (Minsk: Polymia, 1993).

72 'Iakaia mova byla dziarzhaŭnai u Vialikim Kniastve Litoŭskim?', in San'ko, *100 pytanniaŭ i adkazaŭ z historyi Belarusi*, pp. 12–13, at p. 12.

73 Paŭla Urban, 'Pra pakhodzhan'ne naimen'nia "Litva"', in his *Da pytan'nia etnichnai prynalezhnas'tsi starazhytnykh lits'vinoŭ* (Minsk: Bats'kaŭshchyna/ Besiadz', 1994); Vitaŭt Charopka, 'Litviny – slavianski narod', *Belaruskaia minuŭshchyna*, no. 3–4, 1993, pp. 12–14.

74 Stanislaŭ Tsiarokhin, 'Taiamnitsy Kreŭskai unii', *Belaruskaia minuŭshchyna*, no. 3, 1995, pp. 7–10.

75 Anatol' Hrytskevich, 'Barats'ba Vialikaha kniastva Litoŭskaha i Ruskaha (belaruska-litoŭskai dziarzhavy) z Teŭtonskim ordenam u kantsy XIV – pershai palove XV st.', in A. Hrytskevich (ed.), *Adradzhenne: histarychny al'manakh. Vypusk 1* (Minsk: Universitetskae, 1995), pp. 36–61.

76 Anatol' Hrytskevich has criticised even the venerable Belarusian historian Usevalad Ihnatoŭski for failing to note that the Union of Lublin created not 'a single state', but only 'a federation of two states [Poland and Lithuania-Belarus] with one king': 'Pohliady U. M. Ihnatoŭskaha na historyiu Belarusi feadal'naha peryiadu', in M. U. Tokaraŭ (ed.), *Akademik U. M. Ihnatoŭski: materyialy navukovykh chytanniaŭ, prysvechanykh 110-hoddziu z dnia naradzhennia* (Minsk: Navuka i tekhnika, 1993), pp. 48–56, at p. 54. See also Sh. Glava, 'Liublinskaia uniia kak zavershenie protsessa formirovaniia federativnoi Rechi Pospolitoi', in Dzmitryi Karaŭ et al., *Nash Radavod*, vol. VI, no. 2 (Hrodna: Belarusian State Museum on the History of Religion et al., 1994), pp. 318–48.

77 Maksim Bahdanovich, *Belaruskae adradzhenne* (Minsk: Universitetskae, 1994).

78 Kanstantsin Ezavitaŭ, 'Pershy Usebelaruski Kanhres', *Belaruskaia minuŭshchyna*, no. 1, 1993, pp. 25–9.

79 Anatol' Hrytskevich, 'Slutskae paŭstanne 1920 – zbroiny chyn u barats'be za nezalezhnasts' Belarusi', *Spadchyna*, no. 2, 1993, pp. 2–13.

80 Colin Williams and Anthony D. Smith, 'The National Construction of Social Space', *Progress in Human Geography*, vol. 7 (4), 1983, pp. 502–18, at p. 509.

81 Petro Lavriv, *Istoriia pivdenno-skhidnoï Ukraïny* (L'viv: Slovo, 1992), pp. 9–14.

82 Iaroslav Isaievych, 'Do pytannia pro zakhidnyi kordon Kyïvs'koï Rusi', in *Ukraïna: davna i nova*, pp. 81–104.

83 Dmitro Bilyi, *Malynovyi Klyn: narysy z istoriï ukraïntsiv Kubani* (Kiev: Ukraïna, 1994), pp. 5–11.

84 D. I. Bahalii, *Istoriia Slobids'koï Ukraïny* (Kharkiv: Del'ta, 1993), a reprint of the 1918 edition; S. M. Kudelko and S. I. Posokhov, *Kharkiv: nauka, osvita, kul'tura* (Kharkiv: Oko, 1996), p. 5. According to the latter (at p. 4), although the Kharkiv region was first occupied by the Siverianians in the eighth century AD and was mentioned in Rus' chronicles, 'the founders of the town were Ukrainian Cossacks and peasants, who arrived on the territory in the middle of the seventeenth century during the war for the liberation of the Ukrainian people led by Bohdan Khmel'nyts'kyi against the [Polish] Rzeczpospolita'. On the Don basin, see Andrew Wilson, 'The Donbas Between Ukraine and Russia: The Use of History in Political Disputes', *Journal of Contemporary History*, vol. 30 (2), April 1995, pp. 265–89.

85 Feliks Shabul'do, 'Ukraïna v derzhavotvorchykh protsesakh u Krymu v kintsi XIV – pershii polovyni XV st.', *Suchasnist'*, no. 5 (May), 1996, pp. 82–8; V. V. Stanislavs'kyi, 'Zaporoz'ka Sich u politychnykh vidnosynakh z Kryms'kym khanstvom (pochatok XVIII st.)', *Ukraïns'kyi istorychnyi zhurnal*, no. 6, 1995, pp. 3–21.

86 Ahatanhel Krymsk'yi, *Istoriia Turechchyny* (L'viv: Olip, 1996), a reprint of the original 1924 edition.

87 See, for example, 'Krym ot drevneishikh vremen do nachala XX v.', in R. G. Nevedrova (ed.), *Krym mnogonatsional'nyi* (Simferopol': Tavriia, 1988), pp. 5–42.

88 Iaŭhen Nasytka, '"Tyia zh belarusy . . . ": etnichnyia mezhy belarusaŭ u XIX–pachatku XX st.', *Belaruskaia minuŭshchyna*, no. 4, 1994, pp. 11–15; Leŭ Kasloŭ and Anatol' Tsitoŭ, *Belarus' na siami rubiazhakh* (Minsk: Belarus', 1993), p. 25.

89 See for example the maps in Vitaŭt Charopka, 'Liublinskaia uniia', *Belaruskaia minuŭshchyna*, no. 2, 1995, pp. 31–4, between pp. 32 and 33.

90 Ermalovich, *Starazhytnaia Belarus': vilenski peryiad*, p. 5, and 'Tsi praŭda, shto litoŭtsy zavaëŭvali Belarus'?', in San'ko, *100 pytanniaŭ i adkazaŭ z historyi Belarusi*, pp. 10–11. Vil'nia was the main centre of the Belarusian national revival until 1917, after which it was seized by the Poles, before being transferred to Lithuania in 1940.

91 Iaroslav Dashkevych, 'Etnichni psevdomenshyny v Ukraïni', in Volodymyr Ievtukh and Arnold Suppan (eds.), *Etnichni menshyny Skhidnoï ta Tsentral'noï Ievropy* (Kiev: INTEL, 1994), pp. 65–79, at pp. 76–7.

92 Iaroslav Isaievych, 'Cultural Relations Between Belarusians, Russians and Ukrainians (Late Sixteenth Through Early Eighteenth Centuries)', in *Ukraïna: davna i nova*, pp. 198–213.

93 'Nova Ukraïna chy nova koloniia?', *Holos Ukraïny*, 12 December 1995.

94 Leonid Zalizniak, 'Ukraïna i Rosiia: rizni istorychni doli', *Starozhytnosti*, no. 19, 1991. Cf. Stepan Rudnyts'kyi, 'Ukraïns'ka sprava zi stanovyshcha polity-chnoï heohrafiï', in his *Chomu my khochemo samostiinoï Ukraïny?* (L'viv: Svit, 1994; first published in 1920), pp. 93–208.

95 Volodymyr Serhiichuk, *Mors'ki pokhody zaporozhtsiv* (Kiev: Biblioteka Ukraïntsia, no. 5, 1992); Andrii Panibud'laska and Borys Kantseliaruk, *Istoriia ukraïns'koï zbroï* (Kiev: Biblioteka Ukraïntsia, no. 3-7, 1993); and Vladimir Kravtsevych, *Ukrainskii derzhavnyi flot* (Kiev: Krai, 1992).

96 Iazep Iukho, 'Shto takoe mahdeburhskae prava?', in San'ko, *100 pytanniaŭ i adkazaŭ z historyi Belarusi*, pp. 20–1.

97 Levko Luk''ianenko, 'Ukraïntsi i ïkh konstytutsiia', *Samostiina Ukraïna*, no. 11 (August), 1991; Olena Apanovych, 'Demokratyzm derzhavnoho ustroiu i zhyttia Zaporoz'koï Sichi', in V. F. Huzhva (ed.), *Demokratiia v Ukraïni: mynule i maibutnie* (Kiev: Ukraïns'kyi pys'mennyk, 1993), pp. 93–102.

98 A. H. Sliusarenko and M. V. Tomenko, *Istoriia ukraïns'koï konstytutsiï* (Kiev: Znannia, 1993), p. 9. See also Iryna Kresina and Oleksii Kresin, *Het'man Pylyp Orlyk i ioho konstytutsiia* (Kiev: Biblioteka Ukraïntsia, no. 3-9, 1993).

99 Arsen Zinchenko, 'Ukraïns'ke pravoslav''ia iak natsional'no-istorychnyi fenomen', *Heneza*, no. 2, 1994, pp. 242–8, at p. 244.

100 Volodymyr Kisyk, 'Pro shliakhy rozvytku tserkvy v Ukraïni i Rosiï (XI–XVI st.)', *Ukraïns'kyi istorychnyi zhurnal*, nos. 2–3, 1993, pp. 76–85; V. I. Ul'ianovs'kyi, *Istoriia tserkvy ta relihiinoï dumky v Ukraïni*, vol. I (Kiev: Lybid', 1994), pp. 43–78.

101 Nataliia Kochan, 'Florentiis'ka uniia i Kyïvs'ka mytropoliia: do kharak-terystyky rozvytku ta vtilennia ideï uniï tserkov', *Ukraïns'kyi istorychnyi zhurnal*, no. 1, 1996, pp. 28–45.

102 O. S. Onyshchenko et al. (eds.), *Istoriia khrystyians'koï tserkvy na Ukraïni (Relihiieznavchyi dovidkovyi narys)* (Kiev: Naukova dumka, 1992), pp. 8–12; Kost' Panas, *Istoriia Ukraïns'koï tserkvy* (L'viv: Transintekh, 1992), pp. 45–68; and V. V. Haiuk et al. (eds.), *Istoriia relihii v Ukraïni* (Kiev: Akademiia nauk Ukraïny, 1993), pp. 28–30 and 38–9.

103 Borys Gudziak (ed.), *Istorychnyi kontekst, ukladennia Beresteis'koï uniï i pershe pouniine pokolinnia* (L'viv: Instytut istoriï tserkvy, 1995).

104 N. Tsisyk (ed.), *Ukraïns'ke vidrodzhennia i natsional'na tserkva* (Kiev: Pam''iatky Ukraïny, 1990).

105 Serhii Zdioruk, 'Natsional'na tserkva u konteksti derzhavotvorennia v Ukraïni', *Rozbudova derzhavy*, no. 1, 1994; and Serhii Bilokin', 'Dukhovnist' – nadbannia natsiï: derzhavnyts'ka ideolohiia Kyïvs'koho patriarkhatu', *Samostiina Ukraïna*, no. 7 (March), 1994.

106 Sylenko, *Maha vira*; Shylov, *Brama bezsmertia*.

107 Ihnat Abdziralovich, *Advechnym shliakham: das'ledziny belaruskaha s'vetahliadu* (Minsk: Navuka i tekhnika, 1993); I. V. Kazakova, *Etnichnyia tradytsyi ŭ dukhoŭnai kul'tury belarusaŭ* (Minsk: Universitetskae, 1995); I. I. Salivon, *Fizichny typ belarusaŭ: uzrostavaia, typalahichnaia i ekalahichnaia zmenlivasts'* (Minsk: Navuka i tekhnika, 1994).

108 'Tsi byla na Belarusi manhola-tatarskaia niavolia?', in San'ko, *100 pytanniaŭ i adkazaŭ z historyi Belarusi*, pp. 8–9, at p. 9.

109 Vitaŭt Charopka, 'Liublinskaia uniia', *Belaruskaia minuŭshchyna*, no. 2,

1995, pp. 31–4; and '"Braterskaia liuboŭ"', *Belaruskaia minuŭshchyna*, no. 1, 1995, pp. 7–10.

110 Author's interviews with Anatol´ Hrytskevich and Valentin Hrytskevich, 2 September 1995. See also Yaŭhen Filipovich, 'Khto zh peremoh u Arshanskai bitve?', *Nasha slova*, no. 18, 4 May–7 June 1995.

111 Henadz´ Sahanovich, *Neviadomaia vaina: 1654–1667* (Minsk: Navuka i tekhnika, 1995), p. 130.

112 Anatol´ Hrytskevich, 'Relihiinae pytanne i zneshniaia palitika tsaryzmu perad padzelami Rechy Paspalitai', *Vestsi AN BSSR*, no. 6, 1973, pp. 62–71, at p. 63; and Hrytskevich, 'Uniiatskaia tsarkva ŭ kantsy XVII–pachatku XIX stahodz´dzia', *Khrys´tsiianskaia Dumka*, no. 3, 1993, pp. 18–32; author's interviews with Anatol´ Hrytskevich, 2 and 5 September 1995.

113 Mark R. Beissinger, 'The Persisting Ambiguity of Empire', *Post-Soviet Affairs*, vol. 11 (2), April–June 1995, pp. 149–84.

114 According to Iurii Badz´o, for example, 'the words "war" and "occupation" . . . are understood by many to be metaphors or publicists' exaggerations. Unfortunately they represent the real state of affairs' between Ukraine and Russia: 'Ukraïna: chetverta sproba, abo chy vyzhyvut´ ukraïntsi?', *Rozbudova derzhavy*, no. 9 (September), 1995, p. 9. See also Levko Luk´´ianenko, 'Zvitna dopovid´ z´´ïzdovi Ukraïns´koï hel´sins´koï spilky', in *Viruiu v boha i v Ukraïnu* (Kiev: Pam´´iatky Ukraïny, 1991), pp. 278–90, esp. pp. 278–81.

115 Stanislaŭ Stankevich, *Rusifikatsyia belaruskae movy ŭ BSSR i supratsiŭ rusifikatsyinamu pratsesu* (Minsk: Navuka i tekhnika, 1994); Oleksandr Serbezhs´koï (ed.), *Anty-surzhyk* (L´viv: Svit, 1994).

116 Iurii Badz´o and Ivan Iushchyk (eds.), *Naibil´shyi zlochyn imperiï: materialy naukovo-praktychnoï konferentsiï 'Slobozhanshchyna: Holodomor 1932–1933 rokiv'* (Kiev: Prosvita, 1993). See also the open letter to Kravchuk signed by leading nationalists in *Poklyk sumlinnia*, no. 18 (May), 1992.

117 Iurii. I. Shapoval, *Ukraïna 20–50-kh rokiv: storinky nenapysanoï istoriï* (Kiev: Naukova dumka, 1993); 'Stalinizm i Ukraïna', *Ukraïns´kyi istorychnyi zhurnal*, 1991 and 1992 *passim*; *Liudyna i systema (shtrykhy do portretu totalitarnoï doby v Ukraïni* (Kiev: Akademiia nauk Ukraïny, 1994); Mikhas´ Kastsiuk, 'Stalinshchyna i Belarus´´', *Belaruski histarychny chasopis*, nos. 1 and 2, 1995, pp. 9–14 and 98–106; Uladzimir Adamushka, *Palitychnyia represii 20–50-ykh hadoŭ na Belarusi* (Minsk: Belarus´, 1994).

118 'Ekonomika i derzhavna nezalezhnist´´', *Samostiina Ukraïna*, no. 9 (July), 1991; L. P. Horkina, *Narysy z istoriï politychnoï ekonomiï v Ukraïni* (Kiev: Naukova dumka, 1994).

119 Oleksandr Boldyrev (ed.), *Istorychni postati Ukraïny* (Odesa: Maiak, 1993); I. Boitsekhivs´ka et al., *Istoriia Ukraïny v osobakh: XIX–XX st.* (Kiev: Ukraïna, 1995); and Soldatenko et al., *Ukraïns´ka ideia: pershi rechnyky*.

120 Iu. O. Ivanchenka (ed.), *Mazepa* (Kiev: Mystetstvo, 1993); Larysa Bondarenko (ed.), *Ivan Mazepa i Moskva* (Kiev: Rada, 1994); Valerii Shevchuk, 'Vyzvol´na aktsiia Ivana Mazepa ta ioho systema derzhavotvorennia', and 'Borot´ba Pavla Polubotoka za zberezhennia reshtok ukraïns´koï avtonomiï', *Rozbudova derzhavy*, no. 2 (February), 1993, and no. 9 (September), 1994.

121 V. H. Sarbei, 'Stanovlennia i konsolidatsiia natsiï ta pidnesennia natsional'noho rukhu na Ukraïni v druhii polovyni XIX st.', *Ukraïns'kyi istorychnyi zhurnal*, no. 5, 1991, pp. 3–16; Taras Hunchak, *Ukraïna: persha polovyna XX stolittia. Narysy politychnoï istoriï* (Kiev: Lybid', 1993), pp. 7–78.

122 See the critique by Iaroslav Hrytsak, 'Reabilitatsiia Hrushevs'koho i legitymatsiia nomenklatury', *Den'*, no. 12, 1996.

123 Anatolii Rusnachenko, 'Iak Ukraïna zdobuvala nezalezhnist' i shcho z toho vykhodyt'', *Suchasnist'*, no. 3–4 (March–April), 1996, pp. 58–64; Ievhen Sverstiuk et al., *Oksana Meshko, kozats'ka matir* (Kiev: URP, 1995); Bohdan Horyn', 'Tykhyi i hromovyi holos Vasylia Symonenka', *Samostiina Ukraïna*, nos. 3 and 4 (January), 1995. In particular the poet Vasyl' Stus, who died in the Gulag in 1985, has been turned into something of a national icon: Dmytro Stus, *Zhyttia i tvorchist' Vasyla Stusa* (Kiev: Biblioteka Ukraïntsia, no. 7, 1992); and Iurii Bedryk, *Vasyl' Stus: problema spryimannia* (Kiev: Biblioteka Ukraïntsia, no. 2-5, 1993).

124 Liubov Holota (ed.), *Symon Petliura: vybrani tvory ta dokumenty* (Kiev: Dovira, 1994); Natalia Kychyhina, 'Politychna kontseptsiia V. K. Vynnychenka', *Politolohichni chytannia*, no. 2, 1994, pp. 83–95.

125 V. A. Smolii, 'Deiaki dyskusiini pytannia istoriï Koliïvshchyny (1768 r.)', *Ukraïns'kyi istorychnyi zhurnal*, no. 10, 1993, pp. 21–9.

126 Oles' Kozulia, *Zhinky v istoriï Ukraïny* (Kiev: Ukraïns'kyi tsentre dukhovnoï kul'tury, 1993).

127 O. P. Reient, *Robitnytstvo Ukraïny i Tsentral'na Rada* (Kiev: Akademiia nauk Ukraïny, 1993), p. 45, and Reient, 'Stavlennia proletariatu Ukraïny do Tsentral'noï Rady', *Ukraïns'kyi istorychnyi zhurnal*, no. 4, 1994, pp. 13–18.

128 The literature on the OUN-UPA is voluminous; the following are only examples: M. Bar and A. Zalens'kyi, 'Viina vtrachenykh nadii: ukraïns'kyi samostiinyts'kyi rukh u 1939–1945 rr.', *Ukraïns'kyi istorychnyi zhurnal*, no. 6, 1992, pp. 116–22; M. V. Koval', 'OUN-UPA: mizh "tretim reikhom" i stalins'kym totalitaryzmom', *Ukraïns'kyi istorychnyi zhurnal*, no. 2–3, 1994, pp. 94–102; Oleh Bahan, *Natsionalizm i natsionalistychnyi rukh: istoriia ta ideï* (Drohobych: Vidrodzhennia, 1994); Stepan Mechnyk, *U vyri voiennoho lykholittia: OUN i UPA u borot'bi z hitlerivs'kymy okupantamy* (L'viv: Krai, 1992); and Bohdan Zalizniak (ed.), *Zdaleka pro blyz'ke: zbirnyk statei* (L'viv: Memorial, 1992). For a Polish critique, see Wiktor Poliszczuk, *Legal and Political Assessment of the OUN and UPA* (Toronto: n.p., 1997).

129 Volodymyr Serhiichuk, 'V UPA – vsia Ukraïna', *Viis'ko Ukraïny*, no. 6, 1993, pp. 74–84.

130 The total includes members of other underground groups: Koval', 'OUN-UPA', p. 101. For some Western estimates, see David R. Marples, *Stalinism in Ukraine in the 1940s* (London: Macmillan, 1992), pp. 72–9.

131 Mykhailo Slaboshpyts'kyi and Valerii Stetsenko, *Ukraïns'ka dyviziia 'Halychyna': istoryko-publitsystychnyi zbirnyk* (Kiev and Toronto: Visti z Ukraïny, 1994).

132 See for example the rolling cycle of fiftieth anniversary commemorations in *Holos Ukraïny*, January to July 1995, *passim*.

133 Anatol' Hrytskevich, 'Paŭstanne 1794 h.: peradumovy, khod i vyniki', *Belaruski histarychny chasopis*, no. 1, 1994, pp. 39–47.

134 'Iaki sled u historyi Belarusi pakinuŭ A. Suvoraŭ?', in San´ko, *100 pytanniaŭ i adkazaŭ z historyi Belarusi*, pp. 50–1.

135 Viachaslaŭ Shal´kevich, 'Apostal svabody i nezalezhnastsi – Kastys´ Kalinoŭski', *Belaruskaia minuŭshchyna*, no. 1, 1993, pp. 30–3.

136 Iaŭhen Siamashka, *Armiia Kraëva na Belarusi* (Minsk: Khata, 1994).

137 Robert F. Byrnes, *V. O. Kliuchevskii, Historian of Russia* (Bloomington: Indiana University Press, 1995), pp. 145–50.

138 Paul Bushkovitch, 'The Ukraine in Russian Culture, 1790–1860: The Evidence of the Journals', *Jahrbücher für Geschichte Osteuropas*, vol. 39 (1), 1991, pp. 339–63. The quote is at p. 361.

139 S. N. Shchegolev (then the Kiev censor), *Ukrainskoe dvizhenie kak sovremennyi etap yuzhno-russkogo separatizma* (Kiev: L. Idzikovskogo, 1912), and *Sovremennoe ukrainstvo* (Kiev: L. Idzikovskogo, 1914); Petr Struve, 'Obshcherusskaia kul´tura i ukrainskii partikuliarizm: otvet ukrainstu', *Russkaia mysl´*, vol. 33 (1), January 1912. Cf. Vladimir Vernadskii's 1916 essay, 'Ukrainskii vopros i russkoe obshchestvo', reprinted in V. P. Volkov (ed.), *V. I. Vernadskii: publitsisticheskie stat´i* (Moscow: Nauka, 1995), pp. 212–21.

140 On the civil war period, see Anna Procyk, *Russian Nationalism and Ukraine: The Nationality Policy of the Volunteer Army During the Civil War* (Edmonton: CIUS, 1995).

141 Aleksandr Volkonskii, *Istoricheskaia pravda i ukrainofil´skaia propaganda* (Turin: Vicenti Bona, 1920), published in English as Prince Alexandre Wolkonsky, *The Ukraine Question: The Historic Truth Versus the Separatist Propaganda* (Rome: Ditta E. Armani, 1920); V. M. Levitskii, *Chto kazhdyi dolzhen´ znat´ ob´ Ukrainie* (Paris: n.p., 1939); Andrei Dikii, *Neizvrashchennaia istoriia Ukrainy–Rusi*, 2 vols. (New York: Pravda o Rossii, 1960–1); and Nikolai Ul´ianov, *Proiskhozhdenie ukrainskogo separatizma* (Moscow: Indrik, 1996). Significantly, this one modern work is a reprint of an edition first published in New York in 1966. See also the article by Ian Zamoiski, 'Otnoshenie "beloi" russkoi emigratsii k ukrainskim voprosam (1919–1939)', *Slavianovedenie*, no. 4 (July–August), 1993, pp. 39–48.

142 Lowell Tillet, *The Great Friendship: Soviet Historians on the Non-Russian Nationalities* (Chapel Hill: University of North Carolina Press, 1969), provides a useful survey of Soviet historical myths concerning the non-Russian nations. See also the volume produced in Kiev for the 300th anniversary of Pereiaslav in 1954, *Vikovichna druzhba rosiis´koho i ukraïns´koho narodiv* (Kiev: Radians´ka shkola, 1954), and official Soviet Ukrainian histories such as the 1948 magnum opus, and the volumes produced in 1965–7 and 1977–9. See the commentary in Velychenko, *Shaping Identity in Eastern Europe and Russia*, pp. 155–8 and 164–76.

143 Dikii, *Neizvrashchennaia istoriia Ukrainy–Rusi*, vol. I, p. 15; Alexander Solzhenitsyn, *Rebuilding Russia* (London: Harvill, 1991), pp. 17–18.

144 Dikii, *Neizvrashchennaia istoriia Ukrainy–Rusi*, vol. I, p. 28.

145 Wolkonsky, *The Ukraine Question*, pp. 45, 43, 51 and 12; Dikii, *Neizvrashchennaia istoriia Ukrainy–Rusi*, vol. I, p. 40. Cf. Lev Gumilev, *Ot Rusi k Rossii* (Moscow: Ekopros, 1992).

146 Wolkonsky, *The Ukraine Question*, p. 77. Cf. B. N. Floria, 'Istoricheskie

sud′by Rusi i etnicheskoe samosoznanie vostochnykh slavian v XII–XV vekakh (k voprosu o zarozhdenii vostochnoslavianskikh narodnostei)′, *Slavianovedenie*, no. 22 (March–April), 1993, pp. 42–66. Pavel Miliukov and the nineteenth-century 'Moscow school' of Russian historians tended to pass over the period of 'common development' at the time of Kievan Rus′; see Miliukov's *Ocherki po istorii russkoi kul′tury*, 3 vols. (Moscow: Progress, 1993–5).

147 Wolkonsky, *The Ukraine Question*, p. 72.
148 Dikii, *Neizvrashchennaia istoriia Ukrainy–Rusi*, vol. I, p. 55; Solzhenitsyn, *Rebuilding Russia*, p. 18.
149 Alexander Solzhenitsyn, *The Russia Question at the End of the Twentieth Century* (London: Harvill, 1995), p. 26; Dikii, *Neizvrashchennaia istoriia Ukrainy–Rusi*, vol. I, pp. 83 and 87.
150 Solzhenitsyn, *The Russia Question*, p. 29–31.
151 Wolkonsky, *The Ukraine Question*, p. 99.
152 Dikii, *Neizvrashchennaia istoriia Ukrainy–Rusi*, vol. I, pp. 99–101.
153 Ul′ianov, *Proiskhozhdenie ukrainskogo separatizma*, p. 22; Dikii, *Neizvrashchennaia istoriia Ukrainy–Rusi*, vol. I, pp. 338–9.
154 Wolkonsky, *The Ukraine Question*, pp. 136–8, 121 and 236.
155 Dikii, *Neizvrashchennaia istoriia Ukrainy–Rusi*, vol. I, pp. 362–6; Wolkonsky, *The Ukraine Question*, p. 132.
156 Nikolai Trubetskoi, 'The Ukrainian Problem', in the collection of his essays, *The Legacy of Genghis Khan and Other Essays on Russia's Identity* (Ann Arbor: Michigan Slavic Publications, 1991), pp. 245–67, at p. 251. Emphases in original.
157 'Zaiavlenie Grazhdanskogo kongressa Ukrainy [on the 340th anniversary of the Treaty of Pereiaslav]', *Grazhdanskii kongress*, no. 2, 1994.
158 Ul′ianov, *Proiskhozhdenie ukrainskogo separatizma*, p. 5.
159 Wolkonsky, *The Ukraine Question*, pp. 160 and 158.
160 Ul′ianov, *Proiskhozhdenie ukrainskogo separatizma*, p. 205.
161 Dikii, *Neizvrashchennaia istoriia Ukrainy–Rusi*, vol. II, pp. 4 and 36; Ul′ianov, *Proiskhozhdenie ukrainskogo separatizma*, pp. 4–5.
162 Dikii, *Neizvrashchennaia istoriia Ukrainy–Rusi*, vol. II, pp. 120, 123–4 and 136–9.
163 Ibid., vol. II, p. 67; Solzhenitsyn, *Rebuilding Russia*, p. 18.
164 I. M. Ihnatsenka, 'Belarus′ napiaredadni i ŭ pershyia hady savetskai ulady', in M. P. Kastsiuk et al., *Narysy historyi Belarusi*, vol. II (Minsk: Belarus′, 1995), pp. 8–76, at pp. 58, 59, 51, 60 and 73. Ihnatsenka was a former Soviet procurator.
165 Ihnatsenka, 'Belarus′ napiaredadni i ŭ pershyia hady savetskai ulady', pp. 65–6 and 73. Ihnatsenka also denies the 'so-called Slutsk rebellion' against Soviet power ever took place (as there were no Soviet troops in the region at the time to fight against): ibid., pp. 71–2.
166 Petro Symonenko, '"Natsional′na ideia": mify i real′nist′', *Holos Ukraïny*, 21 March 1996; Volodymyr Hyrn′ov, *Nova Ukraïna: iakoiu ia ïï bachu* (Kiev: Abrys, 1995), p. 62.
167 Solzhenitsyn, *Rebuilding Russia*, p. 18
168 A. M. Litvin and Ya. S. Paŭlaŭ, 'Belarus′ u hady Vialikai Aichynnai vainy', in

Kastsiuk et al., *Narysy historyi Belarusi,* vol. II, pp. 265–323. See also the view of Myroslav Popovych, a liberal Ukrainian centrist, *Ievropa–Ukraïna – pravi i livi* (Kiev: Kyïvs´ke bratstvo, 1997), pp. 93–4.

169 Oleksandr Moroz, *Vybir* (Kiev: Postup, 1994), pp. 60–2; Symonenko, '"Natsional´na ideia": mify i real´nist''.

170 Solzhenitsyn, *The Russia Question,* p. 87.

171 See for example V. I. Kozlov, *Istoriia tragedii velikogo naroda* (Moscow: n.p., 1996). For an analysis of the views of Gennadii Ziuganov and the Russian communists, see David Remnick's essay in the *New York Review of Books,* 23 May 1996, pp. 45–51.

172 A. Luzan, 'Kakoe gosudarstvo my stroim i chemu my uchim nashikh detei?', *Grazhdanskii kongress,* no. 1, 1994; Fedor Gorelik and Ivan Karachun, 'Shkola snova v "miasorubke" ideologii', *Donetskii kriazh,* no. 30, 3–9 September 1993. Crimea is an exception, as it still possesses an autonomous 'ministry of education'.

173 See the Ministry of Education's *Historyia Belarusi* (Minsk: Narodnaia asveta, 1993), one volume each for the fifth to ninth grades.

174 See Wilson, 'Myths of National History', for a fuller treatment.

175 Considerable use has been made of the following school texts as source materials: M. V. Koval´, S. V. Kul´chyts´kyi and Iu. O. Kurnosov, *Istoriia Ukraïny* (Kiev: Raiduha, 1992), exam primer for tenth and eleventh classes; Iu. M. Alekseev, A. H. Vertehel and V. M. Danylenko, *Istoriia Ukraïny* (Kiev: Teal, 1993), exam primer for final classes and students; *Istoriia Ukraïny dlia ditei shkil´noho viku* (Kiev: Znannia, 1992), a reprint of a 1934 L´viv edition; R. D. Liakh and N. R. Temirova, *Istoriia Ukraïny: z naidavnishykh chasiv do seredyny XIV stolittia* (Kiev: Heneza, 1995), seventh class; F. H. Turchenko, *Novitnia istoriia Ukraïny: chastyna persha (1917–1945 rr.)* (Kiev: Heneza, 1994), tenth class; and Turchenko, P. P. Panchenko and S. M. Tymchenko, *Novitnia istoriia Ukraïny: chastyna druha (1945–1995 rr.)* (Kiev: Heneza, 1995), eleventh class.

176 See Kuchma's speeches in *Holos Ukraïny,* 28 August 1995; *Literaturna Ukraïna,* 28 December 1995 (on the 400th anniversary of the birth of Khmel´nyts´kyi); and *Uriadovyi kur´´ier,* 29 August 1996.

3 NATIONAL IDENTITY AND MYTHS OF ETHNOGENESIS IN TRANSCAUCASIA

1 Milton Esman, 'Two Dimensions of Ethnic Politics: Defence of Homelands, Immigrant Rights', *Ethnic and Racial Studies,* vol. 8 (3), 1985, pp. 438–9.

2 Colin Williams and Anthony D. Smith, 'The National Construction of Social Space', *Progress in Human Geography,* vol. 7 (4), 1983, pp. 502–18, at p. 502.

3 Stephen Velychenko, 'National History and the "History of the USSR": The Persistence and Impact of Categories', in D. V. Schwartz and R. Panossian (eds.), *Nationalism and History: The Politics of Nation-Building in Post-Soviet Armenia, Azerbaijan and Georgia* (Toronto: Center for Russian and East European Studies, University of Toronto, 1994), pp. 13–39.

4 Eric Hobsbawm and Terrence Ranger (eds.), *The Invention of Tradition*

(Cambridge: Cambridge University Press, 1983); B. C. Shafer, *Faces of Nationalism: New Realities and Old Myths* (New York: Harcourt, Brace, Jovanovich, 1972), pp. 313–42; Anthony D. Smith, 'National Identity and Myths of Ethnic Descent', *Research in Social Movements, Conflict and Change*, no. 7, 1984, pp. 95–130; A. D. Smith, *The Ethnic Origins of Nations* (Oxford: Blackwell, 1988), pp. 24–31 and 174–208; A. D. Smith, *National Identity* (London: Penguin, 1991), p. 78; T. Eriksen, *Ethnicity and Nationalism: Anthropological Perspectives* (London: Pluto Press, 1993), pp. 70–3.

5 Michael Walzer, *The National Question Revised* (Oxford: Tanner Lectures, 1989), p. 35; Yael Tamir, *Liberal Nationalism* (Princeton, NJ: Princeton University Press, 1993), p. 94.

6 Victor A. Shnirelman, *Who Gets the Past? Competition for Ancestors Among Non-Russian Intellectuals in Russia* (Washington, DC, and Baltimore: Woodrow Wilson Center Press and Johns Hopkins University Press, 1996), p. 60.

7 Yuri Slezkine, *Arctic Mirrors: Russia and the Small Peoples of the North* (Ithaca and London: Cornell University Press, 1994), p. 387.

8 B. R. Posen, 'The Security Dilemma and Ethnic Conflict', in M. E. Brown (ed.), *Ethnic Conflict and International Security* (Princeton, NJ: Princeton University Press, 1993), pp. 103–24, at p. 107.

9 Gerhard Brunn, 'Historical Consciousness and Historical Myths', in Andreas Kappeler (ed.), *The Formation of National Elites: Comparative Studies on Governments and Non-Dominant Ethnic Groups in Europe, 1850–1940*, vol. VI (New York: New York University Press, 1992), pp. 327–38.

10 William Graham Sumner, *Folkways* (London: Constable, 1958), pp. 12–14; Sumner, 'War', in L. Bramson and S. Goethals (eds.), *War: Studies from Psychology, Sociology and Anthropology* (New York: Basic Books, 1964), pp. 205–27.

11 C. H. Wedgwood, 'Some Aspects of Warfare in Melanesia', *Oceania*, vol. 1 (1), 1930, pp. 5–33.

12 Robert LeVine and Donald Campbell, *Ethnocentrism: Theories of Conflict, Ethnic Attitudes and Group Behavior* (New York: John Wiley and Sons, 1972).

13 See also Viktor Shnirelman, 'The Past as a Strategy for Ethnic Confrontation', *Helsinki Citizens' Assembly Quarterly*, no. 14, Summer 1995, pp. 20–2; Nora Dudwick, 'The Case of the Caucasian Albanians: Ethnohistory and Ethnic Politics', *Cahiers du monde russe et soviétique*, vol. 31 (2–3), 1990, pp. 377–84; Dudwick, 'The Pen and the Sword: Intellectuals, Nationalism and Violence in Armenia and Azerbaijan', unpublished manuscript, 1994; Stephan H. Astourian, 'In Search of Their Forefathers: National Identity and the Historiography and Politics of Armenian and Azerbaijani Ethnogenesis', in Schwartz and Panossian, *Nationalism and History*, pp. 41–94; and Robert H. Hewson, 'Ethno-History and the Armenian Influence on the Caucasian Albanians', in Thomas J. Samuelian (ed.), *Classical Armenian Culture: Influence and Creativity* (Philadelphia: Scholars' Press, 1982), pp. 27–40.

14 Astourian, 'In Search of Their Forefathers', pp. 43–5, describes this as 'the classical thesis'.

15 I. M. Diakonov, 'K metodike issledovanii po etnicheskoi istorii', in M. S.

Asimov et al. (eds.), *Etnicheskie problemy istorii Tsentral'noi Azii v drevnosti* (Moscow: Nauka, 1981), pp. 90–100, at p. 91; Diakonov, 'K praistorii armianskogo iazyka', *Istoriko-filologicheskii zhurnal*, no. 4, 1983, pp. 149–78, at p. 157; and author's personal communications with Diakonov, 1993.

16 R. A. Ishkhanyan, 'Novye otkrytiia v sravnitel'nom iazykoznanii i voprosy proiskhozhdeniia i drevneishei istorii armian', *Vestnik Ierevanskogo universiteta obshchestvennye nauki*, no. 2, 1979, pp. 85–111; Ishkhanyan, 'Drevneishye aborigeny', *Kommunist* (Yerevan), 16 February 1980; Ishkhanyan, 'Proiskhozhdenie i drevneishaia istoriia armian v svete novykh dostizhenii linguistiki', *Literaturnaia Armeniia*, no. 4, 1981, pp. 63–78.

17 V. N. Khachatrian, 'Khaiatsy', *Vestnik obschestvennykh nauk Armianskoi SSR*, no. 8, 1972, pp. 32–41; Khachatrian, 'Khaiasa i Nairi', *Vestnik obschestvennykh nauk Armianskoi SSR*, no. 1, 1973, pp. 37–47; Khachatrian, 'Nairi i Armina', *Vestnik obschestvennykh nauk Armianskoi SSR*, no. 8, 1976, pp. 59–72; Khachatrian, 'Strana Khaik v sostave Urartu', *Vestnik obschestvennykh nauk Armianskoi SSR*, no. 6, 1980, pp. 101–12.

18 A. Mnatsakanian, 'Armianskie namestniki Armenii v period vladychestva Urartov i Assiriitsev po Movsesu Khorenatsi (k voprosu ob avtokhtonnosti Armian)', *Vestnik obschestvennykh nauk Armianskoi SSR*, no. 2, 1981, pp. 74–87.

19 S. M. Ayvazian, *Rasshifrovka armianskoi klinopisi* (Yerevan: n. p., 'na pravakh rukopisi', 1963); Ayvazian, *K nekotorym voprosam istorii i metallurgii drevneishei Armenii* (Yerevan and Moscow: VINITI, 1967).

20 Nora Dudwick, 'Armenia: Paradise Regained or Lost?', in Ian Bremmer and Ray Taras (eds.), *New States, New Politics: Building the Post-Soviet Nations* (Cambridge: Cambridge University Press, 1997), pp. 471–500, at pp. 480 and 497, n. 60.

21 A. M. Mamedov, 'Teoreticheskie problemy vosstanovleniia pervichnykh kornei v tiurkskikh iazykakh', in M. Z. Dzhafarov (ed.), *Voprosy azerbaidzhanskoi filologii*, vol. II (Baku: Elm, 1984), pp. 5–21.

22 Iu. B. Iusifov, 'Ob aktual'nykh problemakh etnicheskoi istorii Azerbaidzhana', in T. S. Veliiev (ed.), *Problemy izucheniia istochnikov po istorii Azerbaidzhana* (Baku: Akademiia nauk Azerbaidzhanskogo SSR, 1988), pp. 15–39, at p. 20.

23 Iusifov, 'Ob aktual'nykh problemakh', and Iusifov, 'Kimmery, Skify i Saki v Drevnem Azerbaidzhane', in G. G. Goergadze (ed.), *Kavkazsko-blizhnevostochnii sbornik* (Tbilisi: Metsniereba, 1988), no. 8, pp. 181–92; and Giiaseddin Gejbullaiev and A. Giiaseddin, *K etnogenezu Azerbaidzhantsev* (Baku: Elm, 1991).

24 Mamedov, 'Teoreticheskie problemy'; S. S. Alijarov, 'Ob etnogeneza azerbaidzhanskogo naroda', in M. A. Ismailov (ed.), *K probleme etnogeneza azerbaidzhanskogo naroda* (Baku: Elm, 1984), pp. 4–39; Iusifov, 'Ob aktual'nykh problemakh', and Iusifov, 'K znacheniiu drevnikh toponimov v izuchenii etnicheskoi istorii Azerbaidzhana', *Izvestiia AN Azerbaidzhanskoi SSR, seriia literatury, iazyka i iskusstva*, no. 2, 1987, pp. 101–10; Gejbullaiev and Giiaseddin, *K etnogenezu Azerbaidzhantsev*.

25 P. Muradian, *Istoriia – pamiat' pokolenii: problemy istorii Nagorno Karabakha* (Yerevan: Aiastan, 1990).

26 I. G. Aliev, *Nagornyi Karabakh: istoriia, fakty, sobytiia* (Baku: Elm, 1989).
27 Dudwick, 'The Case of the Caucasian Albanians', p. 378; Dudwick, 'The Pen and the Sword'.
28 Astourian, 'In Search of Their Forefathers', pp. 52 and 62.
29 Dudwick, 'Armenia', p. 483.
30 T. K. Mikeladze, '"Anabasis" Ksenofonta i iego svedeniia o kartvel'skikh plemenakh' (Tbilisi: Avtoreferat kandidatskoi dissertatsii, 1953); Mikeladze, 'Issledovaniia po istorii drevneishego naseleniia Kolkhidy i iugo-vostochnogo Prichernomoriia (15–4 vv. do n.e.)' (Tbilisi: Avtoreferat doktorskoi dissertatsii, 1969); Mikeladze, *Issledovaniia po istorii drevneishego naseleniia Kolkhidy i iugo-vostochnogo Prichernomoriia* (Tbilisi: Metsniereba, 1974).
31 'Kartvelian' is the Georgians' own self-name.
32 Mikeladze, *Issledovaniia po istorii*, p. 184; Mikeladze, *K arkheologii Kolkhidy (epokha srednei i pozdnei bronzy – rannego zheleza)* (Tbilisi: Metsniereba, 1990), p. 80. In most academic literature the proto-Kartvelian community is regarded as giving rise to the Georgians, Mingrelians and Svans, who still live in modern Georgia.
33 V. G. Ardzinba, 'Poslesloviie: o nekotorykh novykh rezul'tatakh v issledovanii istorii, iazykov i kul'tury Drevnei Anatolii', in D. G. Makkuin, *Khetty i ikh sovremenniki v Maloi Azii* (Moscow: Nauka, 1983), pp. 152–80; Ardzinba, 'K istorii kul'ta zheleza i kuznechnogo remesla (pochitaniie kuznitsy u abkhazov)', in L. Bramson and S. Goethal (eds.), *Drevnii Vostok: etnokul'turnyie sviazi* (Moscow: Nauka, 1988), pp. 263–306.
34 In its broad meaning 'Abkhazian–Adyghe' refers to the indigenous peoples who belong to the north Caucasian family of languages and live in the north-western Caucasus (Abkhazians, Abazinians, Kabardinians and others). 'Adyghe' also has a narrow meaning as an ethnonym referring to the inhabitants of the autonomous okrug around the city of Maikop.
35 Mikeladze, *Issledovaniia po istorii*.
36 Phillip Kohl and Gocha Tsetskhladze have criticised this aspect of the Georgian nationalist construction, arguing that the Greek presence in the region was substantial. See their 'Nationalism, Politics and the Practice of Archaeology in the Caucasus', in Kohl and Clare Fawcett (eds.), *Nationalism, Politics and the Practice of Archaeology* (Cambridge: Cambridge University Press, 1995), pp. 149–74, at pp. 165–8.
37 G. A. Melikishvili and O. D. Lordkipanidze (eds.), *Ocherki istorii Gruzii*, vol. I (Tbilisi: Metsniereba, 1989), pp. 195, 205–8, 230–3; M. D. Lordkipanidze, *Abkhazy i Abkhaziia* (Tbilisi: Ganatleba, 1990), pp. 6 and 40.
38 V. Sichinava, 'Po sledam argonavtov', in V. P. Iankov (ed.), *Dorogami tysiacheletii*, book IV (Moscow: Molodaia gvardiia, 1991), pp. 28–62.
39 *Bielaia kniga Abkhazii: dokumenty, materialy, svidetel'stva, 1992–1993* (Moscow: Komissiia po pravam cheloveka i mezhnatsional'nym otnosheniiam Verkhovnogo Soveta Respubliki Abkhaziia, 1993), p. 27.
40 Melikishvili and Lordkipanidze, *Ocherki istorii Gruzii*, p. 188; E. V. Khoshtaria-Brosse, *Mezhnatsional'nye otnosheniia v Gruzii – prichiny konfliktov i puti ikh preodoleniia* (Tbilisi: Metsniereba, 1993), pp. 14–15 and 31.

41 Melikishvili and Lordkipanidze, *Ocherki istorii Gruzii*, p. 326.
42 P. Ingorokva, *Georgii Merchule* (Tbilisi: Fabchota Mtzerali, 1954). For the political connotations of his concept, see S. Lakoba and S. Shamba, 'Kto zhe takiie abkhazy?', *Sovietskaia Abkhaziia*, 8 July 1989, and M. Iu. Chumalov (ed.), *Abkhazskii uzel: dokumenty i materialy po etnicheskomu konfliktu v Abkhazii* (Moscow: Rossiiskaia akademiia nauk, Institut etnologii i antropologii, 1995), pp. 23–5 and 84–5.
43 Mikeladze, 'Issledovaniia po istorii', p. 92.
44 Mikeladze, *K arkheologii Kolkhidy*, p. 79. It is worth noting that there is an alternative Afrocentric view of the Colchians' identity, according to which they were black Africans. The author is grateful to Tim Champion for pointing out this theory.
45 M. D. Lordkipanidze, 'Nekompetentnost´ – v rang istiny?', *Zaria Vostoka*, 21 July 1989; and Lordkipanidze, *Abkhazy i Abkhaziia*.
46 There are some reasons to believe that the Missimians could be identified with the Georgian tribe of the Svans: G. V. Tsulaia, *Abkhaziia i abkhazy v kontekste istorii Gruzii* (Moscow: Rossiiskaia akademiia nauk, Institut etnologii i antropologii, 1995), pp. 20–1.
47 Lordkipanidze, *Abkhazy i Abkhaziia*, pp. 58–9.
48 Lakoba and Shamba, 'Kto zhe takiie abkhazy?'; Lakoba, *Ocherki politicheskoi istorii Abkhazii* (Sukhumi: Alashara, 1990), p. 6; *Bielaia kniga Abkhazii*, pp. 19–21.
49 S. Biguaa, 'Na rodine predkov', *Ekho Kavkaza*, no. 3, 1993, p. 16.
50 M. M. Gunba, *Abkhaziia v pervom tysiacheletii nashei ery* (Sukhumi: Alashara, 1989), pp. 140–50; Lakoba, *Ocherki politicheskoi istorii Abkhazii*, p. 5.
51 Gunba, *Abkhaziia v pervom tysiacheletii*, pp. 139ff.
52 Lakoba and Shamba, 'Kto zhe takiie abkhazy?'; Shamba and Lakoba, 'Narodnyi forum Abkhazii i iego tseli', in Chumalov, *Abkhazskii uzel*, pp. 9–16, at pp. 12–15; *Bielaia kniga Abkhazii*, p. 30.
53 Author's field notes, Abkhazia, autumn 1989.
54 Lordkipanidze, 'Nekompetentnost´ – v rang istiny?'; Lordkipanidze, *Abkhazy i Abkhaziia*; Sh. A. Badridze, 'Nekotorye voprosy politicheskogo i sotsial´no-ekonomicheskogo stroia Abkhazskogo tsarstva', and G. G. Paichadze, 'Nazvaniie "Gruziia" v russkikh pis´mennykh istochnikakh', in G. D. Togoshvili (ed.), *Voprosy istorii narodov Kavkaza* (Tbilisi: Metsniereba, 1988).
55 Lordkipanidze, *Abkhazy i Abkhaziia*, p. 43.
56 Ibid., pp. 46–7.
57 Z. V. Anchabadze, *Ocherk etnicheskoi istorii abkhazskogo naroda* (Sukhumi: Alashara, 1976), pp. 52–4; Anchabadze, G. A. Dzidzariia and A. E. Kuprava, *Istoriia Abkhazii* (Sukhumi: Alashara, 1986), pp. 42–6; Lakoba and Shamba, 'Kto zhe takiie abkhazy?'
58 Gunba, *Abkhaziia v pervom tysiacheletii*, pp. 213–35; Lakoba, *Ocherki politicheskoi istorii Abkhazii*, p. 4. Initially the Abkhazian Kingdom was established as a sovereign power by the Abkhazian princes, but later their independence was restricted by the newly created Georgian state. For an illuminating discussion, see Tsulaia, *Abkhaziia i abkhazy v kontekste istorii Gruzii*, pp. 30–41.

59 Biguaa, 'Na rodine predkov'.

60 Lordkipanidze, *Abkhazy i Abkhaziia*, p. 3.

61 Author's field notes; *Bielaia kniga Abkhazii*, p. 15.

62 Lordkipanidze, 'Nekompetentnost' – v rang istiny?'; Lordkipanidze, *Abkhazy i Abkhaziia*, p. 50.

63 Author's field notes. See also *Bielaia kniga Abkhazii*, p. 24.

64 Gunba, *Abkhaziia v pervom tysiacheletii*, pp. 81ff.; Lakoba, *Ocherki politicheskoi istorii Abkhazii*, p. 5.

65 See the debate between the Abkhazian writer Alexei Gogua, 'Nasha trevoga', *Druzhba narodov*, no. 5, 1989, pp. 157–9, and the Georgian historian Marika Lordkipanidze, 'Nekompetentnost' – v rang istiny?'

66 Cited in Khoshtaria-Brosse, *Mezhnatsional'nye otnosheniia v Gruzii*, p. 128.

67 Z. Chichinadze, *Istoriia Osetii po gruzinskim istochnikam* (Tskhinvali: Nauchnyi otdel kul'turnogo tsentra AMN, 1993), p. 14.

68 G. R. Lazarashvili, 'O vremeni pereseleniia osetin v Gruziiu', *Sovetskaia etnografiia*, no. 2, 1966, pp. 101–9; G. D. Togoshvili, 'K voprosu o vremeni i usloviiakh pereseleniia osetin na territoriiu Gruzii', *Izvestiia Iugo-osetinskogo nauchno-issledovatel'skogo instituta*, vol. 28, 1983, pp. 195–214.

69 Khoshtaria-Brosse, *Mezhnatsional'nye otnosheniia v Gruzii*, p. 84.

70 B. Tuskia, 'K voprosu etnogeneza osetin i ikh pereseleniia v predely Gruzii', *Literaturnaia Gruziia*, no. 4–5, 1992, pp. 395–404, at pp. 400–1.

71 O. Vasil'eva, *Gruziia kak model' postkommunisticheskoi transformatsii* (Moscow: Gorbachev Foundation, 1993), p. 45.

72 Iu. S. Gagloev, 'Tulasy myggag tsaver adema khattei u. uyi tykhkhei', *Fidiueg*, no. 11, 1959, pp. 93–6; Gagloev, 'Svedeniia "Armianskoi geografii" VII v. ob alanakh', *Izvestiia Severo-osetinskogo nauchno-issledovatel'skogo instituta*, vol. 25, 1966, pp. 184–94, at pp. 193–4.

73 V. N. Gamrekeli, *Dvaly i Dvaletiia v I–XV vv. n.e.* (Tbilisi: AN GruzSSR, 1961); Lazarashvili, 'O vremeni pereseleniia', p. 102.

74 Z. N. Vaneev, *Izbrannye raboty po istorii osetinskogo naroda*, vol. I (Tskhinvali: Iryston, 1989).

75 Ibid., pp. 340–3.

76 Ibid., pp. 346–7.

77 Ibid., p. 127.

78 Ibid., pp. 140–3.

79 Ibid., pp. 351–5.

80 Ibid., p. 362.

81 Ibid., p. 364.

82 Ibid., pp. 127–8 and 131–2.

83 Ibid., pp. 133–4 and 145–6.

84 Ibid., p. 139.

85 F. Hill and P. Jewett, *Report on Ethnic Conflict in the Russian Federation and Transcaucasia* (Cambridge, MA: Harvard University, John F. Kennedy School of Government, 1993), pp. 95–9.

86 Victor A. Shnirelman, 'Bor'ba za alanskoe nasledie (etnopoliticheskaia podopleka sovremennykh etnogeneticheskikh mifov)', *Vostok*, no. 5, 1996, pp. 100–13.

87 Chichinadze, *Istoriia Osetii po gruzinskim istochnikam*, p. 3.

88 Ibid., p. 4.
89 Iurii Gagloity, 'Sarmaty i Tsentral'nyi Kavkaz', in A. A. Magometov (ed.), *Tezisy dokladov na mezhdunarodnoi nauchnoi konferentsii po osetinovedeniiu, posviashchennoi 200-letiiu so dnia rozhdeniia A. M. Shegrena* (Vladikavkaz: Izdatel'stvo SOGU, 1994), pp. 44–6.
90 Iurii Dzitstsoity, 'Dialektologiia i drevniaia istoriia iuzhnykh osetin', in Magometov, *Tezisy dokladov*, pp. 58–9.
91 Shnirelman, 'Bor'ba za alanskoe nasledie'.
92 Melikishvili and Lordkipanidze, *Ocherki istorii Gruzii*, pp. 133–5 and 176–7.
93 Boris Tekhov, *Tsentral'nyi Kavkaz v 16–10 vv. do n.e.* (Moscow: Nauka, 1977), pp. 192–3 and 214.
94 Mikeladze, *K arkheologii Kolkhidy*, pp. 75–7. See also the map on p. xii.
95 B. V. Tekhov, *Osetiny – drevnii narod Kavkaza (istoki, kul'tura, etnos)* (Tskhinvali: Yryston, 1993).
96 B. V. Tekhov, 'Koban i Gal'shtat (konets II – nachalo I tys. do n.e.)', in Magometov, *Tezisy dokladov*, pp. 62–6.
97 R. Kh. Gagloity, 'Sarmato-alany v Iuzhnoi Osetii', in Magometov, *Tezisy dokladov*, pp. 59–61.
98 Vaneev, *Izbrannye raboty*, pp. 337, 140 and 144.
99 Chichinadze, *Istoriia Osetii po gruzinskim istochnikam*, p. 8.
100 P. Kozaiev, *Iz drevneishei istorii narodov (assiriitsy, narty, semity)* (St Petersburg: Prilozheniie k gazete Dobryi den', 1993).
101 Ibid., pp. 22–3.
102 A. Chochiiev, *Uroki igry na boine* (n.p.: n.p., n.d.), pp. 81–4.
103 V. L. Khamitsev and A. Ch. Balaev, *David Soslan, Fridrikh Barbarossa . . . Alanija ot Palestiny do Britanii* (Vladikavkaz: IPF Arian, 1992).
104 A. Kh. Bekuzarov, 'Formirovaniie gosudarstva u alan', in Magometov, *Tezisy dokladov*, pp. 61–2.
105 Shnirelman, 'Bor'ba za alanskoe nasledie'.
106 See especially Mikeladze, 'Issledovaniia po istorii'.
107 Vaneev, *Izbrannye raboty*, pp. 134–6, 140 and 365–73.
108 Gogua, 'Nasha trevoga'.
109 Lakoba and Shamba, 'Kto zhe takiie abkhazy?'
110 I. V. Abashidze (ed.), *Gruzinskaia Sovietskaia Sotsialisticheskaia Respublika* (Tbilisi: Gruzinskaia sovietskaia entsiklopedia, 1981).
111 Ralph Premdas, S. W. R. de A. Samarasinghe and Alan Anderson (eds.), *Secessionist Movements in Comparative Perspective* (London: Pinter, 1990).

4 HISTORY AND GROUP IDENTITY IN CENTRAL ASIA

1 Mirza 'Abdal'azim Sami, *Ta'rikh-i salatin-i manghitiya (Istoriia mangytskikh gosudarei)*, copy dated 1906–7 (the year the historian wrote his manuscript), trans. L. M. Epifanova (Moscow: Izdatel'stvo vostochnoi literatury, 1962).
2 Ibid., leaf 108b, p. 118; leaf 110b, p. 120.
3 Mullah 'Alim Makhdum Hajji, *Ta'rikh-i Turkistan* (Tashkent: Turkistan Giniral Gubirnatorigha Tob'e Basmäkhanädä, 1915), pp. 3–4.
4 Hajji Mu'in [Shukrullah Oghli], 'Milliy tä'rikh haqindä', *Ayinä*, no. 10 (28

February 1915), p. 258; 'Turkistan tä'rikhi keräk', *Ayinä*, no. 38 (12 July 1914), p. 898.

5 Edward A. Allworth, *The Modern Uzbeks. From the Fourteenth Century to the Present: A Cultural History* (Stanford, CA: Hoover Institution, 1993), chs. 7 ('History') and 8 ('Education').

6 M. A. Akhunova and B. V. Lunin, *Istoriia istoricheskoi nauki v Uzbekistane: kratkii ocherk* (Tashkent: Akademiia nauk UzSSR, Institut istorii i arkheologii, 1970), pp. 118–19.

7 Imam Qorban'ali Hajji Khalid-oghli, *Täwarikh-i khämsä: shärqi ismindä. Birinchi juz' färghanä khanläri* (Kazan: Ornäk Mätbä'äsi, 1910), 790 pp.; A.-Z. Validov, 'Vostochnyie rukopisi v ferganskoi oblasti', *Zapiski Vostochnogo otdeleniia Imperatorskogo russkogo arkheologicheskogo obshchestva*, vol. 22 for 1913–14 (1915), pp. 303–20.

8 Bolat Saliyif, *Orta asiya tarikhi (11–15inchi 'äsrlär)* (Samarkand and Tashkent: Ozbekistan Däwlät Näshriyati, 1926).

9 Polat Säliyif, *Ozbekistan tarïkhï (XV–XIXinchi äsrlär)* (Samarkand and Tashkent: Ozbekistan Däwlät Näshrïyatï, 1929).

10 O. Akhmeddzhan, 'Predposylki i podgotovka k provedeniiu "Ezhovshchiny" v Turkestane', *Türkeli*, nos. 3–4 (March–April 1952), pp. 25–8, cited in Allworth, *Uzbek Literary Politics* (The Hague: Mouton & Co., 1964), p. 82, n. 1.

11 P. P. Ivanov, *Ocherki po istorii srednei Azii* (Moscow: Izdatel'stvo vostochnoi literatury, 1958).

12 Muzaffar M. Khayrullaew, *Ortä asiyadä IX–XII äsrlärdä mädäniy täräqqiyat (uyghanish däwri mädäniyäti)* (Tashkent: Ozbekistan Respublikäsi Fänlär Äkädemiyäsi, Fän Näshriyati, 1994), pp. 50–4.

13 Ibragim M. Muminov, *Rol' i mesto Amira Timura v istorii srednei Azii v svete dannykh pis'mennykh istochnikov* (Tashkent: Izdatel'stvo Fan UzSSR, 1968); Uzbek version reprinted without change, posthumously, with a new introduction by Muzaffar M. Khayrullayew, director of Uzbekistan's Oriental Institute, under the name and title: Ibrahim Mominaw, *Ämir Temurning Ortä Asiya tärikhidä tutgän orni wä roli: yazmä mänbälär mä'lumati äsasidä* (Tashkent: Ozbekistan Respublikäsi Fänlär Äkädemiyäsi, Fän Näshriyati, 1993).

14 Muzäffär M. Khäyrullaew, 'Ibrahim Mominawning kättä ilmiy jäsaräti', in Mominaw, *Ämir Temurning Ortä Asiya tärikhidä tutgän orni wä roli*, 1993, 2nd edn, pp. 7–9.

15 Aleksandr Iu. Iakubovskii, 'Timur', *Voprosy istorii*, nos. 8–9 (1946); Iakubovskii, in *Istoriia narodov Uzbekistana*, vol. I (Tashkent: Izdatel'stvo AN UzSSR, 1950), p. 356.

16 *Ozbekistan SSR tärikhi*, vols. I–II (Tashkent: Ozbekistan SSR Fänlär Äkädemiyäsi Näshriyati, 1956–8), exemplifies the usual broad history put together collectively.

17 Boris A. Litvinsky et al., *Historiography of Tajikistan* (Moscow: Nauka Publishing House, 1970), p. 40.

18 Sharaf R. Rashidov, 'O zadachakh intelligentsii Uzbekistana v osushchestvlenii istoricheskikh reshenii XXI S''ezda Kommunisticheskoi Partii

Sovetskogo Soiuza', *II s''ezd intelligentsii Uzbekistana, 11–12 dekabria 1959 goda: stenograficheskii otchet* (Tashkent: Gosudarstvennoe izdatel'stvo UzSSR, 1960), p. 48.

19 Ähmädäli Äsqäraw (ed.), *Ozbekistan khälqläri tärikhi*, vols. I–II (Tashkent: Ozbekistan Respublikäsi Fänlär Akädemiyäsining, Fan Näshriyati, 1992–3).

20 G. A. Hidoyätaw, *Mening janäjan tärikhim* (Tashkent: Oqituwchi, 1992).

21 Ibid., p. 2.

22 Sh. Kärimaw (ed.), *Ozbekistan tärikhi wä mädäniyäti: mä'ruzälär toplämi* (Tashkent: Oqituwchi, 1992), p. 9.

23 Toräbek S. Säidqulaw, *Ortä Asiya khälqläri tärikhining tärikhshunasligidän läwhälär* (Tashkent: Oqituwchi, 1993).

24 'The Tashkent Declaration', *Kyrgyzstan Chronicle*, no. 35 (30 October–5 November 1996), p. 10.

25 English-language translations of two examples: Islam Karimov, *Building the Future: Uzbekistan – Its Own Model for Transition to a Market Economy* (Tashkent: Uzbekiston Publishers, 1993), 115 pp.; President Nursultan Nazarbayev, *A Strategy for the Development of Kazakhstan as a Sovereign State* (Washington, DC: Embassy of the Republic of Kazakhstan, 1994), 63 pp.

26 'Biografiia I. A. Karimova', *Pravda Vostoka*, 30 November 1991, p. 1.

27 'Rech' Prezidenta Respubliki Uzbekistan Islama Karimova, desiataia sessiia Verkhovnogo Soveta Respubliki Uzbekistan, dvenadtsatogo sozyva', *Pravda Vostoka*, 4 July 1992, pp. 1–3.

28 *Komsomol'skaia pravda*, 12 February 1993, p. 2.

29 *Ozbekistan awazi*, 14 March 1995, 10 June 1995, 5 September 1995 and 25 November 1995, p. 1 of each issue.

30 *Khälq sozi*, 5 September 1995, p. 1.

31 'Update on Human Rights Violations in Uzbekistan: Helsinki Watch, September 23, 1993', five-page press release of Helsinki Watch, now Human Rights Watch/Helsinki, 27 September 1993, including a copy of a letter addressed to President Islam Karimov, c/o Mission of the Republic of Uzbekistan to the United Nations, signed by Jeri Laber, Executive Director, Helsinki Watch. On 25 April 1995, in a four-page letter over the signature of Holly A. Cartner, Acting Executive Director, Human Rights Watch/Helsinki, the organisation once more communicated to President Karimov its findings about atrocious beatings and other physical violence perpetrated against people he viewed as his political opponents in Uzbekistan.

32 Lowell Bezanis, 'Niyazov for Life', *OMRI Daily Digest*, no. 192, pt I, 2 October 1995, citing BBC; John Anderson, 'Authoritarian Political Development in Central Asia: The Case of Turkmenistan', *Central Asian Survey*, vol. 14 (4), 1995, pp. 512–13.

33 'Ozbekistan Respublikäsi referendumidä awaz berish uchun Biulleten'', 1995 yil 26 märt', *Ozbekistan awazi*, 25 March 1995, p. 1.

34 Bhavna Dave, 'Opposition to Boycott Kazakhstani Elections?', *OMRI Daily Digest*, no. 202, pt II, 17 October 1995; Dave, 'Media Shake-up by Nazarbaev', *OMRI Daily Digest*, no. 203, pt II, 18 October 1995; Dave,

'Nazarbaev Completes Personnel Reshuffle at Top', *OMRI Daily Digest*, no. 206, pt I, 23 October 1995.

35 Bruce Pannier, 'Kyrgyz Movement Demands that President Step Down', *OMRI Daily Digest*, no. 203, pt II, 18 October 1995; Pannier, 'Kyrgyz Authorities Head off Demonstration', no. 211, pt II, 30 October 1995; Pannier, in no. 219, pt I, 9 November 1995.

36 'Topchubek Turgunaliev in Jail Again', *Central Asia Monitor*, no. 2, 1997, p. 38; Iurii Maksimaw, 'Zashchishchat' oppozitsiiu v Kyrgyzstane – delo bez-nadezhnoe', *Res Publica*, no. 37, 22–8 October 1996, p. 2.

37 Special issue, *'Birlik' of Uzbekistan* (Tashkent: Press-Centre of the Popular Movement Birlik, August 1990), pp. 2–3.

38 Herodotus, *The History of Herodotus*, trans. George Rawlinson (New York: Tudor Publishing Co., 1943), Book 1, pp. 75–9.

39 Äsqäraw, *Ozbekistan khälqläri tärikhi*, vol. I, p. 25.

40 Roger Kangas, 'Political Opposition Activity in Uzbekistan', *OMRI Daily Digest*, no. 200, pt I, 13 October 1995.

41 Mukhtar Khudayqulaw (Docent and Writer, Tashkent Darulfununi), '"Äzädlik' abidäsi qändäy bolmaghi keräk?', *Ozbekistan ädäbiyati wä sän'äti*, 8 November 1991, p. 1.

42 Karl-Heinz Golzio begins with Graeco-Bactrians in BC 256 and comes up to the Khwarazmshahs of the tenth to thirteenth centuries AD in his *Kings, Khans and Other Rulers of Early Central Asia: Chronological Tables* (Bonn: Religionswissenschaftliches Seminar der Universität Bonn; Cologne: commissioned by E. J. Brill, 1984). Stanley Lane-Poole's great work restricts itself to the Islamic period, beginning in the seventh (in Central Asia eighth) century AD: *The Mohammadan Dynasties: Chronological and Genealogical Tables with Historical Introductions* (Westminster: Archibald Constable and Co, 1894).

43 Kenneth Petersen, 'Celebrating Amir Timur: A Report from Tashkent', *Central Asia Monitor*, no. 5, 1996, p. 15.

44 Äbdullä Ä'zämaw (comp.), *Mustäqil Ozbekistan – tärikh silsiläläridä: mä'lumat-namä* (Tashkent: Qamuslar Bash Tähririyati, 1992), pp. 11–15, 26–7.

45 'Address by HE Mr Islom Karimov, President of the Republic of Uzbekistan at the 48th Session of the United Nations General Assembly (September 28, 1993)', p. 4 in the typewritten English translation circulated at that time.

46 Mätyaqub Qoshjanaw, 'Eng muhimi – insanpärwärlik', *Ozbekistanning milliy istiqlal mäfkuräsi*, ed. Kärim Boronaw (Tashkent: Ozbekistan, 1993), pp. 101–3.

47 Islam Kärimaw, *'Täfäkkur zhurnali oquwchilärigä'*, *Täfäkkur*, no. 1, 1994, pp. 1, 5.

48 *Natsional'nyi sostav naseleniia SSSR*, proof pages 88, 126.

49 Erkin Yusupaw, interviewed by Arif Muhammad, 'Säadät käliti', *Täfäkkur*, no. 1, August 1994, pp. 9–10.

50 Ahmad Khoja, 'Yuksäk mä'näwiyätsiz keläjäk yoq', *Ozbekistan ädäbiyati wä sän'äti*, 6 September 1996, p. 1.

51 Dr Ahmad Ali, Dr Sherali Turdi, and several colleagues, with their numerous articles and texts showed special, active interest in this revival of the Jadids.

52 Fitrat Bukhara-yi, *Munazira mudarrisi Bukhoroi bo yak nafari farangi dar Hinduston dar borai makotibi jadida* (Istanbul: Matbaa-i Islomiyai Hikmat, H. 1327/AD 1909), pp. 67–8; Fitrat of Bukhara, *Debate Between a Teacher from Bokhara and a European in India about New Schools*, trans. by William L. Hanaway from the Tajik (Istanbul: publication of the author, printed at Matba'a-e Eslamiyya-e Hekmat, H. 1327/AD 1909–10), p. 71; Abduraufi Fitrat, *Munazara: haqiqat natijai tasadumi afkorast* (Dushanbe: TGU, 1992), pp. 52–3.

53 Fitrat, *Bidil: bir mäjlisdä* (Moscow: Millat Ishläri Kämisärligi Qashida Markazi Sharq Nashryati, 15 December 1923 (on outer jacket, 1924)), 54 pp. Although the publisher presented the text in the Turki language and modified Arabic script of the time, on the colophon page a Russian line refers to this subversive work as 'An anti-religious play in one act'.

5 NATION RE-BUILDING AND POLITICAL DISCOURSES OF IDENTITY POLITICS IN THE BALTIC STATES

1 As a consequence, virtually all Lithuania's ethnic Russians have taken up the offer of Lithuanian citizenship. As of 21 May 1996, this amounts to 151,300 people: data from Lithuania's Department of Migration (Vilnius, 1997).

2 According to official government data, 89,973 non-Estonians (as of 31 March 1997) have since 1992 qualified for citizenship under Estonia's naturalisation procedures, of whom 5,721 have been naturalised since the citizenship law of April 1995 came into force. In Latvia the rate of naturalisation is considerably lower; by February 1997 only 1,962 ethnic Russians (out of a total of 4,544 people naturalised in this period) had qualified for citizenship of Latvia through naturalisation. One reason for Latvia's lower figures is that naturalisation procedures began far later than in Estonia: *Kopdakondsus – Ja Migratsiooniamet* (Tallinn, 11 April 1997); Naturalisation Board of the Republic of Latvia (10 June 1996; March 1997) .

3 According to one of the most comprehensive surveys undertaken of the diaspora in the Baltic states, almost 60 per cent of Russians in Estonia and 40 per cent in Latvia have no knowledge of the state language. See Richard Rose and William Maley, *Nationalities in the Baltic States: A Survey Study*, Centre for the Study of Public Policy Paper no. 222, University of Strathclyde, Glasgow, 1994.

4 Adam Przeworski, *Sustainable Democracy* (Cambridge: Cambridge University Press, 1995), p. 17.

5 Lee Metcalf, 'Outbidding to Radical Nationalists: Minority Policy in Estonia, 1988–1993', *Nations and Nationalism*, vol. 2 (2), 1996, pp. 213–34.

6 Alvin Rabushka and Kenneth Shepsle, *Politics in Plural Societies: A Theory of Democratic Instability* (Columbus, OH: Merrill, 1972).

7 Graham Smith, 'The Ethnic Democracy Thesis and the Citizenship Question in Estonia and Latvia', *Nationalities Papers*, vol. 24 (2), 1996, pp. 199–216.

8 Certain civil, political and social rights, however, are enjoyed universally, most notably freedom of the press, access to an independent judiciary, the right to vote in local municipal elections (in Estonia but not Latvia) and within certain prescribed limits (as outlined in their respective national constitutions), the

right of assembly and association. Certain collective rights are also upheld, including particular rights concerning non-titular language schools and newspapers, access to television programmes in the Russian language and the right to organise diasporic cultural associations and clubs (although only citizens of the settler communities have the right to secure cultural autonomy for their local communities).

9 Michael Billig, *Banal Nationalism* (London: Sage, 1995), p. 74.

10 In the first post-independent parliamentary elections in Estonia (1992) and Latvia (1993), both governments were led by centre-right coalitions. In Estonia, the centre-right party, Pro-Patria (Fatherland) dominated, while in Latvia the political faction Latvia's Way formed the government, with far right political parties, Fatherland and Freedom and the Latvian National Independence Party (LNNP) forming the official opposition. In the subsequent 1995 elections in both countries, more moderately minded coalition governments came to power: in Estonia, the Coalition Party/Rural Union formed the government, whereas in Latvia a large coalition of political parties rule, led by the Democratic Party Saimnieks.

11 *Latvijas Republikas Augstakas Padomes un Valdibas Zinotajas* (Riga, 1991), no. 21, 22 pp.

12 Although the independence of the Baltic states was not fully acknowledged until August 1991 by the international community, Baltic politicians predate their restored status to 1990, the year when both Estonia and Latvia declared that they were in transition to reclaiming their full sovereign status as independent states.

13 *Diena*, 23 July 1993.

14 See, for example, Graham Smith (ed.), *The Baltic States: The National Self-Determination of Estonia, Latvia and Lithuania* (London: Macmillan, 1994), ch. 5.

15 Claus Offe, *Varieties of Transition: The East European and East German Experience* (Oxford: Polity Press, 1996), p. 60. See also Leslie Green, 'Rational Nationalists', *Political Studies*, vol. 30 (2), 1984, pp. 236–46.

16 Anton Steen, *Elites, Democracy and Policy Development in Post-Communist States: A Comparative Study of Estonia, Latvia and Lithuania* (Oslo: Forskningsrapport 02, University of Oslo, 1996), p. 332.

17 As a result of the 1995 national elections in Estonia and Latvia, representation of the Russian diaspora has increased only marginally: thus in the Estonian parliament, 4 out of its 101 members are Russian-speakers while in Latvia the proportion remains virtually unchanged.

18 This has been more the case in Estonia than in Latvia because of the smaller proportion of inter-war citizens and their descendants who are not of the titular nation. See, for example, *Eesti Sonumid*, 23 May 1994.

19 See, for example, Erik Andersen, 'The Legal Status of Russians in Estonian Privatisation Legislation, 1989–1995', *Europe–Asia Studies*, vol. 49 (2), 1997, pp. 303–16.

20 Michael Hechter, *Internal Colonialism* (London: Routledge & Kegan Paul, 1975).

21 See, for example, *Diena*, 15 April 1996.

22 *Rossiiskaia gazeta*, 27 January 1993, p. 7.

23 *Izvestiia*, 13 October 1992, p. 7.
24 *Baltic Independent* (henceforth, *BI*), 23–9 July 1993, p. 1.
25 Ibid.
26 24 February 1993, from *BI*, 5–11 March 1993, p. 9.
27 *Izvestiia*, 9 July 1996, p. 1.
28 *Baltic News Service* (henceforth, *BNS*), Tallinn, 11 July 1996.
29 In a 1996 survey, 67 per cent of Estonians felt that criminal activity was increasingly carried from Russia to Estonia. See Tartu University Market Research Team, *Estonia's Experiment: The Possibilities to Integrate Non-Citizens into Estonian Society* (Tallinn, 1997), p. 147.
30 The legal legislation on the position and status of 'identity card holders' in Latvia is embodied in a 1995 law 'On the Status of the Former Soviet Citizens Who Are Citizens of Neither Latvia nor Another State'. The official text of this law can be found in *Latvijas Vestnesis*, 25 April 1995.
31 *Diena*, 15 March 1997.
32 See, for example, Anthony Smith, *The Ethnic Revival in the Modern World* (Cambridge: Cambridge University Press, 1981); Ernest Gellner, *Nations and Nationalism* (Oxford: Basil Blackwell, 1984). However, Gellner also makes the point that, although nationalism demands a form of cultural homogeneity in which national and political spaces should be ideally congruent, 'it is not the case . . . that nationalism imposes homogeneity; it is rather that a homogeneity imposed by objective, inescapable imperative eventually appears on the surface in the form of nationalism' (p. 39).
33 *Po-hjarannik*, 4 September 1996.
34 Alex Grigorievs, 'The Baltic Predicament', in Richard Caplan and John Feffer (eds.), *Europe's New Nationalism: States and Minorities in Conflict* (Oxford and New York: Oxford University Press, 1996), pp. 127–8. See also *Diena*, 18 October 1995, for an account by the OSCE Mission in Latvia on such practices.
35 *Sovetskaia molodezh'*, March 1994.
36 Naturalisation Board of the Republic of Latvia, *On Naturalisation in Latvia* (Riga, 1997), pp. 56–63.
37 Grigorievs, 'The Baltic Predicament'.
38 Demographic data from the Central Statistical Bureau of Latvia, *Demographic Yearbook of Latvia for 1996* (Riga, 1996), p. 28.
39 *Diena*, 3 February 1996; see also *Nacionala neatkariba*, 29 December 1993, p. 7.
40 *Panomara Latvii*, 20 January 1993.
41 *BI*, 12–18 February 1993.
42 See, for example, *Latvijas Vestnesis*, 21 July 1993. However, within official public policy decision-taking circles the question of settler decolonisation has tended to receive far less consideration since the mid-1990s than in the earlier years of statehood.
43 *BI*, 11–17 February 1994, p. 2.
44 Interview with Andrejs Pantelejevs, chair of the Standing Commission on Human Rights and National Question of the Supreme Council of Latvia, Riga, February 1993. A full transcript of this interview is available in G. Smith, A. Aasland and M. Mole, *Nationality and Citizenship in the Baltic States*,

Resource Paper no. 3 (Washington, DC: Department of Geography, University of Cambridge, and Institute of Peace Studies, 1994).

45 See David Millar, *On Nationality* (Oxford: Oxford University Press, 1996).

46 See, for example, Graham Smith, 'The Resurgence of Nationalism', in Graham Smith, *The Baltic States*, pp. 121–43.

47 For accounts of the economic successes of the Baltic states, especially Estonia, in the transition to the market, see Ole Norgaard et al., *The Baltic States After Independence* (Cheltenham: Edward Elgar, 1996), particularly ch. 4.

48 Ibid., p. 180.

49 Quoted by Andrea Hanneman, 'Independence and Group Rights in the Baltics: A Double Minority Problem', *Virginia Journal of International Law*, vol. 32 (2), 1995, p. 511.

50 Juris Boyars, 'The Citizenship and Human Rights Regulation in the Republic of Latvia' (Riga: unpublished manuscript, 1992, 26 pp.), p. 26.

51 *BI*, Tallinn, 8 July 1993, p. 3.

52 Here I draw upon four of the most comprehensive of the public opinion surveys undertaken in this period: a 1993 University of Cambridge survey of the Russian diaspora conducted in all three Baltic states, a survey undertaken by Richard Rose and William Maley that sampled a number of ethnic groups throughout the Baltic states in 1994, and two surveys of ethnic groups in Estonia carried out by sociologists at the University of Tartu, Estonia, in 1995 and 1996. For fuller details of these surveys, see Graham Smith, *Nationality and Citizenship in the Baltic States*, Report to the Institute of Peace Studies, Washington DC, 1994; Graham Smith, Aadne Aasland and Richard Mole, 'Statehood, Ethnic Relations and Citizenship', in Graham Smith, *The Baltic States*, pp. 181–205; Rose and Maley, *Nationalities in the Baltic States*; Tartu University Market Research Team, *Estonia's Experiment*; Tartu Ulikooli Turu-uurimisruhm, *Kirde-Eestil Linnaelanike Suhtumine Eesti Reformidesse Ja Sotsiaalpolitikasse* (Tartu, 1996).

53 Rose and Maley, *Nationalities in the Baltic States*.

54 Graham Smith, Aasland and Mole, 'Statehood, Ethnic Relations and Citizenship'.

55 Tartu University Market Research Team, *Estonia's Experiment*.

56 Graham Smith, Aasland and Mole, 'Statehood, Ethnic Relations and Citizenship'. See also Rasma Karklins and Brigita Zepa, 'Multiple Identities and Ethnopolitics in Latvia', *American Behavioral Scientist*, vol. 40 (1), 1996, pp. 33–45.

57 *Molodezh' Estonii*, 10 August 1996, p. 1; *Vybory Presidenta Rossiiskoi Federatsii 1996: electoral'naia statistika* (Ves'mir: Moscow, 1996), p. 147.

58 Tartu University Market Research Team, *Estonia's Experiment*.

59 Rose and Maley, *Nationalities in the Baltic States*.

60 David Laitin, 'Language and Nationalism in the Post-Soviet Republics', *Post-Soviet Affairs*, vol. 12 (1), 1996, pp. 4–24. See also other articles in this special issue of *Post-Soviet Affairs* that adopt a similar approach to analysing the post-Soviet states.

61 Laitin, 'Language and Nationalism', p. 18.

62 See, for example, *Diena*, 20 February 1995.

63 The above 1993–6 survey data confirm that the younger generation are keener to invest their time in learning the state language than those aged fifty and over, and are also keener to become members of the citizen-polity.

64 In the 1996 Tartu University Survey, just over 40 per cent of non-Estonians declared that they have no intention whatsoever of sitting the language examination. When the diaspora in more cosmopolitan Tallinn were asked if they had passed the Estonian language examination, 35 per cent said they had, 21 per cent said they had not but intended to sit it, 42 per cent said they had no intention of sitting it and 12 per cent gave no answer. See Tartu Ulikooli Turu-uurimisruhm, *Kirde-Eestii*. Official data collected on Adult Education in Latvia for 1996 reveal that only 2,837 non-Latvians are at present engaged in learning Latvian (Riga, Central Statistical Bureau, Review of Adult Education, 1997).

65 Graham Smith, Aasland and Mole, 'Statehood, Ethnic Relations and Citizenship'.

66 Sidney Tarrow, *The Power of Movement* (Cambridge: Cambridge University Press, 1994), p. 81.

67 Of the 465 people in Estonia granted citizenship for 'special services' following the enactment of Estonia's 1992 Law on Citizenship, the overwhelming majority were from the non-Estonian educated classes, including some members of Narva City Council, who, at that time, were openly questioning the future position of the north-east within the new Estonia. In the wake of its citizenship law, similar procedures have also been established in Latvia 'for those who have provided outstanding services' to the state (*Diena*, 31 January 1995).

68 For a fuller discussion, see Graham Smith and Andrew Wilson, 'Rethinking Russia's Post-Soviet Diaspora: The Potential for Political Mobilisation in Eastern Ukraine and North-East Estonia', *Europe–Asia Studies*, vol. 49 (5), 1997, pp. 845–64.

69 *Diena*, 3 May 1994.

70 These seats went to the Russian Party of Estonia and the United National Party of Estonia.

71 See in particular the article by A. Erek in *Molodezh' Estonii*, 8 October 1994, p. 1.

72 The Estonian Round Table comprises fifteen representatives, five from the Russian community, five from the other minorities and five parliamentarians. Latvia's eighteen-member Minorities Consultative Council comprises twelve representatives appointed by the president and six by the Latvian Association of Ethnic Cultural Societies.

73 Interview by Graham Smith with Priit Jarve, plenipotentiary of the president to the Round Table on Minorities, Cambridge, 18 February 1997.

74 Not surprisingly, discontent over the limited remit and thus effectiveness of these bodies is expressed particularly by Russian representatives: personal communication with Boris Tsilevich, a Russian member of the Minorities Consultative Council, 4 April 1997.

75 See, for example, Stanford Lyman (ed.), *Social Movements: Critiques, Concepts, Case Studies* (London: Macmillan, 1995), and D. McAdam, John McCarthy

and Mayer Zald, *Comparative Perspectives on Social Movements* (Cambridge: Cambridge University Press, 1996).

76 *Postimees*, 30 October 1995.
77 The Baltic states are especially important to Russia in this regard given that three-quarters of all the diaspora in the post-Soviet states who have taken out Russian citizenship now reside within Estonia and Latvia.
78 *Pravda*, 15 April 1996.
79 For a consideration of the role of the ethnic patron as a political resource in the Donbas and north-east Estonia, see Graham Smith and Andrew Wilson, 'Rethinking Russia's Post-Soviet Diaspora'.
80 *Izvestiia*, 4 July 1993.
81 For an earlier discussion of far right nationalist groups in Russia and their ties with the diaspora, see *Rossiia*, no. 37, 2 October 1994, p. 3. This contrasts with those Russian political parties in Estonia who are committed to a sovereign Estonia but who want to see the political institutionalisation of a more multi-culturalist society. Such political parties are quite open about their political links with more moderate political parties in Russia, notably with such democratic organisations as Yabloko and the Party of Russian Unity and Concord.
82 For a discussion of the Communist Party in Russia and its post-1991 geographical vision for Russia, see Yevgeny Vinokurov, 'Overdosing on Nationalism: Gennadii Zyuganov and the Communist Party of the Russian Federation', *New Left Review*, 1997, pp. 34–52.
83 Robin Cohen, 'Diasporas and the Nation-State: From Victims to Challengers', *International Affairs*, vol. 72 (3), 1996, pp. 507–20.

6 REDEFINING ETHNIC AND LINGUISTIC BOUNDARIES IN UKRAINE: INDIGENES, SETTLERS AND RUSSOPHONE UKRAINIANS

1 Dominique Arel and Valeri Khmelko, 'The Russian Factor and Territorial Polarization in Ukraine', *Harriman Institute Review*, vol. 9 (1–2), March 1996, pp. 81–91; Khmelko and Andrew Wilson, 'The Political Orientations of Different Regions and Ethno-Linguistic Groups in Ukraine Since Independence', in Taras Kuzio (ed.), *Contemporary Ukraine: Dynamics of Post-Soviet Transformation* (New York: M. E. Sharpe, 1998).
2 See Paul S. Pirie, 'National Identity and Politics in Southern and Eastern Ukraine', *Europe–Asia Studies*, vol. 48 (7), November 1996, pp. 1079–1104, and Yuri L. Shevchuk, 'Citizenship in Ukraine: A Western Perspective', in John S. Micgiel (ed.), *State and Nation Building in East and Central Europe: Contemporary Perspectives* (New York: Columbia University, Institute on East Central Europe, 1996), pp. 351–69, for some preliminary thoughts on the open-ended nature of identities in Ukraine.
3 Iver B. Neumann, 'Self and Other in International Relations', *European Journal of International Relations*, vol. 2 (2), June 1996, pp. 139–74, at p. 162; emphasis in original.
4 See also Andrew Wilson, *Ukrainian Nationalism in the 1990s: A Minority Faith* (Cambridge: Cambridge University Press, 1997), esp. ch. 6.

5 See Iukhym Kachurenko (ed.), *Prava liudyny: mizhnarodni dohovory Ukraïny* (Kiev: Iurinform, 1992). Whereas the 1991 citizenship law allowed for the possibility of dual citizenship if appropriate bilateral agreements were negotiated, this provision was withdrawn in 1996.

6 *Prohrama i statut Narodnoho Rukhu Ukraïny (zminy ta dopovnennia vneseni III Vseukraïnsk´ymy zboramy Narodnoho Rukhu Ukraïny 1 bereznia 1992 r.)* (Kiev: Rukh, 1992), p. 13.

7 Ibid.

8 See the appeal in *Chas/Time*, 28 June 1996; and also Iurii Badz´o, 'Ukraïna: chetverta sproba, abo chy vyzhyvut´ ukraïntsi?', *Rozbudova derzhavy*, nos. 9 and 10 (September–October), 1995; Mykhailo Vivcharyk, 'Etnonatsional´na polityka na etapi ukraïns´koho derzhavotvorennia', *Rozbudova derzhavy*, no. 12 (December), 1994; Ihor Pas´ko, 'Natsional´na ideia: varianty na tli ievropeis´koï kul´tury', *Skhid*, nos. 4 and 5–6, 1996.

9 Volodymyr Doroshkevych, 'Nadiliaiuchy vladoiu, spodivaiut´sia na viddachu', *Holos Ukraïny*, 9 April 1996.

10 'Postanova Konhresu Ukraïns´koï Intellihentsiï', *Literaturna Ukraïna*, 16 November 1995; 'Prohramovi zasady Kongresu natsional´no-demokratychnykh syl', *Samostiina Ukraïna*, no. 31 (August), 1992. In *Ukrainian Nationalism in the 1990s* (at p. 151), I defined this as a form of 'ethnic-led territorialism'. Cf. Oleksii Haran´, 'Ukraïns´ku derzhavu ne mozhna buduvaty na kosmopolitychnii osnovi', *Den´*, no. 5, 9 October 1996.

11 *Prohrama Ukraïns´koï konservatyvnoï respublikans´koï partiï* (Kiev: Party document, 1992).

12 Stepan Khmara, 'Konstytutsiinyi protses i bezpeka natsiï', *Holos Ukraïny*, 30 April 1996. Although Khmara is on the far right, the views expressed by Iurii Badz´o, former leader of the supposedly moderate Democratic Party, are little different; see his 'Osnova pravdy nashoï', *Holos Ukraïny*, 6 May 1996.

13 Hryhorii Prykhod´ko, *Politychni viziï* (L´viv: Ukraïns´kyi chas, 1994), p. 12; Volodymyr Iavors´kyi, 'Vidlunnia velykoï Ukraïny: suchasna kontseptsiia ukraïns´koho natsionalizmu', *Napriam*, no. 3, 1992.

14 Roman Koval´, *Pidstavy natsiokratiï* (Kiev: DSU, 1994). 'Natsiokratiia' was the title of a book published by Mykola Stsibors´kyi in 1942 (Prague: Proboem).

15 'DSU – orhanizatsiia Ukraïntsiv', *Neskorena natsiia*, no. 14, 1993; Ivan Kandyba, 'Khto my?', *Neskorena natsiia*, no. 2, 1992.

16 'Politychna filosofiia DSU', copy in author's possession, dated May 1991.

17 See also Lee Kendall Metcalf, 'Outbidding to Radical Nationalists: Minority Policy in Estonia, 1989–1993', *Nations and Nationalism*, vol. 2 (2), July 1996, pp. 213–34.

18 Wilson, *Ukrainian Nationalism in the 1990s*, ch. 5.

19 Graham Smith (ed.), *The Baltic States: The National Self-Determination of Estonia, Latvia and Lithuania* (London: Macmillan, 1994), p. 189.

20 Volodymyr Zolotor´ov, 'Rubikon ishche poperedu?', *Den´*, no. 1, 1996. See also the discussion in Oleksandr Derhachov and Volodymyr Polokhalo (eds.), *Modeli derzhavnosti ta derzhavnoho ustroiu Ukraïny na porozi XXI stolittia* (Kiev: Politychna dumka, 1996).

21 Some have therefore argued that the phrase 'Ukrainian people [*ukraïns'kyi narod*] now has two meanings – narrow and broad, the traditional-ethnic and the general-civic': Iurii Badz'o, 'Istorychni nebezpeky na nashomu shliakhu do hromadians'koho suspil'stva', *Literaturna Ukraïna*, 6 March 1997.

22 *Konstytutsiia Ukraïny* (Kiev: Secretariat of the Ukrainian Parliament, 1996), p. 3; also in *Zerkalo nedeli*, 13 July 1996.

23 'Concept of the National Policy of Ukraine in Relation to Indigenous Peoples (Draft)', English version, p. 1; emphasis added.

24 Rogers Brubaker, *Nationalism Reframed: Nationhood and the National Question in the New Europe* (Cambridge: Cambridge University Press, 1996); Dominique Arel, 'Ukraine: The Temptation of the Nationalizing State', in Vladimir Tismaneanu (ed.), *Political Culture and Civil Society in Russia and the New States of Eurasia* (London: M. E. Sharpe, 1995), pp. 157–88.

25 See for example the statement by the veteran dissident Levko Luk''ianenko at the spring 1992 congress of Rukh that, until 1991, 'we were a colony and regarded our government as an occupying administration': *III Vseukraïns'ki Zbory Narodnoho Rukhu Ukraïny 28 liutoho–1 bereznia 1992 roku (Stenohrafichnyi svit)* (Kiev: Rukh, 1992), p. 97.

26 Serhii Zhyzhko, 'Meta i zavdannia ukraïns'koho natsionalistychnoho rukhu', in *Materiialy pershoho zboru Kongresu Ukraïns'kykh Natsionalistiv* (Kiev: Holovnyi Provid Kongresu Ukraïns'kykh Natsionalistiv, 1995), pp. 31–4, at p. 32.

27 Author's interview with Pavlo Movchan, 26 October 1994.

28 *Prohrama i statut Narodnoho Rukhu Ukraïny*, pp. 12–13.

29 The Ukrainian version of this myth is considered in more detail in my *Ukrainian Nationalism in the 1990s*, ch. 7. See also Ivan Dziuba, 'Ukraïna i svit' and 'Ukraïna i Rosiia', in Ihor Ostash (ed.), *Quo vadis, Ukraïno?* (Odesa: Maiak, 1992), pp. 10–54.

30 Ievhen Hutsalo, *Mental'nist' ordy* (Kiev: Prosvita, 1996); Leonid Zalizniak, 'Ukraïna na Evraziis'komu rosdorizzi', *Vechirnii Kyïv*, 16 August 1996.

31 Cf. Ihor Ševčenko, *Ukraine Between East and West: Essays on Cultural History to the Early Eighteenth Century* (Edmonton: Canadian Institute for Ukrainian Studies (CIUS), 1996).

32 Roman Koval', *Chy mozhlyve Ukraïno-Rosiis'ke zamyrennia?* (L'viv: Stryi, 1991).

33 Roman Szporluk, 'Des marches de l'empire à la construction d'une nation', *L'autre Europe*, no. 30–1, 1995, pp. 134–50; and his 'The Ukraine and Russia', in Robert Conquest (ed.), *The Last Empire: Nationality and the Soviet Future* (Stanford, CA: Hoover Institution Press, 1986), pp. 151–82.

34 Valerii Soldatenko, Volodymyr Kryzhanivs'kyi, Iurii Levenets' et al., *Ukraïns'ka ideia: istorychnyi narys* (Kiev: Naukova dumka, 1995); and Soldatenko et al. (eds.), *Ukraïns'ka ideia: pershi rechnyky* (Kiev: Znannia, 1994).

35 The key works of Stepan Rudnyts'kyi, the founder of Ukrainian political geography, are reprinted in *Chomu my khochemo samostiinoï Ukraïny* (L'viv: Svit, 1994).

36 See the letter to President Kuchma signed by over 170 parliamentary

deputies, 'Hrikh smiiatysia nad matir˝iu', in *Holos Ukraïny*, 4 February 1995, and Mykhailo Kosiv, 'Bez movy nemaie narodu: bez narodu nemaie derzhavy', *Holos Ukraïny*, 16 September 1994.

37 Pavlo Movchan, 'Bula, ie i bude!', *Visnyk Prosvity*, special issue no. 1, 1994, p. 3. See also Tamila Pan´ko and Mariia Bilous, *Slovo v dukhovnomu zhytti natsiï* (Kiev: Znannia, 1995).

38 Survey evidence analysed by Dominique Arel and Valeri Khmelko shows that Russophone Ukrainians are closer to ethnic Russians on the language issue, but lie between Ukrainophones and ethnic Russians on political issues, such as the maintenance of statehood: 'The Russian Factor and Territorial Polarization in Ukraine', at pp. 86–8.

39 Badz´o, 'Istorychni nebezpeky'.

40 Vasyl´ Lyzanchuk, *Navichno kaidany kuvaly: fakty, dokumenty, komentari pro rusyfikatsiiu v Ukraïni* (L´viv: Akademiia nauk Ukraïny, Instytut etnolohiï, 1995), pp. 17–19. See also Leonid Poltava (ed.), *Rosiishchennia Ukraïny* (New York: Ukrainian Congress Committee of America, 1984; reprinted in Kiev, 1992).

41 The first term is from the article by Iurii Badz´o, 'Ukraïna: chetverta sproba, abo chy vyzhyvut´ ukraïntsi?', *Rozbudova derzhavy*, no. 9 (September), 1995, p. 5; the second from the polemic, 'Nova Ukraïna chy nova koloniia?', signed by sixteen nationalist deputies and academics and designed as a rebuttal of the book published by Volodymr Hryn´ov (see nn. 72–3), published, *inter alia*, in *Holos Ukraïny*, 12 December 1995. Cf. Mykola Zhulyns´kyi, 'Ukraïna: formuvannia dukhovnoï nezalezhnosti', *Suchasnist´*, no. 5 (May), 1995, pp. 90–9, at pp. 96–7.

42 Levko Luk˝ianenko, 'Ne dai smiiatys´ voroham nad ridnym kraiem', *Holos Ukraïny*, 3 September 1995.

43 Dmytro Pavlychko, 'Pro robotu rady natsional´nostei rukhu', speech to the second Rukh congress, October 1990, in author's possession.

44 Oleh Rudakevych, 'Polityko-kul´turna ukraïnizatsiia iak suspil´nyi fenomen i naukove poniattia', *Rozbudova derzhavy*, no. 11 (November), 1996, pp. 60–2.

45 Author's interview with Levko Luk˝ianenko, 23 October 1994. One prominent centrist, the philosopher Myroslav Popovych (the original spokesman for Rukh in 1988) has written that 'the problems of "Ukrainianisation" or, as it is beginning to be called, "de-Russification", provoke [*zachipaiut´*] Russophone Ukrainians more than Russians': *Ievropa–Ukraïna – pravi i livi* (Kiev: Kyïvs´ke bratstvo, 1997), p. 97.

46 Dmytro Dontsov, *Rosiis´ki vplyvy na ukraïns´ku psykhiku* (L´viv: Russica, 1913); *Rosiia chy Evropa?* (London: Union of Ukrainians of Great Britain, 1955); *Za iaku revoliutsiiu?* (Toronto: League for the Liberation of Ukraine, 1957) – most available in modern Ukrainian reprints.

47 Mykola Khvyl´ovyi, 'Kul´turnyi epigonizm', in his 'Dumky proty techiï'; and 'Ukraïna chy malorosiia?', in the collection of essays *Ukraïna chy malorosiia?* (Kiev: Smoloskyp, 1993), pp. 83–154 and 219–66, at pp. 110 and 241. The former essay was originally published in 1926, the latter circulated only in manuscript. Selections from some of Khvyl´ovyi's main works can be found in English in Myroslav Shkandrij (ed.), *The Cultural Renaissance in Ukraine*.

Mykola Khvylovy: Polemical Pamphlets, 1925–1926 (Edmonton: CIUS, 1986).

48 Ievhen Malaniuk, *Malorosiistvo* (New York: Visnyk ODFFU, 1959), pp. 10, 12, 13 and 8.

49 Ibid., pp. 6–7.

50 Ibid., p. 9.

51 For similar themes in Kazak nationalism, see Bhavna Dave, 'National Revival in Kazakhstan: Language Shift and Identity Change', *Post-Soviet Affairs*, vol. 12 (1), 1996, pp. 51–72.

52 'Shchob ne zhasla svicha: z Konhresu Ukraïns'koï Intellihentsiï', *Literaturna Ukraïna*, 23 November 1995.

53 'Manifest ukraïns'koï inteligentsiï', in *Literaturna Ukraïna*, 12 October 1995. See also *Literaturna Ukraïna*, 16 and 23 November 1995, and Mykola Tomenko, *Iaku Ukraïnu buduie komanda Prezydenta Leonida Kuchmy?!* (Kiev: Ukraïns'ka perspektyva, 1996).

54 Andrew Wilson, 'The Donbas Between Ukraine and Russia: The Use of History in Political Disputes', *Journal of Contemporary History*, vol. 30 (2), April 1995, pp. 265–89. For some typical examples of such claims, see Dmitrii Kornilov, 'Zemlia – uteriannykh bogov', *Donetskii kriazh*, 5 March 1993; and the series *Problemy politicheskoi istorii Kryma* (Simferopol': Ministerstvo obrazovaniia respubliki Krym, 1996–).

55 I. B. Pogozhinkov, 'Russkie v nashem gosudarstve – eto ne natsional'noe men'shinstvo, poetomu russkii iazyk i literatury nado ne zapreshchat', a berech', leleiat' . . .', *Vidrodzhennia*, no. 1, 1994.

56 'Deklaratsiia o natsional'nom edinstve Russkogo Naroda (proekt)', document prepared for the founding congress (s''ezd) of the Congress of the Russian People in Simferopil', Crimea, on 5 October 1996, Article 2. See also Sergei Kiselev and Natal'ia Kiseleva, *Razmyshleniia o Kryme i geopolitike* (Simferopil': Krymskii arkhiv, 1994), p. 26.

57 'Zakon Ukrainy (proekt) "Ob osobom poriadke ispol'zovaniia russkogo iazyka kak iazyka odnogo iz korennykh narodov Ukrainy"' (draft in author's possession). Articles 10 and 11 of the constitution refer to language and minority rights.

58 E. I. Golovakha and N. V. Panina, 'Natsional'no-gosudarstvennaia identifikatsiia i formirovanie sotsial'no-politicheskikh orientatsii russkogo men'shinstva v Ukraine', in Golovakha and I. M. Pakhomov (eds.), *Politicheskaia kul'tura naseleniia Ukrainy: resul'taty sotsiologicheskikh issledovanii* (Kiev: Naukova dumka, 1993), pp. 98–111, at p. 104. The sample size was 95 in Crimea and 276 in eastern Ukraine.

59 Ludmila Chizhikova, *Russko-Ukrainskoe pogranich'e: istoriia i sud'by traditsionno-bytovoi kul'tury (XIX–XX vv.)* (Moscow: Nauka, 1988).

60 Valentin Mamutov, 'Dikoe pole – ne terra-inkognita', *Donetskii kriazh*, 8–14 October 1993; V. A. Pikro, 'Zaselenie v XVI–XVIII vv.', in A. A. Slin'ko (ed.), *Novye stranitsy v istorii donbassa* (Donets'k: Donbas, 1992), pp. 26–43.

61 Iaroslav Hrytsak, 'Ukraïna, 1991–1995 rr.: nova politychna natsiia', *Skhid*, no. 4, 1996, pp. 12–19, at p. 15.

62 Iurii Iurov, 'Kryms'ka karta v donbas'komu pas'iansi', *Heneza*, no. 1, 1995, pp. 188–93, at p. 188.

63 Maria Popovych, '*The Days of the Turbins* by Mikhail Bulgakov in the Light of

the Russian–Ukrainian Literary Discussion', in Lesley Milne (ed.), *Bulgakov: The Novelist-Playwright* (Luxemburg: Harwood Academic Press, 1995), pp. 50–60.

64 V. B. Liubchenko, 'Teoretychna ta praktychna diial'nist' rosiis'kykh natsion-alistychnykh orhanizatsii v Ukraïni (1908–1914 rr.)', *Ukraïns'kyi istorychnyi zhurnal*, no. 2, 1996, pp. 55–65, at p. 63. See also Don C. Rawson, *Russian Rightists and the Revolution of 1905* (Cambridge: Cambridge University Press, 1995), pp. 91–103.

65 Dmytro Vydrin, 'Rosiiany v Ukraïni: pid chas referendumu, do i pislia', *Politolohichni chytannia*, no. 1, 1992, pp. 237–49. See also Valentyna Ermolova, '"Russkii vopros" v Ukraine', *Vseukrainskie vedomosti*, 6 December 1994.

66 Kiselev and Kiseleva, *Razmyshleniia o Kryme i geopolitike*, pp. 16, 18 and 21–5; 'Ievraziiskii soiuz: kontseptsiia (proekt)', *Grazhdanskii kongress*, no. 1, 1993. For a foreign policy view backed by the Communist Party of Ukraine, see V''iacheslav Kudin, 'Ukraïna v systemi suchasnoï heopolityky', *Komunist*, nos. 12–15 (April), 1996.

67 See also Myroslav Popovych, *Istoriia ukraïns'koï kul'tury* (forthcoming).

68 Zenon E. Kohut, 'The Development of a Little Russian Identity and Ukrainian Nationbuilding', *Harvard Ukrainian Studies*, vol. 10, 1986, pp. 559–76.

69 See Paul Robert Magocsi, 'The Ukrainian National Revival: A New Analytical Framework', *Canadian Review of Studies in Nationalism*, vol. 16 (1–2), 1989, pp. 45–62, and Ivan Lysiak-Rudnyts'kyi, 'Rusyfikatsiia chy malorosiianizatsiia?', *Journal of Ukrainian Graduate Studies*, Spring 1978, pp. 78–84. See also Linda Colley, *Britons: Forging the Nation, 1707–1837* (New Haven: Yale University Press, 1992).

70 Oleksandr Derkachov et al., *Ukraïns'ka derzhavnist' u XX stolitti* (Kiev: Politychna dumka, 1996), pp. 55–72.

71 Orest Subtelny, 'Russocentrism, Regionalism and the Political Culture of Ukraine', in Tismaneanu, *Political Culture and Civil Society in Russia and the New States of Eurasia*, pp. 189–207.

72 Hryn'ov was deputy chairman of parliament from 1990 to 1993, stood for president in 1991 and received 4.2 per cent of the vote, and co-founded the Interregional Block in the winter of 1993–4 with Leonid Kuchma. Kuchma appointed him an advisor on regional affairs after he became president in July 1994. Hryn'ov is bilingual, but in identity terms is an archetypal Russophone Ukrainian.

73 Volodymyr Hyrn'ov, *Nova Ukraïna: iakoiu ia ïï bachu* (Kiev: Abrys, 1995), p. 60.

74 Ivan Shapovalov and Volodymyr Aleksieiev, 'Demokratychnyi pohliad na rosiis'ku movu ta Ukraïns'ku derzhavu', *Holos Ukraïny*, 27 July 1995.

75 Popovych, *Ievropa–Ukraïna*, pp. 49 and 97.

76 Hyrn'ov, *Nova Ukraïna*, p. 61. See also Petro Tolochko, 'Imeet li Ukraina natsional'nuiu ideiu?', *Kievskie novosti*, 20 October 1995; the interview with Tolochko in *Kievskie vedomosti*, 12 February 1996; and the attack on 'Russophobia' by Oleksii Tolochko, 'Mental'nist' Iasyru', in *Den'*, 25 December 1996.

77 Andrei Derkach, Sergei Veretennikov and Andrei Iermolaiev, *Beskonechno dliashcheesia nastoiashchee. Ukraina: chetyre goda puti* (Kiev: Lybid', 1995), pp. 43–5. See also Dmytro Vydrin and Dmytro Tabachnyk, *Ukraïna na porozi XXI stolittia: politychnyi aspekt* (Kiev: Lybid', 1995), pp. 37 and 126–36.

78 Popovych, *Ievropa–Ukraïna*, pp. 48–9.

79 Myroslav Popovych, 'Shcho poperedu: ievropeistvo chy fundamentalizm?', *Heneza*, no. 1, 1994, pp. 35–7, at p. 35.

80 Petr Rabinovich, 'O zakonodatel'nom reshenii iazykovykh problem v Ukraine', *Sovest'*, no. 19 (November), 1992. See also the material from the conference 'Russian Culture in the Context of the Social-Historical Realities in Ukraine at the End of the Twentieth Century', held in Kiev in October 1993, in *Vidrodzhennia*, no. 1, 1994.

81 Hryn'ov, *Nova Ukraïna*, p. 62.

82 Popovych, *Ievropa–Ukraïna*, p. 80.

83 Iu. G. Morozov, 'Russkie Ukrainy – nositeli dvukh iazykovykh kul'tur – russkoi i ukrainskoi . . .', *Vidrodzhennia*, no. 1, 1994.

84 Eleonora Vilens'ka and Vasyl' Poklad, 'Natsional'no-kul'turni oriientatsiï meshkantsiv Luhans'koï oblasti', *Filosofs'ka i sotsiolohichna dumka*, no. 4, 1993, pp. 48–59, at pp. 52 and 54. The survey questioned 968 residents of Luhans'k, the more easterly and more radical of the two oblasts of the Donbas.

85 Pirie, 'National Identity'.

86 Analiticheskii otdel Partii Slavianskogo Edinstva Ukrainy, 'Rusichi – novaia slavianskaia natsiia?', *Slavianskoego edinstvo*, no. 2 (March), 1995.

87 'Vse my – brat'ia', *Brat'ia slaviane* (a paper published in Luhans'k by the Rus' society), no. 9 (December), 1996.

88 On the persistence of a 'Soviet' identity, particularly in eastern and southern Ukraine, see Iaroslav Hrytsak, Oksana Malanchuk and Nataliia Chernysh, 'Ukraïna: skhid i zakhid', *Sovremennoe obshchestvo* (Kharkiv), no. 3, 1994, pp. 70–5, at p. 73; 45 per cent of their sample in Donets'k identified themselves as 'Soviet'.

89 Arel and Khmelko record 38 per cent of Russophone Ukrainians supporting the assertion that 'Ukraine and Russia must unite in one state', as against 22 per cent of Ukrainophones and 56 per cent of ethnic Russians: 'The Russian Factor and Territorial Polarization in Ukraine', p. 87.

90 I. L. Mykhailyn (ed.), *Panteleimon Kulish i ukraïns'ke natsional'ne vidrodzhennia* (Kharkiv: Kharkivs'kyi derzhavnyi universitet, 1995).

91 *Grazhdanskii kongress*, no. 3, 1995, p. 1. The Civic Congress Party used as its emblem Mikhail Mikeshin's statue of Khmelnyts'kyi in St Sophia Square, Kiev (finished in 1888), with his mace pointing north towards Moscow.

92 Vernads'kyi founded the Ukrainian Academy of Sciences in 1918; Kotsiubyns'kyi was a leading Bolshevik. See also Elizabeth Luchka Haigh, 'Was V. I. Vernadsky a Ukrainian Nationalist?', *Ukrainian Review*, vol. 43 (2), Summer 1996, pp. 55–62.

93 Dmitrii Kornilov, 'Tak kto zhe bol'she liubit Ukrainu?', *Donetskii kriazh*, no. 50, 21–7 January 1994; Natal'ia Shapiro, 'Russkoe dvizhenie v Galitsii (1848–1939)', *Sovest'*, no. 17 (September), 1992.

94 Cf. the statement by the Christian-Democratic Party of Ukraine that

'Ukrainian culture without Gogol is unimaginable, as is Russian [culture]': 'Slovo pro khrystyians´ku demokratiiu', *Khrystyians´ko-demokratychna partiia Ukraïny: prohrama i statut* (Kiev: Party publication, 1994), pp. 1–4, at p. 2.

95 See also Graham Smith and Wilson, 'Rethinking Russia's Post-Soviet Diaspora'.

96 V. Iakovlev, 'Obshchenatsional´nye idei sovremennoi Ukrainy', *Tovarysh*, nos. 1 and 2 (January), 1996.

97 Speech of Petro Symonenko to the June 1993 congress of the Communist Party of Ukraine, *Partiia Kommunistov vozrozhdaetsia: dokumenty i materialy vtorogo etapa Vseukrainskoi konferentsii kommunistov i s´´ezd Kommunist-icheskoi partii Ukrainy* (Kherson: Party document, 1993), p. 23.

98 'Statut Liberal´noï partiï Ukraïny (proekt)' (Kiev: Party document, 1996), p. 2.

99 'Programme of the Socialist Party of Ukraine' (Kiev: Party document, 1995; in English), p. 13.

100 Petro Symonenko, '"Natsional´na ideia": mify i real´nist´', *Holos Ukraïny*, 21 March 1996, p. 7; Heorhii Kriuchkov, 'Shche odyn krok do dyktatury? (Pro novyi variant proektu Konstytutsiï Ukraïny)', *Komunist*, no. 49 (December), 1995, p. 5.

101 See for example Kuchma's inauguration address, *Holos Ukraïny*, 21 July 1994.

102 'Osnovy derzhavnoï etnonatsional´noï polityky', in Mykola Tomenko, *Ukraïns´ka perspektyva: istoryko-politolohichni pidstavy suchasnoï derzhavnoï stratehiï* (Kiev: Ukraïns´ka perspektyva, 1995), pp. 60–7, at pp. 65 and 66.

103 In a 1995 survey, 33 per cent of a sample of 402 in Donets´k still considered themselves first and foremost 'population of the former USSR': 'Sotsial´no-politychnyi portret chotyr´okh mist Ukraïny', *Politychnyi portret Ukraïny* (Kiev: Demokratychni initsiatyvy, no. 13, 1995), p. 46. See also the 1994 survey by Viktor Nebozhenko and Iryna Bekeshkina, 'Politychnyi portret Ukraïny (skhid, pivden´)', *Politychnyi portret Ukraïny*, no. 9, 1994, when the figure was 34 per cent (at p. 45).

104 *Krasnoe znamia* (the organ of the Kharkiv branch of the Communist Party of Ukraine), no. 8 (August), 1996, p. 1, refers to 'our [Soviet] homeland' in the present tense.

105 *Konstitutsiia respubliki Krym* (Simferopil´: Verkhovnyi sovet Kryma, 1993), p. 2.

106 Svetlana In´shakova, 'Odeskie Mankurty', *Pravda Ukrainy*, 6 February 1991; author's interview with Dmitrii Kornilov, 31 April 1994.

107 *Partiia Kommunistov vozrozhdaetsia*, p. 25.

108 Dmitrii Kornilov, interviewed by the author and Dominique Arel, 14 July 1993; Kornilov, 'Federatsiia – de-fakto. A de-iure?', *Donetskii kriazh*, no. 23, 25 June–1 July 1993. Samuel Huntington also argues that there is a *civilisational*, rather than an ethnic divide in Ukraine; see his *The Clash of Civilizations and the Remaking of World Order* (New York: Simon and Schuster, 1996), pp. 165–8.

109 Natalia Dinello, 'Religious Attitudes of Russian Minorities and National Identity', in Vladimir Shlapentokh, Munir Sendich and Emil Payin (eds.),

The New Russian Diaspora: Russian Minorities in the Former Soviet Republics (New York: M. E. Sharpe, 1994), pp. 195–205.

110 Mykhailo Hrushevs'kyi, 'Halychyna i Ukraina', *Literaturno-naukovyi vistnyk*, vol. 36, 1906, pp. 489–96.

111 'Rusichi – novaia slavianskaia natsiia?'

112 V. Popov of the Congress of Russian Organisations of Ukraine, 'Prishla pora ob''ediniat'sia', *Brat'ia slaviane*, no. 9 (December), 1996.

113 Khmelko and Wilson, 'The Political Orientations'.

114 *Grazhdanskii kongress*, no. 3, 1995, p. 3.

115 *Ustav Kongressa Russkikh Organizatsii Ukrainy* (Kiev: private document, dated 1996), p. 2.

116 Interview with Baziliuk, 'S Rossiei – na vechnye vremena!', *Brat'ia slaviane*, no. 4 (July), 1996; 'Partiia Grazhdanskii kongress Ukrainy, Kongress Russkikh Organizatsii Ukrainy – obrashchenie k grazhdanam Ukrainy i ikh ob''edineniiam', dated 2 February 1997.

117 Popov, 'Prishla pora ob''ediniat'sia'.

118 Khmelko and Wilson, 'The Political Orientations'.

119 Information provided by Dr Khmelko. The survey size was 3,479, with 3,327 answering the national identity question. A total of 58.8 per cent saw themselves as 'only Ukrainian' and 10.8 per cent as 'only Russian'.

120 Taras Kuzio, 'National Identity in Independent Ukraine: An Identity in Transition', *Nationalism and Ethnic Politics*, vol. 2 (4), Winter 1996, pp. 582–608.

7 THE CENTRAL ASIAN STATES AS NATIONALISING REGIMES

1 Rogers Brubaker, *Nationalism Reframed: Nationhood and the National Question in the New Europe* (Cambridge: Cambridge University Press, 1996), pp. 79–106.

2 This study excludes the Central Asian state of Tajikistan from examination for the simple reason that, since the outbreak of civil war there in 1992, regional identities have become consolidated and any concept of a unified national identity has been eroded.

3 Although primary identification may lie with the local language and culture, most members of the native intelligentsias are none the less fluent in Russian.

4 The terms 'Kazakstani', 'Uzbekistani', 'Turkmenistani' and 'Kyrgyzstani' are used in this chapter to refer to citizens in those states, irrespective of their ethnic nationality. 'Kazak', 'Uzbek', 'Turkmen' and 'Uzbek' refer to members of those ethnic groups, irrespective of their citizenship.

5 Nurlan Amrekulov and Nurbulat Masanov, *Kazakhstan mezhdu proshlym i budushchim* (Almaty: Beren, 1994), pp. 165–7.

6 *Mankurt* is a term of chastisement and derision used by nationalist-minded Central Asians (primarily Kazaks and Kyrgyz) to describe their Russified, urban co-ethnics who have only a superficial knowledge of the customs and language of their elders. It originally referred to a character in a novel (*I dol'she veka dlit'sia den'*) of the renowned Kyrgyz writer Chinggis Aytmatov.

7 The Kazaks achieved a simple majority of the population in their state only in 1997; and the Kyrgyz achieved majority status only in the mid-1980s. In 1989, ethnic Kyrgyz constituted 52.4 per cent of Kyrgyzstan's total population, while they formed only 47 per cent of the total population as late as 1980. Kyrgyz currently make up 60.8 per cent of Kyrgyzstan's population (see table 7.1).

8 For fuller information, see Annette Bohr, 'Kyrgyzstan and the Kyrgyz', in Graham Smith (ed.), *The Nationalities Question in the Post-Soviet States* (London: Longman, 1996), pp. 385–409.

9 For an examination of the triadic relationship between nationalising states, national minorities and external 'historic homelands', see Brubaker, *Nationalism Reframed*, pp. 55–76.

10 Interview with the then chairman of the Kazakstani State Committee on Nationalities Policy Georgii Kim: 'Natsional′naia politika – sfera delikatnaia: ona ne terpit naskokov i vysokomeriia', *Kazakhstanskaia pravda*, 7 September 1996.

11 Valeriy Tishkov, *Ethnicity, Nationalism and Conflict in and After the Soviet Union: The Mind Aflame* (London: Sage, 1997), p. 35.

12 Bearing in mind that only 46.8 per cent of Russians resident in Kazakstan were born in that republic, according to 1989 census data. In Uzbekistan the corresponding figure was 48.3 per cent; in Tajikistan 43.3 per cent; in Turkmenistan 47.1 per cent; and in Kyrgyzstan 45.3 per cent. Approximately another 40 per cent have lived in the Central Asian region for more than twenty years: Leonid Rybakovskii, 'Tsentral′naia Aziia i Rossiia: mezhgosudarstvennyi migratsionnyi obmen', in Galina Vitkovskaia (ed.), *Migratsiia russkoiazychnogo naseleniia iz Tsentral′noi Azii: prichiny, posledstviia, perspektivy* (Moscow: Carnegie Endowment for International Peace, 1996), p. 72.

13 Mikhail Guboglo, 'Trudno byt′ bratom: bolevie tochki etnopoliticheskoi situatsii v Kazakhstane', *Segodnia*, 25 November 1995.

14 See, for example, 'O vyrublennykh sadakh i unizhennykh liudiakh', *Lipetskaia gazeta*, 14 September 1996, and 'Po kom trubiat karnai i surnai', *Neva*, no. 9, 1992, p. 227.

15 Mark R. Beissinger, 'The Persisting Ambiguity of Empire', *Post-Soviet Affairs*, vol. 11 (2), 1995, p. 150.

16 As articulated by Lieutenant-Colonel K. Ershkov of the Semirech′e Cossack Host on *Vesti*, 12 November 1995.

17 Brubaker, *Nationalism Reframed*, p. 63.

18 While the *guls* of the Ahal-Tekke and Yomud tribes are easily discernible, it is not completely clear to which tribes the other three *guls* on the flag belong. Moreover, the *gul* of the Ersary tribe is missing altogether, a circumstance that is reported to have caused some consternation amongst members of that tribe living in Germany and Sweden.

19 'Kazhdyi den′ budut pet′ o vozhde', *Pravda-5*, 26 September 1996; and *Turkmenistan*, 29 August 1996.

20 ITAR-TASS, 24 November 1992, in *FBIS SOV*, 25 November 1992. According to the Turkmen constitution, the Halq Maslakhaty is the supreme representative organ of power in the country. Although the Halq Maslakhaty is alleged to be neither an executive nor a legislative body, its decisions take

precedence over those of the parliament and the president, and the Cabinet of Ministers is required to accept the Council's decisions for mandatory implementation.

21 *Izvestiia*, 18 July 1994.

22 The Turkmen also emphasise historical continuity, but to a lesser degree. President Niyazov has claimed on several occasions that 'the last Turkmen state existed eight centuries ago', and that the current Turkmen nation is 'the successor to the world's most ancient civilisations'. See, for example, Niyazov's speech to the fiftieth session of the United Nations General Assembly on 22 October 1995.

23 For an account of the Soviet historiographical treatment of Temur and the Temurids, see Edward Allworth, *The Modern Uzbeks* (Stanford, CA: Hoover University Press, 1990), pp. 242–8.

24 In rural regions alone, some 320 collective and state farms and other organisations carry the name of Amir Temur: 'Starie nazvaniia otvlekaiut ot idei nezavisimosti', *Nezavisimaia gazeta*, 2 August 1996.

25 Nation-building can require heavy financial backing: the Uzbekistani government reportedly spent more than US $9 million to erect the Temur Museum and US $2.5 million to celebrate the country's fifth year of independence.

26 'Kontseptsiia stanovleniia istoricheskogo soznaniia v Respublike Kazakhstan', *Kazakhstanskaia pravda*, 30 June 1995.

27 'Starie nazvaniia'.

28 *Kyrgyz Rukhu*, no. 2, 2 December 1992, pp. 2–3.

29 The wide-reaching constitutional amendments adopted in January 1996 did not affect this article.

30 In 1990, Kyrgyz and Uzbeks clashed over housing and land rights in the Osh valley, leaving 171 dead and several hundred injured. For an analysis of the conflict, see Tishkov, *Ethnicity, Nationalism and Conflict*, pp. 135–54.

31 The Korean and Dungan diasporas in Kyrgyzstan have also traditionally worked the land. The representatives of those groups in the Assembly of the Peoples of Kyrgyzstan asked the government to allot their communities additional land plots in September 1996. See 'Problemy est', no budut reshat'sia', *Slovo Kyrgyzstana*, 5 September 1996.

32 The percentage was later reduced to one-quarter before the idea was dropped: personal communication by Valeriy Petrovich Zhivoglyadov, the rector of the Kyrgyz–American International University in Bishkek; and Ol'ga Vasil'eva, *Sredniaia Asiia: god posle putcha* (Moscow: Tsentr Sever–Iug, 1993), p. 49.

33 A. D. Nazarov and S. I. Nikolaev, 'Russkie v Kirgizii: est' li al'ternativa iskhodu?', in S. S. Savoskul, A. I. Ginzburg, L. V. Ostapenko and I. A. Subbotina, *Russkie v novom zarubezh'e: Kirgiziia* (Moscow: Rossiiskaia akademiia nauk, Institut etnologii i antropologii, 1995), p. 18.

34 Martha Brill Olcott, *Central Asia's New States* (Washington, DC: United States Institute of Peace Press, 1996), p. 77; Nurlan Amrekulov, 'Inter-Ethnic Conflict and Resolution in Kazakstan', in Roald Z. Sagdeev and Susan Eisenhower, *Central Asia: Conflict, Resolution and Change* (Washington, DC: Center for Post-Soviet Studies, 1995), pp. 161–3.

35 Ermias Abebe, 'Kazakstan and Russia: Foreign Policy, Ethnicity and

Economics', Former Soviet South Project Briefing Paper no. 7, Royal Institute of International Affairs, March 1996.

36 The Central Asian republics kept pace in this regard with the other Soviet union republics: nine out of fifteen union republics adopted language laws in 1989, and two more did so in 1990. For more details and the texts of all the laws, see Mikhail Guboglo (ed.), *Perelomnye gody*, vol. II, *Iazykovaia reforma – 1989: dokumenty i materialy* (Moscow: Rossiiskaia akademiia nauk, Institut etnologii i antropologii, 1994).

37 See, for example, Eugene Huskey, 'The Politics of Language in Kyrgyzstan', *Nationalities Papers*, vol. 23 (3), 1995, pp. 549–72; Michael Ochs, 'Turkmenistan: The Quest for Stability and Control', in Karen Dawisha and Bruce Parrott (eds.), *Conflict, Cleavage and Change in Central Asia and the Caucasus* (Cambridge: Cambridge University Press, 1997), pp. 334–5; Bhavna Dave, 'Kazaks Struggle to Revive Their "Language of Folklore"', *Transition*, 29 November 1996, pp. 23–5; William Fierman, 'Problems of Language Law Implementation in Uzbekistan', *Nationalities Papers*, vol. 23 (3), 1995, pp. 573–95.

38 Witness the illustrative statement made by a Kyrgyzstani Russian to a Moscow researcher: 'Study Kyrgyz? You can break your tongue on it! And what will they do without Russian anyway?' (N. P. Kosmarskaia and S. A. Panarin (eds.), *Etnosotsial'nye protsessy v Kyrgyzstane* (Moscow: Rossiiskaia akademiia nauk, Institut vostokovedeniia, 1994), p. 72).

39 For fuller information, see ch. 9 in this volume.

40 *Panorama*, 22 November 1996, and 'Spory vokrug novogo zakona o iazykakh', *Inostranets*, no. 47, 4 December 1996.

41 Grigorii Piadukhov, 'Kirgiziia: politicheskii faktor kak prichina vynuzhdennoi migratsii', in Vitkovskaia, *Migratsiia russkoiazychnogo naseleniia*, p. 136.

42 In March 1996 the People's Assembly, the lower house of the Kyrgyzstani parliament, passed a draft constitutional amendment at Akaev's urging granting Russian the status of an official language in the country. The proposed amendment was approved by the Constitutional Court at the end of the year, but still needed to be passed by both houses of parliament in order to become law. When the People's Assembly took up the issue again in June 1997, however, it failed to muster the two-thirds majority needed to pass it. The amendment never reached the upper house of parliament for discussion. The proposed constitutional amendment stated that 'the Russian language is used in the Kyrgyz Republic in the capacity of an official language': *Vechernii Bishkek*, 8 January 1997. The author is grateful to Naryn Idinov for information provided on this subject.

43 L. V. Ostapenko, 'Voprosy trudovoi zaniatosti', in Savoskul, *Russkie v novom zarubezh'e*, pp. 94–5.

44 Ian Bremmer, 'Understanding Nationalism in the Post-Communist States', in Bremmer (ed.), *Understanding Nationalism: Ethnic Minorities in the Post-Communist States* (London: forthcoming from Routledge).

45 Vitkovskaia, *Migratsiia russkoiazychnogo naseleniia*, p. 141.

46 Sally N. Cummings, 'Kazakstan's Parliamentary Elections and After', Former Soviet South Project Briefing Paper no. 5, Royal Institute of International Affairs, February 1996. In the Kazakstani parliament elected in 1994, Kazaks occupied 59 per cent and Russians 27 per cent of all seats.

47 *Qanun Nami Bilän: Ozbekistan Respublikäsi Aliy Sudining Äkhbaratnamäsi*, (Bulletin of the Supreme Court of Uzbekistan), nos. 1–2, 1995, pp. 7–13.

48 See, for example, 'U kazhdogo svoi rezony', *Karavan*, 17 June 1994, and *Prava cheloveka*, vol. 2, no. 4, 31 January 1994.

49 A. Dokuchaeva, 'O gosudarstvennom iazyke, i ne tol'ko o nem . . .', *Etnopoliticheskii vestnik*, vol. 2 (8), 1995, p. 157.

50 Nurbulat Masanov and Igor Savin, *Model' etnologicheskogo monitoringa: Kazakhstan* (Moscow: Rossiiskaia akademiia nauk, Institut etnologii i antropologii, 1997). The directive issued by the board ordering the dismissals went into effect only after having been approved by the head of the municipal department of education.

51 See, for example, 'Pochemu russkie begut iz Uzbekistana', *Komsomol'skaia pravda*, 16 November 1994.

52 Brubaker, *Nationalism Reframed*, pp. 26–32.

53 'Chuzhie sredi svoikh', *Pravda*, 21 March 1996.

54 *Bulletin*, Network on Ethnological Monitoring and Early Warning of Conflict, vol. 2 (4), September 1996, pp. 19–20.

55 In Turkmenistan, Soviet passports are still in use and full circulation of the new Turkmenistani passports has not gone into effect: written communication to the author by the Embassy of Turkmenistan, Washington, DC, 8 May 1997. In Kazakstan, while a passport is necessary only for foreign travel (other than to CIS member states), all Kazakstani citizens are required to obtain a personal identification card, which also includes a line denoting ethnic nationality. See 'Ia-grazhdanin', *Kazakhstanskie novosti*, 1 July 1995.

56 *Kazakhstanskaia pravda*, 4 March 1997.

57 'Pochemu Kazakhstanu nuzhna novaia stolitsa', *Kazakhstanskaia pravda*, 21 September 1995.

58 *Demograficheskii ezhegodnik Kazakhstana* (1994), cited in Ian Bremmer and Cory Welt, 'The Trouble with Democracy in Kazakhstan', *Central Asian Survey*, vol. 15 (2), 1996, p. 181.

59 The third paragraph of Article 3 (removed in October 1995) recognised 'the right of all Kazaks who were forced to leave the territory of the republic and reside in other states to hold citizenship of the Republic of Kazakstan together with the citizenship of other states, if this does not contradict the laws of those states of which they are citizens'.

60 The fourth paragraph of Article 3 states: 'The Republic of Kazakstan creates the conditions for the return to its territory of persons who were forced to leave the territory of the republic during periods of mass repressions and forced collectivisation, and as a result of other inhumane political actions; and of their progeny as well as Kazaks living on the territory of former union republics.'

61 Adam Dixon, 'Kazakstan: Political Reform and Economic Development', in Roy Allison (ed.), *Challenges for the Former Soviet South* (London: Royal Institute of International Affairs, 1996), p. 84; interview with Kazakstani President Nazarbaev: 'Zalozhnikom krovi sebia ne chuvstvuiu', *Trud*, 3 October 1996.

62 Jiger Janabel, 'When National Ambition Conflicts with Reality: Studies on Kazakhstan's Ethnic Relations', *Central Asian Survey*, vol. 15 (1), 1960, p. 7.

63 Nazarbaev, 'Zalozhnikom krovi sebia ne chuvstvuiu'.

64 Interview with the Mongolian ambassador extraordinary and plenipotentiary to the Republic of Kazakstan: 'Chuzhie sredi svoikh', *Karavan*, 24 October 1996.

65 *Demograficheskaia situatsiia v Kazakhstane* (Moscow: Informatsionno-ekspertnaia gruppa 'Panorama', January 1995), pp. 5–7.

66 Ibid. and 'Chuzhie sredi svoikh'.

67 The most celebrated cases were those of Boris Suprunyuk, the chairman of the North Kazakstan branch of the Russian Community; and Nina Sidorova, the leader of the Russian Centre.

68 See, for example, 'Strannii sud-strannii prigovor', *Komsomol'skaia pravda*, 22 November 1995, and *Nezavisimaia gazeta*, 14 November 1995.

69 The Cossacks were a military formation that annexed and guarded the borderlands of the Russian Empire. The Cossack movement, banned during Soviet rule, has been rejuvenated since the break-up of the USSR. Nikolai Gunkin, the ataman of the Semirech'e Cossack Host, was arrested in Almaty in October 1995 as he was attempting to register as a candidate in the upcoming elections to Kazakstan's lower house of parliament. Authorities accused Gunkin of organising an unsanctioned meeting at which participants called for the annexation of the northern regions of Kazakstan to Russia. He was sentenced to three months' imprisonment and was allegedly physically assaulted by police officers during his arrest. See 'Kazakstan: Ill-Treatment and the Death Penalty, a Summary of Concerns', Amnesty International Country Report, July 1996.

70 Interview with the chairman of Uzbekistan's Russian cultural centre, Sergei Zinin: 'Russkii iazyk v Tashkente ne zabyli', *Kontinent*, 26 October–1 November 1995.

71 'Qudrätimiz-dostlikdä', *Ozbekistan awazi*, 20 August 1994.

72 'V Tashkente zakryta russkaia gazeta', *Nezavisimaia gazeta*, 24 January 1996.

73 See, for example, 'Bezhentsy i vynuzhdennye pereselentsy v gosudarstvakh SNG-puti resheniia problem mnogostoronnimi usiliiami', *Res Publika*, 19 September 1995.

74 Paul Kolstoe, *Russians in the Former Soviet Republics* (London: Hurst & Company, 1995), p. 236.

75 At that time Russia required all states wishing to remain within the ruble zone to turn over their gold reserves. As Uzbekistan contains approximately a quarter of the former Soviet Union's proven reserves, it opted instead to introduce its own national currency, thereby sending the economy into an inflationary spiral.

76 'Uzy i uzli integratsii', *Pravda*, 23 May 1996.

77 Shirin Akiner, *The Formation of Kazak Identity: From Tribe to Nation-State* (London: Royal Institute of International Affairs, 1995), p. 63.

78 For more on this subject, see the excellent historical overview by Shirin Akiner, 'Islam, the State and Ethnicity in Central Asia in Historical Perspective', *Religion, State and Society*, vol. 24 (2–3), 1996, pp. 91–132.

79 *Biulleten' Obshchestva sodeistviia sobliudeniiu prav cheloveka v Tsentral'noi Azii* (Moscow), no. 8, 10 May 1994, in *Prava cheloveka*, 23 May 1994.

80 Kazakstan passed a law on citizenship in December 1991 that went into effect in March 1992. Laws on citizenship were passed in Uzbekistan in July 1992,

in Kyrgyzstan in 1993 and in Turkmenistan in September 1992 (supplemented by an agreement on dual citizenship with Russia signed in December 1993).

81 Igor Zevelev, 'Russia and the Russian Diasporas', *Post-Soviet Affairs*, vol. 12 (3), 1996, pp. 271–2.

82 There are, none the less, many instances of 'illegal' dual citizens who have managed to obtain Russian passports without renouncing their local citizenship. See '. . . A grazhdaninom byt´ obiazan!', *Slovo Kyrgyzstana*, 31 May 1996.

83 Permanent residents of Kazakstan were given until 1 March 1994 to decline, in writing, the automatic conferral of Kazakstani citizenship upon them. This deadline was prolonged for a year to 1 March 1995 by presidential edict. Thereafter, they were obliged to renounce Kazakstani citizenship by way of the formal procedure. See paragraph 3 of the resolution of the Kazakstani Supreme Soviet on the implementation of the law on citizenship, and the presidential edict on citizenship matters in *Sovet Kazakhstany*, 25 December 1993.

84 Zevelev, 'Russia and the Russian Diasporas', pp. 268–71.

85 Tajikistan signed an agreement with Russia on dual citizenship in September 1995: *OMRI Daily Digest*, 8 September 1995. The accord was ratified by the Tajik parliament in November 1995, although the Russian Duma has not yet ratified the accord.

86 In addition, Turkmenistan and Russia signed an agreement in May 1995 regulating the status of their respective citizens who are living on the other's territory.

87 Vitkovskaia, *Migratsiia russkoiazychnogo naseleniia*, p. 35.

88 'Soglashenie mezhdu Respublikoi Kazakhstan i Rossiiskoi Federatsiei ob uproshchennom poriadke priobreteniia grazhdanstva grazhdanami Respubliki Kazakhstan, pribyvaiushchimi dlia postoiannogo prozhivaniia v Rossiiskuiu Federatsiiu, i grazhdanami Rossiiskoi Federatsii, pribyvaiushchimi dlia postoiannogo prozhivaniia v Respubliku Kazakhstan', *Kazakhstanskaia pravda*, 21 January 1995.

89 'Soglashenie mezhdu Respublikoi Kazakhstan i Rossiiskoi Federatsiei o pravovom statuse grazhdan Respubliki Kazakhstan, postoianno prozhivaiushchikh na territorii Rossiiskoi Federatsii, i grazhdan Rossiiskoi Federatsii, postoianno prozhivaiushchikh na territorii Respubliku Kazakhstan', *Kazakhstanskaia pravda*, 21 January 1995.

90 Aleksei Arapov and Iakov Umanskii, 'Tsentral´naia Aziia i Rossiia: vyzovy i otvety', *Svobodnaia mysl´*, no. 5, 1995, p. 77.

91 Despite his attempt, Russian foreign minister Yevgenii Primakov was unable to conclude these agreements with his Uzbekistani counterpart during his visit to Tashkent in February 1996.

8 LANGUAGE MYTHS AND THE DISCOURSE OF NATION-BUILDING IN GEORGIA

1 Patrick Sériot, 'Le cas russe: anamnèse de la langue et quête identitaire (la langue – mémoire du peuple)', *Langages*, vol. 114, 1994, pp. 84–97, remarks

upon the 'massive presence of the theme of language' in the political discourse of post-1991 Russia on the part of democrats and patriots alike (p. 91).

2 Patrick Sériot, 'La linguistique spontanée des traceurs de frontières', in Sériot (ed.), *Langue et nation en Europe centrale et orientale du XVIIIème siècle à nos jours* (Lausanne: Université de Lausanne, 1996), pp. 277–304.

3 Already in 1860, more than twenty-five years before Renan's celebrated pronouncement, Moritz Lazarus and Heymann Steinthal had underscored the importance of 'subjective notions' rather than objective criteria such as descent and language in defining a *Volk*: 'Descent is of no significance in itself; what matters is the notion bound up with it of the shared identity of the persons sharing common descent, their forebears, their fate, their destiny, their whole past and consequently their future too. It is not the identity of the words used which matters but the awakening awareness and feeling of shared identity common to speaker and hearer in mutual understanding' ('Einleitende Gedanken über Völkerpsychologie', *Zeitschrift für Völkerpsychologie und Sprachwissenschaft*, vol. 1, 1860, pp. 1–73, at p. 41, reprinted in W. Bumann (ed.), *Heymann Steinthal: kleine sprachtheoretische Schriften* (Hildesheim: Georg Olms, 1970), pp. 307–79, at p. 347).

4 This factor is exacerbated by the fact that a number of the scholars currently studying the reshaping of national identities on the territory of the former Soviet Union are conversant only with Russian. By the nature of the thing, language myths tend to be documented only *in* the language concerned, as part of the 'secret knowledge' that binds the community together and sets it apart from the heteroglossic other.

5 The cautionary words of Eric Hobsbawm – 'At all events problems of power, status, politics and ideology and not of communication or even culture, lie at the heart of the nationalism of language', *Nations and Nationalism Since 1780* (Cambridge: Cambridge University Press, 1992), p. 110 – serve as a salutary reminder.

6 Of course no one would wish to claim that language is the sole defining feature of Georgian nationalism or the construction of Georgian identity. Fairy von Lilienfeld, 'Reflections on the Current State of the Georgian Church and Nation', in Stephen K. Batalden (ed.), *Seeking God: The Recovery of Religious Identity in Orthodox Russia, Ukraine, and Georgia* (DeKalb, IL: Northern Illinois University Press, 1993), pp. 220–31, makes some suggestive comments on the ambivalent status of religion and the Church in contemporary Georgia.

7 The magnificent study by Joshua A. Fishman, *In Praise of the Beloved Language: A Comparative View of Positive Ethnolinguistic Consciousness* (Berlin: Mouton de Gruyter, 1997), reached us only after this chapter had been sent to press. I wish to thank my colleagues for their stimulating comments on this chapter, and also the many Georgians who have contributed in one way or another ever since I first got to know their remarkable country and ever-challenging people. Because many of them would not agree with the interpretation I have placed upon the data they have so kindly supplied me with – often at considerable inconvenience to themselves – I have deemed it better not to thank them by name. My gratitude is none the less very deep. They and any other Georgians who might happen to read this are asked to remember that this chapter was written for *Western* readers, whose interests and assumptions

are very different from those of their Georgian counterparts. In particular, the notion of taking seriously *all* the beliefs that constitute the mental universe of a group of people, no matter how outrageous they might seem to serious scholars, is one which puzzles many Georgians of my acquaintance, who regard the search for absolute truth ('What is the origin of the Georgian language?') as the only valid pursuit, and consider subjective truth ('What ideas do people hold about the origin of the Georgian language?') as futile and uninteresting. The pursuit of objective truth does not lose its interest or importance through the study of subjective beliefs such as language myths; the two are complementary. Thus, Georgian readers should remember that this chapter was written in answer to a contemporary Western question – what image do we have of the world? – and not in answer to the question my Georgian friends find more urgent: what is the world really like?

8 The younger generation do not invariably hold this tradition in the same high esteem as their elders and, with the rapid changes now taking place in Georgian society, its days may be numbered. In particular, as increasing numbers of young people study business abroad and seek to import an American-style business culture to Georgia, this traditional form of social interaction may disappear from the business and professional scene.

9 History is the only exception in current British practice.

10 *Gosudarstvennaia programma gruzinskogo iazyka*, reprinted in M. N. Guboglo (ed.), *Perelomnye gody 2. Iazykovaia reforma – 1989. Dokumenty i materialy* (Moscow: Rossiiskaia akademiia nauk, Tsentr po izucheniiu mezhnatsional'nykh otnoshenii instituta etnologii i antropologii im. N. N. Miklukho-Maklaia, 1994), pp. 164–70, at p. 168. See further p. 172.

11 E. Fuller, 'Manifestations of Nationalism in Current Georgian-Language Literature', *Radio Liberty Research*, 106/80, 14 March 1980, p. 4, gives the example of Nodar Jalagonia's 'Chemi ena k'art'uli' (1979). The May 1997 issue of *Burji erovnebisa*, a popular monthly dealing with language, literature, history and religion, printed Lado Asatiani's (1917–43) poem on the Georgian language ('K'art'uli ena') on its front page in dual commemoration of Georgian Language Day and of the eightieth anniversary of the poet's birth.

12 *Country Data – Georgia*, section 'Ethnic Issues', accessed from the homepage of the Georgian parliament, version of 29 January 1996 (http://www.parliament.ge); *Ethnologue Database* gives an estimate of half a million.

13 Strabo, *Geographica*, XI 498; Pliny, *Naturalis Historia*, VI v.

14 Quoted with a minor modification from Besarion A. Jorbenadze, *The Kartvelian Languages and Dialects* (Tbilisi: Mecniereba, 1991), p. 10.

15 Jorbenadze, *The Kartvelian Languages and Dialects*, pp. 11–12. B. G. Hewitt expands upon this passage in 'Languages in Contact in NW Georgia: Fact or Fiction?', in his edited volume, *Caucasian Perspectives* (Unterschleissheim/ Munich: Lincom Europa, 1992), pp. 244–58, on pp. 256–7.

16 An early version of this story is to be found in S. R. Gorgadze, *Sak'art'velos istoria*, vol. I (Tbilisi: printed by Shroma for *Jejili*, 1910/11; see n. 37 below), pp. 3–4: 'Of the languages of the Japhetic family, only Georgian today has a writing system; Svan- and Mingrelian-speaking peoples use Georgian as their literary and ecclesiastical language; and because they share a common descent with the Georgians, they call themselves Georgians. In this way Georgian is

today the national [*erovnuli*] language of all Japhetids; this language unites every branch of the Georgian [*k'art'uli*] race and makes of them a single people which is today known as the Georgian people.'

17 Abel Kikvidze, *Sak'art'velos istoria XIX–XX ss.*, vol. II (Tbilisi: Stalinis sakhelobis t'bilisis sakhelmts'ip'o universitetis gamomtsemloba, 1959), p. 139. Wolfgang Feurstein gives a well-documented account from the minority perspective in 'Mingrelisch, Lazisch, Swanisch: alte Sprachen und Kulturen der Kolchis vor dem baldigen Untergang', in Hewitt (ed.), *Caucasian Perspectives*, pp. 285–328; see also B. G. Hewitt, 'Aspects of Language Planning in Georgia (Georgian and Abkhaz)', in M. Kirkwood (ed.), *Language Planning in the Soviet Union* (London: Macmillan, 1989), pp. 123–44.

18 See, for example, A. Jik'ia, 'Sheteva k'art'ul enaze' [Attack on the Georgian language], *Sakhalkho ganat'leba*, August 1990, part 2, basing his outline on Kikvidze's no less polemical account.

19 Nat'ela Kereselidze, 'Saark'ivo masala: damoukidebeli sak'art'velo da k'art'uli enis movla-patronobis sakit'khi', *Sakhalkho ganat'leba*, 9 August 1990. This article, which reprints two pieces of correspondence from 1918 on the provision of Georgian typewriters, is itself a prime example of history being pressed into the service of the present: at the time, nationalist fervour and calls for independence from the USSR were increasing in strength. Articles such as this one drew welcome parallels between the revered era of independence, 1918–21, and the strivings for independence led by the then very popular dissident Zviad Gamsakhurdia.

20 Stephen F. Jones, 'Georgia: A Failed Democratic Transition', in Ian Bremmer and Ray Taras (eds.), *Nations and Politics in the Soviet Successor States* (Cambridge: Cambridge University Press, 1993), pp. 288–310.

21 N. Sh. Vasadze, O. K. Baliashvili and L. V. Chkhenkeli, 'Prepodavanie russkogo iazyka v vuzakh natsional'nykh respublik: Gruziia', in V. V. Ivanov et al. (eds.), *Russkii iazyk v natsional'nykh respublikakh Sovetskogo Soiuza* (Moscow: Nauka, 1980), pp. 188–95, at pp. 190–1.

22 N. Sh. Vasadze et al., 'Prepodavanie russkogo iazyka v vuzakh natsional'nykh respublik', p. 192.

23 Roman Solanchyk, 'Russian Language and Soviet Politics', *Soviet Studies*, vol. 34, 1982, pp. 23–42. On the language situation during the 1970s, see J. W. R. Parsons, 'National Integration in Soviet Georgia', *Soviet Studies*, vol. 34, 1982, pp. 547–69, at pp. 556–7; for an official account, see D. S. Chanturishvili, 'Russkii iazyk v Gruzii', in Ivanov et al., *Russkii iazyk v natsional'nykh respublikakh Sovetskogo Soiuza*, pp. 78–87. Note in particular the statement 'The Georgian language occupies a leading position in all spheres of the multifaceted life of the republic, although in institutions, large enterprises and workplaces with a staff of diverse national composition Russian is to be heard alongside Georgian on an equal footing' (p. 86). Peter Trudgill, *Sociolinguistics: An Introduction to Language and Society* (Harmondsworth: Penguin, 1974; revised edn, 1983), reports that native speakers of Ossetic 'receive all their education in Russian apart from one hour a week in Ossetic' (p. 155).

24 On language issues around this time, see Elizabeth Fuller, 'Expressions of Official and Unofficial Concern over the Future of the Georgian Language', *Radio Liberty Research*, 149/81, 7 April 1981. George Hewitt gives a brief

account of the relationship between Georgian and Russian in 'Georgian: A Noble Past, A Secure Future', in Isabelle T. Kreindler (ed.), *Sociolinguistic Perspectives on Soviet National Languages: Their Past, Present and Future* (Berlin, New York, and Amsterdam: Mouton de Gruyter, 1985), pp. 163–79, at pp. 168–70. More generally, see E. Glyn Lewis, *Multilingualism in the Soviet Union: Aspects of Language Policy and Its Implementation* (The Hague and Paris: Mouton, 1972).

25 See n. 10 above. On the language laws adopted in eleven of the fifteen republics (excluding Russia and the Transcaucasian republics) of the Soviet Union in 1989 and 1990, see Albert S. Pigolkin and Marina S. Studenikina, 'Republican Language Laws in the USSR: A Comparative Analysis', *Journal of Soviet Nationalities*, vol. 2, 1991, pp. 38–76.

26 As B. G. Hewitt suggests in *Georgian: A Structural Reference Grammar* (Amsterdam and Philadelphia: John Benjamins, 1995), p. 14.

27 Amongst the accounts of the events lying behind the recent resurgence of Georgian nationalism are Jonathan Aves, *Paths to National Independence in Georgia, 1987–1990* (London: School of Slavonic and East European Studies, 1991); Stephen Jones, 'Georgia: The Long Battle for Independence', in Miron Rezun (ed.), *Nationalism and the Breakup of an Empire: Russia and Its Periphery* (Westport, CT, and London: Praeger, 1992), pp. 73–96; Naira Gelaschwili, *Georgien: ein Paradies in Trümmern* (Berlin: Aufbau Taschenbuch Verlag, 1993); John Russell, 'The Georgians: The Two-Edged Sword of Independence', in José Amodia (ed.), *The Resurgence of Nationalist Movements in Europe* (Bradford: University of Bradford, Department of Modern Languages, n.d. (c. 1994)), pp. 79–95; Stephen Jones and Robert Parsons, 'Georgia and the Georgians', in Graham Smith (ed.), *The Nationalities Question in the Post-Soviet States* (Harlow: Longman, 1996), pp. 291–313; Jonathan Aves, *Georgia: From Chaos to Stability?* (London: Royal Institute of International Affairs, 1996). Summary accounts of political, economic and social aspects of the country may be found in Glenn E. Curtis (ed.), *Armenia, Azerbaijan and Georgia: Country Studies* (Washington, DC: Government Printing Office, 1995); *Human Development Report: Georgia 1996* (Tbilisi: United Nations Development Programme, 1996), published annually.

28 'Kidev ert'khel vizeimet' (?!)', *Burji erovnebisa*, 5 (22), 1997, p. 2. This was not the first time such a call had appeared, as the editor remarks à propos of the fate of the State Programmes on Language and History (*Burji erovnebisa*, 3 (20), 1997, p. 14, col. 3).

29 *Burji erovnebisa*, 5 (22), 1997, p. 12. On the brief of the commission and its sub-committees, see Besarion Jorbenadze, 'Sametsniero mushaoba enat'met-snierebis institutshi', *Iberiul-kavkasiuri enat'metsniereba*, vol. 30, 1991, pp. 7–15, on pp. 13–14. A call for an improvement in the official status of Georgian concludes an article on the activities of the Department for the Cultivation of Georgian Speech in the same issue: Lia Lezhava and Shuk'ia Ap'ridonidze, 'K'art'uli metqvelebis kulturis ganqop'ileba' (pp. 66–73, at p. 73).

30 Gerhard Brunn, 'Historical Consciousness and Historical Myths', in Andreas Kappeler (ed.), *The Formation of National Elites* (New York: New York University Press, and Aldershot: Dartmouth Publishing Company for the European Science Foundation, 1992), pp. 327–38, stresses the important role played by outsiders in popularising the ideas of professional historians (p. 331).

31 The two scholarly communities signalled here are not the same as those described by Patrick Sériot, 'La théorie des deux sciences dans la linguistique russe et soviétique', in David Cram, Andrew Linn and Elke Nowak (eds.), *Proceedings of the Seventh International Conference on the History of Linguistics (ICHoLs VII)* (Amsterdam: John Benjamins, forthcoming), and in P. Sériot and Natalja Bocadorova, 'Avant-propos', *Histoire épistémologie langage*, vol. 17 (2), 1995, pp. 7–15; nor the same as the 'deux cultures' outlined in Sériot's 'Changements de paradigmes dans la linguistique soviétique des années 1920–1930', *Histoire épistémologie langage*, vol. 17 (2), 1995, pp. 235–51, and in his 'Le cas russe', at pp. 88–91. Sériot's 'deux sciences' constitute the scholarly orthodoxy of their respective communities, Western and Soviet respectively. Each of them exists in relation to the other, to some degree, even though the amount of contact and mutual knowledge has often been slight; far more active and significant for the purposes of self-definition is the other constituted by fringe scholars within their respective communities. 'Fringe' scholarship (or 'pseudo-science') is the yardstick against which 'true' scholarship is measured within a given culture, whereas different national scholarly cultures – Sériot's 'deux sciences' – may turn out to be incommensurable, occupied with different questions and inclined to recognise different kinds of answers as satisfying. A case in point is signalled in n. 7 above.

32 Anthony D. Smith, *National Identity* (London: Penguin, 1991), p. 83.

33 See especially A. D. Smith, *The Ethnic Origins of Nations* (Oxford: Blackwell, 1986), and the older but still useful book by Joshua Fishman, *Language and Nationalism: Two Integrative Essays* (Rowley, MA: Newbury House, 1972), reprinted in his *Language and Ethnicity in Minority Sociolinguistic Perspective* (Clevedon: Multilingual Matters, 1989), pp. 97–175 and 269–367. Much relevant material is to be found in Arno Borst, *Der Turmbau von Babel: Geschichte der Meinungen über Ursprung und Vielfalt der Sprachen und Völker*, 4 vols. (Stuttgart: Anton Hiersemann, 1957–63).

34 Johannes Goropius Becanus, *Hermathena* (Antwerp: Plantinus, 1580), pp. 25–7.

35 Richard W. Bailey, *Images of English: A Cultural History of the Language* (Ann Arbor: University of Michigan Press, 1991), p. 268, reports the striking case of Robert Claiborne's *Our Marvelous Native Tongue* (1983), in which English is all but identified with proto-Indo-European, existing as a distinct entity some 8,000 years ago, and borrowing from 'modern members of the family' only when it was fully consolidated.

36 From amongst the voluminous bibliography on Marr and Marrism, see Lawrence L. Thomas, *The Linguistic Theories of N. Ja. Marr*, University of California Publications in Linguistics 14 (Berkeley and Los Angeles: University of California Press, 1957); Gisela Bruche-Schulz, *Russische Sprachwissenschaft: Wissenschaft im historisch-politischen Prozeß des vorsowjetischen und sowjetischen Rußland*, Linguistische Arbeiten 151 (Tübingen: Max Niemeyer, 1984), pp. 60–7; René l'Hermitte, *Marr, marrisme, marristes: une page de l'histoire de la linguistique soviétique* (Paris: Institut d'études slaves, 1987); V. M. Alpatov, *Istoriia odnogo mifa: Marr i marrizm* (Moscow: Nauka, 1991).

37 (Tbilisi: printed by Shroma for *Jejili*, 1910/11). According to the title page it
    was published in 1910, but the cover bears the date 1911.

38 A comparable unexamined item of linguistic belief is the oft-repeated *myth of
    the fourteen scripts*. In one source after another, from tourist brochures and
    posters to university textbooks, one meets the statement: 'The Georgian
    script is one of the fourteen scripts in the world.' Once again, the listing of
    more than fourteen scripts – by no means a difficult feat – confronts
    Georgians with an unanticipated disjunction between what they have been
    taught and the worldview of respected foreigners, both apparently empirically
    based.

39 Both were (re)printed in his *Ts'erilebi, esseebi* (Tbilisi: Khelovneba, 1991), pp.
    191–227 and 3–45 respectively.

40 Ibid., pp. 192–3.

41 Ibid., p. 29.

42 Thomas, *The Linguistic Theories of N. Ja. Marr*, p. 47.

43 Anna Meskhi, 'New Etymological Approach to the Study of the English Word
    "Day"', *Big Ben*, 1 (13), 1997, pp. 2–3, and 2 (14), 1997, pp. 4–5.

44 The current lively debate over the origin and affiliations of the Georgian
    alphabet is surveyed by N. Kemertelidze in Cram, Linn and Nowak,
    *Proceedings of the Seventh International Conference on the History of Linguistics
    (ICHoLS VII)*. See also p. 184.

45 Suzanne Goldenberg, *Pride of Small Nations: The Caucasus and Post-Soviet
    Disorder* (London: Zed Books, 1994), p. 12.

46 The Library of Congress catalogue gives the title of volume I in a somewhat
    different form: *Lithuanian History, Philology and Grammar* (Chicago: Peoples
    Printing Co., 1941). Although both book and pamphlet were published under
    the name of 'Theodore S. Thurston', in the text of the pamphlet 'Mr
    Theodore S. Thompson' is repeatedly named as the author.

47 Cf. Jones' original text: 'The Sanskrit language, whatever be its antiquity, is of
    a wonderful structure; more perfect than the Greek, more copious than the
    Latin, and more exquisitely refined than either, yet bearing to both of them a
    stronger affinity, both in the roots of verbs and in the forms of grammar, than
    could possibly have been produced by accident; so strong indeed, that no
    philologer could examine them all three, without believing them to have
    sprung from some common source, which, perhaps, no longer exists: there is a
    similar reason, though not quite so forcible, for supposing that both the
    Gothic and the Celtic, though blended with a very different idiom, had the
    same origin with the Sanskrit' (quoted from Winfred P. Lehmann, *A Reader in
    Nineteenth-Century Historical Indo-European Linguistics* (Bloomington and
    London: Indiana University Press, 1967), p. 15).

48 The case quoted in ch. 2 above, n. 22, of the claim that Sanskrit was the
    ancient Ukrainian language and therefore the basis of all Indo-European lan-
    guages, is a still more egregious example of the rewriting of linguistic history
    to suit political ends.

49 Raphael Loewe, 'Hebrew Linguistics', in Giulio Lepschy (ed.), *History of
    Linguistics*, vol. I, *The Eastern Traditions of Linguistics* (London and New York:
    Longman, 1994), pp. 97–163, esp. pp. 102–6.

50 *Commentaire d'Išo'dad de Merv sur l'Ancien Testament*, vol. I, *Genèse*, trans.

Ceslas Van den Eynde, *Corpus Scriptorum Christianorum Orientalium* 156, *Scriptores Syri* 75 (Louvain: L. Durbecq, 1955), p. 150.

51 Translated by Donald Rayfield, *The Literature of Georgia: A History* (Oxford: Clarendon, 1994), pp. 19–20.

52 Gamsakhurdia, *Ts'erilebi, esseebi*, p. 43.

53 Alina Chaganava, 'O, enav chemo, dedao enav!', *Horizonti*, 14 (32), 14–20 April 1993, p. 1, quoting from Gamsakhurdia, *Ts'erilebi, esseebi*, p. 43.

54 *Archevani*, 2, 14 April 1993, p. 1.

55 See the studies in L. Hinton, J. Nichols and J. J. Ohala (eds.), *Sound Symbolism* (Cambridge: Cambridge University Press, 1994), esp. T. Priestly's 'On Levels of Analysis of Sound Symbolism in Poetry, with an Application to Russian Poetry' (pp. 237–48).

56 For examples, see J. Jolivet, 'Quelques cas de "platonisme grammatical" du VIIe au XIIe siècle', in Pierre Gallais and Yves-Jean Riou (eds.), *Mélanges offerts à René Crozet*, vol. I (Poitiers: Société d'études médiévales, 1966), pp. 93–9.

57 Aves, *Paths to National Independence in Georgia*, p. 57.

58 Joh. Petrus Ericus, *Renatum è mysterio principium philologicum, in quo vocum, signorum et punctorum, tum & literarum maxime ac numerorum origo . . . forma dialogi propalatur* (Passau: Ex Typographia Seminarii, 1686).

59 It is only in the relatively recent past that the Georgian alphabet has been used to record the other languages used upon the territory of Georgia; consequently, the association of the alphabet with the Georgian language remains strongly embedded in popular consciousness.

60 For the link between Sumerians and Georgians, see p. 177 above.

61 T. V. Gamqrelidze [Gamkrelidze], *Alphabetic Writing and the Old Georgian Script* (Tbilisi: Publishing House of the Djavakhishvili State University, 1990). Although the jacket and title page bear an English title, and the contents are briefly outlined in English on the flaps of the jacket, the work is in fact in Georgian with an extensive Russian summary (pp. 207–306).

62 Z. K'ap'ianidze, 'Sikvdilis shemdeg maints nugha ats'amebt' Ivane Javakhishvils' [Ivane Javakhishvili – posthumously tortured yet again], *Nat'lisveti*, 2, 1995. This article is one in a series of exchanges apparently sparked off by the publication of Zurab Sarjveladze's complimentary review of Gamqrelidze's book in *Literatuli Sak'art'velo*, 1 June 1990, pp. 5, 6 and 10.

63 Gamqrelidze's attempt to cover himself in the afterword ('Bolot'k'ma') to the Georgian text of his book (p. 206) – by pointing out that the imminent anniversary of the creation of the Georgian alphabet and establishment of Georgian Christianity was an event of as much significance to Christendom as the recently celebrated anniversary of East Slavonic Christianity and the creation of the associated scripts (Cyrillic and Glagolitic) – failed to redeem him in the eyes of extreme nationalists. Needless to say, this section was not included in the Russian summary, a fact which throws into relief the uneasy path he found himself treading between Russian scholarly orthodoxy on the one hand, and more radical Georgian opinion on the other.

64 W. Camden, *Remaines concerning Britaine* (London: John Legatt for Simon Waterson, 1614), p. 28.

65 Chaganava, 'O, enav chemo, dedao enav!'.

66 These examples convey a different nuance from most of those reported by

Hewitt, *Georgian: A Structural Reference Grammar*, pp. 167–8, who, basing himself on a study by A. Potskhishvili, translates almost all his examples using the adverb 'unwittingly'. Intention, rather than knowledge, is clearly what is at issue in the examples supplied by this author's informants.

67 Avtandil Sakvarelidze, Anzor Totadze and Nicoloz Cherkezishvili, *On Ethnic Composition of Population of the Georgian Republic (Information Material)* (Tbilisi: Samshoblo, for Staff of the Head of the Georgian Republic 1993), p. 9. Naira Gelaschwili, *Georgien: ein Paradies in Trümmern*, writes: 'The Caucasus was always a model of religious and national tolerance' (p. 10), and follows this up with a page of historical instances, leading into a discussion of the traditional code of honour of the Caucasian peoples.

68 In principle, speakers of Italian during the sixteenth century and of French in the seventeenth and eighteenth might have been expected to make such claims in view of the cultural supremacy of their respective languages and literatures and their consequent attractiveness to foreigners, but in practice allusions to foreign interest and approbation are largely lacking.

69 Kita Tschenkéli, *Einführung in die georgische Sprache*, 2 vols. (Zürich: Amirani, 1958). See p. 189 for Tschenkéli's use of quotations from foreign authorities to support a necessarily subjective view as to the euphoniousness of the Georgian intonation pattern.

70 G. I. Tsibakhashvili, *Samouchitel' gruzinskogo iazyka (elementarnyi kurs)* (Tbilisi: Izdatel'stvo Tbilisskogo universiteta, 1981): the preface occupies pp. 4–9.

71 'O, enav chemo, dedao enav!', col. 1.

72 On the history of these and similar arguments, see Fishman, *Language and Nationalism*; Maurice Olender, *The Languages of Paradise: Race, Religion, and Philology in the Nineteenth Century* (London and Cambridge, MA: Harvard University Press, 1992).

73 See p. 180 above.

74 Reported by Chenciner in a talk in the Post-Soviet States in Transition seminar programme, Cambridge, 8 May 1996.

75 There is no bar to different writers' claiming diametrically opposing virtues for their language, as Bailey makes vividly clear in *Images of English*, pp. 1–2.

76 'O, enav chemo, dedao enav!'.

77 Tschenkéli, *Einführung in die georgische Sprache*, p. lix, n. 1.

78 G. P. Harsdörffer, *Schutzschrift für die teutsche Spracharbeit und derselben Beflissene*, reprinted in Harsdörffer, *Frauenzimmer Gesprächspiele*, vol. I, ed. Irmgard Böttcher (Tübingen: Max Niemeyer, 1968), p. 13 (p. 356).

79 *Coopers Grammatica linguae anglicanae (1685)*, ed. John D. Jones (Halle a. S.: Max Niemeyer, 1912), p. ix.

80 Tsibakhashvili, *Samouchitel' gruzinskogo iazyka*, p. 3.

81 Dzidziguri, *Gruzinskii iazyk: kratkii obzor* (Tbilisi: Izdatel'stvo Tbilisskogo universiteta, 1968), p. 3.

82 As Bailey points out (*Images of English*, p. 278), such claims are in truth a tribute to the labours of English lexicographers, who have made it possible for the native speaker to view the extent of the resources available to him or her as a member of a particular speech community. In practice, of course, very many of the entries in the celebrated *New (Oxford) English Dictionary* are words

which went out of use centuries ago, or which belong to the specialised vocabulary of farriers, miners or astronauts. Any individual native speaker would need to master only a tiny subset of these terms during his/her life. In other languages the same situation obtains, even if it has not been so fully documented.

83 On this theme, see Patrick Sériot, 'L'un et le multiple: l'objet-langue dans la politique linguistique soviétique', in *Etats de langue* (Paris: Fayard, 1986), pp. 119–57.

84 Conrad Gesner, *Mithridates* (Zurich: Froschauer, 1555), p. 3r.

85 Lewis, *Multilingualism in the Soviet Union*; Michael Kirkwood (ed.), *Language Planning in the Soviet Union* (London: Macmillan, 1989).

86 George Thomas, *Linguistic Purism* (Harlow: Longman, 1991).

87 The role of Belarusian in the Grand Duchy of Lithuania is emphasised by many Belarusian writers today. See, apart from Stanislaŭ Stankevich, *Rusifikatsyia belaruskae movy ŭ BSSR i supratsiŭ rusifikatsyinamu pratsesu* (Minsk: Navuka i tekhnika, 1994), p. 72, the following: Z'mitser San'ko, *100 pytanniaŭ i adkazaŭ z historyi Belarusi* (Minsk: Zviazda, 1993), pp. 12–13, 43, 67–8; Ivan Laskoŭ, 'Adkul' paishla belaruskaia mova', in *Z historyiai na 'vy'* (Minsk: Mastatskaia litaratura, 1994), pp. 298–312; A. Ia. Mikhnevicha, *Belaruskaia mova: entsyklapedyia* (Minsk: Belaruskaia entsyklapedyia, 1994), esp. pp. 147–8, 534–6; Uladzimir Sviazhynski, 'Belaruskaia mova', *Nasha slova*, 16, 1995.

88 See ch. 3 above.

89 Quoted by Fuller, 'Manifestations of Nationalism in Current Georgian-Language Literature', p. 4. Cf. the comparable statement in a survey of Armenian history: 'The alphabet was a powerful weapon for national self-preservation and it was used against the policy of assimilation pursued by the Persian kings': *Pages from History* (http://www.sci.am/armenia/hist.html).

90 Cf. the appropriation of religious symbolism by Shevardnadze in November 1992, when he was baptised as a member of the Georgian Orthodox Church and took the name of the patron saint of Georgia, Giorgi. For an analogous process of appropriation of nationalist mythology by Leonid Kravchuk, see Andrew Wilson, 'Myths of National History in Belarus and Ukraine', in Geoffrey Hosking and George Schöpflin (eds.), *Myths and Nationhood* (London: Hurst, 1997), pp. 182–97, at p. 197, n. 76.

91 See the examples quoted by Tony Crowley, *Language in History: Theories and Texts* (London and New York: Routledge, 1996), ch. 4.

9 LANGUAGE POLICY AND ETHNIC RELATIONS IN UZBEKISTAN

1 Donald Horowitz, *Ethnic Groups and Conflict* (Berkeley: University of California Press, 1985).

2 Likewise, the constitution of the Uzbek SSR did not ascribe state or official status to any language. Exceptions amongst the constitutions of the union republics were those of Georgia (Article 156), Armenia (Article 119) and Azerbaijan (Article 151), which explicitly named their respective titular languages as the official languages of those republics.

3 See, for example, *RFE/RL Special*, 'Central Asian Intellectuals Push for the State Language Status of Mother Tongues', 22 December 1988. Following the publication of the draft legislation in June 1989, a group of twenty-five members of the USSR's Writers' Union in Uzbekistan proposed a version of the language law that would have made the use of Uzbek compulsory in the public sector within one year: James Critchlow, 'Uzbek Language Bill Sets Tongues Loose', *Report on the USSR*, vol. 1 (38), 22 September 1989.

4 Although Uzbek was part of the curriculum for children studying in schools in which Uzbek was not the medium of tuition, the language was treated as an unimportant subject. See William Fierman, 'Independence and the Declining Priority of Language Law Implementation in Uzbekistan', in Yaacov Ro'i (ed.), *Muslim Eurasia: Conflicting Legacies* (London: Frank Cass, 1995), p. 209. For a chronological overview of Soviet language planning, see Isabelle T. Kreindler, 'Soviet Muslims: Gains and Losses as a Result of Soviet Language Planning', in Ro'i, *Muslim Eurasia*, pp. 187–204, and Kreindler, 'Soviet Language Planning Since 1953', in Michael Kirkwood (ed.), *Language Planning in the Soviet Union* (London: Macmillan, 1989), pp. 46–63.

5 'Ozbekistan Respublikasining Qanuni: Dävlät tili häqidä (yängi tährirdä)', *Khälq sozi*, 29 December 1995; and 'Zakon Respubliki Uzbekistan: O gosudarstvennom yazyke (v novoi redaktsii)', *Narodnoe slovo*, 29 December 1995.

6 'Novyi zakon – novye vozmozhnosti', *Narodnoe slovo*, 16 January 1996.

7 For fuller information, see ch. 7 in this volume.

8 Some of the 1989 text's more important provisions concerning the spheres of use of Russian were as follows: the law guaranteed the right to receive a general education in Russian (Article 13), and professional-technical institutes, secondary specialised and higher educational establishments were to offer instruction in both Uzbek and Russian (Article 14). Article 15 made the study of Russian compulsory for all school children. Office work (*ish yuritish*; *deloproizvodstvo*) was to be carried out in the state language as well as in Russian or other languages in enterprises and organisations where the majority did not know Uzbek (Article 7). Article 3 guaranteed the right to address governmental and social organisations in the state language and in other languages and 'to receive answers in the state language and in the language of inter-ethnic communication'. The official press was to publish translations of laws, resolutions and other official documents in Russian, Karakalpak, Tajik, Kazak, Kyrgyz, Turkmen and other languages (Article 6). Statistical and financial documentation in enterprises and organisations was to be carried out in the state language and in the language of inter-ethnic communication (Article 8). Organs of state power and administration were to conduct business with all-union organisations in Russian (Article 9).

9 As William Fierman has pointed out, however, this provision was rarely if ever enforced; see Fierman, 'Independence and the Declining Priority of Language Law', p. 217.

10 *Ozbekistan Respublikasining Qanuni Latin yazuwigä äsaslängän ozbek alifbasini jariy etish toghrisidä* (Tashkent: Ozbekistan, 1993).

11 The *Current Digest of the Soviet Press*, vol. 47 (23), 1995. Uzbekistan is making the shift to the Latin script in order to 'speed the republic's all-round progress and its entry into the system of world communications'.

12 For an excellent examination of constraints on language law implementation,

see William Fierman, 'Problems of Language Law Implementation in Uzbekistan', *Nationalities Papers*, vol. 23 (3), 1995, pp. 573–95.

13 'Novyi zakon – novye vozmozhnosti'.

14 The modern literary Uzbek language, adopted in 1923, was based on the strongly Iranised dialects of Tashkent and Farghana. These urbanised dialects were sharply distinguished by their loss of vowel harmony from the dialects spoken at the time by the nomadic Uzbeks. See Karl H. Menges, 'Peoples, Languages and Migrations', in Edward Allworth (ed.), *Central Asia: 130 Years of Russian Dominance* (Durham, NC: Duke University Press, 1994), p. 69. For more information on dialects, see A. B. Dzhuraev, *Teoreticheskie osnovy areal'nogo issledovaniia uzbekoiazychnogo massiva* (Tashkent: Fan, 1991); and Shirin Akiner, 'Uzbekistan: Republic of Many Tongues', in Kirkwood, *Language Planning in the Soviet Union*, pp. 110–11.

15 Fierman, 'Problems of Language Law Implementation in Uzbekistan', p. 579.

16 Fierman, 'Independence and the Declining Priority of Language Law Implementation', p. 205.

17 The prominent Uzbek poet Erkin Vahidov called the draft bill, which was entitled the Law of the Uzbek SSR on Languages (rather than one Uzbek language), a string of 'obsequious phrases resembling a long-winded apology for other languages'. See Critchlow, 'Uzbek Language Bill Sets Tongues Loose'.

18 'Tanlagan yolimizning toghriligigä ishonchimiz komil', *Khälq sozi*, 5 March 1996.

19 Fierman, 'Independence and the Declining Priority of Language Law Implementation', p. 206.

20 Fierman, 'Problems of Language Law Implementation in Uzbekistan', p. 580.

21 'Novyi zakon – novye vozmozhnosti'.

22 'Sosedey ne vybiraiut – sosedi ot boga', *Segodnia*, 29 February 1996.

23 Fierman, 'Problems of Language Law Implementation in Uzbekistan', pp. 576–7. Of the 8,877 general education schools in Uzbekistan in 1995, Russian was the medium of instruction in 998. Another 1,462 schools used either Kazak, Tajik, Karakalpak, Turkmen, Kyrgyz or Korean as the language of tuition: 'Mnogoiazychie – davniaia traditsiia', *Pravda Vostoka*, 21 February 1995.

24 Fierman, 'Independence and the Declining Priority of Language Law Implementation', p. 227.

25 Bhavna Dave, 'National Revival in Kazakhstan: Language Shift and Identity Change', *Post-Soviet Affairs*, vol. 12 (1), 1996, p. 52.

26 As delineated by Albert O. Hirschman in his study of the same title *Exit, Voice and Loyalty* (Cambridge, MA: Harvard University Press, 1970).

27 Graham Smith and Andrew Wilson, 'Rethinking Russia's Post-Soviet Diaspora: The Potential for Political Mobilisation in Eastern Ukraine and North-East Estonia', *Europe–Asia Studies*, vol. 49 (5), July 1997, pp. 845–64.

28 'V Tashkente zakryta russkaia gazeta', *Nezavisimaia gazeta*, 24 January 1996. See also ch. 7 in this volume.

29 Figures and percentages in this section have been calculated on the basis of data provided to the author by the State Committee of the Russian Federation on Statistics (Goskomstat of Russia) in November 1996 and May 1997. As

many migrants fail to register and thus cannot be counted, however, actual figures are likely to be much higher.

30 Total losses of ethnic Russians are in fact larger since about 20 per cent of Russian migrants from the Central Asian region have chosen Ukraine and Belarus as their country of destination rather than Russia. See Zhanna Zaionchkovskaiia, 'Istoricheskie korni migratsionoi situatsii v Srednei Azii', in Galina Vitkovskaia (ed.), *Migratsiia russkoiazychnogo naseleniia iz Tsentral'noi Azii: prichiny, posledstviia, perspektivy* (Moscow: Carnegie Endowment for International Peace, 1996), p. 46.

31 A major study on migrational trends in Central Asia undertaken by experts at the Institute of Economic Forecasting of the Russian Academy of Sciences in 1994–5 found that, in contrast to the answers given by potential migrants in Kazakstan and Kyrgyzstan, potential migrants from Uzbekistan cited the 'language barrier' as inducement to emigration more often than any other single ethnopolitical, ethnosocial or ethnocultural motive. Galina Vitkovskaia, 'Migratsionnoe povedenie netitul'nogo naseleniia v strankakh Tsentral'noi Azii', in Vitkovskaia, *Migratsiia russkoiazychnogo naseleniia*, pp. 100–2 and p. 122.

32 See n. 12 in ch. 7.

33 Hilary Pilkington, 'Going Home? The Implications of Forced Migration for National Identity Formation in Post-Soviet Russia', paper presented to the BASEES Annual Conference, Fitzwilliam College, Cambridge, 1 April 1996, p. 7.

34 'Sem´ raz otmerit´', *Vechernii Bishkek*, 18 July 1996.

35 Sergei Panarin, 'Tsentral'naia Aziia: integratsionnyi potentsial i perspektivy migratsii' in Vitkovskaiia, *Migratsiia russkoiazychnogo naseleniia*, p. 36.

36 *OMRI Daily Digest*, no. 26, pt I, 6 February 1997.

37 David Laitin, 'Marginality: A Micro Perspective', *Rationality and Society*, vol. 7 (1), January 1995, p. 35.

38 Horowitz, *Ethnic Groups and Conflict*.

39 David Laitin, 'Language and Nationalism in the Post-Soviet Republics', *Post-Soviet Affairs*, vol. 12 (1), 1996, p. 19.

40 Ibid., p. 12; and Laitin, 'Language Normalization in Estonia and Catalonia', *Journal of Baltic Studies*, vol. 23 (2), 1992, pp. 149–66.

41 Muriel Atkin, 'Religious, National and Other Identities in Central Asia', in Joann Gross (ed.), *Muslims in Central Asia: Expressions of Identity and Change* (Durham, NC: Duke University Press, 1992), p. 48. See also Ludmila Chvyr, 'Central Asia's Tajiks: Self-Identification and Ethnic Identity', in Vitaly Naumkin (ed.), *State, Religion and Society in Central Asia: A Post-Soviet Critique* (Reading: Ithaca Press, 1993), pp. 244–61.

42 Victoria Koroteyeva and Ekaterina Makarova, 'The Assertion of Uzbek National Identity', paper presented to the European Seminar on Central Asian Studies (ESCAS) V, Copenhagen, August 1995.

43 The Chaghatay literary language, used primarily but not exclusively by poets and historians in Central Asia until the early twentieth century, was far removed from the spoken dialects of the region. European scholars gave the name 'Chaghatay' to the written language based upon eastern Turkic that flowered in the Temurid period of the fifteenth and sixteenth centuries. Soviet

sources generally refer to this language as 'Old Uzbek'. For more information on the Chaghatay language, see the introductory chapter to Janos Eckmann's *Chagatay Manual* (Bloomington: Indiana University's Uralic and Altaic Series, vol. 60, 1966), 340 pp.

44 Kazak, Uzbek and Turkmen had achieved a certain literary form by 1917, however. See Geoffrey Wheeler, *The Modern History of Soviet Central Asia* (New York: Frederick A. Praeger), p. 193.

45 Brian Silver, 'The Ethnic and Language Dimensions in Russian and Soviet Censuses', in Ralph S. Clem (ed.), *Research Guide to the Russian and Soviet Censuses* (Ithaca: Cornell University Press, 1986), p. 78.

46 At the time of the National Delimitation, most of the Tajik population was residing in areas that fell within the borders of the newly created Uzbek SSR. The mountainous terrain of eastern Bukhara was given to Tajikistan in 1924, which was an autonomous republic within the Uzbek SSR until 1929. Samarkand was the capital of the Uzbek SSR until 1930.

47 Richard Foltz, 'The Tajiks of Uzbekistan', *Central Asian Survey*, vol. 15 (2), 1996, p. 213.

48 Alisher Il'khamov, 'Uzbekistan: etnosotsial'nye problemy perekhodnogo perioda', *Sotsiologicheskie issledovanie*, no. 8, 1992, p. 14.

49 Atkin, 'Religious, National and Other Identities', pp. 50–1.

50 'Sredniaia Aziia posle Fergany i Osha', *Moskovskie novosti*, no. 18, 1992.

51 'Znakom'tes': novie dissidenty', *Moskovskie novosti*, no. 30, 1992; and Richard Foltz, 'Uzbekistan's Tajiks: A Case of Repressed Identity?', *Central Asia Monitor*, no. 6, 1996. The 'Samarkand' Social-Cultural Organisation of Tajiks and Tajik-Speaking Peoples was one of several associations that was not allowed to re-register under the 1993 decree requiring all public organisations and political organisations officially registered in Uzbekistan to re-register or face suspension. Rather than a distinct assault on Tajik culture, the crackdown on Tajik activists was in keeping with the general Uzbekistani approach towards dissidence that is reminiscent of Soviet policy in the 1970s.

52 See Foltz, 'The Tajiks of Uzbekistan', *Central Asia Survey*, vol. 15 (2), 1996, pp. 213–16.

53 The first three localities selected (Tashkent, Farghana and Samarkand) are strongholds in Uzbekistan of Russian, Uzbek and Tajik culture, respectively. In Khwarazm, which was the most ethnically homogeneous region in Uzbekistan in 1989 (with a population that was 95 per cent Uzbek), knowledge of Uzbek amongst Russians was more than twice as high as in any other region of the country (1989 census data).

54 Interviewers were instructed to record the subjective, self-identified nationality of the respondent, which may or may not necessarily correspond to the official nationality registered in his or her passport.

55 The group of respondents referred to as 'Russophone minorities' in this chapter consisted of Tatars (Volga and Crimean), Koreans and other linguistically Russified groups who immigrated to the region within the last century. While the Russians and other Slavs migrated voluntarily, the Koreans and Crimean Tatars were deported en masse to the region in 1937 and 1944, respectively.

56 A higher proportion of Russian respondents in the 1996 survey sample

claimed a good or excellent knowledge of the language in comparison with the 1989 census results. It is interesting to note in this regard that a major survey carried out by experts at the Institute of Economic Forecasting of the Russian Academy of Sciences in 1994–5 amongst 2,400 Russians and linguistically Russified minorities in Uzbekistan (see n. 31) yielded results that were very similar to the ones produced by the present survey: a good command of Uzbek was claimed by 9.5 per cent of respondents compared to 11 per cent in the present survey, an average knowledge by 29.9 per cent (compared to 28 per cent) and weak or no Uzbek skills by 57.4 per cent (compared to 60 per cent). See Vitkovskaiia, *Migratsiia russkoiazychnogo naseleniia*, p. 103.

57 'Tanlagan yolimizning toghriligigä ishonchimiz komil'.
58 Aleksei Arapov and Iakov Umanskii, 'Tsentral′naia Aziia i Rossiia: vyzovy i otvety', *Svobodnaia mysl′*, no. 5, 1995, p. 77.

Index

Printed in the United Kingdom
by Lightning Source UK Ltd.
1341

9 780521 599689